THE INTERCULTURAL APPROACH TO COVID 19 MANAGEMENT

Cultures juridiques et politiques
Vol. 19

Cultures juridiques et politiques   Vol. 19

Les conceptions du pouvoir, du droit et de l'ordre se réfèrent inévitablement à l'ensemble du système de représentations qu'est la culture de chaque société. Toute forme de culture ayant donc nécessairement une dimension politique et juridique, la collection « Cultures juridiques et politiques » publie des travaux, tels que des thèses, synthèses de recherches, ouvrages collectifs et actes de colloques, se proposant de faire connaître les systèmes politiques et juridiques des pays européens, d'évaluer les grandes tendances des processus d'intégration politique et d'harmonisation juridique en cours dans l'Union européenne et d'éclairer les interférences entre le politique, le juridique et les autres aspects « culturels » dans le contexte de ces processus.

Collection dirigée par Stephanie Rohlfing-Dijoux et Otmar Seul.

Comité de lecture:

Tilman BEZZENBERGER (Universität Potsdam)
Raphaël CALLSEN (Georg-August Universität Göttingen)
Dorothée CAILLEUX (Université Paris-Nanterre)
Birgit DAIBER (Université Nationale de Séoul (SNU))
Tomas DAVULIS (Vilniaus Universiteto)
Géraldine DEMME (Université Paris-Nanterre)
Romuald DI NOTO (École nationale de la Magistrature (Auditeur de justice) Bordeaux)
Heinrich DÖRNER (Westfälische Wilhelms-Universität Münster)
Joachim GRUBER (Fachhochchule Zwickau)
Peter JANSEN (Fachhochschule Brandenburg)
Jörg LUTHER (Università del Piemonte Orientale Vercelli)
Jean-Pierre MORELOU (Université Paris-Nanterre)
Volker NEUMANN (Humboldt Universität zu Berlin)
Kerstin PEGLOW (Université Paris-Nanterre)
Götz SCHULZE (Universität Potsdam)
Annette SOUSA COSTA (Université Paris-Nanterre)

STÉPHANIE ROHLFING-DIJOUX,
RAJENDRA PARSAD GUNPUTH (EDS.)

THE INTERCULTURAL APPROACH TO COVID 19 MANAGEMENT

IN GERMANY, FRANCE AND THE INDIAN OCEAN COUNTRIES

PETER LANG

Lausanne - Berlin - Bruxelles - Chennai - New York - Oxford

Cofinancé par l'Université franco-allemande et le Centre de Recherches Pluridisciplinaires Multilingues.

The book was subject to a double blind refereeing process.

No part of this book may be reproduced in any form, by print, photocopy, microfilm or any other means, without prior written permission from the publisher. All rights reserved.

© 2024, Peter Lang Group
Published by Peter Lang Éditions scientifiques internationales - P.I.E.A, Brussels, Belgium
www.peterlang.com, info@peterlang.com

ISSN 2235-1078
ISBN 978-2-87574-790-7
ISBN 978-2-87574-793-8 ePub
D/2023/5678/54

ISBN 978-2-87574-792-1 eBook
DOI 10.3726/b21272

Bibliographic information published by "Die Deutsche Nationalbibliothek". "Die Deutsche Nationalbibliothek" lists this publication in the "Deutsche National-bibliografie"; detailed bibliographic data is available on the Internet at <http://dnb.d-nb.de>.

CIP available at the British Library and the Library of Congress.

Table des matières

Preface 11

Préface 15

PART I EPIDEMIC AND EMERGENCY LEGISLATION: *LÉGISLATION SUR LES EPIDÉMIES ET LES SITUATIONS D'URGENCE*

Law-making and rule of law during the COVID-19-pandemic in Germany 21
Kerstin PEGLOW

Concerns regarding the restrictions on freedom and discrimination measures during the recent health crisis in Germany and France – What perspective for the rule of law? 33
Géraldine DEMME

Les conséquences du mensonge sur son statut vaccinal en droits civil et pénal 47
Sabir KADEL

German fundamental rights in times of a global health crisis 59
Marie ROSSIER

The Covid (miscellaneous provision) act et The Quarantine Act à l'Ile Maurice 75
Rajendra Parsad GUNPUTH and Ambareen BEEBEEJAUN

La mise mettant en otage des municipalités : la réforme du Local Government Act (LGA) et le renvoi des élections municipales en raison de la crise sanitaire 99
Didier MICHEL

Part II Management of COVID: La gestion du Covid

The management of Covid, a comparative analysis of German federal and French centralized management of the crisis 113
Berquis BESTVATER

Covid and the risk culture: Understanding the different strategies in covid management 125
Régis LANNEAU

Responses to the Covid crisis in antitrust and merger control 139
Gleb FROMM

The impact of COVID-19 on the public debt of countries in Sub-Saharan Africa 159
Essohanam PELENGUEI, Benoit KAFANDO, Kokouvi Kunalè MAWUENA, Joseph Essèmou-Abalè Kossi ASSOGBAVI, Abdoulaziz ALHASSANE GARBA, Soumaïla WONI and Rajendra Parsad GUNPUTH

Part III COVID-19 and Economic and Social Law: *COVID-19 et le droit économique et social*

The effects of COVID-19 on quality auditor's report 181
Mootooganagen RAMEN and Aslam R. SAIB

COVID-19 and new working conditions as the new normal: The domino effect – The Mauritian and African human rights comparative case study 199
Rajendra Parsad GUNPUTH and Ambareen BEEBEEJAUN

L'avenir du travail et le contrat de travail face au COVID-19 – l'expérience mauricienne 223
Goran GEORGIJEVIC

An empirical study on socio economic status of Indians in
turbulent times of COVID-19 241
    Sid CHOUDARY

PART IV COVID-19, MEDIA, TECHNOLOGY AND
DIGITISATION: *COVID-19 MEDIEN, TECHNOLOGIE ET DIGITALISTION*

The protection of employee personal data in times of COVID-19
health crisis 263
    Victoria ROUX

The technology acceptance model post COVID-19 275
    Rajendra Parsad GUNPUTH and Ashwin Michael
    Claudius THODDA

The COVID-19 crisis in the EU, France and Germany: Between
data sovereignty and GAFAM dependency 297
    Danielle-Josée BOUTOILLE

Freedom of expression and the spread of misinformation during
COVID-19 in Mauritius 309
    A. BEEBEEJAUN and R. P. GUNPUTH

PART V HEALTH, END OF LIFE AND COVID-19/*SANTÉ, FIN DE VIE
ET COVID-19*

The right to life and care in a crisis situation with limited
resources 333
    Stephanie ROHLFING-DIJOUX

The challenge of vulnerability in the health crisis: Comparative
study of the French and German health laws on the protection of
vulnerable adults 347
    Charles WALLEIT

Brand experience in the COVID-19 age-health and safety as the key factors 357
Adjnu Damar LADKOO

Response to domestic violence due to COVID-19 at international and national levels 369
Dhan Devi SOOKUR and Nishita Devi HORILL

Hommage à Pierre Rosario Domingue 383
Sabir Kadel

Preface

Managing COVID-19 was an enormous challenge for the whole world. No country has been spared. The huge upheaval in daily activity has affected every area of life: family life, training and education, work, economic life, health and psychology. The extent of the consequences and side-effects, which often persist in the long term, cannot yet be fully assessed. This colloquium, co-organized by the Universities of Paris Nanterre, Potsdam and Mauritius, with the collaboration of the Law Reform Commission and the support of the Franco-German University, was an opportunity to bring together research professors from these different countries and from different disciplines, lawyers and economists, to compare the different forms of pandemic management in a multidisciplinary and comparative way.

Some countries have been more affected than others, because of their climate, demographics, population density and various other factors. It has to be said that there has been no equality in the face of the pandemic. A country's geographical location and culture therefore had a major influence on government measures during the pandemic. The various contributions in this volume highlight these differences, particularly between small island and developing countries and the countries of the European Union.

Some countries, particularly small island states, were particularly hard hit because medical resources and structures quickly proved inadequate. The fear of being overwhelmed by the influx of hospitalisations had a strong influence on the measures taken by governments to protect their populations as much as possible from the harmful consequences of the pandemic.

These measures, which were numerous and varied, were exceptional in their scale and coercive nature: closure of borders, closure of shops, schools and universities, closure of hotels, ban on leaving the house and various curfew operations. No one would have imagined, before this pandemic, that such restrictions on individual freedoms could be envisaged by democratic governments.

Public reaction to these measures has also varied greatly from country to country. In some countries, the courts have been inundated with freedom applications and proceedings to challenge the constitutionality of government measures. In others, there have been few, if any, challenges. This behaviour in the face of the pandemic is also a factor that reveals the sociological culture of the country and was the subject of this study.

Finally, we need to distinguish between different periods in the management of the crisis. The surprise effect and the failure of governments to prepare for a health crisis of this scale was significant for the beginning of the management of Covid, a period marked by the imitation of measures from one country to another, confusion and contradictory, uncoordinated measures. As new waves of Covid appeared over a period of two years, with the emergence of new variants, advances in research into the virus and the discovery of a vaccine, protective measures changed and were adapted to the new situation. During this phase, there were more differences between countries in the way they managed the crisis.

It is certain, in hindsight, that with the scientific knowledge acquired during this period and the assessment of the need for and effectiveness of 'anti-COVID' measures, the assessment would have been very different today.

The title of this publication of the proceedings of a 2022 symposium suggests the existence of a link between a country's culture and its management of COVID. The conference provided an opportunity to look back at the decisions taken in several countries and to examine how their cultural and geographical contexts had influenced the choices made by their leaders.

The first part of the conference was devoted to emergency measures restricting freedoms and their conflict with constitutions and fundamental freedoms. This part enabled a comparative approach between France, Germany and Mauritius.

The second part concerns the management of Covid in a comparative study between the countries examined and the influences in several areas of economic and social life.

The serious measures taken to combat the pandemic have had side-effects that were not fully anticipated by those responsible. In particular, the economic and social consequences have been far-reaching, plunging many countries into serious crisis. These consequences are discussed in Part 3.

Preface

One of the major consequences of the pandemic and the resulting confinement is that life has largely been reduced to a digital one. To a certain extent, this digitalisation has enabled certain activities to continue, but it has not been without risk. The heavy use of the internet during this period meant that data protection had to be strengthened, an issue addressed in Part 4. This part also deals with the role of the media during the pandemic and the consequences for employment law.

Part 5 deals specifically with health issues related to the pandemic, in particular the protection of vulnerable people and the problem of allocating resources in a context of insufficient capacity to care for all patients, which makes 'triage' inevitable.

Stephanie Rohlfing-Dijoux
Paris Nanterre, Mauritius, July 2023

Préface

La gestion du COVID-19 a représenté un énorme défi pour le monde entier. Aucun pays n'a été épargné. L'immense bouleversement de l'activité quotidienne a touché tous les domaines de la vie : La vie familiale, la formation et l'éducation, le travail, la vie économique, la santé, la psychologie. L'ampleur des conséquences et des effets secondaires qui subsistent souvent à long termes ne peut pas encore être totalement évalué. Ce colloque, co-organisés par les Universités Paris Nanterre, Potsdam et University of Mauritius et avec la collaboration de la Law Reform Commission et le soutien de l'Université franco-allemande, a été l'occasion de réunir des enseignants chercheurs de ces différents pays et de disciplines différentes, juristes et économistes qui ont permis de confronter les différentes formes de gestion de la pandémie de manière pluridisciplinaire et comparatif.

Certains pays ont été plus touchés que d'autres, en raison de leur climat, de leur démographie, de la densité de leur population et de divers autres facteurs. Force est de constater qu'il n'y a pas eu d'égalité face à la pandémie. La situation géographique et la culture du pays a exercé donc une grande influence sur les mesures gouvernementales pendant la pandémie. Les différentes contributions de ce volume mettent en lumières ces différences, notamment entre les petits pays insulaires et en développement et les Etats de l'Union européenne.

Certains Etats, en particulier les petits Etats insulaires, ont été particulièrement affectés car les moyens et structures médicaux se sont avérés très vite insuffisants. La peur d'être dépassés par des flux d'hospitalisation a fortement influencé les mesures prises par les gouvernants afin de protéger le plus possible leurs populations des conséquences néfastes de la pandémie.

Nombreuses et diversifiées, ces mesures ont été exceptionnelles par leur ampleur et leur caractère coercitif : fermeture des frontières, fermeture des commerces, des écoles et Universités, des hôtels, interdiction de sortir de chez soi et diverses opérations de couvre-feu. Personne n'aurait imaginé, avant cette pandémie, que de telles restrictions des libertés individuelles pourraient être envisagées par des gouvernants démocratiques.

Les réactions de la population face à ces mesures ont été également très différentes d'un pays à l'autre. Dans certains pays, les tribunaux ont été submergés de référés liberté et de procédures en anti-constitutionnalité des mesures gouvernementales. Dans d'autres, les contestations ont été rares, voire inexistantes. Ce comportement face à la pandémie est aussi un facteur qui révèle la culture sociologique du pays et qui a fait objet de cette étude.

Enfin, il faut distinguer des différentes périodes dans la gestion de la crise. L'effet surprise et la non-préparation des Etats à une crise sanitaire d'une telle ampleur a marqué le début de la gestion du Covid, période qui a été marqué par l'imitation des mesures d'un Etats à l'autre, la confusion, des mesures contradictoires et non coordonnées. Au fur et à mesure des nouvelles vagues de Covid pendant une durée de deux ans, l'apparition de nouvelles variantes, l'avancement de la recherche sur le virus et la découverte du vaccin, les mesures de protection ont changées et ont été adaptées à la nouvelle situation. Dans cette phase on peut constater plus de différences entre les pays dans la gestion de la crise.

Il est certain, *a posteriori*, qu'avec les connaissances scientifiques acquises pendant cette période ainsi que l'évaluation de la nécessité et de l'efficacité des mesures « anti-COVID », l'appréciation aurait été très différente aujourd'hui.

Le titre de cette publication des actes d'un colloque de 2022 suggère l'existence d'un lien entre la culture d'un pays et sa gestion du COVID. Ce colloque a, en effet, permis de revenir sur les décisions prises dans plusieurs pays et d'examiner de quelle manière leur contexte culturel et géographique avait influencé les choix des dirigeants.

La première partie du colloque a été consacré aux mesures d'urgence, limitatives de libertés et leur conflit avec les constitutions et libertés fondamentales. Cette partie a permis une approche comparative entre la France, l'Allemagne et l'Ile Maurice.

La deuxième partie concerne la gestion du Covid dans une étude comparative entre les pays examinés et l'influences dans plusieurs domaines de la vie économique et sociale.

Les graves mesures contre la pandémie ont eu des effets secondaires qui n'ont pas été anticipées à leur juste mesure par les responsables. Notamment les conséquences économiques et sociales ont été très importantes et ont plongé beaucoup de pays dans de graves crises. Ces conséquences font l'objet de la troisième partie.

Une des conséquences importantes de la pandémie et du confinement qui en a résulté est liée au fait que la vie en grande partie a été réduite à une vie digitale. Cette digitalisation a, d'une certaine manière, permis de poursuivre certaines activités mais elle ne s'est pas faite sans risques. La forte utilisation d'internet pendant cette période a nécessité un renforcement de la protection des données, question traitée dans la quatrième partie. Celle-ci traite aussi le rôle des médias pendant la pandémie ainsi que les conséquences en droit du travail.

La partie 5 traite spécifiquement les questions de santé liées à la pandémie, notamment la protection des personnes vulnérables ainsi que la problématique de la répartition des moyens dans un contexte d'insuffisance de capacités de prise en charge de l'ensemble patients qui rend le « triage » inévitable.

Stephanie Rohlfing-Dijoux
Paris Nanterre, Mauritius, Juillet 2023

PART I

EPIDEMIC AND EMERGENCY LEGISLATION

LÉGISLATION SUR LES EPIDÉMIES ET LES SITUATIONS D'URGENCE

During the COVID-19 pandemic, most countries resorted to exceptional emergency legislation, often without going through the democratic channels of the legislature. This part analyses the rationale behind these laws, distinguishing between the different periods of the pandemic when they were enacted. It also looks at the constitutional basis for these laws and respect for fundamental freedoms.

Pendant la pandémie du COVID-19 la plupart des pays ont eu recours à des législations exceptionnelles prises en urgence, souvent sans passer par les voies démocratiques de législateur. Cette partie propose une analyse de la justification de ces législations en distinguant les différentes périodes de la pandémie où elles ont été décidées. L'analyse porte également sur le fondement constitutionnel de ces législations et sur le respect des libertés fondamentaux.

Law-making and rule of law during the COVID-19-pandemic in Germany

Kerstin PEGLOW[1]

Abstract

The COVID-19-pandemic presented a challenge for law-making and the Rule of law all over the world. In Germany, individual liberty and fundamental rights have been restricted to an unprecedented extent. Crisis legislation has therefore been subject to strong criticism. In particular, the respect of the Rule of law was a highly discussed topic. This paper addresses the question of whether Germany was in a 'state of exception' during the pandemic and whether the separation of powers – on the one hand between the legislative and the executive branch and on the other hand between the federal and the regional authorities – was observed.

La pandémie de COVID-19 a constitué un défi pour l'État de droit et les législateurs dans le monde entier. En Allemagne, la liberté individuelle et les droits fondamentaux ont été restreints dans une mesure sans précédent. La législation relative à la crise sanitaire a donc fait l'objet de vives critiques. En particulier, le respect de l'État de droit a été un sujet très discuté. Ce document aborde la question de savoir si l'Allemagne était en 'état d'exception' pendant la pandémie et si la séparation des pouvoirs – d'une part entre les pouvoirs législatif et exécutif et d'autre part entre les autorités fédérales et régionales – a été respectée.

Introduction

No country in the world was prepared for the COVID-19 pandemic which appeared in early 2020. The rapidly spreading virus forced governments on every continent to take swift and efficient action to deal with a public health emergency, which was a challenge for law-making and the Rule of Law in each country. Worldwide, the legal approaches and

---

[1] Professor Université Paris Nanterre.

practical measures used to combat the pandemic have been substantial; society and state institutions were called upon to respond immediately to a health crisis of unknown extent. The COVID-19 pandemic was a surprise, but pandemics are, historically speaking, not new: Since the origins of mankind there have always been pandemics. In recent times, there has been in the early 20th century the plague of the Spanish flu causing millions of deaths, the AIDS epidemic of the 1980s and now we are facing the COVID-19. Globalized and industrialized living conditions, especially human mobility, play a major part in worldwide spread of these pandemics which are transmitted mainly from animals to humans. The reactions of states and societies to the current pandemic have been similar, but they have not been identical.

If you are consulting legal publications on the COVID-19 pandemic measures very often you can read about a 'state of emergency' or the use of 'legal emergency powers'. State of emergency laws or a state of exception declared by the government usually frighten the population, as they generally signal a neglect of democratic decision-making processes in favour of authoritarian measures. When a 'state of emergency', a 'state of exception' or a 'state of disaster' is declared, a government is allowed to suspend laws to restore normal conditions within its territory. In legal terms, this is a significant encroachment on the rights of citizens and the separation of powers. In the context of the COVID-19 pandemic, it should be noted that the use of the terms 'state of emergency' or 'state of exception' often did not match the legal means by which the health crisis was to be addressed. Thus, extreme caution should be exercised when using emergency terminology.

Concerning the European Union, the tools adopted by the Member States for the COVID-19 legislation were not coordinated. Each member state had its own legal method to combat the pandemic using constitutional or ordinary legal instruments. Despite this, there was also convergence in the legal approach: the crisis was the 'hour of the executive'[2], Governments and health ministers made use of extensive powers and parliaments were only gradually involved in the development of legal

---

[2] European Parliament, States of emergency in response to the coronavirus crisis, Normative response and parliamentary oversight in EU Member States during the first wave of the pandemic, 4 December 2019, p. 10.

https://www.europarl.europa.eu/RegData/etudes/STUD/2020/659385/EPRS_STU(2020)659385_EN.pdf – accessed on 18 July 2022; Michael Fuchs, Corona, „Gesundheitsdiktatur" und „Legiszid", DÖV 2020, 653, 656.

instruments to tackle the crisis. In the heat of the moment, democratic and constitutional elements often fell by the wayside, at least temporarily. In the 27 Member States, there was a certain consistency in the concrete measures imposed on citizens and the economy: variously designed curfews, like in France with a self-issued '*attestation de déplacement dérogatoire*[3] with a time specification, or in Germany with the restriction of meetings to a certain number of selected people, the prohibition of staying overnight in hotels for private purposes, travel bans within and outside the country, mandatory Covid tests, restricted shopping opportunities, closure of schools, etc.

In France, in response to the health crisis caused by the COVID-19 virus, the emergency law of 23 March 2020[4] introduced into the public health code the possibility of establishing a 'state of health emergency' in the event of a health disaster. It could be qualified as a *statutory regime* because it refers to a regime provided by statute, rather than by the constitution[5]. The state of health emergency is an exceptional measure that can be decided by the Council of Ministers in the event of a health disaster, in particular a pandemic, that endangers the health of the population. The provisions of the Public Health Code organising the state of health emergency were adopted on a temporary basis. They were to expire on 1 April 2021 and were extended until 31 December 2021. The law of 10 November 2021[6] on various health protection measures maintained them in force until 31 July 2022 although the government had the power to decide to lift restrictions earlier in case of a favourable evolution of the epidemic.

In Germany, regarding its normative responses to the crisis, the pandemic has been seen as a challenge to state institutions and constitutional requirements: not since the founding of the Federal Republic of Germany have there been such far-reaching restrictions on public and

---

[3] Certificate of exemption.
[4] Loi n° 2020-290 du 23 mars 2020 d'urgence pour faire face à l'épidémie de covid-19, Art. 4. Journal officiel de la République française, n° 72 du 24/03/2020.
[5] European Parliament, States of emergency in response to the coronavirus crisis, Normative response and parliamentary oversight in EU Member States during the first wave of the pandemic, 4 December 2019, p. 24. https://www.europarl.europa.eu/RegData/etudes/STUD/2020/659385/EPRS_STU(2020)659385_EN.pdf, accessed on 18 July 2022.
[6] Loi n° 2021-1465 du 10 novembre 2021 portant diverses dispositions de vigilance sanitaire, Journal officiel de la République française, n° 0263 du 11/11/2021.

private life[7]. Crisis management and crisis legislation have therefore been subject to strong criticism since March 2020. Respect for the Rule of law[8] in particular has been a highly discussed topic. In this presentation we will first have a look at the German crisis legislation and the question of whether we may speak of a 'state of emergency' or of a 'state of exception'. Then we will address the so-called 'federal emergency brake' and problems caused by it to the vertical distribution of power in Germany which is a federal state where the power is divided between federal authorities and those of the 16 federal states, the *Länder*. Finally, we will briefly discuss the respect of the distribution of power between the legislative and executive branches during the pandemic crisis.

I. German crisis legislation

The legal basis for German crisis legislation is the Infection Protection Act (Act on the Prevention and Control of Infectious Diseases in Humans, IPA), which has been modified several times since the beginning of the crisis. On 25 March 2020[9], the German Parliament recognized for the first time an 'epidemic situation of national scope' with the

---

[7] Cf. v. Münch/Kunig/Kotzur, 7th ed. 2021, GG Art. 20 n° 174–176.

[8] Rule of Law – *Rechtsstaatsprinzip* in German: "In Germany, the principle of the rule of law is based on the separation of powers (legislative, executive and judiciary). The mutual control, restraint and moderation of the partial powers is intended to limit the state's exercise of power and secure the freedom of the individual ("checks and balances"). At the same time, the division of powers is intended to ensure that state tasks are performed by the bodies best suited to do so." (Andreas Voßkuhle, Ann-Kathrin Kaufhold, Grundwissen – Öffentliches Recht: Das Rechtsstaatsprinzip, JuS 2010, 116, 117).

The terms *Rechtstaatsprinzip* and rule of law might not have the same meaning in Germany as it does in the USA, the United Kingdom or other English language-based legal systems. However, if this presentation refers to the "Rule of Law", it is possible because this term is nowadays characteristic for the use of language in international organizations and in international law. Even at the level of the European Union, a supranational concept is gradually emerging, so there is a minimum of consistency in the use of the term "Rule of law." (v. Mangoldt/Klein/Starck/Sommermann, 7th ed. 2018, GG Art. 20 n° 242–247; cf. https://eur-lex.europa.eu/legal-content/EN/TXT/?uri=CELEX%3A52020DC0580 – accessed on 3 August 2021.

[9] *Gesetz zum Schutz der Bevölkerung bei einer epidemischen Lage von nationaler Tragweite, Bundesgesetzblatt Jahrgang 2020 Teil I Nr. 14, ausgegeben am 27.03.2020, Seite 587* (Federal Law Gazette Volume 2020 Part I N°. 14, issued on 27.03.2020, p. 587).

entry into force of Section 5 (1) Sentence 1 of the Infection Protection Act due to the spread of the new Coronavirus in Germany. In resolutions of 18 November 2020, 4 March 2021, and 11 June 2021, the Parliament (*Bundestag*) again stated that the 'epidemic situation of national scope' persisted.

The Infection Protection Act (IPA) is a federal law that relates to publicly dangerous or transmissible diseases in humans. It regulates the necessary cooperation and collaboration among federal state and local authorities, physicians, veterinarians, hospitals, scientific institutions, and other involved parties. It is intended to prevent transmissible diseases, detect infections at an early stage and prevent their further spread. According to this law, the federal government and the 16 states cooperate in the fight against infectious diseases. Since the pandemic broke out, the law has been amended several times to meet the exceptional situation. The second-to-last, very freedom-restricting version of the IPA dates from 24 April 2021. The law, which for the first time provided uniform rules for all of Germany, was limited in time until 30 June 2021. Since then, the number of cases has declined, so that the IPA continued to apply, but with modified rules. The 'epidemic situation of national scope' expired definitively on 25 November 2021. The protective legal measures, which remained possible, were limited until 19 March 2022 and could be extended once by three months upon a resolution of the German Parliament.

With regard to the crisis legislation under the IPA, since the beginning of the crisis there has been frequent talk in the media, blogs and legal texts of a 'state of emergency' or a 'state of exception'. But what does a 'state of exception' (*Ausnahmezustand*) or 'state of emergency' (*Notstand*) mean? In a state of exception, the applicable law, the separation of powers and the constitution are suspended. This was not the case in Germany. First, unlike other states or Article 48 of the Weimar Republic, the German Constitution does not provide such a 'state of exception'[10]. In addition,

---

[10] Horst Dreier, Rechtsstaat, Föderalismus und Demokratie in der Corona-Pandemie, DÖV 2021, p. 229. The Weimar Constitution provided for a state of exception in crisis situations. The right to issue emergency decrees under Article 48 of the Weimar Constitution gave the German president (*Reichspräsident*) the option of bypassing parliamentary control and governing by emergency decree. Particularly in the last crisis-ridden years of the Weimar Republic, the legislative power of the Parliament was thus undermined, and power was shifted to a presidential cabinet, which ultimately heralded the end of the Weimar Republic.

parliamentary laws, executive decrees, and individual administrative acts by the authorities have been enacted in accordance with predetermined constitutional procedure. Finally, fundamental rights have not been suspended in whole or in part[11]. On the contrary, there have been numerous court cases for violations of certain fundamental rights, such as the nighttime curfew, in which the courts have used these fundamental rights as a benchmark for the constitutionality of a state measure. Suspending fundamental rights would have made judicial verification impossible[12].

Contrary to a 'state of exception', a 'state of emergency' is provided for by the German constitution. But in the context of the COVID-19 pandemic, the federal government did not invoke this constitutional *state of emergency*. The provisions of Article 35 (2) and (3) and Article 91 of the German constitution are not really suitable for this purpose. They are intended to combat natural or other disasters, or to counter insurrections or civil war-like situations that threaten the survival of the free democratic constitutional order. After all, the health crisis caused by the COVID-19 pandemic does not fit this pattern.

As a result, it is incorrect legally speaking and can even be confusing to refer to constitutional 'states of exception or of emergency'. In Germany was only applied an *emergency statutory regime* provided by statute, meaning by ordinary security laws[13].

II. The 'federal emergency brake' from April 2021

In April 2021, the federal legislature felt compelled to introduce a nationwide federal coronavirus regulation – the so-called 'federal emergency brake' – because the 16 German federal states were not consistently implementing the measures agreed upon with the Chancellor in their weekly federal-state conferences[14]. At that time the infection situation was still very dynamic, and the calls for uniform requirements were

---

[11] Jens Kersten/Stephan Rixen, Der Verfassungsstaat in der Corona-Krise, 2nd ed., C.H. Beck, München 2021, III.1.
[12] Dreier, op. cit., p. 229, 230.
[13] Cf. Kersten/Rixen, op. cit., III.3.
[14] Cf. Simone Kuhlmann, Das neue Infektionsschutzgesetz: Verfassungsmäßigkeit der Bundesnotbremse (A. Einleitung).

https://www.juris.de/jportal/nav/juris_2015/aktuelles/magazin/infektionsschutzgesetz-verfassungsmaessigkeit.jsp, accessed on 18 July 2022.

growing louder. In this regard, it is important to know that, in principle, each of the 16 states determines the specific regulations for containing the pandemic as part of their own competencies. This is due to the distribution of powers between the federal authorities and the states. As a result, there has been a patchwork of measures put in place to combat the Coronavirus, with different regulations applying from one federal state to the next, causing confusion for citizens. This has been met with criticism, though some have welcomed a response tailored to the regional risk of infection[15].

The 'federal emergency brake', which was in effect from 23 April to 30 June 2021, meant that the same protective regulations would automatically apply nationwide to cities or regions with an incidence of 100 or more new cases of the disease per week over three consecutive days. With the creation of the 'federal emergency brake' in the IPA, the federal legislature was taking back the responsibility for infection protection that was institutionally incumbent on it but had been outsourced to the 16 states.

In addition to a uniform minimum standard of protective measures, the amendment authorized the federal government to order further measures by decree. To this extent, the *federal emergency brake* temporarily suspended the *vertical division of powers* between the federal authorities and the states[16]. However, this did not result in a permanent shift in the federal power structure; in any case, the substantive scope of the shift to the Federal Ministry of Health was limited to the COVID-19 pandemic and did not apply to other infectious diseases. Furthermore, the *Bundesrat*, i.e., the federal body involved in legislation and representation of the 16 states at the federal level, approved the issuing of decrees by the Federal Minister of Health on the occasion of the amendment of the IPA. Finally, within the framework of the IPA, the 16 federal state governments were still free to issue some legal provisions on pandemic control.

Protective measures of the 'federal emergency brake' included (Section 28b IPA):

---

[15] Dreier, op. cit., 229, 237, 238.
[16] Cf. Dreier, op. cit., who concludes that there is a lack of administrative competence on the part of the federal government, making the issuance of orders by the federal Minister of Health unconstitutional (229, 238 et seq.).

1. Contact restriction to private gatherings with only one other person outside the household
2. Curfew between 10 p.m. and 5 a.m.
3. Restrictions on shop openings.
4. Closure of cultural institutions (museums) and bans on events (e.g., concerts)
5. Restrictions on recreational and competitive sports (e.g., closing fitness clubs)
6. Closure of restaurants, cafes, etc., prohibition of personal services (e.g. cosmetic treatments; exception: hairdressers)
7. Restriction of passenger transportation
8. Prohibition of overnight accommodation for the purposes of tourism.

The law contained various exceptions (e.g., private gatherings with spouses or partners, leaving the home for work-related reasons, opening of zoos, sale of food and beverages outside the home).

The regulations were subject to strong criticism because they allowed substantial restrictions on the *fundamental rights* guaranteed by the Constitution[17]. However, in various decisions, the Federal Constitutional Court dismissed requests for a suspension asserted against these regulations, in view of the disadvantages such a suspension could have on combating the pandemic. In some cases, the main proceedings are still pending. Due to the declining incidence figures, more flexible regulations apply since the end of the 'federal emergency break' on 30 June 2021, and the states can once again issue their own decrees to a greater extent.

III. Unlawful transfer of competences in favour of the executive power?

Another point of criticism has been the transfer of competences between the legislative and executive powers by the IPA: one of the issues at stake here is whether the parliamentary legislature neglected its powers in the heat of crisis management in favour of the regulations issued by the Minister of health. Did they transfer too much power, in violation of the

---

[17] See for example: Kyrill-A. Schwarz, Zur Frage der Verfassungsmäßigkeit der bundeseinheitlichen „Corona-Notbremse ", COVuR 2021, 258.

Rule of law?[18] Or, on the contrary, were the constitutional requirements of the separation of powers observed in the crisis legislation?[19]

At the beginning of the crisis, all government measures were based on Section 28 IPA, which was originally intended for disease outbreaks that were limited in space and time. The provision was a kind of general clause which was very vague. However, during the COVID-19-crisis, a crisis of unforeseen proportions, it was employed to legally justify extremely far-reaching restrictions on liberty and fundamental rights. Nevertheless, in the first weeks of the pandemic, the provision alone was used as an enabling clause by the competent authorities to issue executive legal decrees, which brought the entire country to a quasi-standstill[20].

In principle, in Germany, in the case of restrictions on fundamental rights, the Parliament itself must regulate the requirements or consequences of such restrictions[21]. It may not issue a general clause or leave decisions on such matters to the executive authorities. Finally, in November 2020, the parliamentary legislator reacted, and Coronavirus-specific laws were passed. The newly inserted Section 28a IPA provided detailed examples of rules such as the distance requirement, mask obligation, exit and contact restrictions, entry bans, closures of businesses and stores, prohibition of events, etc. For the first time, the objectives of the measures to be taken were now explicitly named (e.g., the protection of life and health as well as the functioning of the health system). This improved specification of measures and objectives resulted in a considerable gain in legal certainty and democratic legitimacy. Therefore, the amendment of the Infection Protection Act took the Rule of law into greater account.

It remains the case, however, that both the Federal Ministry of Health and the executive branch of the 16 states had considerable authority to issue legal decrees. In this respect, it should be noted that the Rule of

---

[18] The situation in Germany is made more complicated by the fact that there are different legislative and executive bodies: at the federal level, the *Bundestag* and the Federal Ministry of Health; at the *Länder* level, the Parliaments of the *Länder* and the responsible executive bodies of the *Länder*, i.e. ministers, districts and local communities.
[19] Cf. Fuchs, op. cit., 653, 657.
[20] Dreier, op. cit., p. 229, 231.
[21] Dreier, on the so-called "*Wesentlichkeitstheorie*", 229, 232, 233; Lars Brocker: Exekutive versus parlamentarische Normsetzung in der Corona-Pandemie, NVwZ 2020, 1485, 1486.

law also includes compliance with the hierarchy of norms. According to this hierarchy, the legislative power is bound by the provisions of the constitution, and the executive power is bound by parliamentary laws. Legal decrees must therefore remain within the framework of the legal requirements set by the parliament.

What is important, therefore, is the extent to which the Parliament authorizes the executive power to manage the crisis and the instruments it makes available to it for this purpose. During the COVID-19-crisis, the authorization contained in Section 5 (2) of the IPA for the Federal Ministry of Health to issue numerous orders and measures, which many considered too extensive, was particularly controversial[22]. Although some improvements have been made here as well, constitutional concerns remain. However, parliamentary control also comes into play here, in that the extensive authorizations granted to the Federal Ministry of Health were limited in time, unless the pandemic measures had already been previously repealed by the federal Parliament (*Bundestag*) pursuant to Section 5 (1) Sentence 2 IPA. As a result, the federal Parliament has the power to determine the duration of the power exercised by the executive, to put an end to it, and to initiate a return to a normal situation if it deems this appropriate and justified[23].

Conclusion

The COVID-19 pandemic has presented a major challenge to lawmaking in Germany and the respect of the Rule of law. The creation of crisis legislation was not the result of a constitutional 'state of exception or emergency'; rather, regular legislative instruments were sufficient. Since the beginning of the crisis, the German legislator has been in a learning process that required constant adaptation to a mutating virus and the continuing infectious process. Over time, the federal legislator has been increasingly active in providing legal safeguards for the measures and Coronavirus decrees, although it had to be called upon to take greater account of the parliamentary prerogative regarding the delegation of law-making to the executive branch. The courts, and especially the

---

[22] Andrea Kießling, Infektionsschutzgesetz, IFSG, 2nd ed. C.H. Beck, München, 2021, n° 22, 24.
[23] Cf. Fuchs, op. cit., 653, 659.

Federal Constitutional Court, had a critical look at the legal measures that have been decided. Fundamental rights were restricted but in compliance with constitutional limits. In conclusion, we may say that the Rule of law has resisted the crisis, but the crises have also shown us that our legal system must be better prepared to deal with similar situations.

Bibliography

Brocker, Lars, 'Exekutive versus parlamentarische Normsetzung in der Corona-Pandemie', *NVwZ (Neue Zeitschrift für Verwaltungsrecht)*, 2020, 1485.

Dreier, Horst, 'Rechtsstaat, Föderalismus und Demokratie in der Corona-Pandemie', *DÖV (Die Öffentliche Verwaltung)*, 2021, 229.

Fuchs, Michael, Corona, "Gesundheitsdiktatur' und 'Legiszid' ', *DÖV (Die Öffentliche Verwaltung)*, 2020, 653.

Kersten, Jens/Rixen, Stephan, *Der Verfassungsstaat in der Corona-Krise*, 2nd ed., C.H. Beck, München, 2021.

Kießling, Andrea, *Infektionsschutzgesetz, IFSG*, 2nd ed., C.H. Beck, München, 2021.

Kuhlmann, Sabine, 'Das neue Infektionsschutzgesetz: Verfassungsmäßigkeit der Bundesnotbremse', https://www.juris.de/jportal/nav/juris_2015/aktuelles/magazin/infektionsschutzgesetz-verfassungsmaessigkeit.jsp, accessed on 18 July 2022.

Schwarz, Kyrill-A., 'Zur Frage der Verfassungsmäßigkeit der bundeseinheitlichen "Corona-Notbremse"', *COVuR (Covid-19 und Recht)*, 2021, 258.

Von Mangoldt, Hermann/Kunig, Philipp/Kotzur, Markus, *Kommentar zum Grundgesetz: GG*, 7th ed., C.H. Beck, München, 2018.

Von Münch,Ingo/Klein, Friedrich/Stark, Christian, *Grundgesetz Kommentar: GG*, 7th ed., C.H. Beck, München, 2021.

Voßkuhle, Andreas/Kaufhold, 'Ann-Kathrin, Grundwissen – Öffentliches Recht: Das Rechtsstaatsprinzip', *JuS (Juristische Schulung)*, 2010, 116.

Concerns regarding the restrictions on freedom and discrimination measures during the recent health crisis in Germany and France - What perspective for the rule of law?

Géraldine DEMME[1]

Since 2020 the health crisis has presented serious challenges for our nations on a number of levels. Notably, governments were caught unprepared and reacted by taking stringent measures that were unprecedented in time of peace. Numerous restrictions on fundamental rights were imposed in Germany and France, including restrictions on freedom of movement (in the form of confinements, curfews, and perimeter limitations), freedom to work (with forced closures of shops and restaurants), and freedom to gather or demonstrate. Vaccination passports were implemented in some countries and became a condition to access certain everyday places or activities and so effectively discriminate between vaccinated and non-vaccinated citizens. People, through communication campaigns and because of rooted fears, were made gradually accustomed to these restrictions.

This contribution deals with the adequacy of the recent measures taken in Germany and France with respect to the fundamental rights as guaranteed under the constitutions. The contributor wishes to highlight the importance of protecting the rule of law and of enhancing this paramount principle in the common consciousness.

Depuis 2020, la crise sanitaire a confronté nos nations à de sérieux défis et ceci à plusieurs niveaux. De nombreux gouvernements ont été pris au dépourvu et ont réagi en prenant des mesures draconiennes sans précédent en temps de paix. De nombreuses restrictions aux droits fondamentaux ont été imposées en Allemagne et en France, notamment des restrictions à la liberté de circulation (sous la forme de confinements, de couvre-feux et de limitations du périmètre de sortie), à la liberté de profession (avec des fermetures forcées de magasins et

---

[1] Ass. Prof., University Paris Nanterre.

de restaurants) et à la liberté de se rassembler ou de manifester. Des passeports de vaccination ont été mis en place dans plusieurs pays et sont devenus une condition d'accès à certains lieux ou activités de la vie quotidienne, établissant ainsi une discrimination entre les citoyens vaccinés et non vaccinés. Grâce à des campagnes de communication et en raison de peurs profondément ancrées, les citoyens se sont progressivement habitués à ces restrictions.

Cette contribution s'intéresse à la compatibilité des récentes mesures prises en Allemagne et en France par rapport aux droits fondamentaux garantis par nos constitutions. L'auteur souhaite souligner l'importance de protéger l'État de droit et de renforcer ce principe primordial dans la conscience commune.

The health crisis that the global community has been experiencing for over two years now is unprecedented. Humanity has had to fight epidemics before. For instance, the plague epidemics that struck several times in Athens from 430 to 426 BC or in the Roman Empire, between 165 and 180 AD, or the cholera epidemic, identified in India in ancient times and arriving in Europe in the 19th century. Or the smallpox epidemic, first recorded as far back as the 4th century AD in China and then in the 10th century in southwest Asia. The disease was imported to the West in the early 16th century[2].

A 'pandemic' occurs when the epidemic is widespread and affects an entire continent or the entire world[3]. Throughout history, pandemics have been closely linked to the globalization of trade and human contact, such as in the days of the Roman Empire with the establishment of vast trade networks. Today, globalization has reached an unprecedented level, whether it is for commercial exchanges or private travel, which has become trivial. It goes without saying that we exchange not only our goods, our knowledge, and our cultures, but also our strains of diseases that circulate at great speed all over our planet, without any real chance of containing them. Our modern world is particularly at risk from any infectious disease despite a higher level of hygiene, health knowledge and medicine.

---

[2] Michael S. Rosenwald, "History's deadliest pandemics, from ancient Rome to modern America", *The Washington Post*, 7 April 2020.
[3] Miquel Porta (ed.), *Dictionary of Epidemiology*, Oxford University Press, 2014, p. 179.

If the recent sanitary crisis, seen on a global-scale, is without precedent, then reactions of the leaders of our nations were not any less radical. Caught off guard, most leaders resorted to measures that were unprecedented in times of peace. In this regard, it is interesting to note that in his solemn address to the French people on March 16, 2020, French President Macron hammered home the message that 'we are at war' six times, and continued with martial vocabulary, such as 'general mobilization' against an 'invisible enemy'.[4] This assimilation of the situation to a state of war made by the President of the Republic is not without inducing the possibility of absolute infringement of liberties.

I will look first at the fundamental rights and freedoms that have been restricted by Covid crisis management measures (I). Then in part 2, I will highlight certain characteristics that are essential to protect the free rule of law for us and our future generations (II).

I. Interventions in our fundamental rights

Before we start with the core analysis, I would like to give a brief historical overview of the protection of our fundamental rights in Germany and France.

A. About the protection of fundamental rights

With the Constitution of the Weimar Republic of 1919, the German Empire had a republican and democratic constitution in which a catalog of fundamental rights was integrated. However, with the Emergency Law (*Notstandsgesetze*) of March 24, 1933, the National Socialists declared a permanent state of emergency and suspended these fundamental rights[5]. This experience of the weakness of the Weimar Constitution and the perversion of law and morality during the National Socialist dictatorship played an important role in the formulation of the present German Constitution, the so-called Basic Law (*Grundgesetz*).

---

[4] <https://www.elysee.fr/emmanuel-macron/2020/03/16/adresse-aux-francais-covid19>.

[5] According to Article 48 (2) Constitution of the Weimar Republic, the President had the power to suspend fundamental rights in order to restore the peace and to take the measures necessary to restore public security and order.

In the *Grundgesetz*, fundamental rights were placed at the very beginning, symbolizing their primacy over the rest of the law. No one can undermine their essence[6]. They are not merely programmatic propositions but, as Article 1 (3) of the *Grundgesetz* makes clear, their binding effect applies directly to all public authorities, legislation, executive power and jurisdictions. From their historical development, fundamental rights are primarily intended to secure the sphere of freedom of the individual from encroachment by public authority: they are defensive rights of the individual against the state. By designating these fundamental rights 'as the foundation of every human community, of peace and justice in the world' (Art. 1 (2) *Grundgesetz*), the constitution emphasizes the primacy of fundamental rights and connects with their natural law tradition.

In contrast to the *Grundgesetz*, the French Constitution of 1958 does not itself contain a list of fundamental rights. The constitutional guarantee of fundamental rights and freedoms in France is ensured by the preamble of the current constitution, which refers to three sources: the Declaration of the Rights of Man and of the Citizen of 1789, the preamble of the Constitution of 1946 and the Charter of the Environment of 2004[7]. If in 1958 the Constitution was the only text with constitutional value, in 1971 the Constitutional Council (*Conseil constitutionnel*) attributed constitutional value to the preamble and the sources named therein, which is now called the bloc of constitutionality[8]. This jurisprudence allows the Constitutional Council to refer to other texts and principles of constitutional value than the Constitution, by giving them an equal value. Through the integration of the block of constitutionality and its progressive extension to fundamental principles, the jurisprudence of the Constitutional Council has thus strongly contributed to ensuring the respect of fundamental rights and has thus established itself as the guarantor of the rule of law.

---

[6] The "*Wesensgehaltstheorie*" is guaranteed by Article 19 (2) *Grundgesetz*: "In no case may the essence of a fundamental right be affected."

[7] The Preamble of the French Constitution of 1958 states: "The French people solemnly proclaim their attachment to the Rights of Man and the principles of national sovereignty as defined by the Declaration of 1789, confirmed and complemented by the Preamble to the Constitution of 1946, and to the rights and duties as defined in the Charter for the Environment of 2004."

[8] Xavier Pretot, Pascal Jan, « Bloc de constitutionnalité », *Juris-Classeur administratif*, Paris, éd. du Juris-Classeur, 2002, fasc. 1418, p. 16.

Concerns regarding the restrictions on freedom 37

At European Union level, the European Convention on Human Rights of 1950[9] and the Charter of Fundamental Rights of the European Union, declared in 2000[10], are also worth mentioning. They contain rights that are now binding for member states and institutions of the European Union. The national courts and the Court of Justice of the European Union are responsible for ensuring their application.

Our states have thus committed themselves to respecting our rights and freedoms. However, the emergence and rapid spread of the coronavirus brought the need for measures to cope with situations affecting the lives of individuals and the health of populations. These measures that were taken undeniably interfered with inalienable rights. In this context, the Council of Europe and the European Parliament published two documents in 2020, 'Respecting democracy, rule of law and human rights in the framework of the COVID-19 sanitary crisis'[11], and 'The impact of COVID-19 measures on democracy, the rule of law and fundamental rights'[12].

Let us now take a look at some of the measures taken in the light of guaranteed fundamental freedoms and rights.

B. Interventions in fundamental rights due to the health crisis

Let us start here with the restrictions on freedoms. Again, I will focus primarily on measures taken by the German and French states, which I have witnessed most closely. I will however briefly mention interventions from other countries as well.

1. Restrictions on liberties

Because of the Covid Crisis, curfews and lockdowns were imposed on people in many countries. For example, in France, curfews took place from March 2020 at the initiative of mayors. From October 2020, extended curfews were introduced by the government and, finally – a

---

[9] As amended by Protocols Nos. 11, 14 and 15 supplemented by Protocols Nos. 1, 4, 6, 7, 12, 13 and 16.
[10] *Official Journal of the European Communities*, 2000/C 364/01.
[11] 7 April 2020, *SG/Inf(2020)11*.
[12] 13 November 2020, *P9_TA(2020)0307*.

general curfew between 6 p.m. and 6 a.m. was imposed across the entire country over a period of 6 months from December 15, 2020, to June 20, 2021.

Between March 17, 2020, and May 3, 2021, in France, a complete lock-down forced the population to stay at home. During this period people were authorized to leave their homes for only 1 hour per day for essential activities (such as work when remote working was not possible, essential shopping, medical needs, family emergencies…). Those who went out had to present upon request of the police a certificate of exemption, justifying their reasons for leaving their homes.

These rules interfere both with the general freedom of action and with the fundamental right of freedom of movement, as guaranteed, for example, in Article 11 *Grundgesetz*[13].

At the same time, curfews, lockdowns and contact bans almost suspended freedom of assembly (Article 8 *Grundgesetz*, Article 12 of the European Charter of Fundamental Rights, Article 11 of the European Convention on Human Rights[14]). Restrictions on contact between people went as far as to encroach on the private sphere: in Germany for example, private gatherings were limited to a maximum of 10 vaccinated or fully recovered people. However, if an unvaccinated person was present, they were only allowed to gather with two other people from the same household. Children under 14 years of age did not count towards this total, and couples were considered as one household. It was questionable to what extent the number of people gathered in one place could effectively be controlled by the police, which would lead the measures to be considered harmful to the principle of inviolability of the home guaranteed by Article 13 of the German *Grundgesetz*[15].

The ban on contact already restricted certain discussions and the exchange of opinions among the population. But the free exchange of ideas was also being prevented by the closures of online accounts and blacklisting of people who did not conform to the government line.

---

[13] Article 11 *Grundgesetz* provides: "(1) All Germans shall have the right to move freely throughout the federal territory."

[14] For example, Article 11 (1) of the European Convention on Human Rights states: "Everyone has the right to freedom of peaceful assembly and to freedom of association with others, including the right to form and to join trade unions for the protection of his interests."

[15] Article 13 (1) *Grundgesetz*: "(1) The home is inviolable."

Physicians, virologists, lawyers, political scientists and economists who were challenging the mainstream opinion were rarely invited in the public media and, in doing so, their ideas and knowledge were excluded from the public discussion. These are violations of freedom of expression, of information and of the freedom of the press (Article 5 *Grundgesetz*, Article 10 of the European Convention on Human Rights[16], Article 11 European Charter of Fundamental Rights).

In some countries, general mandatory vaccination has been introduced, such as in Austria (from 14 years old), Indonesia (from 18 years old), Ecuador (from 5 years old). Other countries have adopted compulsory corona vaccination for certain age groups (Italy over 50 years old, Greece over 60 years old) or for specific occupational groups, for example USA and Canada for government employees, Germany and France for employees in hospitals or nursing homes[17]. In addition, indirect compulsory vaccination has been implemented in many countries. Even if the obligation to vaccinate did not exist formally there, the measures adopted were able to restrict the lives of non-vaccinated people so massively that they came very close to an obligation to vaccinate. Like in France, where proof of vaccination was required from the age of 16 to enter any restaurant, cinema, museum, coffee shop, or even to travel by train or to practice sports in clubs.

Given that these cases of obligation or quasi-obligation do not allow for the individual to weigh out the pros and cons for themselves, the general freedom of action (Article 2 *Grundgesetz*) and the right to self-determination (Articles 2 (1), 1 (1) *Grundgesetz*) are massively restricted[18].

The emergence of test obligations (PCR or antigen tests), providing results which are stored electronically, the collection of personal data saved after a test, the creation of a digital vaccination passport with apps

---

[16] For example, Article 10 (1) of the European Convention on Human Rights provides: "Everyone has the right to freedom of expression. This right shall include freedom to hold opinions and to receive and impart information and ideas without interference by public authority and regardless of frontiers. This Article shall not prevent States from requiring the licensing of broadcasting, television or cinema enterprises."

[17] Articles 12–19, Loi n° 2021-1040 *relative à la gestion de la crise sanitaire*, 5 August 2021.

[18] Article 1 (1) *Grundgesetz*: "Human dignity shall be inviolable. To respect and protect it shall be the duty of all state authority.", Article 2 (1) *Grundgesetz*: "Every person shall have the right to free development of his personality insofar as he does not violate the rights of others or offend against the constitutional order or the moral law."

(e.g. '*Tous anti-Covid*'), and the tracking of individuals to find contact cases, all encroach on the right to informational self-determination (data protection). In Austria, the mobile phone provider A1 made the movement data of all Austrian citizens available to the government[19].

China, after the Coronavirus outbreak, required its citizens to install software on their smartphones that provides information about their health, tracks their whereabouts, and determines whether they can enter a public place. The software shares this information with police, creating a template for new forms of control that could exist long after the epidemic has subsided.

Businesses and stores that do not serve daily needs (such as food, drink, press, and hygiene items) have been forced to close in many countries. This includes restaurants, cinemas, theaters, museums, and so on. This represents an infringement on entrepreneurial freedom (Article 12 *Grundgesetz*[20]).

In both Germany and France, there were closures of schools and universities. Classes were held remotely, which was detrimental to some of the pupils and students who slipped from school education or dropped out of their studies which disturbed the right to school education (article 2 (1) in conjunction with Article 7 (1) *Grundgesetz*).

These are only examples of the restrictions. The list is not exhaustive. Further restrictions like mandatory mask-wearing, and compulsory PCR testing, were made. No matter how many examples we use, it becomes clear that the Covid crisis has led to many encroachments on fundamental rights.

Let us now turn to the question of equal treatment.

2. Violations of equality

Article 3 *Grundgesetz* guarantees equal rights: '*All human beings are equal before the law.*' Despite this, countless measures have been taken

---

[19] European Parliament, *Tracking mobile devices to fight coronavirus*, https://www.europarl.europa.eu/RegData/etudes/BRIE/2020/649384/EPRS_BRI(2020)649384_EN.pdf.

[20] Article 12 (1) *Grundgesetz*: "All Germans shall have the right freely to choose their occupation or profession, their place of work and their place of training. The practice of an occupation or profession may be regulated by or pursuant to a law."

during the health crisis which discriminates between the vaccinated and the unvaccinated.

In France, for example, an unvaccinated person could not go to a restaurant, cinema, sports club, amusement park, public swimming pool, etc. They were not even allowed to use the railway. Citizens who did not want to be vaccinated had to sacrifice a huge part of their life to remain so.

With the exception for some groups, vaccination was not compulsory in France but the described measures were intended to force the population to get vaccinated. This is what French President Macron explained in a not-so-nice way: he told Le Parisien newspaper in an interview that 'as for the non-vaccinated, I really want to piss them off' with new measures that would bar them from much of public life[21].

As well as the unequal treatment, this situation leads to division among the population. The vaccination/non-vaccination issue divides. Non-vaccinated people are becoming the scapegoats of the crisis situation. At the beginning the French president spoke of an 'invisible enemy'. Now it seems that a visible enemy has been found. This is all very disquieting.

Let us now turn to the question of the conditions under which interventions in fundamental rights can be lawful.

II. Proportionality and time limitation as necessary characteristics

Of course, no fundamental right is granted without limits. Fundamental rights must find their limits where they interfere with the rights of others. For this reason, the legislature reserves, where necessary, the right to limit the scope of fundamental freedoms and rights by means of legislation.

In Germany, for example, this has been done primarily by the Infection Protection Act, which came into force on January 1, 2001[22]. Measures to combat pandemics which interfered with fundamental rights were provided and regulated.

---

[21] *Le Parisien newspaper*, 4 January 2022.
[22] *Infektionsschutzgesetz*, 20 July 2000, *BGBl.* I, 1045.

In France, the Emergency Law of March 23, 2020[23] introduced the possibility of imposing a health emergency in the event of a health disaster. During this health emergency, the government is allowed to resort to exceptional measures, such as restricting freedom of movement, banning citizens from leaving their homes except when absolutely necessary, stopping assemblies, closing stores and all establishments open to the public, etc. At the national level, the health emergency has been declared twice in France: between March 24 and July 10, 2020, and between October 17, 2020 and July 1, 2021. As of June 2, 2021, 'phase-out' regulations have been applied until July 31, 2022.

Measures meant to protect can hurt, it is a difficult balancing act.

A. An unstable situation between protection and injury

The goal of the health of the world population is an outstanding goal of general interest, this is indisputable.

From this point of view, the German Federal Constitutional Court (*Bundesverfassungsgericht*), which we also refer to as the guardian of the German Constitution, has ruled that many of such measures, despite the infringement on fundamental rights that they represent, are compatible with the German constitution 'in the extreme danger of the pandemic'[24]. Thus, the judges of the Federal Constitutional Court leave politicians with an enormous amount of in making decisions in uncertain times[25].

In France too, the Constitutional Council (*Conseil constitutionnel*) emphasized that 'the measures provided for in the framework of the public health state of emergency, in any case, can only be taken in order to preserve public health.' The Council specified that 'it cannot call into question the legislator's evaluation of the existence of a public health catastrophe (…), when, as in this case, this evaluation is not, to current knowledge, clearly inadequate concerning the current situation.'[26]

---

[23] LOI n° 2020-290 *d'urgence pour faire face à l'épidémie de covid-19*, 23 March 2020, *JORF* n°0072, 24 March 2020.

[24] Desicions 1 BvR 781/21, 1 BvR 889/21, 1 BvR 860/21, 1 BvR 854/21, 1 BvR 820/21, 1 BvR 805/21, 1 BvR 798/21, 19 November 2021.

[25] Also very critical of this attitude of the German Federal Constitutional Court: Boehme-Neßler, Volker „Bundesverfassungsgericht zu Corona-Politik: Der Rückzug der Verfassungshüter", *Die Zeit*, 30 November 2021.

[26] Decision no. 2021-824 DC of 5 August 2021.

Despite the current anxiety-provoking situation, we must continue to keep in mind that the state can only interfere with fundamental rights if such interference is proportionate. Not all measures intended to control the infection rate, no matter how well-intentioned they are, are automatically lawful. Even such measures which pursue a legitimate public purpose, must not only be suitable and necessary, but also proportionate. No fundamental right may be affected in its essence (Article 19 (2) *Grundgesetz*). In addition, such measures have to be limited in time.

It is questionable why the Covid crisis management was not more targeted and, moreover, better applied to the groups at risk (the elderly, people with certain pre-existing conditions, and the immunocompromised), since these groups had been identified very early at the start of the Covid disease.

It is also regrettable that some developed countries have not built upon the strong foundations of our society. For example, public hospitals in France have reduced capacity by 79,896 beds since 2000[27]. This is a quarter of their admission capacity. Hospital staff is poorly paid. This led to France being caught unprepared, lacking vigilance and prevention, which shows a weak point in the state's management. What about hospital capacity in the event of a nuclear attack, a major natural disaster or major chemical plant failure?

In the Covid crisis, the responsibility of contagion and disease was often shifted to the population. In France, clips were shown on television in which grandchildren visited their grandparents, and these grandparents died and were buried shortly thereafter. Before a state places such burden and fear on its citizens, shouldn't it first create solid foundations that will allow citizens to face such situations more calmly?

And as far as the principle of equality is concerned, it is true that only what is equal must be treated equally, while what is unequal must be treated unequally. But what gives us today the unquestionable knowledge that non-vaccinated people are sources of danger to such an extent that they have nothing in common with the danger of vaccinated people? Can the vaccinated not also become infected and be contagious? Even if we assume a greater danger potential of the non-vaccinated, alternative

---

[27] https://data.drees.solidarites-sante.gouv.fr/ For more details on this reduction, see Bauduin, Noé, „Comment la France a perdu près de 80,000 lits d'hospitalisation publics en vingt ans", franceinfo, 9 November 2021.

measures are possible, such as a negative antigen test. During a period, in France, non-vaccinated people with a negative test were prevented from travelling from Paris to Marseille by train, whereas a vaccinated Covid sufferer would have no problem boarding the train. The discrimination suffered by non-vaccinated people seems difficult to classify as proportionate. Moreover, it is very important to avoid the division of citizens and finger pointing at some groups of people.

There is no clear evidence to suggest that a more positive outcome could be achieved by excluding the rule of law than would have been achieved in the reverse scenario. But beyond the question of how to combat the Coronavirus, my concern is first of all to emphasize our commitment to a fundamental free legal order in a system based on the rule of law.

B. A challenge also for our future value system

States understandably tend to welcome emergency powers because they make rapid actions possible. However, there is always a danger that these exceptional powers, or at least parts of them, will remain in place even after the dangers have passed. Also, because citizens do not react sufficiently and accept the situation as it has been imposed on them.

Human beings are by nature rather docile and can become accustomed to many things. That is why we are so adaptable, which is certainly an advantage. However, adaptability is also a risk in certain settings. I would like to tell you a little personal anecdote about this: My 9-year-old son, who had become accustomed to his mask in the classroom and in the schoolyard, and whose class was only allowed to play within a confined rectangle in the schoolyard so that there were no contact with different class groups, told me that he stopped once and looked around. He no longer found it strange – like at the beginning of this regulation – to be only allowed to play in a few designated square meters, and not with all children. Meanwhile, he found it bizarre that just a few weeks ago he was allowed to romp around in the entire schoolyard. At the same time, this thought scared him (and rightly so!).

What can we all get used to if we don't stop sometimes to gain some perspective and distance? A healthy distance also from the information submerging us from the media and social networks, which, almost obsessively, provide constant negative facts such as the number of dead people or the number of sick people, without a substantial search for a future perspective? Distance from the majority opinion of which we would prefer to join right away, because humankind has always been dependent on belonging to a group and it is clearly easier to swim with the current than against it. Distance from one's own fear, which can be partly justified, but also partly exaggerated. As a republic we also have to take our fate into our own hands.

Conclusion

Deliberations leading to restrictions of fundamental rights should be explained more transparently and comprehensively to the population, so that these issues do not escape the common consciousness. How many adults have I spoken to during the pandemic who either had not taken the time to seriously think about the restrictions to fundamental rights that were being imposed on them or who considered these restrictions to be trivial? If the older generation, which has at least heard of struggles for liberties, already reacts in this way, how will today's younger generation build the future?

It is for this reason that, in my opinion, the challenge of the Covid crisis does not take place only with regard to health. It is also a situation – and I fear not the last – that challenges us to question which values we subscribe to. This is why I wanted to highlight the importance of protecting the rule of law, to enhance this paramount principle in the common consciousness in order to ensure a very healthy future for our societies.

Bibliography

Boehme-Neßler, Volker, „Bundesverfassungsgericht zu Corona-Politik: Der Rückzug der Verfassungshüter", *Die Zeit*, 30 November 2021.

Charter of Fundamental Rights of the European Union, *Official Journal of the European Communities*, 2000/C 364/01, https://www.europarl.europa.eu/charter/pdf/text_en.pdf (11 July 2023).

European Parliament, 'The impact of COVID-19 measures on democracy, the rule of law and fundamental rights', 13 November 2020, *P9_TA(2020)0307*, https://www.europarl.europa.eu/doceo/document/TA-9-2020-0307_EN.html (11 July 2023).

European Parliament, *Tracking mobile devices to fight coronavirus*, https://www.europarl.europa.eu/RegData/etudes/BRIE/2020/649384/EPRS_BRI(2020)649384_EN.pdf (11 July 2023).

Grogan, Joelle, 'Respecting democracy, rule of law and human rights in the framework of the COVID-19 sanitary crisis', Document requested by the European Parliament's special committee on the COVID-19 pandemic, 7 April 2020, *SG/Inf(2020)11*.

Porta, Miquel (ed.), *Dictionary of epidemiology*, Oxford University Press, 2014.

Pretot, Xavier/Jan, Pascal, 'Bloc de constitutionnalité', *Juris-Classeur administratif*, Paris, éd. du Juris-Classeur, 2002, fasc. 1418.

Rosenwald, Michael S., 'History's deadliest pandemics, from ancient Rome to modern America', *The Washington Post*, 7 April 2020.

Les conséquences du mensonge sur son statut vaccinal en droits civil et pénal

Sabir KADEL[1]

Le mensonge est diversement appréhendé par le droit. Pris très au sérieux quand il s'agit d'un faux en écriture publique, plus légèrement quand il s'agit d'une parole à la dérobée, il ne répond pas non plus aux mêmes exigences de sévérité dépendant s'il est saisi par le droit civil ou le droit pénal, ou sur l'objet sur lequel il porte. Si le mensonge a toujours fait partie de la société, employé souvent de manière bénigne dans la vie de tous les jours, il s'est transformé, en ces temps de Covid, en véritable enjeu sociétal, surtout de la part de personnes non vaccinées, parfois par peur de stigmatisation, souvent pour tout simplement ne plus être aliéné d'une vie sociale qui leur est désormais interdite.

En effet, on le sait, restaurants, bars, hôtels, hôpitaux, crèches, institutions d'enseignement, club de gym, et même salons de coiffure, ont été interdits aux personnes non-vaccinées. De ce fait, la tentation est grande de mentir sur son statut vaccinal, mensonge qui n'est pas sans conséquences. Mais nous sommes ici dans le droit public; qu'en est-il du mensonge de son statut vaccinal en droit privé, c'est-à-dire dans sa relation avec d'autres personnes et non sanctionné par les différentes lois spéciales promulguées ces derniers temps? Le droit y est-il insensible ou alors ce mensonge-là également sera-t-il réprimé?

L'on examinera ainsi le mensonge en droit civil et en droit pénal, et plus particulièrement, pour ce qui est du premier, le mensonge sur son statut vaccinal lors du mariage, et, pour le second, lors des rapports sexuels.

The consequences of lying about one's vaccination status in civil and criminal law

Lies are variously captured by the law. Taken very seriously when it is a forgery in public writing, more lightly when it is a verbal utterance, lying does not face the same harshness depending on whether it is seized by civil law or criminal law, or on the subject matter to which it relates. If lying has always

---

[1] CEO Law Reform Commission Mauritius.

been part of society, often committed in a benign way in everyday life, it has turned, in these times of Covid, into a real societal issue, especially on the part of unvaccinated people, sometimes for fear of being stigmatized, often simply to no longer be alienated from a social life that is now forbidden to them.

Indeed, as we are aware, restaurants, bars, hotels, hospitals, nurseries, educational institutions, gym clubs, and even hair salons, have been prohibited to unvaccinated people. As a result, there is a great temptation to lie about one's vaccination status, a lie which is not without consequences. But we are here in public law, what about lying about one's vaccination status in private law, that is to say in one's relationship with other people and not sanctioned by the various special laws enacted in recent times? Is the law insensitive to this or will this lie also be sanctioned?

We will thus examine lying in civil law and in criminal law, and more particularly, with regard to the former, lying about one's vaccination status prior to marriage, and, for the latter, pertaining to sexual intercourse.

Introduction

Talleyrand disait que la parole a été donnée à l'homme pour déguiser sa pensée. Et selon les dires du Dr House dans la série éponyme, tout le monde ment. Le mensonge est diversement appréhendé par le droit. Pris très au sérieux quand il s'agit d'un faux en écriture publique[2], plus légèrement quand il s'agit d'une parole à la dérobée, il ne répond pas non plus aux mêmes exigences de sévérité dépendant s'il est saisi par le droit civil ou le droit pénal, ou sur l'objet sur lequel il porte.

Si le mensonge a toujours fait partie de la société, employée souvent de manière bénigne pour faire preuve de courtoisie dans la vie de tous les jours, il s'est transformé, en ces temps de Covid par lesquels nous passons, en sport national, surtout de la part de personnes non vaccinées, parfois par peur de stigmatisation, souvent pour tout simplement ne plus être aliéné d'une vie sociale qui leur est désormais interdite.

En effet, on le sait, restaurants, bars, hôtels, hôpitaux, crèches, institutions d'enseignement, club de gym, et même salons de coiffure, ont été interdits aux personnes non-vaccinées à Maurice[3]. De ce fait, la tentation est grande de mentir sur son statut vaccinal, mensonge qui n'est pas sans conséquences. Mais nous sommes ici dans le droit public ;

---

[2] Voir Section 107 du Code pénal mauricien
[3] Voir les *Consolidated COVID-19 (Amendment No. 3) Regulations* 2021

qu'en est-il du mensonge de son statut vaccinal en droit privé, c'est-à-dire dans sa relation avec d'autres personnes et non sanctionné par les différentes lois spéciales promulguées ces derniers temps ? Le droit y est-il insensible ou alors, de par une gymnastique intellectuelle, et en étirant les jurisprudences actuelles, ce mensonge-là également sera réprimé ?

L'on s'intéressera successivement au mensonge en droit civil et en droit pénal, et plus particulièrement, pour ce qui est du premier, le mensonge sur son statut vaccinal lors du mariage, et, pour le second, lors des rapports sexuels.

I. Le mensonge sur son statut vaccinal lors du mariage

Nous l'avons tous appris, et en avons débattu lors de nos études de droit, le mariage est autant une convention qu'une institution. Institution, car il fut intimement lié à la citoyenneté de la ville dans la Grèce antique, tout comme il fut réservé aux seuls citoyens de Rome[4]. Geste politique, le mariage fut aussi longtemps au cœur des alliances et des guerres en Europe[5]. Convention aussi cependant, car il est aussi l'union de deux personnes qui passent un contrat entre elles, solennel certes, mais surtout consensuel[6].

Plusieurs conditions sont attachées au mariage afin que celui-ci ne soit pas entaché d'illicéité ; on pense ainsi à la capacité des époux, qui doivent être capables de conclure des actes juridiques. Ainsi ne peuvent se marier les mineurs, sans exception possible à Maurice depuis la promulgation du *Children's Act*[7], mais également les majeurs incapables.

Autre condition essentielle de la validité du mariage, et c'est ce qui nous intéresse en premier lieu en l'espèce, c'est le consentement, comme le prévoit l'article 149 de notre Code civil. En cas de défaut de consentement, la sanction prévue par notre article 180, c'est la nullité du mariage[8].

---

[4] P. F. GIRARD, *Manuel élémentaire de droit romain*, par LÉVY, 2003, Dalloz.
[5] A. LEFEBVRE-TEILLARD, *Introduction historique au droit des personnes et de la famille*, 1996, PUF
[6] A. COSTE-FLORET, *La nature juridique du mariage, ce qu'elle est dans le code civil, ce qu'elle devrait être*, thèse, Montpellier, 1935
[7] Voir Section 12 du *Children's Act* 2020
[8] MALAURIE et FULCHIRON, Droit civil. La famille, 4e éd., 2011, Defrénois, n° 252

La nullité est l'une des trois causes de dissolution du mariage, les deux autres étant le décès de l'un des époux ainsi que le divorce. La différence entre le divorce et l'annulation consiste dans le fait que le premier n'a d'effet que pour l'avenir tandis que le second produit des effets rétroactifs, comme si le mariage n'avait jamais eu lieu.

L'annulation permet ainsi, par un de ces nombreux tours de passe-passe dont le droit a le secret, de remonter le temps et de défaire ce qui a été fait, par le biais d'une fiction juridique. Et l'une des causes de nullité du mariage est l'erreur. En effet, selon notre article 180, alinéa 2 : s'il y a eu erreur dans la personne, ou sur des qualités essentielles de la personne, l'autre époux peut demander la nullité du mariage.

Nous connaissons tous cette célèbre formule de Loysel, selon qui « en matière de mariage, trompe qui peut » ; en effet, le dol ne constitue pas *de facto* un vice du consentement, puisqu'à en croire les auteurs Fulchiron et Malaurie : « admettre que le dol soit une cause de nullité serait permettre à tous les déçus de la vie matrimoniale de sortir du lien conjugal »[9].

Les choses ne sont cependant pas si simples, puisque certaines tromperies peuvent avoir été déterminantes dans la liberté de l'autre époux de contracter mariage. Si l'erreur sur la personne ne semble pas poser de problème[10], « Louis croit épouser Marie mais en fait il épouse Antoinette », la question de l'erreur sur les qualités essentielles est davantage épineuse[11].

De nombreuses décisions ont été rendues sur l'erreur portant sur les qualités essentielles de la personne tant en droit français que mauricien: notamment, il a été jugé qu'il peut y avoir erreur sur une qualité essentielle quand un époux a ignoré que son conjoint avait la qualité de divorcé, ou lorsqu'il s'est trompé sur son aptitude à avoir des relations sexuelles normales, ou encore sur son état de santé mentale.

En revanche, l'époux tenu dans l'ignorance d'une liaison antérieure à l'union ne justifiait pas l'annulation du mariage pour erreur sur les

---

[9] H. FULCHIRON et Ph. MALAURIE, *La famille*: Defrénois, 2e éd., 2006, n° 179
[10] DEKEUWER-DÉFOSSEZ, Nullité pour erreur sur les qualités essentielles du conjoint: la leçon de droit de la cour de Douai, RLDC 2009/57
[11] BARDOUT, De la persistance de l'ordre public en matière d'annulation du mariage: regain d'intérêt pour un mode de dissolution judiciaire qui n'appartient pas qu'aux époux, AJ fam. 2008. 339

qualités essentielles, car l'infidélité était antérieure à la célébration du mariage.

Ainsi, le conjoint qui sollicite la nullité de son mariage doit prouver que l'erreur prétendue était déterminante pour que le juge accède à sa demande. En d'autres termes, il doit convaincre le juge que s'il n'avait pas commis cette erreur, il ne se serait pas marié.

Pendant longtemps en jurisprudence française, l'erreur sur la virginité de l'épouse pouvait être retenue pour que l'époux demande l'annulation du mariage. Cette position a tenu jusqu'à la désormais célèbre décision de la Cour d'appel de Douai du 17 novembre 2008.

Et c'est bien cette décision, et la *ratio legis* qu'elle invoque, qui nous sera utile pour déterminer si le mensonge sur son statut vaccinal peut donner lieu à l'annulation du mariage.

Jusqu'à cette décision, l'erreur était appréciée *in concreto*, c'est-à-dire en fonction de l'appréhension que s'en fait la partie qui se prétend induite en erreur, et de l'importance qu'elle revêt pour elle, qu'elle juge déterminante dans sa décision de contracter le mariage.

Mais la Cour d'appel de Douai dit « stop » ! Selon elle, dans une société moderne, où doit prévaloir l'égalité des sexes, la virginité de l'épouse ne saurait être prise en compte. Elle se prononce donc pour une interprétation *in abstrato* de l'erreur, autrement dit, en tenant compte des valeurs de la société dans son ensemble et non de l'un des époux.

Mais rappelons les faits de l'affaire. Le 1er avril 2008, le tribunal de grande instance (TGI) de Lille a annulé un mariage pour « erreur sur les qualités essentielles du conjoint » en vertu de l'article 180, alinéa 2 du Code civil. Selon le tribunal, la femme n'est pas vierge alors qu'elle savait que cette condition avait un caractère déterminant dans la motivation et le consentement de l'homme qu'elle épousait[12].

Fin mai 2008, une polémique s'en est suivie et de nombreuses personnalités, politiques, religieuses ou encore intellectuelles ont réagi à la décision. À la suite de ces événements, la garde des Sceaux Rachida Dati a demandé au ministère public, c'est-à-dire au procureur général de Douai, de faire appel, et ce à l'encontre de l'avis des conjoints. L'appel a été interjeté auprès de la cour d'appel de Douai, le 3 juin 2008.

---

[12] TGI Lille, 1er avr. 2008, D. 2008. 1389, note Labbée.

Le 17 novembre de la même année, la cour d'appel a infirmé le jugement du tribunal de grande instance.

Il est important de noter qu'en l'espèce, l'épouse a donné son approbation à la procédure de nullité. Ainsi, la Cour d'appel fait fi de la volonté de la femme au profit du bien public de toutes les femmes, essentialisant ainsi le concept de la femme.

Que nous faut-il donc retenir de cette décision et quelles leçons pouvons-nous en tirer concernant la question qui nous interpelle, c'est-à-dire, le fait de mentir sur son statut vaccinal.

Cette décision annonce un recul de la notion d'autonomie de la volonté, notion si chère au doyen Carbonnier, qui trouvait, dans cette théorie, une justification de l'existence de l'erreur en droit contractuel ; en effet, selon lui, la volonté est altérée en cas d'erreur, puisque celle-ci amène à une fausse représentation de la réalité. Dès lors, le consentement donné par l'une des parties ne serait pas complètement autonome, ce qui justifierait de sanctionner l'erreur, en l'espèce par la nullité.

La Cour d'appel bat en brèche cette théorie, la seule réalité qui compte c'est celle nourrie par la société dans son ensemble, qu'importe la représentation qu'en font les parties au contrat.

Suite à cette décision, tout en prenant en compte la jurisprudence traditionnelle, et pour en revenir au statut vaccinal, nous pouvons supputer qu'un mensonge portant sur ce sujet devrait être sanctionné par la nullité du mariage. Et ce, que nous adhérions à l'interprétation *in concreto* ou *in abstracto*[13].

En effet, si c'est l'appréciation *in concreto* que l'on retient, l'on s'attardera uniquement sur ce qui est considéré important aux yeux de l'une des parties. En ce sens, si l'un des époux considère qu'il ne veut épouser qu'une personne vaccinée, et qu'il l'a bien fait comprendre à l'autre avant le mariage que pour lui c'est un critère essentiel, alors un mensonge ayant trait à cela devrait emporter l'annulation de l'union.

Idem, si tant est que ce soit l'appréciation *in abstracto* qui l'emporte auprès du juge. En effet, en ces temps où en France comme à Maurice, le *pass vaccinal* a cours, et qu'il est essentiel de prouver être vacciné pour avoir accès à une pléthore de services, et où la fraude d'un tel statut entraîne des sanctions pénales, il convient de subodorer que le juge

---

[13] TGI Rennes, 9 nov. 1976, D. 1977. 539, note Cosnard.

serait enclin d'en déduire que la société dans sa majorité a assimilé la vaccination à une norme de santé publique. Et qu'en conséquence, un tel mensonge serait à même de constituer un critère essentiel aux termes de l'article 180 du Code civil.

II. Le mensonge sur son statut vaccinal lors de rapports sexuels

Venons-en maintenant aux conséquences du mensonge sur son statut vaccinal dans la sphère pénale, et plus précisément aux infractions sexuelles.

On l'a dit, mentir sur le fait que l'on est vacciné peut entraîner la nullité du mariage. Mais si on peut défaire un mariage, l'on ne peut pas défaire des rapports sexuels.

Quelles seraient donc les conséquences pour la personne qui mentirait sur son statut de vacciné afin d'avoir des rapports sexuels et quelle qualification juridique retenir en l'espèce ?

La licéité de tout rapport sexuel est marquée par le consentement qu'expriment les parties en présence. Si c'est le consentement qui fait défaut, nous serions alors en présence d'un viol.

Si pendant longtemps, c'est l'honneur des familles que le droit pénal a entendu protéger en incriminant le viol[14], un changement paradigmatique a été amorcé au siècle dernier, du moins en France, et c'est maintenant l'autonomie de la volonté qui est au cœur de la question des relations sexuelles.

Mais avant de pénétrer au cœur du sujet, des prolégomènes s'imposent pour délimiter et définir la question du viol et le distinguer des autres infractions sexuelles. Le viol fait partie des infractions sexuelles impliquant un contact physique entre l'auteur et la victime, au même titre que l'attentat à la pudeur, mais au contraire du harcèlement sexuel ou encore de l'exhibition sexuelle.

Ce qui différencie le viol de l'attentat à la pudeur, c'est que le premier consiste, du moins à Maurice, en une pénétration vaginale de la femme par le pénis de l'homme[15]. Tout autre acte sexuel relèverait soit de

---

[14] Bull. crim. n° 240; S. 1857, 1, p. 711; DP 1857, 1, p. 314.
[15] B. BOULOC, Répertoire de droit pénal, Dalloz, *Viol*, n° 4.

l'attentat à la pudeur, soit de la sodomie, visée par la Section 250 de notre Code pénal, section au cœur de tant de controverses. Je dis à Maurice, car la définition juridique du viol diffère sensiblement en France[16] où le législateur en a élargi considérablement le champ d'incrimination. Mais nous ne nous attarderons pas sur ce point, car ce qui nous intéresse, pour la question qui nous taraude en l'espèce, ce sont les modalités de commission du viol, et celles-ci sont les mêmes tant à Maurice qu'en France.

Ces modalités sont au nombre de quatre. Le viol peut être commis par : violence, contrainte, menace, ou surprise. Relevons que certains auteurs assimilent la menace à la contrainte, mais ce sont là des controverses jésuitiques dont nous ferons fi pour cette présentation. La violence, la contrainte, et la menace, ne posent pas de problème conceptuel ; dans les trois cas, ces comportements contraignent la victime à l'acte sexuel dont l'absence de consentement n'est pas prise en compte.

Il en va autrement de la surprise, où le consentement est donné, mais qu'il n'est pas éclairé, car la victime se fait une fausse représentation de la réalité. Il ne faut point considérer la surprise dans son sens commun, qui s'entend comme l'émotion, le sentiment provoqué par quelque chose d'inattendu. Il n'est pas ici question de l'étonnement, ou de stupéfaction. Au regard des éléments constitutifs du viol, la surprise n'est pas à « prélever dans le domaine du sentiment, mais dans celui du consentement » nous dit Mayaud[17].

Selon une jurisprudence constante[18], la surprise, comme élément constitutif du viol, consiste à surprendre le consentement de la victime et ne saurait se confondre avec la surprise exprimée par cette dernière. De ce fait a été cassé un arrêt qui, pour déclarer le prévenu coupable d'agression sexuelle (dont les manifestations du défaut de consentement de la victime sont identiques à celles du viol), avait énoncé qu'après « les avances poussées » du prévenu, la victime était « tombée des nues ».

L'absence de consentement fondé sur la surprise a, en revanche, été admise pour un médecin qui s'était servi de son autorité professionnelle pour abuser sexuellement d'une patiente en lui imposant des investigations

---

[16] E. GARÇON, Code pénal annoté, ss. art. 331 à 333, n° 6, 2e éd.
[17] Y. MAYAUD, Les qualifications relatives aux atteintes sexuelles, AJ pénal 2004.
[18] Crim. 25 avr. 2001, n° 00-85.467.

vaginales et anales non nécessaires[19]. Le consentement de la victime avait été surpris, en raison du caractère fallacieux des examens pratiqués sur la patiente, en ce qu'ils furent présentés comme relevant naturellement du cadre de la consultation.

Ainsi, selon la professeure Valérie Malabat, le consentement surpris est donc celui qui est donné, à la différence du consentement forcé par la violence, la contrainte ou la menace, mais qui n'est pas donné en connaissance de cause, qui manque de lucidité[20].

La liberté sexuelle n'est pas totalement supprimée, elle est seulement altérée, la victime n'ayant pas parfaitement conscience des actes qu'elle est en train de subir.

Dès lors, la surprise est avérée si la victime est inconsciente, en état d'alcoolémie, sous l'empire d'un narcotique, ou encore aliénée mentale.

En outre, la surprise peut résulter d'un stratagème, lorsque celui-ci vise à surprendre le consentement de la victime. La ruse remplace alors l'usage de la force par l'agresseur. Le mensonge est à même de constituer un stratagème quand il permet de renvoyer une fausse image de la réalité et ainsi tromper la victime[21].

Comme pour le mariage, le mensonge sur l'identité de la personne a été, selon une jurisprudence constante, constitutive de viol par surprise. Et ce depuis une célèbre affaire datant de 1857. En l'espèce, un individu, après s'être introduit dans la chambre et le lit d'une femme encore endormie dont le mari était absent, profite de l'erreur de cette femme en consommant sur elle l'acte de pénétration.

Mais qu'en est-il du mensonge portant sur les qualités du partenaire sexuel ? Est-ce que mentir sur son niveau d'études, son titre, son travail, ou même sur sa fertilité, seraient à même de relever de la surprise telle que l'entend le droit pénal ?

En droit britannique, la poursuite a refusé à aller de l'avant avec l'acte d'accusation de « *rape by deception* », le pendant anglais du viol par surprise, dans le cas d'un policier infiltré ayant menti sur sa véritable identité. De plus, en 2020, la Cour d'appel d'Angleterre et du Pays de

---

[19] Cass., ass. plén., 14 févr. 2003, n° 96-80.088.
[20] V. Malabat, *Droit pénal spécial*, 4ᵉ éd., 2009, coll. HyperCours, Dalloz, n° 303.
[21] P. Conte, Dr. pén. 2017, comm. 71.

Galles a jugé que mentir sur le fait qu'on ait fait une vasectomie n'était pas à même de constituer l'infraction.

Que pouvons-nous en déduire du mensonge sur son statut vaccinal afin d'entretenir des rapports sexuels. Une comparaison qui peut être faite, même si comparaison n'est pas raison, c'est avec le mensonge sur sa séropositivité. Une partie de la doctrine française[22], certes minoritaire, considère que la qualification idoine devrait être le viol, que le partenaire sexuel qui était dans l'ignorance se retrouve contaminé ou non. Le problème serait toutefois probatoire et consisterait à prouver que sachant la vérité l'autre partie n'aurait pas accepté d'avoir des rapports sexuels.

Si dans le cas du statut vaccinal, le partenaire sexuel avait bien fait comprendre qu'il ne veut entretenir des relations sexuelles qu'avec des personnes vaccinées, et que la poursuite parvient à prouver ce point, alors, l'on serait tenté de considérer que son consentement a été surpris, c'est-à-dire qu'il a été donné, mais basé sur une perception altérée de la vérité, et donc qu'il y a bien viol.

Une telle exégèse peut paraître exagérée et la doctrine comme la jurisprudence, française ou étrangère, semblent la balayer. En effet, la jurisprudence française paraît n'admettre que la surprise ne peut être retenue que lorsque le mensonge véhiculé par l'auteur porte sur son identité (par exemple l'auteur se fait passer pour le mari) ou sur ses fonctions (l'auteur se fait passer pour un médecin). De même la jurisprudence étrangère ne semble se ranger du côté du viol par surprise que lorsque le mensonge est lié aux modalités des rapports sexuels.

On en veut pour preuve l'exemple de Julian Assange, le fondateur de Wikileaks, poursuivi pour viol en Suède. En l'espèce une femme l'a accusé d'avoir accepté de mettre un préservatif, une condition qu'elle a érigée comme impérative pour avoir des relations sexuelles, pour qu'ensuite Assange ne le perce ce qui fait qu'il aurait éjaculé à l'intérieur d'elle.

En revanche, mentir sur sa santé ou certaines dispositions physiologiques ne paraissent pas à même de réunir les conditions nécessaires pour que la qualification de viol par surprise ne soit constituée.

---

[22] B. Chapleau, 'La pénalisation de la transmission du virus de l'immunodéficience humaine par voie sexuelle', Droit pénal n° 10, Octobre 2006, étude 18.

Conclusion

N'est pas Diogène qui veut ; en effet le philosophe présocratique grec ayant un goût prononcé pour la vérité, lui qui s'exprimait sans filtre[23], allant jusqu'à narguer Alexandre le Grand.

Le commun des mortels cependant, dont vous et moi faisons partie, mentons, à longueur de temps. Entre mon réveil du matin et le moment où je me tiens devant vous, j'ai dû mentir une bonne dizaine de fois. Mais certains mensonges ne sont pas sans conséquences sur les rapports humains. Et le droit prend acte de ce fait.

En ces temps où le monde entier passe par une crise sanitaire sans commune mesure, et où la vaccination contre le COVID-19 est ouverte à tous, et permettrait, selon la majorité des experts, d'endiguer la pandémie, il est fort à parier que le droit ne resterait pas insensible au mensonge y ayant trait, surtout sur des actes aussi importants que le mariage. Mais si le droit civil était enclin à le considérer pour annuler un mariage, le droit pénal pourrait se montrer plus réticent à envisager une qualification aussi lourde que le viol et portant une charge symbolique aussi forte.

---

[23] J-M ROUBINEAU, *Diogène: l'antisocial*, Presses Universitaires de France, 2020

German fundamental rights in times of a global health crisis

Marie ROSSIER[1]

During the Covid crisis, many crucial fundamental freedoms have been restricted and even partially completely removed temporarily. The outbreak of the Corona virus has put fundamental rights to the test, but despite the crisis, one must continually ask the question: what is justified, what measures are proportional to the pandemic? Numerous applications have been made to the administrative courts as well as to the German constitutional court. This presentation will give an overview of the German case law on fundamental freedoms in times of crisis.

Les droits fondamentaux en temps de crise sanitaire mondiale

Pendant la crise actuelle due à la pandémie, beaucoup de libertés fondamentales cruciales ont été restreintes et même partiellement complètement supprimées temporairement. L'apparition du Covid a mis les droits fondamentaux à l'épreuve, mais malgré la crise, on se doit de continuellement poser la question ce qui est justifié, quelles mesures sont proportionnelles vis-à-vis de la pandémie ? De nombreuses requêtes ont été portées devant les tribunaux administratifs ainsi que devant la cour constitutionnelle allemande. Cette présentation a comme objectif de donner un aperçu de la jurisprudence allemande concernant les libertés fondamentales en temps de crise.

Introduction

The global Corona virus pandemic has created entirely new challenges with regards to the protection of fundamental rights. In response to the high infection risk, general curfews, far-reaching contact bans, assembly restrictions and distance regulations, school closure and finally the

---

[1] Doctorante, Université Paris Nanterre et Potsdam.

obligation to wear mouth-to-nose coverings have been installed on the basis of relevant laws, ordinances and general orders in Germany.

The legal measures were initiated to contain infection with the Corona virus as far as possible, but above all to avoid overburdening the health care system. This involved considerable encroachment on fundamental rights. Personal freedom (Article 2 I, Article 2 II 2, Article 104 I German Constitution) was restricted, in particular to protect the right to physical integrity (Article 2 II 1 German Constitution). Congregations to churches, mosques and synagogues claimed that Article 4 I of the German Constitution had been violated by the fundamental ban of religious gatherings. The temporary closure of daycare centres and schools was criticized as a violation of Article 6 I of the German Constitution. The general restrictions on freedom of assembly encroached on Article 8 I of the German Constitution. The economic consequences of the legal measures were condemned as a violation of the freedom of occupation (Article 12 I German Constitution) and the guarantee of property (Article 14 I German Constitution). Insofar as the State subsequently provided financial aid, the principle of equal treatment under Article 3 I German Constitution was targeted[2].

To address the problematic issues regarding Covid restrictions and the German Constitution, firstly an overview of the German fundamental rights system will be given. Secondly, the response of the German Federal Constitutional Court towards legislative action limiting certain fundamental rights will be addressed.

German law detains a precise systematic examination scheme concerning constitutional rights[3]: firstly, the scope of protection of the respective fundamental right needs to be examined, where a distinction is made between the factual and the personal scope of protection. The personal scope of protection looks at the question whether the individual can invoke this fundamental right, i.e. there are certain fundamental rights which are called 'German fundamental rights', which means that people without German nationality cannot invoke them[4]. The substantive scope

---

[2] R. Zuck, Prof. Dr. H. Zuck, *Die Rechtsprechung des BVerfG zu Corona-Fällen*, NJW 2020, 2302.

[3] S. Kielmansegg Graf, *Die Grundrechtsprüfung*, JuS 2008, 23; U. J. Schröder, *Der Schutzbereich der Grundrechte*, JA 2016, 641.

[4] v. Mangoldt/Klein/Starck/Starck, 7. Aufl. 2018, GG Art. 1 Rn. 207.

of protection clarifies what is protected in terms of content by the specific fundamental right. The specific fundamental right answers the question 'who' and 'what' is protected.

If both aspects of the specific case are affirmed, the next step is to ask whether this fundamental right has been restricted[5]. This question can usually be answered relatively quickly. The definition of the restriction is as follows: 'any state measure[6] that makes it difficult or impossible to act in a way that is protected by a fundamental right'. The intervention in the classical sense is a goal-determined, directly effective legal command, which can be a norm or an individual act[7].

The state can restrict or even prohibit certain rights, but in this context the so-called constitutional justification must be examined. As far as the state restricts a fundamental right it requires a special justification to do so which is enrooted in the Constitution[8].

Thus, the examination scheme is the following: scope of protection, infringement, constitutional justification.

On this basis, the case law of the Federal Constitutional Court regarding the Corona virus pandemic will be examined, using examples of freedom of religion, freedom of assembly, freedom of movement and the right to education. The Federal Constitutional Court has always stated that the COVID-19 measures have led to severe encroachments on fundamental rights. A whole series of aspects play an important role in weighing of the encroachments on the applicants' fundamental rights[9]:

– Is the challenged measure limited in time or would it have to be abolished?
– Are restrictions/exceptions provided for the measures in question and have they been observed by the authority/court?
– Are the challenged measures mitigated by government assistance programs?

---

[5] M. Sachs, Grundgesetz, Vorbemerkungen zu Abschnitt I, 9. Auflage 2021, Rn. 78 ff.
[6] BVerfG, Beschluß vom 16.12.1983 – 2 BvR 1160/83 u. a.
[7] v. Mangoldt/Klein/Starck/Starck, *op. cit.* 3, Rn. 265.
[8] M. Sachs, *op. cit.* 4, Rn. 78 ff.
[9] R. Zuck, H. Zuck, *op. cit.* 1.

- Has the petitioner perceived that the agency responsible for issuing the COVID-19 regulations has discretion to assess, evaluate, and design?

I. Freedom of religion

The Federal Constitutional Court had to examine different legislative measures to determine if the legislator had sufficiently considered the fundamental rights. One of the most discussed issues within the Covid restriction was the freedom of religion, Article 4 of the German Constitution[10]. In personal terms, the scope of protection of Article 4 of the German Constitution includes everyone[11], i.e. all people within the scope of the Constitution and thus also children. In the case of children, however, it is necessary to consider if they are in a position to assert freedom of religion themselves, i.e. without or against the will of their parents. Generally, the law on the religious upbringing of children is taken as a guide, therefore children can be assumed to have reached the age to assert the freedom of belief and conscience by the age of 14 years[12]. Furthermore, the personal scope of protection of Article 4 of the German Constitution also includes associations of persons, since faith can not only be exercised personally but also collectively. Regardless of the legal capacity or form, faith congregations are thus also covered by the scope of protection[13].

---

[10] Article 4 [Freedom of faith and conscience]

1. Freedom of faith and of conscience and freedom to profess a religious or philosophical creed shall be inviolable.

2. The undisturbed practice of religion shall be guaranteed.

3. No person shall be compelled against his conscience to render military service involving the use of arms. Details shall be regulated by a federal law.

[11] Jarass/Pieroth/Jarass, 17. Aufl. 2022, GG Art. 4 Rn. 10, 18.

[12] BVerfGE 30, 415 (31.03.1971 – 1 BvR 744/67); Jarass/Pieroth/Jarass, *op. cit.* 10, Rn. 18.

[13] vgl. BVerfGE 19, 129 [132] = NJW 1965, 2339; BVerfGE 42, 312 [323] = NJW 1976, 2123; BVerfGE 99, 100 [118] = NVwZ 1999, 753 = NJW 1999, 2430 Ls.; BVerfGE 105, 279 [292 f.] = NJW 2002, 2626 = NVwZ 2002, 1495 Ls.; BVerfGE 125, 39 [79] = NVwZ 2010, 570; stRspr.

The term faith is to be understood as a view of man's position in the world and his relations to higher powers and deeper layers of being[14]. Freedom of belief is guaranteed in principle irrespective of the cultural predetermination of the community[15]. Accordingly, the numerical strength and social relevance of a religious association are also irrelevant.

From a factual point of view, the scope of protection of Article 4 of the German Constitution can be divided into a general and a concrete scope of protection. Generally speaking, Article 4 of the German Constitution represents a uniform fundamental right[16] that has two areas of protection: on one hand it serves to protect the internal formation of convictions (*forum internum*)[17] and, on the other hand, it protects the external realization and activity of convictions (*forum externum*)[18]. In order to assess the concrete scope of protection, it is necessary to differentiate between the individual paragraphs of Art. 4 German Constitution. However, Art. 4 I German Constitution and Art. 4 II German Constitution coincide and serve to protect faith, religion and ideology[19], while Art. 4 III German Constitution covers freedom of conscience.

The freedom of religion and belief from Article 4 I, II German Constitution can be divided into a positive and a negative scope of protection. According to this, the freedom to form, have, express and act according to a belief, i.e. a religious conviction or an ideology, including an areligious conviction, is positively protected[20]. In negative terms the freedom not to have to profess a belief or worldview, to be able to conceal it, and to refrain from actions that accompany belief is equally protected. In part, some aspects were already contained in Articles 136 and 137 of the Weimar Constitution and continue to apply today via Article 140[21] of the German

---

[14] ErfK/Schmidt, 22. Aufl. 2022, GG Art. 4, Rn. 7; Jarass/Pieroth/Jarass, 17. *op. cit.* 10, Rn. 7.
[15] BVerfG 17.12.1975, NJW 1976, 947; BVerfG 19.10.1971, NJW 1972, 327.
[16] BVerfGE 32, 98 (107 f.); 33, 23 (30 f.); 108, 282 (297); Dürig/Herzog/Scholz/Di Fabio, 96. EL November 2021, Art. 4 GG, Rn. 85.
[17] v. Mangoldt/Klein/Starck/Starck, 7. Aufl. 2018, GG Art. 4 Rn. 34, 35.
[18] ErfK/Schmidt, *op. cit.* 13, Rn. 62.
[19] Jarass/Pieroth/Jarass, *op. cit.* 10, Rn. 2.
[20] vgl. BVerfGE 19, 129 [132] *op. cit.* 12; BVerfGE 24, 236 [246 f.] = NJW 1969, 31; BVerfGE 53, 366 [387] = NJW 1980, 1895; BVerfGE 105, 279 [293 f.] = NJW 2002, 2626 = NVwZ 2002, 1495 Ls.
[21] Article 140 [Law of religious denominations]

Constitution[22].

Article 4 I, II German Constitution do not contain any restrictions[23]. Isolated barriers to fundamental rights and a reservation of general laws are contained in the provisions of the Weimar Reichsverfassung, which applies via Article 140 German Constitution. However, the Federal Constitutional Court has consistently rejected this construction and instead assumes that freedom of faith and conscience is guaranteed without reservation[24]. However, the freedom of faith must not lead to the unreasonable restriction or impairment of other important constitutional goods or fundamental rights of others[25]. For this reason freedom of faith is subject to a constitutional barrier, whereby a legal basis must be required due to the principle of the reservation of the law[26].

Even if Article 4 German Constitution can be restricted in individual cases by conflicting constitutional law, this does not mean that Article 4 German Constitution can be unreasonably limited or impaired. Rather, a detailed proportionality test must be carried out with the aspect of practical concordance[27] of the affected constitutional values playing a particularly prominent role under the test of reasonableness. Accordingly, a careful balance must be sought between the fundamental rights or other constitutional values so that – as far as possible – no fundamental right or constitutional value will be unreasonably limited or impaired.

Under this scope, the Federal Constitutional Court had to seek a balance between freedom of religion and protection from the infection with the Corona virus. In the Federal state Hesse, religious gatherings in churches, mosques and synagogues were banned[28]. The Federal Constitutional Court stated that the ban on these celebrations constituted an extremely serious encroachment on the right to freedom of belief

---

The provisions of Articles 136, 137, 138, 139 and 141 of the German Constitution of 11 August 1919 shall be an integral part of this Basic Law.

[22] ErfK/Schmidt, *op. cit.* 13 Rn. 2.
[23] ErfK/Schmidt, *op. cit.* 13, Rn. 13.
[24] BVerfG 11.4.1972, NJW 1972, 1183.
[25] BVerfG 14.1.2020, NJW 2020, 1049 Rn. 86.
[26] BVerfGE 52, 223/246 f; 93, 1/21; BVerwGE 116, 359/360 f.
[27] Sachs/Kokott, 9. Aufl. 2021, GG Art. 4 Rn. 28.
[28] Vierte Verordnung zur Bekämpfung des Corona-Virus vom 17. März 202 https://www.rv.hessenrecht.hessen.de/bshe/document/aiz-jlr-CoronaVVHE4rahmen%4020200318.

and confession under Article 4 I and II of the German Constitution[29]. According to the plausible statements of the plaintiffs, this applies even more insofar as the ban also extended to the Easter holidays as the high point of the religious life of Christians. The common celebration of the Eucharist is, according to Catholic conviction, a central component of faith, the absence of which cannot be compensated for by alternative forms of practicing the faith, such as the broadcasting of church services on the Internet or individual prayer[30].

The Federal Constitutional Court ruled that freedom of religion, i.e. the constitutionally protected right to the joint celebration of religious services, must step back regarding the state's duty to protect the fundamental right to life and physical integrity. Yet, the ban must be limited in time and the state is obliged to subject the ban to a strict proportionality test on an ongoing basis. Under these circumstances the blanket ban is compatible with the constitution. In weighing freedom of religion against the protection of health, the Federal Constitutional Court ruled that if the constitutional complaint were unsuccessful, a large number of people would be likely to gather in churches for religious services – especially over the Easter holidays. This would significantly increase the risk of infection with the virus, the illness of many people, the overloading of the health facility in the treatment of serious cases and, in the worst case, the death of people according to the authoritative risk assessment of the Robert Koch Institute of March 2020. These dangers would not remain limited to those persons who voluntarily participated in the religious services but would extend to a considerably larger group of persons due to possible secondary infections and the concern of treatment capacities. Yet, this could be avoided by a ban on religious services in a constitutionally permissible manner[31].

Compared to these dangers to life and limb, against which the state is also obligated to protect according to the basic right to life and physical integrity (Article 2 II German Constitution), the constitutionally protected right to the joint celebration of religious services must currently take a back seat[32]. It is interesting that here a right of defense

---

[29] BVerfG, Beschluss vom 10.4.2020 – 1 BvQ 28/20.
[30] BVerfG, *op. cit.* 28, Rn. 11.
[31] BVerfG, *op. cit.* 28 Rn 13.
[32] BVerfG, *op. cit.* 28, Rn 14.

(*Abwehrrecht*) in the form of Art. 4 German Constitution collides with a stately duty to protect (*Schutzpflicht*). In the case of rights of defense, the so-called prohibition of excessiveness applies, i.e. the state must keep the encroachment as limited as possible. In the case of the state's duty to protect, the principle of inadequacy applies, meaning that the Federal Constitutional Court can only sanction the legislator based on the latter's broad discretionary powers and if the legislator as a result fails to comply with its duty to protect.

The extremely serious encroachment on freedom of belief to protect health and life is also justifiable because the ordinance of March 17, 2020, and thus also the ban on meetings in churches at issue here, was limited in time until April 19, 2020. This ensured that the ordinance would have to be updated in the light of new developments in the Corona virus pandemic. In this context – as with any further update of the ordinance – a strict proportionality test must be carried out with regard to the ban on meetings in churches. Also, it must be examined whether in view of new findings, for example on the ways in which the virus is spread or on the risk of overloading the healthcare system, it is justifiable to relax the ban on religious services subject to – possibly strict – conditions and possibly also on a regionally limited basis. In summary, this means that the intervention was constitutional from the perspective of the Federal Constitutional Court but only under the premise of the time limitation and as far as the case numbers of the disease remain the same.

In another chamber decision of April 10, 2020, the emergency application of a Berlin association for the promotion of religion with the aim of permitting public religious services with a limited number of participants while observing concrete protective measures was also rejected[33].

II. Freedom of assembly

Another central fundamental right was severely curtailed during the acute Corona virus pandemic: the freedom of assembly from Article 8 German Constitution[34]. An assembly is the local gathering of several

---

[33] BVerfG *op. cit.* 28.
[34] Article 8 [Freedom of assembly]
   1. All Germans shall have the right to assemble peacefully and unarmed without prior notification or permission.

persons for the purpose of collective discussion or demonstration aimed at participating in the formation of public opinion. An assembly is peaceful if it does not take or is not expected to take a violent or inflammatory course[35]. According to its wording ('All Germans'), freedom of assembly is a fundamental right of Germans. Consequently, only Germans within the meaning of Article 116 of the Constitution[36] fall within the personal scope of protection of freedom of assembly.

The Federal Constitutional Court was confronted with the following case: the plaintiff filed a constitutional complaint for temporary legal protection against a ban on assembly[37]. He registered several assemblies with the respondent in the original proceedings under the motto 'Strengthen health instead of weakening fundamental rights – protection from viruses, not from people'. He indicated an approximate expected number of participants of 30 persons. The assembly participants would be instructed by signs to observe safety distances and would be directed by helpers to appropriately marked starting positions. The markings of the starting positions would be at a distance of 10 meters to the front and to the back and 6 meters to the side. They would each be occupied by individuals or groups of apartments or families. Speeches would be transmitted via each speaker's own cell phone to a public address system. During the elevator, the designated distances would be maintained, and care would be taken to ensure that newly arriving assembly participants joined the line at the back. Suggestions for further infection control

---

    2. In the case of outdoor assemblies, this right may be restricted by or pursuant to a law.

[35] v. Mangoldt/Klein/Starck/Gusy, *op. cit.* 3, Art. 8 Rn. 15 ff.

[36] Article 116 [Definition of "German" – Restoration of citizenship]

    1. Unless otherwise provided by a law, a German within the meaning of this Basic Law is a person who possesses German citizenship or who has been admitted to the territory of the German Reich within the boundaries of 31 December 1937 as a refugee or expellee of German ethnic origin or as the spouse or descendant of such person.

    2. Former German citizens who, between 30 January 1933 and 8 May 1945, were deprived of their citizenship on political, racial or religious grounds and their descendants shall, on application, have their citizenship restored. They shall be deemed never to have been deprived of their citizenship if they have established their domicile in Germany after 8 May 1945 and have not expressed a contrary intention.

[37] BVerfG, Beschluss vom 15.4.2020 – 1 BvR 828/20.

measures would be appreciated; corresponding requirements would be followed.

The competent authority ordered the ban of the assembly. Public safety and public order would be directly endangered if the assemblies were held. The assemblies would violate § 1 of the Ordinance of the Hessian State Government for the Control of the Corona virus of 14 March 2020 in the version of the Ordinance of 30 March 2020. According to this regulation, contacts with people outside of one's own household were to be reduced to the absolute minimum necessary. The stay in public was only allowed with one other person not belonging to the own household. In the case of – unplanned – encounters with other persons, a minimum distance of 1.5 meters was to be maintained. Public behaviour that could endanger the distance requirement were prohibited, regardless of the number of people. The authority claimed that experience had shown that minimum distances were not observed at gatherings of all kinds. The plaintiff could not ensure this either. A direct threat to public order resulted also from the fact that the assemblies were perceived as a provocation by the majority of the city's population, which for the most part complied with the Corona ordinances of the state.

The above mentioned application against the ban was partially successful. The Federal Constitutional Court ruled since the competent authority had not read the Hessian regulation in the light of the fundamental rights. § 1 of the 3rd Ordinance on the Control of the Corona Virus (Hesse) grants the assembly authority a margin of discretion precisely to take into account the freedom of assembly protected by fundamental rights[38]. The assembly authority incorrectly assumed that the ordinance of the Hessian state government to combat the Corona virus contained a general ban on assemblies of more than two persons who did not belong to the same household. In doing so, it violated the freedom of assembly protected by fundamental rights, because it did not take into account that there was room for maneuver in the decision to protect it[39]. By the decision to ban the assembly, the significance and scope of the complainant's fundamental right under Article 8 of the German Constitution were not adequately taken into account. The competent

---

[38] BVerfG, Beschluss vom 15.4.2020 – 1 BvR 828/20, BeckRS 2020, 5766.
[39] BVerfG, *op. cit.* 37, Rn. 12.

authority did not decide with sufficient consideration of the concrete circumstances of the individual case.

In another case, the Federal Constitutional Court refused to overrule a municipal ban on unregistered corona 'walking tours'[40]. The Assembly Act stipulates that 'open-air assemblies' must be notified to the authorities at least 48 hours in advance. The 'walking tours' by opponents of the Corona measures were often not reported within the 48-hour delay. The municipalities saw this as an attempt to avoid charges and to avoid having to name any responsible parties. Like several other municipalities, the town of Freiburg had issued a general decree on January 7, 2022, which expired at the end of the month. In it, 'all meetings and meetings of shareholders that are not reported and not subject to official approval and that are connected with regular meetings' were prohibited. The plaintiff had unsuccessfully filed urgent applications with the administrative courts.

Federal Constitutional Court stated that decisions of the municipality were not 'obviously erroneous'. It was 'an obvious observation' that the main purpose of the participation of these 'corona-walks' was to circumvent regulations. The judges could also assume that the initiators and participants of such 'walks' were not willing to wear protective masks or to keep their distance to each other. The clarification of the question of whether a precautionary ban on assembly can be reconciled with the meaning and scope of the constitutionally protected freedom of assembly is, however, reserved for the main proceedings.

III. Corona 'Federal emergency brake'

Another crucial question regarding Covid restriction and fundamental rights was the decision of the Federal Constitutional Court on the so-called Corona 'emergency brake' which was deemed to be constitutional[41]. Two major sets of issues were examined by the judges: the exit and contact restrictions, on the one hand, and the school closures, on the other. The spring curfews and school closures were deemed to be constitutional. With this decision, the Federal Constitutional Court has

---

[40] BVerfG, Beschluss vom 31.1.2022 – 1 BvR 208/22; NJW 2022, 612, BeckRS 2022, 808 , LSK 2022, 808 (Ls.).
[41] BVerfG Beschluss vom 19.11.2021 – 1 BvR 781/21 ua.

rejected several lawsuits – and at the same time provided a sort of guideline for political decisions. According to the Federal Constitutional Court the regulations of the federal government during the pandemic in April 2020 were constitutional. Neither the exit restrictions nor the school closures had violated the constitution. There were significant interferences with fundamental rights but justified by the states duty to protect citizens from major dangers to life and health.

Regarding the curfews, federal Constitutional Court stated that it was understandable that politicians in Berlin were worried in the spring that the health system would be overburdened. Yet, the night-time curfew restrictions have a profound impact on people's living conditions[42]. Its effects do not only limit the possibilities to stay outside one's accommodation and the associated pacified property at any time according to one's own ideas and to pursue a wide variety of activities in public space. Rather, it brings about considerable changes in the everyday lives of many of those affected, who are no longer able to maintain their previous way of life unchanged during the period of validity of the curfew.

This affects the entire range of life plans, as can be seen from the statements of the plaintiffs. The consequences of the exit restriction affect almost all areas of private, family and social contacts as well as the timing of working hours. If those affected wanted to maintain their social contacts, especially family contacts, to the same extent as before under the conditions of nighttime curfew, in addition to the time commitments resulting from their office or job, this was accompanied by considerable burdens. In the case of those affected, who were already vulnerable due to age or illness, for example, the restriction on leaving may further exacerbate existing impairments with considerable effects on mental and physical health, because existing contacts were no longer possible to the same extent due to the restrictions.

Yet many health experts had again confirmed that the situation was critical at the time[43]. Contact restrictions were also a suitable way to protect people. At the time, the legislature had rightly not considered any other means to be just as effective. According to the court, one must also see that the federal emergency brake had already expired again at the end

---

[42] BVerfG, *op. cit.* 40, Rn 291 ff.
[43] Wortprotokoll der 154. Sitzung des Ausschusses für Gesundheit, Protokoll-Nr. 19/154, 10 f.

of June[44]. The shorter the duration of the measures, the more likely it is that freedom can be limited.

According to the explanatory memorandum to the draft bill, legislature was pursuing the goal of protecting life and health and ensuring the functioning of the health care system as an overriding public good and thus at the same time the best possible health care with the Fourth Act for the Protection of the Population in the Event of an Epidemic Situation of National Significance in fulfilment of its constitutional duty to protect[45]. To this end, measures were needed to prevent the exponential spread of the virus, especially that of viral variants that might call into question previous vaccination successes[46]. This goal was to be achieved by effective measures to reduce interpersonal contact[47]. According to the legislator, the exit restriction under § 28 b I 1 No. 2 IfSG that was challenged served in particular to control and promote compliance with the general contact regulations[48]. It thus served a fundamentally legitimate purpose.

Furthermore, with regard to the consequences of a continuation of the initial restriction, the Federal Constitutional Court emphasized that it must be considered that its validity was linked to the threshold value of the seven-day incidence of 100. Since the legislature had also mitigated the effects of the restrictions on freedom associated with the initial restriction by means of exceptions and the period of validity of the challenged regulation is relatively narrowly limited in terms of time under the current legal situation, the regulation was deemed constitutional.

The fact that schools were closed was also constitutional according to the Federal Constitutional Court. However, the Court accentuated that extensive encroachments on fundamental rights such as through school closures can only be considered in an extreme situation of danger. For the first time, the judges explicitly recognize a right of children to schooling[49]. If children could not go to school this right would be seriously impaired: there would be learning deficits and deficits in personality

---

[44] BVerfG, *op. cit.* 40, Rn 297.
[45] BT-Drs. 19/28444, pp. 1 and 8, https://dserver.bundestag.de/btd/19/284/1928 444.pdf.
[46] BT-Drs. 19/28444, *op. cit.* 45, pp. 8, 10.
[47] BT-Drs. 19/28444, *op. cit.* 45, p. 8.
[48] BT-Drs. 19/28444, *op. cit.* 45, p. 12.
[49] BVerfG, *op. cit.* 40.

development, especially in socially disadvantaged families[50]. However, with regard to the school issue the court again stressed that it was a matter of maintaining the functioning of the healthcare system. According to the experts, the children could transmit the virus even if they themselves rarely became seriously ill. Other equally effective measures such as ventilation systems had not been sufficiently researched at the time and were not available.

In addition, there had been an aid of 1.5 billion euro in total to the Federal States to enable the creation of online instruction[51]. And as with the exit restrictions, the court pointed out that the whole situation lasted only a relatively short time. In the case of children, the court emphasized that the more people are vaccinated, the less likely the measure to close schools can be deemed as constitutional. In the case of older students, it is more likely to happen because they are more likely to cope with distance learning. However, the closing of elementary schools requires a particular justification[52].

Conclusion

For the future, the jurisprudence clarified that restrictions on freedom in times of pandemic are only feasible as long as they can be justified by suitable reasons and no milder measures are conceivable. However, next to this classical scheme, the Federal Constitutional Court has added some new aspects regarding the possibility of the legislator to limit fundamental rights.

The decisions of the Federal Constitutional Court accentuate that although fundamental rights can be restricted, blanket prohibitions not taking into account the specific individual case thereby violate the Constitution. The legislature can severely restrict certain fundamental rights and even abolish them completely, but this must be limited in time, there must be means to mitigate the result by an exception system, there must be an ongoing test regarding the current circumstances of the virus spreading and each individual case must be examined separately.

---

[50] BVerfG, *op. cit.* 49, Rn. 145.
[51] BVerfG , *op. cit.* 49, Rn 189.
[52] BVerfG , *op. cit.*, Rn. 49, 145 ff.

Equally, the recent development has shown that the legislator can and will fundamentally restrict Constitutional rights if there are values which a qualified as more worthy and those measures will not necessarily be restricted to individual cases but can constitutionally affect society as a whole. Nevertheless, the border between a protective state and a paternalistic government can be very thin. Consequently, a clear and consequent jurisprudence of Constitutional Courts is crucial.

Different case law of the Federal Constitutional Court, exact references in the footnotes.

Bibliography

Di Fabio, Udo in Dürig/Herzog/Scholz, *Grundgesetz Kommentar,* 96. Lieferung, 2021.

Jarass, Hans in Jarass/Pieroth/Jarass, *Grundgesetz für die Bundesrepublik Deutschland,* 17. Aufl. 2022.

Kielmansegg Graf, Sebastian, *Die Grundrechtsprüfung,* JuS 2008, 23.

Sachs, Michael in Sachs, *Grundgesetz Kommentar,* 9. Auflage 2021.

Schmidt, Ingrid in *Erfurter Kommentar zum Arbeitsrecht,* 22. Aufl. 2022.

Schröder, Ulrich Jan, *Der Schutzbereich der Grundrechte,* JA 2016, 641.

Starck, Christian in Mangoldt, v./Klein/Starck/Starck, *Grundgesetz Kommentar,* 7. Aufl. 2018.

Zuck, Rüdiger, Zuck, Holger, *Die Rechtsprechung des BVerfG zu Corona-Fällen,* NJW 2020, 2302.

The Covid (miscellaneous provision) Act et The Quarantine Act à l'Ile Maurice

Rajendra Parsad GUNPUTH[1] and Ambareen BEEBEEJAUN[2]

This article explains the confinement in Mauritius and how the legislator reacted swiftly to control activities, salaries, holiday requests and the right to work from home. The fact remains that the right to travel and the right to come and go are a challenge to the fundamental rights of every citizen, while foreign employees are stranded during the health and economic crisis and without residence permits on Mauritian territory. While air and sea flights have been banned on the island, basic products and medicines have been in short supply among the population. Added to this are the seriously ill who have to travel abroad to receive the care they need for their illnesses and/or undergo emergency surgery. As for the students, as is the case just about everywhere else, they are stuck at home, and there are major questions to be asked: how the exams will be conducted, some are in quarantine and others are stuck in Rodrigues, many are salaried employees who work at home and cannot take part in the courses available online. The interest of this article is to find out whether The COVID-19 (Miscellaneous) Act 2020 and The Quarantine Act 2020 contain the regulatory provisions needed to make up for the legal, financial and socio-economic shortcomings in order to deal with the health crisis on a national and international scale at a time when tourism is at its lowest ebb.

Cet article explique le confinement à Maurice, comment le législateur a réagi avec célérité dans le but de contrôler les activités, les salaires, les demandes de congés et le droit de travailler à domicile. Il reste que les droits à la circulation et les droits d'aller et venir font défi aux droits fondamentaux de chaque citoyen alors que les salariés étrangers sont bloqués pendant la crise sanitaire et économique et sans titre de séjour sur le territoire mauricien. Si les vols aériens et maritimes sont interdits sur l'île, les produits de base et des médicaments se

---

[1] Professor, Université de Maurice, Doyen de la Faculté de Droit et de Gestions.
[2] Lecturer Departement de Droit, Dr., Université de Maurice.

sont vite fait sentir parmi la population. A cela s'ajoutent les malades graves qui devraient se rendre à l'étranger pour recevoir les soins nécessaires à leurs maladies et/ou pour se faire opérer d'urgence. Quant aux étudiants, comme c'est le cas un peu partout ailleurs, ils sont bloqués à domicile, et d'importantes questions se posent: comment se feront les examens, certains sont en quarantaine et d'autres sont bloqués à Rodrigues, beaucoup sont des salariés qui travaillent à leur domicile et ils ne peuvent participer aux cours disponibles en ligne. L'intérêt de cet article nous permet alors de découvrir si The COVID-19 (Miscellaneous) Act 2020 et The Quarantine Act 2020 prévoient les dispositions normatives nécessaires pour pallier des lacunes à la fois juridique, financière et socio-économique afin de faire face pendant la crise sanitaire aux envergures nationales et internationales alors que le tourisme est au plus bas.

Introduction

La pandémie de COVID-19 a un impact, entre autres, sur les droits des travailleurs à une rémunération et à un traitement équitable. Il y avait également des risques de chômage et de licenciement des travailleurs, provoquant des inégalités entre les sexes sur le marché du travail, en particulier lorsque le législateur mauricien a proposé de nouvelles législations et réglementations. Le gouvernement mauricien et le législateur mauricien ont commencé à adopter de nouvelles législations à partir de 2019 pour répondre aux nouvelles des conditions telles que le travail à domicile (WFH) avec un « effet domino » qui porte atteinte à leurs droits fondamentaux, et ont été détectées et signalées dans les médias. En effet, des individus ont commencé à souffrir du confinement suite au couvre-feu et à sa propagation au sein de la population. La plupart des droits humains et fondamentaux ont été restreints comme dans la plupart des pays du monde.

Cet article contextualisé traite de la situation réelle de la petite République de Maurice avec ses quelque 1,3 million d'habitants. Il permet également de mieux comprendre la dernière tendance dans le développement de nouvelles législations et réglementations (infra, Tab. 1) pour protéger les travailleurs, et il a signé et ratifié pratiquement la plupart des pactes internationaux et régionaux pour renforcer les droits humains de tous ses individus. Cependant, la pandémie de COVID-19 a également commencé à imposer de nouvelles conditions de vie avec diverses limitations aux droits de l'homme contre la volonté de la plupart des habitants de l'île. A titre d'illustration, et comme de nombreux pays, la petite République de Maurice, en tant que membre du Programme des Nations Unies pour le Développement (PNUD) s'est engagé envers les 17 Objectifs de Développement Durable (ODD) qui ont été mis en place par le PNUD afin de « protéger la planète, éradiquer la pauvreté et faire en sorte que tous jouissent de la paix et de la prospérité » à atteindre d'ici 2030.

Pour atteindre ces ODD, le répéter mauricien a adopté The Equal Opportunities Act 2008, The Employment Relations Act 2008 (Act 32/ 2008) et le récent Workers' Rights Act 2019 (Act 20/2019) pour réduire les inégalités, protéger tous les travailleurs contre la victimisation. et la discrimination sur le lieu de travail. La nouvelle loi de 2019 sur les droits des travailleurs (loi 20/2019) est entrée en vigueur et prévoit également des dispositions suffisantes pour promouvoir le travail décent et la croissance économique grâce à une croissance économique soutenue, des niveaux de productivité plus élevés et des innovations technologiques conformément à l'ODD 8. Le préambule de la loi de 2008 sur l'égalité des chances stipule que cette loi a été adoptée pour : « promouvoir l'égalité des chances entre les personnes, interdire la discrimination fondée sur le statut et par la victimisation, établissant une commission et un tribunal pour l'égalité des chances et pour les questions connexes ». La partie II de la Constitution mauricienne (1968) prévoit des droits fondamentaux et la plupart de ces droits sont inspirés de la Déclaration universelle des droits de l'homme de 1948 et de la Convention européenne des droits de l'homme de 1950 et ils sont très utiles pour protéger les droits constitutionnels de tous les individus à Maurice sans exception (Tab. 1).

Bientôt, des syndicats se sont créés avec des partis politiques et quelques fédérations également. Et tous les Mauriciens bénéficient d'une élection libre et équitable expliquant la stabilité politique de l'île, les investisseurs étrangers ont commencé à investir à Maurice couplés aux investissements directs étrangers (IDE) de l'Inde, de la Chine, de l'Afrique du Sud, du Royaume-Uni et d'autres grandes nations du monde à travers le Convention d'évitement de la double imposition (DTAA). Le prix du sucre a chuté et Sir Anerood Jugnauth a commencé à construire une nouvelle nation plus axée sur la technologie moderne et l'île est devenue une république le 12 mars 1992. Elle reste très active en termes de développement régional et est devenue membre de blocs régionaux (COMESA, SADC de l'IORA) et est également devenue un tremplin pour que la Chine et l'Inde investissent en Afrique.

En raison de son développement socio-économique soudain, le législateur mauricien a commencé à adopter des projets de loi et des lois du Parlement, basés sur le modèle de Westminster, pour le bien-être de tous les travailleurs à Maurice et ils ont vu la promulgation du Workmen's Compensation Act 1931, du Labour Act 1975, Loi de 1976 sur les relations professionnelles, Loi sur les zones franches d'exportation ou Loi sur l'expansion industrielle. Certaines d'entre elles ont été abrogées et remplacées par de nouvelles législations pour faire face à une île plus moderne avec l'adoption de l'Employment Rights Act 2008 (Act 38/2008), de l'Employment Relations Act 2008 (Act 32/2008), de l'OSHA 2005 et de ces législations sont constamment modifiés pour être en phase avec les exigences et les besoins de la population car Maurice est devenue un centre d'exportation, d'importation, de commerce, de commerce et d'échanges attirant des travailleurs étrangers pour travailler dans ses industries et usines avec exportation de textile vers les États-Unis sous le Loi sur la croissance et les opportunités en Afrique (AGOA).

Cependant, bien que la maladie pandémique de COVID-19 soit sous contrôle à Maurice, elle a néanmoins eu un impact très négatif sur les droits des travailleurs de diverses manières à travers la quarantaine, les confinements, les restrictions de mouvement, la liberté individuelle, la liberté d'expression et la liberté d'association et assemblée pour n'en nommer que quelques-uns. Pour la première fois et par inadvertance, les travailleurs ont commencé à découvrir de nouvelles législations et réglementations telles que The Prevention and Mitigation of Infectious Disease Coronavirus Regulations 2020, qui a imposé un couvre-feu de 21 jours pour contenir la propagation de la pandémie de coronavirus-19 à Maurice, et tout manquement entraînerait pour toute personne une peine d'emprisonnement d'une durée maximale de 6 mois et une amende (Rs 500 000). Dès le départ, il est important de savoir que la pandémie de COVID-19 n'est certainement pas un cas de force majeure et qu'il existe diverses obligations et devoirs implicites pour un employé et un employeur, indépendamment du fait que les travailleurs travaillent sur leur lieu de travail ou à domicile. Les deux parties doivent être de bonne foi, que tout travailleur est apte à travailler et que l'employeur doit leur fournir du travail et une rémunération bien qu'il puisse rencontrer des difficultés financières, en particulier pendant le verrouillage et le confinement, a jugé la Cour suprême dans l'affaire Ismael c. Jay Fashions Co. Ltd contre 1988 SCJ 497, où il a été jugé que : 'La question s'est posée de savoir si un employeur qui prétendait ne pas pouvoir subvenir aux besoins de ses travailleurs en raison de difficultés financières entraînant la fermeture de l'entreprise, bien que temporairement, pourrait se prévaloir de ce motif pour justifier le licenciement de son travailleur. Il a été jugé que le licenciement des travailleurs dans les circonstances ci-dessus était injustifié'.

Les auteurs s'appuieraient sur de nouvelles législations et réglementations votées récemment par le législateur mauricien pour démontrer que la propagation de la maladie pandémique COVID-19 a un « effet domino » sur tous les secteurs du développement socio-économique de la petite île de Maurice. Mais l'article est plus axé sur les questions de droits de l'homme dans une approche comparative. Afin de démontrer la même chose, la structure de cet article est de comprendre comment la République de Maurice a réagi lorsque de nouvelles législations et réglementations ont été adoptées : après une introduction (I), il y a une revue de la littérature sur le sujet (II), COVID-19 et Les nouvelles conditions de travail sous de nouvelles législations: le cadre juridique et institutionnel mauricien (III), l'impact du COVID-19 sur les droits des travailleurs aux mesures de santé et de sécurité (IV), l'impact du COVID-19 sur Les droits des travailleurs: l'impact socio-économique (V) et cet article se termineront par une liste de références (IV) pour approfondir la recherche dans ce domaine émergent du droit.

En ce qui concerne la revue de la littérature sur l'impact du COVID-19 sur l'économie mauricienne et l'impact des nouvelles législations et réglementations, il existe déjà des données très larges et importantes qui ont été rapportées, entre autres, par la Wealth Health Organization (OMS), le rapport d'enquête de la Banque mondiale sur les ménages, l'évaluation de l'impact socio-économique du COVID-19 à Maurice, l'Organisation internationale du travail (OIT) a également publié ses normes de l'OIT et COVID-19 (Coronavirus), Business Mauritius Report, Afrasiabank, KPMG et Rogers Capital, et Central Statistics Mauritius, et il est donc important de faire une étude pour savoir comment certaines législations et pactes de la petite République de Maurice ont joué un rôle important dans leur participation en donnant un coup légal pour contenir le COVID-19 maladie pandémique. Divers cabinets, locaux et internationaux, ont également publié des recherches qu'ils ont entreprises pour mieux comprendre l'impact de la maladie COVID-19 sur les droits des travailleurs dans les petites et moyennes entreprises, les grandes entreprises et les sociétés: le cabinet britannique Burges and Salmon a publié le COVID-19 Burges And Salmon's Commitments to

Client Service (burges-salmon.com), et dans pratiquement le même lien l'University of Cambridge Press sur son article sur COVID-19: Resting the limits of Human Rights. Cependant, les buts et objectifs de ce document sont de combler certaines lacunes en ce qui concerne les législations et réglementations, leur mise en œuvre et dans quelle mesure les droits de l'homme sont affectés sur leur lieu de travail.

I. COVID-19 et les nouvelles conditions de travail sous de nouvelles législations: le cadre juridique et institutionnel mauricien

Cet article, sur les législations et réglementations mauriciennes en vue de porter un coup juridique contre la propagation de la maladie pandémique COVID-19 sur la petite île, reflète à quel point la maladie pandémique COVID-19 avait exacerbé le chômage et diverses formes de crise et abus, comme expliqué, sur le petit État insulaire lorsque le gouvernement mauricien a adopté diverses législations et réglementations telles que, entre autres, The COVID-19 (Miscellaneous Provisions) Act 2020, The Prevention and Mitigation of Infectious Disease Coronavirus Regulations 2020, The Public Règlement de 2021 sur la santé (vaccins COVID-19 à usage d'urgence), loi de 2020 sur la quarantaine, règlement de 2021 modifiant le règlement sur la quarantaine (COVID-19), règlement de 2020 sur le travail à domicile, règlement de 2021 sur les droits du travailleur (rémunération supplémentaire), règlement de 2021 sur les droits du travailleur (Paiement de l'allocation spéciale 2021) Règlement 2021 ou Règlement 2020 sur les droits des travailleurs (prolongation du temps pendant la période COVID-19) couplé à divers schémas messages et communiqués envoyés par le gouvernement en place tels que The Government Wage Assistance Scheme ou The Self-Employed Assistance Scheme.

Table 1

	The Mauritian Legislations and Its Adaptability on Some Human Rights Issues			
1	The COVID-19 (Miscellaneous Provisions) Act 2020	16	The Government Wage Assistance Scheme	
2	The Prevention and Mitigation of Infectious Disease Coronavirus Regulations 2020	17	The Self-Employed Assistance Scheme.	
3	The Public Health (COVID-19 Vaccines for Emergency Use) Regulations 2021	18	The Additional Remuneration and Other Allowances (2019) Regulations 2019	
4	The Quarantine Act 2020	19	Constitution of Mauritius 1968	
5	The Quarantine (COVID-19) Amendment Regulations 2021	20	The Employment Relations Act 2008 (Act 32/2008)	
6	The Work from Home Regulations 2020	21	The Employment Relations (Amendment) Act 2019	
7	The Worker's Rights (Additional Remuneration) 2021 Regulations 2021	22	The Equal Opportunities Act 2008	
8	The Workers' Rights (Extension of Time During COVID-19 Period) Regulations 2020	23	The Industrial Relations Act 1973 (repealed)	
9	The Industrial Court Act 1973	24	The Workers' Rights 2019 (Act 20/2019)	
10	The Occupational Safety Health and Welfare Act 1988	25	The Occupational Heal and Safety Act 2005	
11	The End of Year Gratuity Act 2001.	26	Public Bodies Appeal Tribunal Act 2010	
12	Public Service Commission (PSC) Act	27	The Protection of Human Rights Act	
13	The Registration of Association Act 1979	28	The Workers' Rights (Payment of Special Allowance 2021) Regulations 2020	
14	The Public Health Act 1925	29	The Workers' Rights (Extension of Time during COVID-19 Period) Regulations 2020	
15	The Code Civil Mauricien, The Code de Commerce Mauricien and the Code Pénal	30	The Public Gathering Act	

En outre, la République de Maurice a signé et ratifié la plupart des conventions, traités et protocoles internationaux relatifs aux droits de l'homme et en vue de protéger ses citoyens contre le travail forcé (Convention sur le travail forcé de 1930), ainsi que d'autres pactes internationaux tels que, entre autres, la Déclaration universelle des droits de l'homme de 1948, Pactes internationaux relatifs aux droits civils et politiques ou Pacte international relatif aux droits économiques, sociaux et politiques. Elle est également membre de l'Organisation internationale du travail. Cependant, la plupart des citoyens mauriciens, tout comme tous les citoyens d'Afrique ou d'ailleurs, se sont retrouvés confrontés à une nouvelle maladie pandémique et à de nouvelles conditions de travail lorsque la loi sur la quarantaine 2020 et le règlement sur le travail à domicile 2020 ont été adoptés, provoquant certaines perturbations, chaos, frictions. et le désordre chez les ouvriers et les employés parce que ces nouvelles conditions et modalités sur les conditions de travail ont été imposées soudainement pour renforcer les mesures sanitaires et de précaution d'un côté et les effets socio-économiques de l'autre.

Table 2

\multicolumn{4}{l}{The Mauritian International Covenants and Its Adaptability on Some Human Rights Issues}
1	*The Universal Declaration on Human Rights 1948*	4	*The International Covenants on Economic, Social and Cultural Rights* (ICESR)
2	*The International Covenant on Economic, Social and Political Rights* (ICCPR)	5	ILO Conventions
3	*Forced Labour Convention, 1930 (No. 29) and its 2014 Protocol*	6	*European Convention on Human Rights 1950*

En effet, la Constitution écrite mauricienne de 1968 (supra) est de droit colonial, en tant que loi suprême de l'île, dont Maurice a hérité lors de la colonisation britannique (1810–1968) mais elle a aussi un droit hybride très fort avec la Common Law anglaise et le Civil Civil français. Loi lorsque, encore une fois, Maurice était sous la colonisation française (17155–1810) où le Code français Napoléon 1804 a été imposé aux habitants de la petite île couplé avec le Code de commerce français et le Code pénal français de sorte qu'en réalité, le législateur mauricien emprunte et s'inspire encore des législations et des précédents anglais et français de la Cour de cassation française. Par conséquent, outre les législations adoptées par le Parlement, il existe The Workers' Rights 2019 (Act 20/2019) et The Employment Relations Act 2008 (Act 32/2008) qui s'inspirent du droit anglais, des législations et réglementations parmi lesquelles d'importants des législations telles que la loi de 2008 sur l'égalité des chances, la loi de 1988 sur la sécurité, la santé et le bien-être au travail ont été abrogées et remplacées par la loi de 2005 sur la santé et la sécurité au travail ou la loi de 2001 sur les gratifications de fin d'année pour être conformes aux politiques gouvernementales de lutte contre le COVID-19 maladie pandémique. La loi de 2020 sur le COVID-19 (dispositions diverses) a modifié un large éventail de 56 paramètres de santé publique existants afin de s'aligner sur les politiques gouvernementales.

Et lorsque Maurice a signé et ratifié la Convention internationale du travail, elle a également mis en œuvre diverses conventions, conventions collectives, ordonnances de rémunération et législation syndicale inspirées du droit du travail anglais auprès de divers tribunaux en cas de violation des droits des travailleurs sous toutes ses formes, de sorte que tout un citoyen résidant à Maurice peut avoir recours à diverses instances ; allant des appels, des injonctions et des révisions judiciaires (basées sur les injonctions britanniques et l'ordonnance 53 du Royaume-Uni) ; avec sa juridiction compétente, comme le tribunal du travail (loi de 1973 sur les tribunaux du travail), le tribunal des relations du travail (loi de 2008 sur les relations du travail) pour connaître des conflits du travail, le tribunal d'appel des organismes publics (loi de 2010 sur le tribunal d'appel des organismes publics) pour connaître des griefs des agents publics, et la Cour suprême (La Constitution, 1968) en tant que plus haute cour avec des compétences illimitées dans les procédures civiles et pénales. En outre, il existe divers conseils et commissions pour répondre à toute violation des droits de l'homme sur le lieu de travail et ils comprennent, entre autres, la Commission de conciliation et de médiation (CCM), la Commission de la fonction publique (PSC) qui est habilitée à imposer des mesures disciplinaires à l'encontre des agents publics en vertu de la loi sur la Commission de la fonction publique, du Conseil national des rémunérations (NRB), de la Commission des droits de l'homme (HRC) ou de la Commission pour l'égalité des chances (EOC) et ils sont habilités à conseiller, guider ou protéger les travailleurs et les employés conformément à les différentes législations et réglementations en place en cas d'abus sous toutes leurs formes et de fortes violations des droits des travailleurs sur le lieu de travail.

Et lorsque le Workers' Rights Act 2019 est entré en vigueur récemment, les buts et objectifs du législateur mauricien étaient de protéger tous les travailleurs et employés à Maurice contre la discrimination, de fournir une rémunération égale pour un travail égal; protection contre le licenciement injustifié, abusif, abusif, déguisé y compris le licenciement, droit d'être entendu devant une commission de discipline, droit d'être représenté par tout représentant légal de son choix et membre de son syndicat, droit aux congés, diverses formes d'accords ou droit à un programme de workfare. Tous ces droits sont bien entendu en stricte conformité avec le chapitre II de la Constitution de 1968, qui contient diverses dispositions relatives aux droits fondamentaux et qui s'inspirent de la Déclaration universelle des droits de l'homme de 1948.

Lorsque l'Organisation mondiale de la santé (OMS) a proclamé une urgence sanitaire internationale publique dans le monde entier, le gouvernement mauricien, tout comme la plupart des pays du monde, a imposé une période de confinement, mais les citoyens mauriciens ont dû faire face à plusieurs restrictions liées, entre autres, à la santé humaine. Droits et liberté de mouvement et de liberté, confinement sanitaire ou travail à domicile (WFH) mais dans l'ensemble des activités économiques et d'emploi sur la petite île a reçu un coup juridique sévère avec la fermeture soudaine et inattendue de toutes les activités et secteurs importants du pays (hôpitaux publics, aéroports, éducation ou secteur du tourisme) sauf à certains services essentiels en cas de crise nationale aiguë où des cas de COVID-19 ont été signalés.

Il y a eu plusieurs confinements, déconfinements; plusieurs fermetures et reprises d'activités ont été autorisées avec de nouvelles réglementations imposées par le gouvernement mauricien aux restrictions de liberté des individus sur la petite île malgré l'ordonnance de restriction temporaire de mouvement et par conséquent ces nouvelles législations, réglementations, communiqués et ordonnances ont fortement impacté sur le travailleur droits; restrictions et limitations à l'accès au lieu de travail et à l'information, limitations de leur droit au travail, droit à la santé et à la sécurité, droit au droit à des congés, inégalité de travail entre les sexes, discrimination, traitement injuste, risque de licenciement sans aucune indemnisation de sorte que toutes ces questions pertinentes compromettre directement tous les droits fondamentaux et constitutionnels de tous les individus à Maurice lorsque tous les tribunaux locaux étaient fermés, les conseillers juridiques n'étaient pas disponibles en raison du confinement, et au-delà d'autres droits importants tels que, entre autres, le droit à la vie privée, le droit à la sécurité de l'individu, le droit à la vie, la liberté de circulation, la liberté d'association et de réunion, le droit d'être jugé devant un tribunal impartial dans un délai raisonnable ou le droit à la protection contre la discrimination étaient compromis. Par conséquent, les travailleurs et les employés de Maurice se sont retrouvés dans de nouvelles conditions de travail lorsque le règlement sur le travail à domicile 2020 a été adopté, ainsi que divers communiqués et un plan de préparation du lieu de travail ont tous deux étés mis en place et adoptés rapidement pour arrêter la propagation de la pandémie de COVID-19 sur l'Ile.

Néanmoins, il y a eu des plaintes des sociétés civiles, des lignes de front et d'autres combattants des droits de l'homme qui ont plaidé pour la protection des travailleurs, et que leurs droits devraient être maintenus parce que tous les êtres humains naissent libres et égaux en dignité et en droits, et deuxièmement pendant le couvre-feu les travailleurs et les employés ont été licenciés, en particulier dans certains secteurs clés tels que le tourisme et le secteur aéroportuaire, bien que la République de Maurice ait signé et ratifié les conventions de l'OIT sur les droits des travailleurs, qui à leur tour fixent les déclarations de l'OIT sur les principes et droits fondamentaux au travail et qui consistent de huit conventions fondamentales (Tab. 3).

Table 3

ILO Declarations on Fundamental Principles and Rights at Work			
1	Forced Labour Convention, 1930 (No. 29) and its 2014 Protocol	5	Abolition of Forced Labour Convention, 1957 (No.105)
2	Freedom of Association and Protection of the Right to Organise Convention, 1948 (No.87)	6	Discrimination (Employment and Occupation) Convention, 1958 (No.111)
3	Right to Organise and Collective Bargaining Convention, 1949 (No.98)	7	Minimum Age Convention, 1973 (No.138)
4	Equal Remuneration Convention, 1951 (No.100)	8	Worst Forms of Child Labour Convention, 1999 (No.182)

En plus des législations; qui sont très souvent modifiées, abrogées ou les deux ; ces nouvelles lois et réglementations (supra) ont été adoptées par la législation mauricienne devant le Parlement, certaines lacunes ont été ressenties dans notre système car pour toute relation de travail il est crucial pour un travailleur de conclure un accord mais la loi mauricienne n'est pas claire du tout quand un contrat de travail est en cause, et il n'y a pas de promulgation sur la définition d'un « contrat de travail » en soi, et notre loi et nos législations prévoient des « travailleurs » à quelques exceptions près telles que la loi sur les pensions nationales de 1976 et la loi de 2005 sur la santé et la sécurité au travail, qui prévoit le terme « employé ». Comme expliqué (supra), mauricien est un droit hybride et basé sur le droit civil français, il n'y a pas de définition appropriée d'un contrat de travail. L'article 2 de la loi de 2019 sur les droits des travailleurs (loi 20/2019) stipule qu'un accord est un contrat de travail qui peut être oral ou verbal, explicite ou implicite, et selon le droit civil français, il s'agit d'un acte consensuel qui peut être convenu même oralement. En conséquence, en l'absence de toute définition d'un contrat de travail, nos tribunaux suivent la définition pertinente et pertinente qui émane, en fait, de la Cour de cassation française, et dans la même ligne de pensée, notre île Maurice a retenu les différents les formes de contrat qui existent en France, les diverses formes de fautes qui prévalent en France et les formes anglaises de licenciement.

Cependant, comme expliqué (supra), à Maurice, la plupart de nos législations et réglementations prévoient des « travailleurs », et il existe une distinction entre les travailleurs et les employés à Maurice conformément à l'article 2 de la loi sur le travail de 1975 (abrogée), la loi sur l'emploi Right Act 2008 (Act 33/ 2008) (abrogé), et maintenant récemment lorsque le législateur mauricien a adopté The Workers' Rights Act 2019 (Act 20/2019). Si The Workers' Rights Act 2019 (Act 20/2019) a innové en édictant diverses formes de nouvelles formes d'accords, qui n'existaient pas auparavant, il n'existe toujours pas de définition d'un contrat de travail, et ce qui a très souvent été déploré, dans notre pays mauricien loi, législations et réglementations diverses qui ont été adoptées. Très conscient de cette lacune de notre droit, le Tribunal des relations du travail dans l'affaire Balakrishna Kuppan c. Central Electricity Board ERT/RN 32/2019 a déclaré que: « Le contrat de travail n'existe pas Il est soumis aux différentes lois du travail qui ont été édictées par le législateur, qui ont pour objectifs, entre autres, de sauvegarder les droits du travailleur et de protéger le travailleur de tout abus de la part de l'employeur ».

Table 4

Convention	Ratification date	Status
C2 Unemployment Convention 1919	02.12.1969	ratified
C5 Minimum Age (Industry) Convention 1919	02.12.1969	denounced on 30.07.1990
C7 Minimum Age (Sea) Convention 1920	02.12.1969	denounced on 30.07.1990
C8 Unemployment Indemnity (Shipwreck) Convention 1920	02.12.1969	ratified
C11 Right of Association (Agriculture) Convention 1921	02.12.1969	ratified
C12 Workmen's Compensation (Agriculture) Convention, 1921	02.21.1969	ratified
C14 Weekly Rest (Industry) Convention, 1921	02.12.1969	ratified
C15 Minimum Age (Trimmers and Stockers) Convention, 1921	02.12.1969	denounced on 30.07.1990
C16 Medical Examination of Young Persons (Sea) Convention 1921	02.12.1969	ratified
C17 Workmen's Compensation (Accidents) Convention, 1925	02.12.1969	ratified
C19 Equality of Treatment (Accident Compensation) Convention, 1925	02.12.1969	ratified
C26 Minimum Wage-Fixing Machinery Convention (Revised), 1934	02.12.1969	ratified
C42 Workmen's Compensation (Occupational Diseases) Convention (Revised), 1934	020.12.1969	ratified
C50 Recruiting of Indigenous Workers Convention, 1976	02.12.1969	denounced on 02.03.2000
C58 Minimum Age (Sea) Convention (Revised) 1936	02.12.1969	denounced on 30.07.1990
C 59 Minimum Age (Industry) Convention (Revised), 1937		Denounced on 30.07.1990
C63 Convention concerning Statistics of wages and Hours of Work, 1939	02.12.1969	denounced on 14.06.1994
C64 Contracts of Employment (Indigenous Workers) Convention, 1939	02.12.1969	denounced on 08.07.1999
C65 Penal Sanctions (Indigenous Workers) Convention, 1939	02.12.1969	denounced on 08.07.1999
C74 Certification of Able SeamenConvention,1946	02.12.1969	ratified

Convention	Ratification date	Status
C81 Freedom of Association and Protection of the Right to Organise Convention, 1948	01.02.2005	ratified
C81 Labour Inspection Convention, 1947	02.12.1969	ratified
C86 Contracts of Employment (Indigenous Workers) Convention, 1947	02.12.1969	ratified
C87 Freedom of Association and Protection of the Right to Organise Convention, 1948	01.04.2005	ratified
C88 Employment Service Convention, 1948	03.09.2004	ratified
C94 Labour Clauses (Public Contracts) Convention, 1949	02.12.1969	ratified
C95 Protection of Wages Convention, 1949	02.12.1969	ratified
C97 Migration for Employment Convention (Revised), 1949	02.12.1969	ratified
C98 Right to Organise and Collective Bargaining Convention, 1949	02.12.1969	ratified
C99 Minimum Wage Fixing Machinery (Agriculture) Convention, 1951	02.12.1969	ratified
C100 Equal Remuneration Convention, 1951	18.12.2002	ratified
C105 Abolition of Forced Labour Convention, 1957	02.12.1969	ratified
C108 Scafarers' Identity Documents Convention, 1958	02.12.1969	ratified
C111 Discrimination (Employment and Occupation) Convention, 1958	18.03.2003	ratified
C137 Dock Work Convention, 1973	30.07.1990	ratified
C144 Tripartite Consultation (International Labour Standards) Convention, 1976	14.06.1994	ratified
C150 Labour Administration Convention, 1978	05.04.2004	ratified
C156 Workers with Family Responsibilities Convention, 1981	05.04.2004	ratified
C159 Vocational Rehabilitation and Employment (Disabled Persons) Convention, 1983	09.06.2004	ratified
C160 Labour Statistics Convention, 1985	14.06.1994	ratified
C175 Part-Time Work Convention, 1994	14.06.1994	ratified
C182 Worst Forms of Child Labour Convention, 1999	08.06.2000	ratified

II. L'impact du COVID-19 sur les droits des travailleurs aux mesures de santé et de sécurité

Dès que la maladie pandémique de COVID-19 a commencé à se propager sur la petite île de la République de Maurice, le gouvernement mauricien a commencé à adopter de nouvelles législations et réglementations avec des schéma et diverses formes de communiqués (Tab. 1 et Tab. 2) en plus des accords internationaux et instruments juridiques (supra) que le gouvernement mauricien a déjà signés et ratifiés (Tab. 3) qui ont également été communiqués à tous les citoyens et individus du pays, mais ils ont également eu un impact négatif sur les droits humains de tous les individus. Comme expliqué (supra), puisque la maladie est prévisible, la pandémie de COVID-19 n'est pas un cas de force majeure, que toutes les obligations et devoirs implicites du travailleur ou de l'employeur sont maintenus. Dans l'affaire Hosseny v Maico 1970 SCJ 163, la Cour suprême de Maurice a déclaré que: « en l'absence de tout accord ou de toute loi contraire, l'obligation de l'employeur de fournir du travail doit être soumise à l'exception selon laquelle est contenu dans le principe général du Code Civil relatif à la force majeure ».

Comme expliqué (supra), la Constitution mauricienne de 1968, dans son chapitre II, prévoit les droits fondamentaux les plus élémentaires pour tous ses individus sans exception, et ils sont également conformes aux pactes internationaux tels que le Pacte international relatif aux droits civils et politiques. (ICCPR) et le Pacte international relatif aux droits économiques, sociaux et culturels (ICESR). La loi de 2008 sur les relations de travail (loi 32/2008) a été modifiée par la loi de 2019 sur les relations de travail (amendement) et prévoit la liberté d'association et de réunion et la protection contre la discrimination et la victimisation avec des droits dont un travailleur peut jouir en termes de syndicats et la négociation collective à condition que le travailleur soit jugé apte au travail car en présence de la maladie pandémique COVID-19 tout travailleur peut être déclaré inapte au travail.

Suivant les précédents français et anglais pertinents, la Cour suprême de Maurice, dans certaines affaires pertinentes sur l'inaptitude au travail expliquées dans l'affaire New Mauritius Docks Co. Ltd contre PAS Ministry of Labour au nom de Perrine 1974 MR 50, a jugé qu'"Un employeur l tenu de fournir du travail à un ouvrier qui se présente au travail et est jugé apte à travailler, et si l'employeur ne remplit pas son obligation un jour quelconque, l'ouvrier est néanmoins réputé avoir travaillé et avoir gagné son salaire pendant une journée complète".

À Maurice, la loi de 2005 sur la santé et la sécurité au travail prévoit dans son article 5 que « Tout employeur doit. Dans la mesure du possible, assurer la sécurité, la santé et le bien-être au travail de tous ses employeurs ». Et afin que les travailleurs ne soient pas contaminés, ils ont également été encouragés à travailler à domicile (WFH) lorsque le législateur a adopté le règlement sur le travail à domicile 2020. En l'absence de tout cas pertinent quant à savoir si un travailleur peut refuser de reprendre le travail en cas de toute appréhension de risque pour la santé et la sécurité au travail peut être renvoyée à l'affaire Rodgers v Leeds Laser Cutting Limited ET 1803829/2020 où le tribunal du travail a conclu qu'au cas où il serait raisonnable pour l'employé de refuser cette partie du travail qui l'exposent à des risques plus élevés ou de soulever la question auprès de l'employeur pour trouver des solutions appropriées pour un environnement de travail plus sûr, mais qu'une simple circulation du virus COVID-19 dans la société n'est pas une « cause bonne et justifiable » d'absence à travailler. À Maurice, comme dans la plupart des pays du monde, les employeurs fournissent des masques faciaux, des désinfectants et encouragent la distanciation sociale sur le lieu de travail pour encourager les mesures préventives en plus de l'auto-isolement et de l'application de la loi sur la quarantaine de 2020 et d'autres législations et réglementations sur le lieu de travail.

Certes, diverses législations et réglementations ont été adoptées par le législateur mauricien qui a pris toutes les mesures de précaution pour protéger tous ses citoyens à condition qu'elles soient compatibles avec l'article 4(1) du PIDCP, qui prévoit des dérogations aux obligations internationales en matière de droits de l'homme en cas d'urgence publique à condition que ces nouvelles mesures ne « menacent pas la vie de la nation dans la mesure strictement requise par les exigences de la situation, à condition que ces mesures ne soient pas incompatibles avec leurs autres obligations en vertu du droit international et n'impliquent pas de discrimination uniquement fondée sur la race, couleur, sexe, langue, religion ou origine sociale ». Toutefois, ces nouvelles mesures, comme celles qui ont été imposées par le gouvernement mauricien, n'affecteront pas, cependant, le droit inhérent à la vie (article PIDCP), l'interdiction de la torture et des traitements inhumains (article 7 PIDCP), l'interdiction de l'esclavage (article 8 PIDCP), liberté d'emprisonnement pour incapacité à remplir une obligation contractuelle (article 11), droit de ne pas être soumis à l'application rétroactive de la loi pénale (article 15 PIDCP), droit à la reconnaissance de la personnalité juridique (article 16 PIDCP), droit à la liberté de pensée, de conscience et de religion (article 18 PIDCP). Il est bien établi en droit qu'aucun État partie au PIDCP ne peut recourir à l'état d'urgence de manière abusive.

À Maurice, la loi de 1954 sur la quarantaine a été abrogée et la loi de 2020 sur la quarantaine est entrée en vigueur, et l'objet de la loi était : 'de fournir des mesures appropriées pour la prévention et la propagation des maladies transmissibles à Maurice'. Cependant, le Quarantine Act 2020 a été très critiqué car il impose une amende de Rs 500 000 et une peine d'emprisonnement n'excédant pas 5 ans pour les délinquants criminels, et ses articles portent également atteinte aux droits les plus fondamentaux des individus à Maurice. À titre d'illustration, l'article 3 du Quarantine Act 2020 impose des restrictions d'entrée des avions et des navires aux frontières mauriciennes et l'imposition du confinement à domicile et de la fermeture des locaux commerciaux. L'article 7 de la même loi édicte le confinement des personnes dans des installations de quarantaine et l'auto-isolement, l'article 19 de la même loi impose une obligation de fournir des informations, l'article 10 de la même loi prévoit l'obligation de divulguer les maladies transmissibles et l'article 11 de la même loi prévoit que la police a le pouvoir de pénétrer dans des locaux sans mandat et d'arrêter sans mandat. Le Quarantine Act 202 a été adopté pour protéger les citoyens mauriciens de la pandémie de COVID-19, sinon des travailleurs contaminés mettront en danger la vie et la santé d'autres collègues et employés dans un environnement sain. En revanche, de nombreux professionnels, comme les dentistes, les médecins privés ou les avocats ; n'avaient pas accès à leur lieu de travail et il a été déploré que cela constitue un abus d'accès au lieu de travail.

Lorsque la loi de 2008 sur les droits à l'emploi (loi 33/2008) a été abrogée et que la loi de 2019 sur les droits des travailleurs (loi 20/2019) est entrée en vigueur, le but et les objectifs principaux du législateur mauricien étaient d'assurer une rémunération égale pour un travail égal en tant que question d'équité sans distinction de sexe. La plupart des dispositions du Pacte international relatif aux droits économiques, sociaux et culturels (PIDESC) ; que la République de Maurice a signé mais pas ratifié, sont également couverts par la récente entrée en vigueur de la loi de 2019 sur les droits des travailleurs (loi 20/2019) ; prévoit que les États parties reconnaissent le droit de tout individu à des conditions de travail favorables et justes, à assurer une rémunération minimale, juste et égale pour un travail égal sans distinction de sexe, il prévoit également des conditions de travail sûres et saines, la nécessité de reconnaître l'ancienneté et la compétence comme critères d'égalité des chances de promotion au travail, la limitation raisonnable des heures de travail et des vacances et des loisirs pour chaque travailleur et cet État doit remplir certaines conditions telles que la condition de stricte nécessité, de non-discrimination, de notification internationale et de cohérence avec d'autres obligations légales en vertu du droit international.

Le Règlement de 2020 sur la prévention et l'atténuation des maladies infectieuses liées au coronavirus est entré en vigueur avec des sanctions pénales strictes (supra) en cas de violation du règlement et toute personne contaminée a été immédiatement mise en quarantaine conformément à la loi de 2020 sur la quarantaine, et comme souligné, la priorité du gouvernement mauricien était assurer la santé publique de tous après que le pays a subi un confinement (du 19 mars 2020 au 1er juin 2020) et un second confinement (du 10 mars 2021 au 25 mars 2021) avec des zones rouges régulières dans différentes circonscriptions rurales et urbaines pour éviter tout risque de résurgence de la pandémie de COVID-19, sinon cela aurait un impact certain sur les services de santé et l'économie du pays, ainsi que sur ses développements socio-économiques comme la plupart des secteurs clés (tourisme, hôtellerie, importation et exportation de marchandises vers les pays de la SADC, ou étranger direct l'investissement (IDE) a également été touché) mais il y a très souvent eu une levée partielle des blocages pour que le pays respire économiquement et financièrement et de reprendre les activités économiques mais le transport international dans le secteur du tourisme reste proche. Conformément à la loi sur la quarantaine de 2020, seules 10 personnes peuvent se réunir à tout moment et 50 personnes dans des cas exceptionnels (mariage ou rassemblements sociaux importants).

En fait, la plupart des pays ; comme la France, l'Italie, les USA ou la Chine; sont sous l'influence de l'article 4 du PIDCP qui prévoit des dérogations légitimes (supra) et des limitations en cas de sécurité nationale et/ou en cas d'urgence dans l'intérêt de la nation et de son peuple. Dans la loi et les législations mauriciennes, il existe des dérogations similaires qui sont disponibles en vertu de la Constitution de 1968. L'article 4 du PIDCP est conforme à l'article 18 de la Constitution de 1968 qui stipule que: « la loi autorise la prise de mesures qui sont raisonnablement justifiables pour traiter avec la situation qui existe à Maurice durant cette période ». L'article 5(g) de la Constitution de 1968 stipule que: 'dans le but de préserver la propagation d'une maladie infectieuse ou contagieuse'. L'article 15 de la Constitution de 1968 stipule que : 'Nul ne peut être privé de sa liberté de mouvement', comme l'a souligné la Cour suprême dans l'affaire Coorbanally contre la Reine, où le commissaire de police peut imposer une objection au départ à toute personne susceptible d'avoir commis ou soupçonnée d'avoir commis une infraction pénale conformément à l'article 15(3)(a) de la Constitution, 1968 impose des restrictions à Maurice qui sont dans l'intérêt de la défense, de la sécurité publique, de l'ordre public, de la moralité publique ou la santé publique ou d'assurer le respect de toute obligation internationale qui ne sera pas considérée comme incompatible avec ou en contravention avec le présent article.

Il y avait de sérieuses inquiétudes concernant la vaccination à Maurice bien que le règlement de 2021 sur la santé publique (vaccins COVID-19 à usage d'urgence) ait été adopté pour contourner la maladie pandémique et il y aura un programme de vaccination autour de l'île. Les gens se sont plaints qu'ils souffraient d'allergies, certaines personnes sont mortes lorsqu'elles ont été vaccinées, d'autres ont souffert de maux de tête et les travailleurs ont besoin d'un permis d'accès au travail et d'une carte de vaccination pour avoir accès à leur lieu de travail. Les médias ont rapporté que certains travailleurs refusaient de se faire vacciner parce qu'il y avait des risques pour leur santé et leur sécurité. Dès lors, des questions se sont posées quant à la vaccination obligatoire, et devrait-elle être imposée par n'importe quel employeur? À Maurice, tout comme au Royaume-Uni, en Italie, la vaccination est impérative et obligatoire selon les différentes législations et réglementations en vigueur, en particulier pour les frontliners et les personnes qui sont régulièrement en contact avec des patients pandémiques de COVID-19 et d'autres travailleurs de la santé. Cependant, il y a une question juridique pertinente comme Isra Black, a souligné que: « toute autorité publique, qu'il s'agisse de l'État ou d'une fiducie individuelle du NHS, qui rend obligatoire la vaccination devra se conformer aux droits de l'homme et à l'égalité. La vaccination obligatoire porte atteinte au droit à la vie privée protégé par l'article 8 de la Convention européenne des droits de l'homme de 1950, de sorte que les autorités compétentes devront démontrer que l'ingérence est justifiée dans la poursuite d'un but légitime et sa proportionnalité. La dimension des droits de l'homme et de l'égalité de la vaccination obligatoire ne peut être évitée par l'utilisation de la législation sur la santé et la sécurité ».

III. L'impact du COVID-19 sur les droits des travailleurs: l'impact socio-économique

Les ravages et les ravages de la maladie pandémique COVID-19 restent sans précédent dans l'histoire de l'humanité affectant tous les secteurs du développement socio-économique d'un pays affectant, en outre, le taux de chômage (il est passé de 1,1 % à 6,5 % selon l'International l'Organisation du travail) avec, entre autres, une forte augmentation de la pauvreté, des inégalités, des pertes de revenus du travail ou des atteintes aux droits de l'homme notamment sur le lieu de travail. Le gouvernement de la petite République de Maurice a réagi rapidement à la pandémie de COVID-19 en promulguant de nouvelles législations et réglementations (supra), comme expliqué, pour contrôler sa propagation et assurer son développement socio-économique dans des secteurs clés tels que le textile, les secteurs manufacturiers, l'alimentation, le tourisme, le commerce de détail, le commerce de gros et l'agriculture avec un impact direct sur l'économie et la finance mauricienne, et, par conséquent, sur son PIB, qui s'est contracté de 11 % en 2020 selon le Fonds monétaire international.

L'impact psychologique et philosophique a finalement eu un dernier mot car la plupart des Mauriciens pensent qu'ils devront vivre sous la 'nouvelle normalité', c'est-à-dire qu'ils devront désormais vivre avec la maladie pandémique de COVID-19. En effet, la maladie pandémique COVID-19 est venue porter atteinte au droit à la vie et au droit à la santé avec des répercussions sur divers droits humains, entre autres, le droit à la vaccination, le droit d'accès au travail, la liberté d'expression et de parole, la liberté d'association et rassemblement dans un pays démocratique comme la République de Maurice où les tribunaux étaient fermés et les litiges retardés jusqu'au déconfinement mais justice retardée est justice déniée.

Par conséquent, il est important de savoir et de comprendre comment le législateur opère dans d'autres pays africains en adoptant des législations et réglementations pertinentes en vue de contenir la propagation de la maladie pandémique, et comment les gens les considèrent comme une menace pour leur liberté à la vie et à la dignité. Pour éviter tout licenciement, le gouvernement mauricien a mis en place plusieurs mesures pour prévenir les licenciements massifs, notamment parmi les travailleurs peu qualifiés et ceux travaillant dans les petites et moyennes entreprises en raison du confinement.

L'article 72 A (1) de la loi de 2019 sur les droits des travailleurs (loi 20/2019) a été modifié de sorte qu'un employeur ne peut pas pendant la période prescrite commençant le « 1er juin 2021 et se terminant le 31 décembre 2020 (a été prolongé jusqu'au 30 juin 2021) réduire le nombre de travailleurs qu'il emploie de manière temporaire ou permanente ou mettre fin à l'emploi de l'un de ses travailleurs », mais sauf dans les cas où un accord a été conclu concernant la cessation d'emploi pour des raisons économiques, financières, structurelles, et technologiques ou pour toute autre raison similaire, un employeur n'est pas autorisé à réduire ses effectifs pendant la période prescrite. Dans l'affaire Les Frais de l'Artigiano Ltd RB/RN/38/2020, et le Conseil des licenciements a constaté que l'employeur ne s'était pas conformé à l'article pertinent (article 72 A (1) de la loi de 2019 sur les droits des travailleurs (loi 20/2019)) et le licenciement des travailleurs pour cause de licenciement était injustifié. S'appuyant sur le précédent H. Nunkoo Mauritius Biscuit Making Company Ltd 2015 IND 54, le magistrat du tribunal du travail a déclaré : « Il ne suffit pas qu'un employeur prétende que son entreprise est confrontée à un ralentissement économique ou financier. Il doit rapporter des preuves objectives suffisantes de difficultés économiques telles qu'il ne pourrait plus garder tel ou tel salarié sans affecter sa compétitivité. Par conséquent, un état des comptes et une preuve d'expert doivent être produits. Le simple fait que le demandeur ait admis que l'entreprise était confrontée à des difficultés économiques n'est pas en soi une preuve suffisante qu'elle était confrontée à des difficultés économiques n'est pas en soi une preuve suffisante qu'elle était confrontée à des difficultés économiques pour que le poste occupé par le demandeur soit licencié ».

Conclusion et recommandations

On peut en conclure que la maladie pandémique COVID-19 a un effet domino se propageant sur tous les secteurs affectant à la fois le développement socio-économique d'un pays. En outre, il a également affecté les droits fondamentaux les plus élémentaires de tous ses citoyens sans aucune exception lorsque de nouvelles législations et réglementations ont été adoptées en vue de fournir une protection sociale à tous les ménages et individus, en particulier les travailleurs du secteur privé avec l'aide gouvernementale aux salaires. Scheme (GWAS) et le Self-Employed Assistance Scheme (SEAS) pendant la période COVID-19. Bien que le gouvernement mauricien soit confronté à des contraintes financières dues au Covid-19, tous les travailleurs du secteur public ont reçu les mêmes salaires mensuels sans aucune réduction, à l'exception des heures supplémentaires. Étant donné que Maurice est un État-providence avec une éducation gratuite à tous les niveaux, des soins de santé gratuits et des transports gratuits pour les personnes âgées et les étudiants du supérieur, le gouvernement mauricien a immédiatement mis en place un programme gouvernemental d'assistance salariale (GWAS) et un programme d'aide au travail indépendant (SEAS) pendant la COVID-19 pour aider les travailleurs du secteur privé sous forme de salaire de subvention. Et cet effort était fortement recommandé.

Bibliography

Afrasia Bank. (2020, April 17). Retrieved from https://www.afrasiabank.com/en/blog/expert-views/2020/impact-of-covid-19-on-mauritian-economy

Australian Government. (n.d.). Retrieved from https://www.agriculture.gov.au/abares/research-topics/trade/impacts-of-COVID-19-on-Australian-trade

Dentons.com. (2020). *'Force Majeure' and Coronavirus (COVID-19) under the laws of Mauritius–what is force majeure?* [online] Available at: <https://www.dentons.com/en/insights/articles/2020/march/26/force-majeure-and-coronavirus-disease> [Accessed 10 May 2021].

International Labour Organisation. (n.d.). Retrieved from https://www.ilo.org/global/about-the-ilo/newsroom/news/WCMS_742203/lang--en/index.htm

International Labour Organisation. (n.d.). Retrieved from https://www.ilo.org/global/topics/coronavirus/sectoral/lang--en/index.htm

KPMG. (28 April 2020). Retrieved from https://home.kpmg/xx/en/home/insights/2020/04/mauritius-government-and-institution-measures-in-response-to-covid.html

Mardemootoo, S., Balgobin-Bhoyrul, P., Kissoon, G., Guttoo, H., Tung, S. and Desai, J. (2020). *The COVID-19 (Miscellaneous Provisions) Act of 2020 introduced by the Parliament of Mauritius – Amendments and their implications.* [online] Dentons.com. Available at: <https://www.dentons.com/en/insights/articles/2020/may/27/the-covid-19-miscellaneous-provisions-act-of-2020-introduced-by-the-parliament-of-mauritius> [Accessed 7 May 2021].

PLCJ. (2020). *COVID-19(Mauritius): Can companies suspend the payment of commercial rents?*. [online] Available at: <https://plcj.net/en/covid-19mauritius-can-companies-suspend-the-payment-of-commercial-rents/> [Accessed 1 May 2021].

Potayya, S. (2021). *An analysis of force majeure in the context of Mauritian banking law*. [online] Ibanet.org. Available at: <https://www.ibanet.org/article/AA358E1B-028E-4E9A-87B2-6CCAB24DBA70> [Accessed 8 May 2021].

Republic of Mauritius. (n.d.). Retrieved from http://www.govmu.org/English/News/Pages/Efforts-to-boost-tradein-Mauritius-in-response-to-Covid-19.aspx

Richard, N. and Ribet, A. (2020). *COVID-19 and its impact on contractual performance in Mauritius – Force Majeure | DLA Piper Africa, Mauritius | Juristconsult Chambers*. [online] DLA Piper Africa. Available at: <https://www.dlapiperafrica.com/en/mauritius/insights/2020/covid-19-and-its-impact-on-contractual-performance-in-mauritius-force-majeure> [Accessed 5 May 2021].

Rogers Capital. (n.d.). Retrieved from https://www.rogerscapital.mu/9135/key-measures-by-the-government-to-sustain-the-mauritian-economy-amidst-covid-19

UKDiss.com. (14 March 2020). Retrieved from https://ukdiss.com/litreview/financial-crisis-and-tourism-sector-in-mauritian-economy.php

La mise mettant en otage des municipalités : la réforme du Local Government Act (LGA) et le renvoi des élections municipales en raison de la crise sanitaire

Didier MICHEL[1]

Cette contribution permet de faire une évaluation de la gestion des administrations municipales dans le contexte mauricien dans la gestion des villes. Afin d'éviter le prolongement de la crise sanitaire, le législateur a jugé utile de reporter pour deux ans la tenue des élections municipales. Ces dernières auraient dû se tenir en mars 2021 car le mandat des élus municipaux est arrivé à terme. Elle met en avant que le LGA aurait dû être réformé. En application depuis 2011, cette loi n'est plus adaptée aux besoins nécessaires dans la gestion des villes. Elle mérite donc un amendement pour donner aux municipalités plus d'indépendance. Elle conclut sur le fait que ce renvoi met en otage les municipalités car il semble être une stratégie politique de la part de la majorité gouvernementale afin de garder le pouvoir au sein des 5 villes qui sont gérées par des municipalités.

The international symposium organized by the University of Mauritius in partnership with the Paris-Nanterre, Potsdam, Franco-German Universities and the Law Reform Commission on the theme 'The intercultural approach to the management of COVID-19 in Germany, France and in the Indian Ocean islands' coincides with the easing of health restrictions in the Republic of Mauritius.

This contribution makes it possible to make an assessment of the management of municipal administrations in the Mauritian context. In order to avoid the prolongation of the health crisis, the legislator deemed it useful to postpone the holding of municipal elections for two years. These should have been held in March 2021 because the mandate of elected municipal officials has come to an end. She points out that the LGA should have been reformed. In

---

[1] Dr. Senior Lecturer, Faculty of Law and Management, University of Mauritius.

application since 2011, this law has proven itself and deserves an amendment to give municipalities more independence. She concludes on the fact that this dismissal holds the municipalities hostage because it seems to be a political strategy on the part of the government majority in order to keep power within the 5 cities which are managed by municipalities.

Introduction

En mars 2021, les mandats des conseillers et maires des municipalités de la République de Maurice sont arrivés à terme. En vertu de la Section 11 du *Local Government Act* (LGA), des élections municipales devraient être tenues. À cette époque, l'île étant confinée pour la deuxième fois, rendait impossible la tenue des élections sur le plan local.

En mai 2021, un projet de loi a été validé par l'Assemblée nationale apportant deux amendements au LGA. D'une part, les élections municipales ont été renvoyées à une date ultérieure et d'autre part, le mandat des conseillers municipaux élus en juin 2015 a été renouvelé pour une période maximum de deux ans supplémentaires.

Cette contribution a deux objectifs. Premièrement, de démonter qu'en application depuis 2011, cette loi a démontré ses lacunes. Elle ne permet pas aux municipalités de fonctionner comme des autorités locales. Deuxièmement, d'analyser les raisons avancées par le législateur pour renvoyer les élections locales. Les débats parlementaires révèlent plusieurs de ces raisons. En dépit de la crise sanitaire, le moment était propice pour le législateur de donner plus de dynamisme au LGA.

Le plan que propose cette contribution pour traiter la problématique évoquée est le suivant : dans un premier temps, elle définit le concept de décentralisation tel que le prévoit le LGA 2011 (I). Dans un deuxième temps, elle démontre que le LGA 2011 ne suit pas dans le concret l'esprit même de la décentralisation et au lieu de réformer le LGA 2011, le législateur a choisi le renvoi des élections municipales (II).

I. Redéfinir la décentralisation dans le contexte mauricien et les modalités face à la participation féminine aux élections municipales

L'objectif premier d'avoir une nouvelle loi régissant les autorités locales était de démontrer que le législateur était en phase avec l'évolution sociale. Le droit ne peut qu'évoluer que lorsque la réforme ne concerne pas uniquement le droit. Il y a réforme du droit en vue de répondre, d'une façon générale, à un besoin social[2]. Pour pouvoir répondre à cette supposition, il convient de voir la définition de la décentralisation telle que le LGA 2011 la définit (A). L'ouverture qu'il apporte avec la participation féminine aux élections municipales (B).

A. La définition de la décentralisation dans le contexte mauricien : distinction ambiguë entre ville et village

D'un point vue général, la décentralisation peut être définie comme la répartition ou distribution des compétences et des pouvoirs entre un organe central ou national et des organes non centraux ou périphériques de la collectivité[3]. Elle traduit certains intérêts communs à toutes les parties de la nation tels que la formation des lois générales et les rapports du peuple avec les étrangers. D'autres intérêts sont spéciaux à certaines parties de la nation, tels que les entreprises communales[4].

D'après sa Constitution, la République de Maurice est un État unitaire[5]. Ce concept juridique signifie que l'État est gouverné par un gouvernement central avec des pouvoirs extraordinaires que lui confère la Constitution et d'autres dispositions législatives. Sur le plan local, l'île est administrée par cinq conseils municipaux pour la gestion des zones qualifiées urbaines[6]. Pour les régions rurales, leurs administrations sont gérées par neuf Conseils de district et cent-trente Conseils de villages[7].

---

[2] R H Graveson, *Les méthodes de réforme du droit*, In: Revue internationale de droit comparé. Vol. 19 N°2, Avril-juin 1967. pp. 353–361;

[3] H Barnett, *Constitutional & Administrative Law*, Cavendish Publishing Ltd, London 4th Edition 2002, p. 305.

[4] S Sabéran, *La notion d'intérêt général chez Adam Smith : De la richesse des nations a la puissance des nations*, Éditions Choiseul | « Géoéconomie » 2008/2 n° 45 | pages 55 à 71.

[5] La Section première de la Constitution mauricienne définit Maurice comme une République et un État démocratique, « *Mauritius shall be a sovereign democratic State which shall be known as the Republic of Mauritius* ».

[6] Les Sections 4 & 5 du *Local Government Act 2011* définissent les autorités locales administrant les zones urbaines.

[7] Les Sections 6 & 7 du *Local Government Act 2011* définissent les autorités locales administrant les zones rurales.

L'idée d'introduire le LGA 2011 est d'apporter un gouvernement local ou une démocratie de base qui est essentiel au bien-être des communautés[8]. Cela exige que la population soit bien représentée par des élections démocratiques et justes, et que les services attendus des autorités locales soient fournis de manière efficace et efficiente. L'objectif est de pouvoir atteindre un niveau de vie plus élevé pour les communautés locales[9].

En d'autres termes, cela consiste en une répartition du pouvoir entre l'autorité centrale et locale, que l'on peut qualifier de décentralisation par services, ou technique spéciale: l'autonomie juridique et financière[10].

Au niveau du Commonwealth Local Government Forum, il y a une prise de conscience croissante que dans tous les pays, en particulier les pays en développement, le gouvernement local devrait être à l'avant-garde de la lutte contre la pauvreté, dans la lutte contre les taudis, dans l'amélioration de la ville et l'aménagement du territoire, dans la protection de nos valeurs, du cadre de vie et des sites historiques. En raison du défi croissant auquel sont confrontés les gouvernements locaux, les gouvernants doivent toujours revoir en permanence leurs systèmes de gouvernements locaux. Ils doivent repenser les théories, la philosophie et les pratiques de gouvernement local. La législation sur les collectivités locales est donc un outil pour atteindre ces objectifs[11].

Ses objectifs ont été traduits dans la loi de la manière suivante :

L'objet d'une collectivité locale est de:

(a) promouvoir le bien-être social, économique, environnemental et culturel de la communauté locale;

(b) améliorer la qualité de vie globale des habitants de la communauté locale;

(c) veiller à ce que les services et les installations fournis par le Conseil soient accessibles et équitablement répartis;

---

[8] Parliamentary Debates (Hansard), First Session, Tuesday 06 December 2011, [No. 34 of 2011], p. 141.
[9] Ibid.
[10] C Didry, *Leon Duguit, ou Le Service Public en Action*, Belin | « Revue d'histoire moderne & contemporaine » 2005/3 no 52–3 | pages 88 à 97.
[11] Parliamentary Debates (Hansard), First Session, Tuesday 06 December 2011, [No. 34 of 2011], p. 141.

La réforme du Local Government Act 103

(d) veiller à ce que les ressources soient utilisées de manière efficiente et efficace pour répondre au mieux aux besoins de la communauté locale;
(e) assurer la transparence et la responsabilité dans la prise de décision; et
(f) assurer l'utilisation prudente et l'intendance des ressources de la communauté locale[12].

Le LGA ne s'applique pas qu'aux villes, il a aussi force de loi dans la gestion des villages. Dans le concret, les villages connaissent plus de plans de développement que des villes. Au moment de la présentation du projet de loi relatif à l'administration locale et afin de soutenir son projet sur la décentralisation des autorités locales, son auteur a souligné que du fait que d'importants développements immobiliers dans les villages ont vu le jour et que les infrastructures sociales et économiques se sont considérablement améliorées de manière que de nombreux villages ont acquis suffisamment de maturité pour être transformés en villes[13]. Cependant, la structure de la nouvelle législation permet d'envisager un changement de statut de ces gros villages en villes à un stade ultérieur. Une procédure relativement simple a été initiée par la loi. Le Président de la République a le pouvoir de faire une requête au gouvernement central pour transformer un village en une ville. Cela est possible du fait que pour la première fois depuis qu'existe juridiquement les collectivités locales à Maurice, elles sont incluses et définies dans les annexes du projet de loi[14]. Cependant la question sur l'intérêt pratique d'inclure les villes et villages dans les mêmes annexes se pose.

B. Les nouvelles modalités des élections des municipales avec le LGA 2011

L'idée de réformer l'administration des autorités locales provient du fait que le législateur voulait changer le mode de scrutin des élus locaux[15]. Pour qu'une personne puisse se porter candidat aux élections

---

[12] Section 49, Local Government Act 2011.
[13] Parliamentary Debates (Hansard), First Session, Tuesday 06 December 2011, [No. 34 of 2011], p. 144.
[14] Ibid.
[15] Ibid.

municipales, elle devrait être inscrite comme électrice dans le registre dans la commune où elle réside. Avant 2011, n'importe quelle personne pouvait se porter candidat sans être inscrite au registre électoral de sa commune. L'idée d'interdire cette pratique consiste à faciliter la proximité locale entre l'administration et ses administrés. Un conseiller local est considéré comme étant plus proche de ses mandants. Cependant ce dispositif a été amendé en 2021. Les raisons d'enlever ce dispositif n'ont pas été expliquées[16].

Le *Local Government Act 2011* veut assurer une parité entre hommes et femmes au niveau des élus locaux. Lors des dernières élections locales tenues en 2005, il y avait seulement 16 conseillères urbaines sur un total de 126 conseillers. La présence féminine ne représentait que 13 %. Dans les villages, il y avait 97 conseillères rurales sur un total de 1 488 conseillers. Les conseillères rurales ne représentaient que 7 % des élues[17]. C'est loin derrière de l'objectif de 30 % de femmes dans la prise de décision sur le plan de la politique locale. Cet objectif était établi par le Protocole de la SADC sur le genre et le Plan d'action du Commonwealth pour l'égalité des sexes[18]. L'introduction de l'égalité des sexes sur le plan local est de plusieurs ordres. D'abord, cette égalité permet aux femmes de participer aux décisions qui affectent leur vie et celle de leur famille. Ensuite elle garantit leur autonomisation sur le plan politique, social et économique. En dernier lieu, la participation féminine sur le plan local fait partie de l'idéal démocratique qui contribue au développement durable. En effet, puisqu'à Maurice les femmes constituent plus de la moitié de la population, le développement durable ne peut se faire sans elles. La démocratie et le développement doivent donc être considérés comme des objectifs complémentaires essentiels à la réalisation de l'égalité des sexes.

Le *Local Government Act 2011* dispose que pour tout groupement présentant plus de deux candidats dans une circonscription locale, pas plus des deux tiers des candidats du groupement ne doivent pas être du même sexe. En outre, la liste de réserve des candidats présentée par groupements à la Commission de contrôle électoral, destinée à pourvoir les postes vacants, ne doit pas comprendre plus des deux tiers de personnes du même sexe. En outre, la liste doit indiquer l'ordre de

---

[16] Section 11(5) Repealed by [Act No. 5 of 2021], *Local Government Act 2011*.
[17] Parliamentary Debates (Hansard), First Session, Tuesday 06 December 2011, [No. 34 of 2011], p. 151.
[18] Ibid.

La réforme du Local Government Act

préséance de chacun des candidats – dans lequel son nom apparaît sur la liste – à condition que pas plus de deux candidats consécutifs sur la liste soient du même sexe[19].

Il s'avère important de faire la différence entre la situation avant le LGA 2011 et les élections municipales qui se sont tenues après le vote de la loi.

Le premier tableau expose le nombre de femmes qui ont été élues conseillères des villes lors des élections municipales du 07 octobre 2001 et celles du 02 octobre 2005.

TABLEAU 1[20]

Elections municipales	Conseillers	Conseillères	Total des conseillers élus
07 octobre 2001	103	23	126
02 octobre 2005	105	101	126

Le deuxième tableau démontre le nombre Conseillères municipales élues avec le LGA 2001.

TABLEAU 2[21]

Elections municipales	Conseillers	Conseillères	Total des conseillers élus
09 décembre 2012	53	34	87
14 juin 2015	71	41	112

Le LGA 2011 permet à ce que plus de femmes deviennent conseillères municipales. De ce fait, elles arrivent à prendre part activement à la vie politique sur le plan local.

Le LGA 2011 projette une notion de la décentralisation des municipalités dans le contexte mauricien. En matière de participation

---

[19] Parliamentary Debates (Hansard), First Session, Tuesday 06 December 2011, [No. 34 of 2011], p. 151.
[20] Données recueillies sur le site officiel de la Commission électorale de la République de Maurice, https://electoral.govmu.org/oec/?page_id=1644.
[21] Ibid.

féminine aux élections municipales, il offre plus d'ouverture. En contrepartie, le LGA a démontré ses lacunes car la décentralisation ne fonctionne pas. Il s'avère nécessaire de mesurer la justification du législateur l'ayant poussé à renvoyer les élections municipales.

II . De la décentralisation déguisée au renvoi des élections municipales

La décentralisation a une valeur démocratique qui se résume à la gestion d'un maximum d'affaires par les parties intéressées elles-mêmes ou par leurs représentants[22]. L'AGL 2011 ne semble pas atteindre cet objectif de décentralisation. Il mise toujours sur la centralisation déguisée avec le fonctionnaire de Chief Executive Officer (A). Le renvoi des élections municipales s'apparente à une tactique politique visant à maintenir le pouvoir au niveau de la ville plutôt que des raisons de santé (B).

A. La décentralisation déguisée : le Chief Executive Officer

D'après LA Section 49 LGA la ville est gérée par un Conseil municipal élu. L'exemple de la gestion d'un marché démontre la décentralisation déguisée. Un marché est géré par le conseil municipal. Chaque étal et boutique se trouvant dans l'enceinte d'une foire marchande est sous la responsabilité du Conseil Municipal. C'est le Conseil Municipal qui délivre les licences commerciales aux opérateurs économiques des foires marchandes. Dans la mesure où c'est le conseil municipal qui délivre un permis, il doit avoir le pouvoir de le suspendre, de le révoquer ou de ne pas le renouveler. En vertu de la loi, le conseil devrait demander l'approbation du ministre de tutelle pour prendre une telle décision. Quel mécanisme est prévu dans le cas où un commerçant ne respecte pas la condition attachée à sa licence ou omet de payer les frais appropriés au Conseil Municipal? Pourquoi le conseil municipal n'est-il pas habilité à prendre les mesures correctives appropriées dans de telles circonstances? Ceci est un exemple concret qu'une municipalité n'opère pas de manière décentralisée. Dans la mesure où le ministre a le pouvoir sur des sanctions à prendre contre un commerçant à la place d'un Conseil municipal,

---

[22] R Charles. Théorie et réalité de la décentralisation. In: Revue française de science politique, 16e année, n°3, 1966. pp. 445–471;

démontre que le LGA ne va pas dans le sens d'une vraie décentralisation. En plus du ministre de tutelle, il y a le cas du *Chief Executive Officer*, qui est un fonctionnaire qui représente l'exécutif au sein d'un Conseil municipal.

D'après la Section 35 du LGA, le maire émet des directives générales, mais c'est le *Chief Executive Officer* qui organize les affaires du conseil[23]. En d'autres termes, l'interprétation possible à cette Section de la loi signifie que le *Chief Executive Officer* peut refuser de fournir des informations aux conseillers et aux maires élus. Le *Chief Executive Officer* semble concentrer les pouvoirs entre ses mains et dont les décisions n'auront même pas à être approuvées par le conseil, mais il faudra tout simplement en faire rapport au conseil.

Dans l'ancienne loi chaque mairie, selon ces particularités, établissait son mode de fonctionnement avec les *Standing Orders* propre à chaque mairie, désormais cela est aboli. Tout est prévu dans une partie de la loi, *Standing Orders* standardisés. C'est la tendance vers la décentralisation déguisée. Toutes les grandes réformes des administrations régionales entamées dans le passé avaient pour objectif de reconnaître la valeur des collectivités locales, leur confier plus d'autonomie, plus de pouvoir, laisser les citadins décider de leurs représentants et les responsabiliser et les laisser agir. La différence fondamentale entre la loi de 2011 et celui de 2003 est cette tendance inverse à vouloir tout centraliser sur l'État central.

B. Le renvoi des élections municipales : une stratégie politique ?

Il est utile de rappeler que le renvoi des élections tant au niveau législatif qu'au niveau local n'est pas nouveau[24]. La plus grande entorse constitutionnelle a été celle du gouvernement de coalition formé par le Parti-Travailliste de Sir Seewoosagur Ramgoolam et du PMSD de Sir Gaëtan Duval, en 1969. Les deux alliés ont renvoyé toutes les élections (législatives, partielles, locales en 1974). Le Leader de l'opposition d'alors,

---

[23] Section 35, Local Government Act 2011.
[24] Parliamentary Debates (Hansard), First Session, Tuesday 06 May 2021, [No.9 of 2021], p. 98

l'honorable Sookdeo Bissoondoyal, avait commenté ses dérives en ces termes, –

« Aujourd'hui est le jour le plus sombre de l'histoire de l'île Maurice. J'ai honte de voir à l'Assemblée tant de visiteurs, car ils assistent à des funérailles. Nous enterrons la démocratie, et mon cœur se brise »[25].

L'alliance MSM – MMM, menée tantôt par SAJ et Paul Raymond Bérenger de 2000 à 2005, avait décidé de renvoyer les municipales avec pour résultat la perte du pouvoir au bénéfice du Parti-Travailliste mené par Dr Navin Ramgoolam. Celui-ci retint les rênes du pouvoir de 2005 à 2014. Cependant, en renvoyant les municipales de 2010 à 2012, le Parti Travailliste a démontré qu'il n'avait pas tiré de leçon des expériences passées. En 2014, il perdit le pouvoir après ses vaines tentatives pour une alliance avec le MMM.

Toutefois, ils ont tous occulté les conséquences qui ont suivi les renvois des élections dans le passé. En effet, notre histoire politique démontre que tout gouvernement qui a renvoyé les élections municipales a perdu le pouvoir lors des législatives. Cependant, le renvoi des élections municipales a été fait pour les raisons suivantes qui sont en lien avec la crise sanitaire inédite. Une des raisons étaient d'éviter une troisième vague. Comme l'île était confinée partiellement, l'accès dans les lieux publics a été strictement contrôlé.

Le projet de loi modifiant la loi sur les collectivités locales afin de reporter les élections municipales de deux ans maximums a été approuvé par l'Assemblée nationale lors de sa séance du 25 mai 2021. Cependant, le report des élections jusqu'à deux ans soulève des questions. Nos décideurs publics savent bien en quoi consiste une campagne municipale: essentiellement des réunions publiques tôt le matin, le week-end et les jours ouvrables, ainsi que des manifestations en soirée; des campagnes de distribution de tracts en porte-à-porte ciblées; pas d'émissions télévisées comme lors des élections législatives, et quasiment pas de meetings. Et pourtant, que ce soit lors de la première vague en 2020 ou de la seconde en cours cette année, les Mauriciens dans leur ensemble ont démontré qu'ils savaient respecter la loi. Si les rassemblements villageois ont eu lieu l'année dernière, les citadins des cinq villes du pays ne sauront-ils pas prendre leurs responsabilités en

---

[25] Ibid, p. 101.

matière de port de masque et de distanciation sociale? Les Britanniques ont pu voter pour renouveler leurs administrations locales, tout comme les Chiliens lors d'un référendum historique pour réformer leur système politique obsolète. La France se prépare aux élections régionales, très critiquées à l'égard de l'actuel président français.

Conclusion

Le report des élections municipales a des conséquences pour les municipalités qui, en maintenant la même politique dans la gestion des villes, risquent de provoquer le ras-le-bol de la population. Le pouvoir ne cesse de demander à la population de s'adapter à la situation actuelle.

Aucun maire ou conseiller municipal n'a pris position sur cette initiative législative, alors qu'en tant qu'élus locaux, ils ont la possibilité de la contester. Les municipalités disposent de la logistique et des équipements nécessaires pour que les élections puissent se dérouler selon un mode de scrutin alternatif.

Mais il faut se rendre à l'évidence: les conseillers municipaux sont issus de la même famille politique que la majorité gouvernementale.

Le Commissariat aux élections n'a apparemment pas donné d'avis, ni lors des débats parlementaires, ni après le vote de l'amendement par l'Assemblée nationale. D'autant plus que l'amendement voté donne au Premier ministre le droit de décider de la tenue des élections municipales. Il s'agit là d'une atteinte à la démocratie. En vertu de l'article 40 de la Constitution de Maurice, le Commissaire électoral dispose de pouvoirs constitutionnels considérables car il n'est soumis à aucun contrôle. Certes, un contrôle par la Cour suprême est possible, mais il n'est pas automatique: un recours formel est très coûteux. Le report des élections municipales prend les électeurs en otage alors qu'il y avait une opportunité de démontrer que les élections pouvaient se dérouler différemment.

Bibliographie

Barnett, H, *Constitutional & administrative law*, Cavendish Publishing Ltd, London, 4th Edition 2002

Charles, R, Théorie et réalité de la décentralisation. « Revue française de science politique » 1966/16e année, n°3

Commission électorale de la République de Maurice, https://electoral.govmu.org/oec/?page_id=1644.

Constitution de la République de Maurice de 1968

Didry, C, Leon Duguit, ou Le Service Public en Action, Belin | « Revue d'histoire moderne & contemporaine » 2005/3, n° 52–3

Local Government Act 2011

Parliamentary Debates (Hansard), First Session, Tuesday 06 December 2011, [No. 34 of 2011]

Parliamentary Debates (Hansard), First Session, Tuesday 06 May 2021, [No. 9 of 2021]

Sabéran, S, *La notion d'intérêt général chez Adam Smith : De la richesse des nations a la puissance des nations*, Éditions Choiseul | « Géoéconomie » 2008/2, n° 45

PART II

MANAGEMENT OF COVID

LA GESTION DU COVID

In the first phase of the pandemic, COVID-19 management was characterized by contradictory and poorly coordinated measures due to the sudden occurrence of an unknown risk (R. Lanneau). Although the measures taken by neighbouring countries were copied by different countries, the measures were adapted to the specific cultural conditions of each country. A federally organized country like Germany has made it possible to adapt measures according to regional needs (B. Bestvater). In the European Union some borders were temporarily closed and the Schengen space out of order. In countries in Sub-Saharan Africa the measures were different adapted to a different risk.

Durant la première phase de la pandémie, la gestion du COVID-19 a été marquée par des mesures contradictoires et peu coordonnées dues à la survenance subite d'un risque inconnu (R. Lanneau). Bien que l'on ait constaté une imitation des mesures prises par les pays voisins, les mesures ont été par la suite adaptées aux spécificités culturelles de chaque pays. Un pays d'une organisation fédérale comme l'Allemagne a permis d'adapter les mesures en fonction de la nécessité régionales (B. Bestvater). Dans l'Union européenne, certaines frontières ont été temporairement fermées et l'espace Schengen a été mis hors service.

The management of Covid, a comparative analysis of German federal and French centralized management of the crisis

Berquis BESTVATER[1]

La France et l'Allemagne sont peuplées de manière différente et ils ont géré la crise du COVID-19 à leurs manières. La différence commence par la géographie et la démographie des villes des deux pays, la population allemande est répartie de façon bien plus dispersée sur l'ensemble de son territoire. Le fédéralisme et la décentralisation est la clé de voûte des Institutions allemandes puisque la loi fondamentale allemande prévoit une répartition claire des compétences entre le Bund et les Länder. En Allemagne, le dialogue entre l'État Fédéral et les Länder est resté la pierre angulaire de la gestion de la crise. En France, le pouvoir central, lui-même de plus en plus présidentiel, conserve la majeure partie du pouvoir décisionnel. Les prises de décision à l'échelle nationale ont pu être prises rapidement et pour tout le territoire français. Pourtant de manière générale dans tous les pays, la pandémie a été un moment d'affirmation de la centralité du politique, et aussi un moment de retour au national: les pays ont dû gérer seul l'expansion du COVID-19 et prendre des mesures pour tout leur territoire. L'Union européenne s'est effacé brutalement pour un retour de l'État-nation, jusqu'à l'acte souverain de la fermeture des frontières.

France and Germany are differently populated, and they have managed the COVID-19 crisis in their own ways. The difference starts with the geography and demography of the cities in both countries, the German population is much more spread out over its territory. Federalism and decentralization are the keystone of German institutions, as the German Constitutional Law provides for a clear repartition of competences between the Federal Government and the Länder. In Germany, the dialogue between the federal state and the Länder has remained the cornerstone of crisis management. In France, the central government, itself increasingly presidential, retains most of the decision-making power. Decisions at national level could be taken quickly and for the whole French

---

[1] Doctorante en cotutelle à l'Université Paris Nanterre et l'Université Potsdam.

territory. However, in general, in all countries, the pandemic was a moment of affirmation of the centrality of politics, and also a moment of return to the national dimension: countries had to manage the expansion of COVID-19 on their own and take measures for their entire territory. The European Union abruptly stepped aside for a return to the nation-state, up to the sovereign act of closing borders.

Introduction

The objective of my presentation is to document and compare the sanitary mobilization of the states and in particular of France and Germany in the face of the COVID-19 epidemic, to describe and analyse the state interventions on the health systems.

The COVID-19 crisis highlights the advantages and disadvantages of both a highly centralized and a highly decentralized approach. In managing some aspects of the public health emergency, a centralized approach may, for example, facilitate a rapid and uniform response across the country, ignoring possible inequalities, either in terms of available resources or in the treatment of individuals (e.g. quarantining people returning from a particular country, state, region or province). This is the case when national governments decide to transfer hospitalized patients between regions that are highly affected by the epidemic and others that are less so, as was the case in France. At the beginning of the pandemic, for example, the French government transferred patients from hospitals in the most affected regions[2] (such as the Grand Est) to less affected regions in the south. A centralized approach can also facilitate the rapid exchange of information and knowledge that is essential in times of crisis. A decentralized system[3], on the other hand, can provide more flexibility and scope for experimentation in an uncertain context, thus encouraging innovative bottom-up approaches[4] (a way of making corporate decisions

---

[2] BPI France (2020), Covid-19 : les aides régionales, https://bpifrance-creation.fr/encyclopedie/covid-19-mesures-exceptionnelles/autres-mesures/covid-19-aides-regionales.

[3] OCDE (2019), Decentralisation in the health sector and responsibilities across levels of government – Impact on spending decisions and the budget, 7è réunion du Réseau conjoint des Hauts responsables du budget et de la santé de l'OCDE, https://www.oecd.org/officialdocuments/publicdisplaydocumentpdf/?cote=COM/DELSA/GOV(2019)2&docLanguage=En.

[4] Silberzahn, P. (2020 [189])

that starts from the bottom of the hierarchy, rather than at the top) that can be applied elsewhere with the necessary adaptations if successful. Decentralized approaches also allow local and regional authorities to react and intervene quickly. Decentralized networks of laboratories in Germany, for example, have been essential for the implementation of the country's proactive screening strategy. My presentation will be structured in three central points: the first one will discuss the impact of the crisis of COVID-19 and its recovery, my second point concern the territorial approach of the economic and social crisis and finally my last part will focus on support for cooperation between competent authorities. In these different paragraphs I will undertake a comparison between France and Germany[5].

I. Managing the territorial impact of the COVID-19 crisis and recovery

A. *The territorial approach to the health crisis*

The importance of adopting a territorial approach to the health crisis has gradually gained ground in recent months. In many countries, special measures concerning masks[6], school and restaurant closures and strict containment are being applied to certain localities or regions – rather than to the whole territory – in order to limit the economic impact. In line with WHO (World Health Organization) recommendations, testing and tracing are central to all crisis management strategies. An effective screening strategy, combined with social distancing, is less expensive than containment.

– Screening and tracing

At the outset of the pandemic, WHO recommended large-scale screening[7] to control the coronavirus. Frequent testing can identify and

---

[5] Silberzahn, P. (2020), Gérer une situation de crise: faut-il une approche centralisée ou décentralisée? https://beesens.com/contents/78805#!.
[6] OMS (2020), Advice on the use of masks in the context of COVID-19, https://www.who.int/publications/i/item/advice-on-the-use-of-masks-in-the-community-during-home-care-and-in-healthcare-settings-in-the-context-of-the-novel-coronavirus-(2019-ncov)-outbreak.
[7] WHO (2020 [89])

isolate contagious individuals before symptoms appear and prevent the risk of a second wave of infection. This approach requires a significant expansion of testing[8], but the difficulties and costs[9] involved pale in comparison to the costs of lockdown.

European countries[10] considerably increased their capacities and generalized testing for suspicious cases between May and November 2020. The use of auto-test has also been generalized.

In decentralized countries, while central governments need to ensure financial resources and coordination, the actual policy delivery is the responsibility of regional[11] and local governments. Even in countries with more centralized health service delivery, local and regional governments contribute to organizing testing and isolation measures, which leaves room for local initiatives and experimentation.

B. Local and national lockdowns

In order to limit the exorbitant cost of national lockdown, many countries have implemented local lockdowns. This was the case, for example, in Aberdeen (Scotland), Auckland (New Zealand), Barcelona (Spain) and Melbourne (Australia), as well as in some provinces in India and some Länder in Germany. In addition to reducing costs, this territorialized approach allows targeted responses to problems where they occur. In federal countries, policies are differentiated in nature as they are defined at state- Länder level. Effective coordination between local authorities, health agencies and central government is essential to manage local epidemic outbreaks.

---

[8] Lucie Delaporte, « Retard des tests Covid-19: l'ombre des conflits d'intérêts », Mediapart, 21 mai 2020,
  https://www.mediapart.fr/journal/france/210520/retard-des-tests-covid-19-l-ombre-des-conflits-d-interets

[9] OECD (2020)

[10] Council of Europe (2020), Democratic governance and COVID-19, https://rm.coe.int/cddg-2020-20e-final-reportdemocraticgovernancecovid19-for-publication-/1680a0beed.

[11] Coalition for Urban Transitions (2020) COVID-19 and our cities, urbantransitions.global/story/covid-19-and-our-cities/.

The management of Covid, a comparative analysis 117

1. Example from Germany

In Germany, coronavirus testing capacity has increased significantly since the beginning of the crisis. The country was able to perform 500,000 tests per week and has increased this capacity[12] to 200,000 tests per day. Large-scale screening could be organized relatively quickly thanks to the density of the national laboratory network. On 3 November 2020, the German Federal Health Agency, RKI[13] (Robert Koch Institut), changed its screening strategy by deciding not to systematically test all suspected cases but to prioritize vulnerable populations. Decontainment measures are recommended at federal level but are implemented according to different schedules in the Länder. The first local containment was implemented in the Berchtesgadener region in Bavaria in the third week of October. On 28 October 2020, the federal government and the Länder decided on further containment measures by limiting gatherings to 10 people[14] and by ordering the closure of bars and restaurants from 2 November 2020 for at least four weeks.

2. In France

In France, on 11 May 2020, the government announced the gradual exit from a very strict lockdown, provided that the number of coronavirus contaminations decreased. The decontainment took place according to a differentiated territorial approach by classifying departments into green or red zones, depending on whether the virus was under control or not. During the first three weeks, interdepartmental travel to and from red zones was limited to imperative personal or professional reasons. A second phase of decontainment began on 2 June 2020. The Ministry of Health and Santé Publique France set up a 'measure of vulnerability to the virus' in the departments[15], to enable prefectures to limit mass gatherings and impose the wearing of masks on a case-by-case basis. In

---

[12] Government, G. (n.d), *The Federal Government informs about the corona crisis*, https://www.deutschland.de/en/news/german-federal-government-informs-about-the-corona-crisis.
[13] Robert Koch Institute (2020), COVID-19: https://www.rki.de/DE/Home/homepage_node.html.
[14] C. Arentz and F. Wild, « Vergleich europäischer Gesundheitssysteme in der Covid 19-Pandemie » WIP Analyse, Wissenschaftliches Institut der PKV, March 2020.
[15] Covid-19: prise en charge des cas confirmés », Haut conseil de santé publique, https://www.hcsp.fr/Explore.cgi/avisrapportsdomaine?clefr=771

September, as the number of cases increased rapidly, the Bouches-du-Rhône prefecture decided to close restaurants and bars and made it obligatory to wear a mask in the cities of Aix-en-Provence and Marseille[16]. From 17 October 2020, the French state gradually extended the restrictions to other regions by imposing a curfew[17] in 54 departments considered to be at high risk, including the Parisian region.

II. The territorial approach to the economic and social crisis

A. Support for SMEs (small-medium enterprises) and the self-employed at local and regional level

The restrictions put in place to combat the epidemic directly and indirectly affect local businesses and the self-employed. Some businesses, such as restaurants and cafés, close during the lock-downs, while other SMEs and the self-employed could continue to operate, but with much reduced demand. In some cases, their employees are made technically unemployed or even fired. In many countries, local companies were able to resume full activity in June 2020, but the new lockdowns in Europe – as well as partial lockdowns elsewhere in the world – have jeopardized the relaunch, particularly in the service sector.

To avoid cash shortages and bankruptcies among local businesses and the self-employed, most national governments have taken strong measures to support SMEs[18] and micro-enterprises, the self-employed, artisans, liberal professionals and merchants.

---

[16] « Avis n°6 du Conseil scientifique COVID-19 », 20 avril 2020, https://solidarites-sante.gouv.fr/IMG/pdf/avis_conseil_scientifique_20_avril_2020.pdf

[17] CoR-OECD (2020), *CoR-OECD Survey Questionnaire: "How is the COVID-19 affecting regions and cities?"*, https://cor.euroopa.eu/en/news/Pages/ECON-cor-oecd-survey-covid-19.aspx.

[18] COR-CEMR (2021), *The Involvement of municipalities, cities and regions in the preparation of the national recovery and resilience Plans*, https://cor.europa.eu/en/news/Pages/post-COVID-recovery-plans-.aspx.

1. In Germany:

In Germany, in addition to aid the federal government[19], almost all federal states have set up their own regional programs[20] for SMEs, solo self-employed and start-ups[21]. Some of them, such as the 'Coronavirus emergency support programme', are additional to the emergency support programme established by the federal government[22]. The main instruments of these programmes are direct non-repayable grants (Hesse, Thuringia, Schleswig-Holstein, Brandenburg, North Rhine-Westphalia, Hamburg, Bavaria), loans (Rhineland-Palatinate, Saxony, Schleswig-Holstein), liquidity loans or subventions[23](Baden-Württemberg, Bremen, Mecklenburg-Vorpommern), guarantees (Baden-Württemberg) or a combination of all these instruments (Saxony-Anhalt and Lower Saxony).

2. In France

In France, joint action was taken between national and regional governments to manage the crises as part of the new Economic Council established in December 2019. This included regional task forces that incorporate development banks (BPI) in order to accelerate support measures for business.

In addition, regional governments unlocked 250 million EURO[24](in addition to 750 million euros allocated by the State) to participate in

---

[19] S. Partie, « La politique économique allemande face à la crise du COVID-19. Comment l'Allemagne soutient son économie », Notes du Cerfa, n° 154, Ifri, octobre 2020.

[20] F. Osterloh, "Warum Deutschland die Pandemie besser übersteht als viele Nachbarn", *Ärzteblatt*, 28 May 2020; www.aerzteblatt.de

[21] « Fonds de solidarité pour les TPE, indépendants et micro-entrepreneurs: une aide pouvant aller jusqu'à 1 500 € », https://www.economie.gouv.fr/covid19-soutien-entreprises/fonds-de-solidarite-pour-les-tpe-independants-et-micro

[22] Council of State Government (2020), COVID-19 : Fiscal Impact to States and Strategies for Recovery, http://web.csg.org/covid19/wp-content/uploads/sites/10/2020/07/fiscal-impact.pdf.

[23] Deloitte (2020 [111]).

[24] France Government (2021), *Les Investissements d'avenir amplifient leur impact au plus près des territoires : signature d'un accord de partenariat entre le Premier ministre et Régions de France*, https://www.gouvernement.fr/les-investissements-d-avenir-amplifient-leur-impact-au-plus-pres-des-territoires-signature-d-un.

the National Solidarity[25] Fund for artisans, retailers and small businesses. This National Fund has two components:

(i) Monthly aid to very small enterprises, self-employed people, micro-entrepreneurs and liberal professions experiencing turn-over losses of more than 50 %;

(ii) In a one-time additional payment for the most fragile small business. In the regional to identity innovative products and service that could help overcome the crisis and rebound (regional governments websites and BPI France 2020).

III. Support for cooperation between competent authorities

A. Cooperation between municipalities

Horizontal cooperation between competent authorities – countries, regions or local authorities – is just as important as vertical cooperation[26], especially in federal and decentralized countries where approaches are more differentiated across territories. The effects of the coronavirus are so numerous that no single territory or country can manage them alone. Coordination between regions is essential to avoid disparate or contradictory measures, which in the end constitute a collective risk for the population of a country. In federal systems, for example, territorial districts may have little interest in providing assistance[27](pooling of equipment, skilled personnel, etc.) to a neighbouring district if this would compromise their own ability to respond to a crisis situation. However, cooperation is not an option but an imperative. National governments play an

---

BPI France (2020), Covid-19: les aides regionales, https://bpifrance-creation.fr/encyclopedie/covid-19-mesures-exceptionnelles/autres-mesures/covid-19-aides-regionales.

[25] Cour des Comptes (2020), *Les finances publiques locales 2020*, https://www.ccomptes.fr/fr/publications/les-finances-publiques-locales-2020-fascicules-2-et-3.

[26] « Indicateurs d'activité épidémique COVID-19 par département », data.gouv.fr, https://www.data.gouv.fr/fr/datasets/indicateurs-dactivite-epidemique-covid-19-par-departement/

[27] Anne-Katell Peton, « Grippe A(H1N1) – Responsabilités et pouvoirs du maire en matière de police sanitaire », La gazette des communes, 14 septembre 2009, https://www.lagazettedescommunes.com/1244/grippe-ah1n1-responsabilites-et-pouvoirs-du-maire-en-matiere-de-police-sanitaire/

important role in limiting coordination failures and ensuring consistency of approach, even in federal countries.

Cooperation between competent authorities is essential to limit the risk of new outbreaks or, if they occur, to mitigate their impact. Information on new cases and outbreaks needs to be communicated extremely quickly to avoid the spread of the virus between states and regions, and in particular between municipalities within the same functional urban area. Cooperation between competent authorities is also essential to support recovery, including avoiding fragmented approaches to public investment recovery.

In France, intercommunalities have great responsibilities and a large budget fed by their own tax revenues. Since the beginning of the crisis, they have multiplied initiatives to help their member municipalities, citizens, NGOs and local economic actors[28]. Thanks to their federative capacities, their competences and their technical/financial means, these structures often play the role of a platform, but also of an operational actor directly linked to local needs[29].

B. National strategies for recovery through public investment

In Germany, the federal government adopted in early June 2020 a 'plan for the future' focusing on investment in digital and clean technologies, as well as education and health. New spending will focus on research and development projects, electronic mobility, electronic administration and mobile and high-speed networks[30]. With this programme, the government intends to use the stimulus to boost investment and address longer-term challenges such as digital transformation and climate change.

---

[28] Partenaires Finances locales (2020), La crise sanitaire n'affectera pas les recettes de la grande majorité des communes, https://www.lagazettedescommunes.com/683117/la-crise-sanitaire-naffectera-pas-les-recettes-de-la-grande-majorite-des-communes/.

[29] Assemblée des Communautés de France, 2020 [183].

[30] P. Hassenteufel, F.-X. Schweyer, T. Gerlinger, R. Reiter, « Les « déserts médicaux » comme leviers de la réorganisation des soins primaires. Une comparaison France/Allemagne », *revue française des affaires sociales*, n° 1-2020

1. Cross-border cooperation

Pre-existing cooperation agreements between France (Grand Est), Germany (Rhineland-Palatinate and Baden-Württemberg), Switzerland and Luxembourg have enabled cross-border transfers of COVID-19 patients.

2. In Germany

The Minister-President of Rhineland-Palatinate has set up a cross-border working group with the Dutch and Belgian regions to coordinate interventions against the new coronavirus. In France, the State and the Grand Est region are involved in this cooperation.

Conclusion

Another effect of the COVID-19 crisis is to make centralization/decentralization not a goal but a way to achieve objectives (OECD, 2019[190]). This is illustrated by the fact that, in order to manage the crisis, some governments decide to recentralize temporarily and others to decentralize. Many countries have adopted state of emergency laws that transfer some sub-national responsibilities to central or federal governments. Others, on the contrary, have decided to delegate, at least temporarily, additional competences to sub-national authorities. Switzerland, for example, has temporarily re-centralized health management in response to the crisis[31].

The effectiveness of the short-, medium- and long-term response to the coronavirus crisis has little to do with whether the country is federal or unitary, or with its degree of decentralization. What matters is the coordination mechanisms in place and the ability of governments to harmonize priorities, implement joint measures, support each other and share information, including with the public[32].

The crisis also shows the importance of a risk management strategy, of a clear understanding and distribution of responsibilities between the

---

[31] Gereffi G. (2020), « What does the COVID-19 pandemic teach us about global value chains? The case of medical supplies », Journal of International Business Policy, n° 3, pp. 287–301, https://doi.org/10.1057/s42214-020-00062-w.

[32] OECD, 2019[190].

different levels of government – more necessary in the face of a crisis – but also of adequate funding for missions at sub-national level. This not only ensures that the immediate needs that keep arising are covered, but also that they can be covered in the future.

Emergency or crisis situations require a rapid reaction capacity to avoid their aggravation and limit their negative effects. The ability to adapt to change and uncertainty and the capacity to rectify the strategy if necessary, become essential for effective crisis management. As the local level is where the effects of the crisis are first felt, local and regional authorities must have sufficient room for action to respond quickly[33], effectively and responsibly, whether they operate in a centralized or decentralized system.

Finally, the heterogeneity of the effects of the COVID-19 crisis requires flexibility to adopt measures that are territorialized, respond to the most urgent needs, and adapt to the level of preparation of different localities. This can help a region to undertake actions that are not consecutive but coherent, responding to emergency management, lockdown and recovery needs as the pandemic evolves at the regional level. The importance of adopting a territorialized approach to the health crisis has gradually become apparent. In many countries, special measures regarding masks, school and restaurant closures, and total/partial lockdown are being applied in specific localities and regions – rather than nationwide – to limit the economic impact.

---

[33] Rapport Cazeneuve (2020), Évaluation de l'impact de la crise du COVID-19 sur les finances locales, https://www.gouvernement.fr/partage/11683-remise-du-rapport-de-jean-rene-cazeneuve-evaluation-de-l-impact-de-la-crise-du-covid-19-sur-les.

Covid and the risk culture: Understanding the different strategies in covid management

Régis LANNEAU[1]

In 2020, covid represented a risk that countries had to address. To make sense of the diversity of enacted regulation, this paper explores the relevance of the risk culture approach. This approach, which is one among many, reveals itself to be quite insightful to make sense of the debate surrounding covid responses by public authorities.

En 2020, la covid représentait un risque auquel les pays devaient faire face. Pour comprendre la diversité des réglementations adoptées, cet article explore la pertinence de l'approche de la culture du risque. Cette approche, qui n'est qu'une parmi d'autres, se révèle très pertinente pour comprendre le débat sur les réponses apportées par les pouvoirs publics à la covid.

Introduction

If it is relatively easy to predict the past, it is way more complex to anticipate what might happen, especially when an event is surrounded with many uncertainties. It was certainly true regarding the covid crisis. When it hit the planet in December 2019, the virus was unknown. If it was sufficiently worrying to have led China to quarantine part of its population and if some deaths were (under)reported, the risk that it bore was difficult to assess for countries and governments outside of China.

To assess this risk, three questions had to be answered, none of which had clear answers. The first was whether it might spread outside of China, if yes, whether it will hit western countries, and if yes, when. The second set of questions concerned its contagiousness and lethality. Some were considering it was more or less a flue regarding both of these parameters

---

[1] Ass. Professor University Paris Nanterre.

(considering the information we got from China); other were warning about its high lethality (for the USA, few million deaths were expected without government intervention[2]), especially among older people. The third question concerned the length of the sanitary crisis, if such a crisis occurred. Will the virus disappear with warmer weather (like the flu)? Will it be prone to mutate (and if yes, how quickly)?

If we now have more information regarding all of these questions, it was far from being the case during 2020s winter. And of course, the answers given to each question will have an influence on what will be perceived as an appropriate policy response. For some, it was required to act preventively and to focus on lowering the probability that the virus will 'enter' a country or a regional area by closing borders. For others, we should concentrate on preventing the virus to spread through mask mandate, lockdown or quarantine. Some considered that policy intervention should be centred on lowering the damages that the virus might do through investing in respirators, hospital beds, or research and development to develop a vaccine. Of course, it was possible to 'combine' different levels of intervention.

Considering all these uncertainties, a variety of policy responses were to be expected. And indeed, policies chosen in France, Germany, Mauritius, China, USA, Sweden, India or Pakistan were quite different. Even today it is difficult to identify what would have been the best strategy for each country or even if there was an objectively best strategy to follow. It could be possible to make sense of these policies by stressing the relevance of the political system: what can be done in China cannot be done to the same extent in western Europe or in the USA. It could also be possible to stress the influence of state capacity: developed countries could afford over-reaction; developing countries could not. The cost of a quarantine was clearly not the same in France, Germany and India.

In this contribution, I would like to stress the influence of the 'risk culture' to understand differences in policy responses (and criticism addressed to these policy responses) for at least two reasons. First, this concept is not well known within the legal academia. It is nevertheless crucial to understand policy responses to uncertain events (and criticism addressed to them). Second, it makes clear that a policy response should

---

[2] See for example https://www.imperial.ac.uk/media/imperial-college/medicine/sph/ide/gida-fellowships/Imperial-College-COVID19-NPI-modelling-16-03-2020.pdf.

consider the characteristics of a population and should then be contextualized. Transplanting what worked in one country is certainly bound to fail if the population's characteristics are different.

This short paper will proceed as followed. The first section will define the concept of risk culture. The second section will stress the influence of risk culture on regulation. Few concluding thoughts will then be presented.

I. The concept of risk culture

In front of the same danger, opinions will differ on how to regulate. This includes both the 'when' to intervene and the 'how' to intervene. If this statement is common knowledge, it is possible to go one step further. The concept of risk culture is exactly doing that. This concept was developed by Mary Douglas and Aaron Wildavsky in the beginning of the 1980s[3] even if the theory was largely developed in the 1970s by Mary Douglas[4]. Mary Douglas is an anthropologist, known for her work on the social perception of danger[5] and social perception bias[6]. Aaron Wildavsky is a sociologist and a political scientist. The concept of risk culture was developed specially to consider technological and environmental risks (or 'modern' risks).

In *Risk and Culture*, Douglas and Wildavsky identified three types of risk culture: (1) hierarchical and bureaucratic, (2) individualist and competitive, (3) egalitarian (or sectarian). A fourth culture type was added in the 1990s[7] and was labeled 'fatalist'.

This typology is based on the combination of two criteria, grid and group (which explained the requirement to create a fourth category). 'Group means the outside boundary that people have erected between themselves and the outside world'[8]. In other words, how much a person's

---

[3] Mary Douglas and Aaron Wildavsky, *Risk and culture*, Berkley: University of California Press, 1983.
[4] Mary Douglas, *Natural symbols*, London: Routledge, 1970.
[5] Mary Douglas, *Purity and danger*, London: Routledge & Kegan Paul, 1966.
[6] Mary Douglas, *Essays in the sociology of perception*, London: Routledge, 1982.
[7] See Mary Douglas, "Four cultures: the evolution of a parsimonious Model", *Geojournal*, vol 47, 1999, pp. 411–415.
[8] Mary Douglas and Aaron Wildavsky, *Risk and Culture*, op cit, p. 138.

decision will be based on their ties to the community they live in? What is the level of allegiance to the group? Society with low group characteristics will tend to be more 'individualist' (or ego-centred), society with high groups will have a tendency to define individuals by their 'group', and to rely more on social solidarity. 'Grid means all the other social distinctions and delegations of authority that they use to limit how people behave to one another'[9]. In other words, how much a person's decision will be based on (and subject to) societal structures and rules? In high grid society, social roles are well defined (which also implies more heterogeneity within the group), prescriptions are numerous and varied, and individuals will not be as independent. In low grid society, social roles are not as well defined (which also implies more homogeneity within the group), freedom of transaction is a key, and individuals are more independent in their choices.

Four risk cultures naturally derived from these two criteria: high grid/low group (fatalists), low group/low grid (individualist), high grid/low group (egalitarian), high grid/high group (hierarchical).

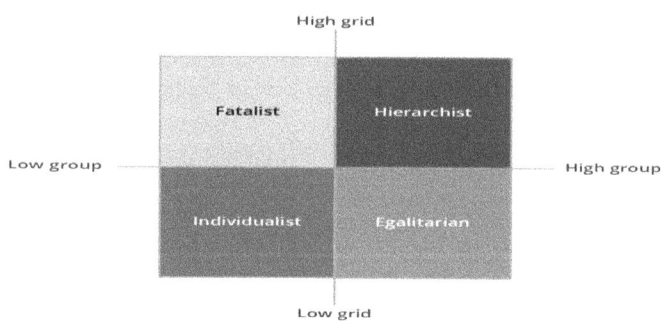

As Douglas and Wildavsky noted, 'A society organized by hierarchy would have many group-encircling and group-identifying regulations plus many grid constraints on how to act. An individualist society would leave to individuals maximum freedom to negotiate with each other, so it would have no effective group boundaries and no insulating constraints on private dealings. A sectarian society would be recognizable by strong barriers identifying and separating the community from nonmembers, but it would be so egalitarian that it would have no leaders and no

---

[9] Mary Douglas and Aaron Wildavsky, *Risk and Culture*, op. cit., p. 138.

rules of precedence or protocol telling people how to behave'[10]. They of course recognized that this typology is relative to a certain context (it will depend on the norm at stake, on the place and period) and is thus quite impressionist.

The vocabulary used by the authors is not transparent for a lawyer and it is possible to reinterpret the above typology in layman's terms in the context of a risk.

In fatalist societies, the motto is clear: nothing can really be done to avoid or lower risks. Individuals are left to themselves and the best they can do is to build resilience. In this society, individuals will stock food, buy guns and prepare for the worst. Certain guidance could be given by 'experts' or government, but this guidance will not be sufficient to solve all problems. If the low group dimension is easy to identify, the high grid is more difficult to explain. It implies that individuals are not independent, and that behaviour is constrained by social roles.

In individualist societies, individuals will be incentivized to take risks, to invest, to find a way and, for that, it is required to let them free to choose their path (nobody knows better since the society is low grid). Some will be rewarded, others will be blamed for non-action. In all situations, individuals will be considered as responsible for their own fate (since the society is low group). Self-regulation is thus the norm.

In egalitarian (or sectarian) societies, individuals do understand that they belong to a group and that they must act as a group. There is no authority supposed to know better (low grid) but individuals understand that their behaviour will not only have an impact on themselves but on the society (high group). This society will rely on social norms (which are not designed by anybody) and exclusion (or punishment) of outsiders (or deviants). If this egalitarian society is a subpart of the society, they will blame outsiders for their 'corrupted' behaviour which is the only reason why they might 'suffer'. Since the society is low grid, there is a belief that nobody knows better.

In hierarchical societies, there is a belief that it is possible to address the problem in a rational way, to address issues through careful management and assessment of costs and benefits. The technocrats (or experts) will then 'teach' individuals how to behave, how to address risks and will try to protect a certain idea of the general interest (by trying to protect

---

[10] Mary Douglas and Aaron Wildavsky, *Risk and Culture*, op. cit., pp. 138–139.

as many people as possible). Everybody knows their place in the society and the society is quite stratified. In such a society most matters are of collective concern.

This typology is of course impressionist (the concepts of grid and group are not easy to define with precision[11]) and only provides ideal typical situation for a world which is naturally far more complex. Nevertheless, this typology, despite all its shortcomings, appears as quite relevant to make sense of what happened during the covid crisis.

II. Risk culture and its relevance for understanding regulation during the covid crisis

This typology appears relevant to account for the diversity of choices in policy strategies, the level of compliance and the criticism which were addressed to implemented policies.

From a purely theoretical point of view, few implications for regulation could be derived regarding policy strategies, compliance and criticism.

Regarding policy strategies, in high grid society, the choice of the policy is likely to be made by experts (since this is their function) and will not tend to be the result of a 'democratic' decision. The policy will thus be justified through 'science' or the expertise of the decision makers. Decision processes will tend to be top down. In low grid societies, we should expect the opposite and probably a higher reliance on status quo, and consensus (since freedom is the default). This does not mean that science will not be considered, but it is expected to be more 'discussed' than in high grid societies. Decision processes will tend to be bottom up. In high group societies, individuals will consider the impact of their actions on the group, informing them of the consequences of their action could then have a real impact (this will have an impact on compliance). Restriction of freedom will be more accepted and will be justified by the influence of this or that behaviour on the group. In low group society, individuals will mostly consider the impact of their actions on themselves; policies are thus expected to stress the individual risk that one is taking by not abiding by a special rule. Nevertheless, in low group society, restrictions for the 'general interest' will be considered with suspicion

---

[11] James Spickard, "A guide to Mary Douglas's Three Versions of Grid/Group Theory", *Sociological Analysis*, vol 50, n°2, 1989, pp. 151–170.

since every individual will assess the relevance of this policy through their individual situation (and this will be even more the case in low grid societies).

Regarding compliance, all things being equal, external legal enforcement is expected to be required in low group societies (since the ties to the group are not strong) and less required in high group societies (since individuals will understand the consequences of their actions on the group). The grid parameter will determine if enforcement relies on social norms (low grid, and especially in high group) or special entities (high grid).

Regarding criticism, restrictions of freedom are expected to lead to harsher criticisms in low group societies (since they value individual freedom) than in high group societies (which value the group). In high grid societies, criticism will tend to concentrate on the expertise and the content of a policy, whereas in low grid societies, regulatory processes will be targeted way more than the content of the policy.

Are these predictions finding any echoes in the real world of the first months of 2020?

To answer this question, it is first required to have an idea of the position of each country on a cultural grid/group map. In 1999, Gunnar Grendstad tried to develop a 'political culture map of Europe'[12] using the group/grid structure. Even if, in this paper, each country is a mix of the four types of society, the author tried to identify the position of some European countries in 1990 on a grid/group table.

---

[12] Gunnar Grendstad, "A political cultural map of Europe: A survey Approach", *Geojournal*, vol 47, n°3, 1999, pp. 463–475.

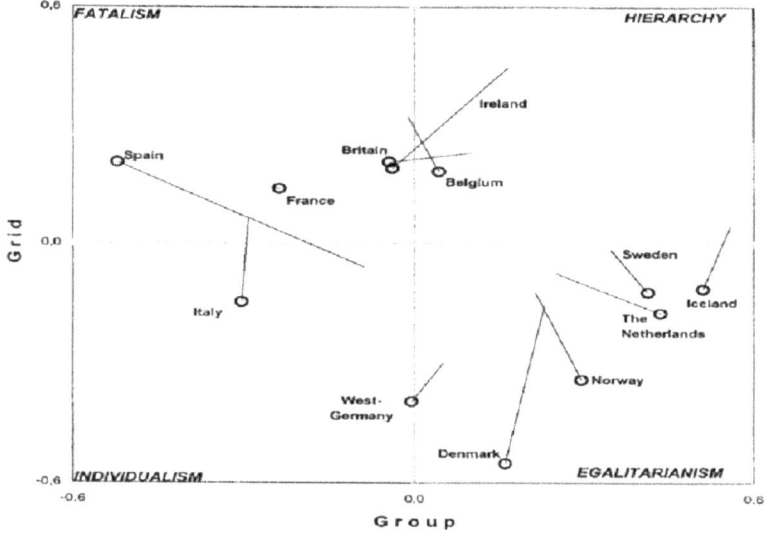

It is certain that in 32 years, things might have evolved. In 2009[13], another study tried to map world countries on a grid group table and some differences can be observed[14]. For example, Britain is no longer in the fatalist group and scored way lower on the grid and group dimension. West Germany is also clearly a low grid low group in the 2009 study. Spain also changed its position. Sweden and Norway on the contrary do not change and stayed high group low grid. We do not have information for other countries.

This is certainly the sign that the grid group approach is imperfect but when the position of a country is relatively non-controversial, it is still possible to verify if the previously made predictions make sense.

---

[13] Sun-Ki Chai, Ming Liu and Min-Sun Kim, "Cultural comparisons of beliefs and values: applying the grid group approach to the world values survey", *Beliefs and Values*, vol 1, n°2, 2009, pp. 193–208.

[14] Note that the axes of the table are different.

Covid and the risk culture 133

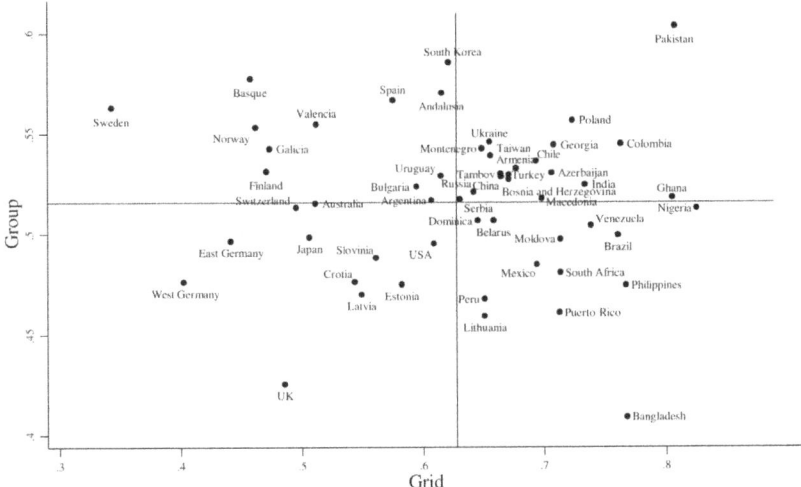

Let's look at Sweden first[15]. It is always considered as a high group low grid society... and the strategy it implemented is certainly the reflection of these features. As a low grid society, Sweden values consensus and the policy implemented by the government was largely accepted by the general population. As a high group country, it will emphasize the consequences of certain behaviour on the group and not on individuals. Combining these two characteristics, Sweden should rely way more on social norms (since low grid) and weak legal enforcement (since the policy will be consensual). And indeed, the government did not order a shutdown, it kept primary school and day care centres opened, it also never mandated face masks in 2020 and only recommended its use by the end of 2020[16]. It merely banned gatherings of more than 50 people and nursing home visits. The high group feature is undeniable when the behaviour of Swedes is considered. They naturally respected social distancing, largely stayed at home (at rates relatively similar to what could have been observed in other European countries with stay-at-home requirements[17]). It is only when someone had symptoms that it was possible for that person to stay at home.

---

[15] See https://www.science.org/content/article/it-s-been-so-so-surreal-critics-sweden-s-lax-pandemic-policies-face-fierce-backlash

[16] See https://www.nature.com/articles/s41598-021-95699-9.pdf

[17] See https://www.science.org/content/article/it-s-been-so-so-surreal-critics-sweden-s-lax-pandemic-policies-face-fierce-backlash

For Norway, if a lockdown was imposed and if a bill transferred powers for the adoption of temporary laws to tackle the spread of covid from the parliament to the executive powers (which might not seem compatible with an egalitarian society), it is to be noted that this bill was heavily criticized mostly for procedural reasons[18]. Hans Petter Graver thus indicates that 'The case of Norway, however, reveals how the process of adopting these measures can compromise democratic discourse and procedure. The main rule of law challenges we have seen here are an overreach of the authorities of their legal powers, a lack of transparency and exclusion of the public from public decision-making and battle over jurisdiction to regulate between the central government and local authorities. In the end, it is not just our health, but the rule of law that is under threat'[19]. This way to criticize the regulation was to be expected from the group/grid framework.

The idea that France is a fatalist society[20] also makes sense. Regulations were implemented on the basis of 'scientific' recommendations made by a 'scientific council'[21] and decision were adopted by a 'public health defense council'[22] (high grid characteristic). The health policies were not determined democratically but through executive orders (high grid characteristic)[23]. Naturally, regulations were criticized (low group characteristic) based on alternative 'scientific knowledge'[24] and implementation relied on the risk of being sanctioned[25] or the perceived individual risk associated with not abiding by a certain regulation (low group characteristic)

---

[18] See for example, https://verfassungsblog.de/fighting-the-virus-and-the-rule-of-law-a-country-report-on-norway/

[19] https://verfassungsblog.de/fighting-the-virus-and-the-rule-of-law-a-country-report-on-norway/

[20] We could also note a tendency for France to be hierarchical (hence its fascination for the "general interest" which is a great justification in high group characteristics but not in low group ones).

[21] See https://www.vie-publique.fr/avis-et-notes-du-conseil-scientifique-covid-19

[22] https://www.elysee.fr/en/french-presidency/public-health-defence-council

[23] See for example Loi n° 2020-290 du 23 mars 2020 d'urgence pour faire face à l'épidémie de covid-19 which habilitates the government to take action through executive orders.

[24] See for example https://www.rfi.fr/en/france/20200625-controversial-french-doctor-slams-government-covid-19-response-parliament-inquiry

[25] See for example https://fr.statista.com/statistiques/1110482/amendes-controles-de-police-confinement-coronavirus-france/

and not on voluntary compliance by French citizens. Even the motto of the anticovid app was 'protect yourself and protect others' (protégez vous et protégez les autres)[26] after having been 'protect yourself, protect your loved one and protect others' (protégez vous, protégez vos proches et protégez les autres[27]) or simply 'protect yourself, protect your loved one' (protégez vous et protégez vos proches)[28] which also stresses the low group characteristic.

Regarding the USA, it is certainly an individualist society (low group, low grid). Nevertheless, we need to consider the federal structure and the culture risk in every state to 'test' the theory. Not surprisingly, covid responses were quite different depending on the grid position (low grid is associated with republican, high grid with democrats). Some red states did not enact stay-at-home orders (to protect liberties) while most blue state did (to protect health)[29]. Not surprisingly, red states were less likely to impose health orders requiring the wearing of masks than blue states (low grid characteristic). Often, these states did not ban the possibility to use a mask, it was considered as a 'personal' choice and people had to bear the consequences of their decision (low group characteristic). Arguments based on the consequences of one's behaviour on others were considered as paternalistic (low group characteristic) and were sometimes considered as not legitimate (low grid characteristic). When the mask mandate was required, a part of the population criticized it for being too strict a requirement (low grid, low group). Some red states even banned vaccine mandates for employees[30] of either the public sector, the private sector or both. States which mandate boosters were, unsurprisingly, largely democratic.

---

[26] For example, https://www.facebook.com/gouvernement.fr/videos/504986060444431/

[27] https://www.ille-et-vilaine.gouv.fr/Actualites/Coronavirus-COVID-19/TousAntiCovid/Protegez-vous-protegez-vos-proches-protegez-les-autres-telechargez-TousAntiCovid

[28] For example, https://www.normandie.ars.sante.fr/vous-proteger-et-proteger-vos-proches-conseils-et-recommandations; https://www.belfort.fr/actualites-109/covid-19-protegez-vous-protegez-vos-proches-7467.html?cHash=ce1539ac6d3b4884a7de285b64e2f940

[29] See for example https://eu.usatoday.com/storytelling/coronavirus-reopening-america-map/

[30] https://leadingage.org/workforce/vaccine-mandates-state-who-who-isnt-and-how

Regarding China which can be considered as a hierarchical society, expectations are also met. Covid policies were determined by experts, enacted quickly, justified by the protection of the group[31]. The problem had to be solved by the government which was considered as a guide and protests were minimum since the role of the government was largely accepted[32].

It would be possible to multiply examples but, for the point this paper tries to make, it is not required. Indeed, this paper does not argue that the grid group approach is able to perfectly predict what happened or what will happen; empirical work would be required to do so. As already stressed the grid and group concepts are relatively fuzzy and the way to 'classify' countries can vary depending on the characteristics considered for identifying the grid and group level of a country. This approach is thus quite 'impressionist'. As such, this paper only tries to stress the fact that this approach can offer some interesting insights to understand the diversity of policy strategies, criticisms of these policies and enforcement levels.

Conclusion

The risk-culture-based approach of regulation is far from being standard in the legal literature to analyse risk regulation. Nevertheless, and despite its limitations, it provides relevant insights to interpret the diversity of regulation. It is even possible to consider that the type of enacted regulation might reveal the type of risk culture, such that it will be possible to anticipate future reactions to uncertain situations. It is also possible to wonder up to what point the risk culture will evolve after the covid crisis, especially when an enacted policy was considered too lenient or too strict (which was the case in Sweden or during the spring of 2020 in the USA). The risk culture approach could also help to make sense of the legal doctrine in reaction to enacted regulation.

---

[31] See for example https://www.fmprc.gov.cn/mfa_eng/topics_665678/kjgzbdf yyq/CERC/

[32] See https://www.reuters.com/article/us-health-coronavirus-china-wuhan-idCAKB N21I0NU. Protests happened in Hong Kong but for other reasons. The zero covid strategy was way more criticized in 2022 (with Shanghai lockdown) than in 2020.

More importantly, the risk culture approach stresses the futility of transplanting a strategy that worked in one country in another country without consideration for the grid group differences between these two countries[33]. If certain people prized Sweden for its liberal policy, simply enacting it in France or in the USA would have led to very different results. For some, this leads to a relative uncomfortable conclusion: the risk culture approach of regulation makes it clear that the best regulation and enforcement strategy to mitigate a risk is highly dependent on a country's characteristics. Thus, judging the strategy enacted in one country relative to the one enacted in another country reveals itself almost impossible since the cultural characteristics of an observer will naturally create bias in his/her assessment of the best strategy.

---

[33] To which we should add state resources and capacity.

Responses to the Covid crisis in antitrust and merger control

Gleb FROMM[1]

Competition policy and its main instrument, competition law, is usually targeting firm or state activity in 'normal times'. Crises however cause turmoil to the markets and thereby displace the basic assumptions on which competition policy works. While the financial crisis 2009 was of endogenous nature, provoked by economic agents themselves, the (post-)Covid crisis has been exogenous, at least in its beginning. Focusing mainly on antitrust and merger control, an analysis of the general approaches taken by competition authorities shows a tension between economic and public interest approaches. Another dichotomy can be established between the interest of firms in reinforced guidance and extraordinary measures with regard to economically uncertain times and the likewise reinforced risk of anticompetitive behaviour of firms abusing the crisis situation and misusing the new temporary framework.

La politique de concurrence et son principal instrument, le droit de la concurrence, ciblent généralement l'activité des entreprises ou des États en 'temps normal'. Les crises provoquent toutefois des turbulences sur les marchés et bouleversent ainsi les hypothèses de base sur lesquelles repose la politique de concurrence. Alors que la crise financière de 2009 était de nature endogène, provoquée par les agents économiques eux-mêmes, la crise (post-)Covid a été exogène, du moins à ses débuts. En se concentrant principalement sur le contrôle antitrust et le contrôle des fusions, une analyse des approches générales adoptées par les autorités de la concurrence montre une tension entre les approches économiques et les approches d'intérêt public. Une autre dichotomie peut être établie entre l'intérêt des entreprises pour des orientations renforcées et des mesures extraordinaires en ce qui concerne les périodes d'incertitude économique et le risque également accru de comportement anticoncurrentiel des entreprises qui abusent de la situation de crise et détournent le nouveau cadre temporaire.

---

[1] Etudiant en Master II, Université Paris Nanterre.

Introduction

Silent enim leges inter arma?[2] The question could also be whether the law is silent in times of crisis: how does law treat a crisis, 'a time of great difficulty, danger, or suffering'[3], is it applicable at all and, if so, does it provide for solutions or does it remain silent? On 11th of March 2020, the World Health Organisation (WHO) declared the spread of the Corona virus to be a pandemic[4]. The disease, provoked by the Corona virus (Covid), has been a cause of difficulties for the international community. This is reflected in law: every branch of law, including competition law, was affected by the new situation.

There are several imaginable approaches to deal with the Covid crisis in competition law: the responses given by the competition authorities to the questions posed by the Covid crisis either try to keep up with the nowadays predominant economic approach to competition law or give preference to the public interest approach[5]. The ways to deal with a crisis may depend on the design of the general competition framework of a given jurisdiction, or also on the nature of crisis in question: enforcers maybe feel less empathy for the endogenous financial crisis than for the exogenous Covid crisis?

The most pressing questions with regards to Covid are: the framework for legal cooperation of firms, including agreements and mergers of firms in difficulties, the increasing prices becoming a burden for consumers,

---

[2] Albert Curtis Clark (ed), 'M. Tulli Ciceronis Orationes: Recognovit breviqve adnotatione critica instrvxit Albertus Curtis Clark Collegii Reginae Socius' (1918) para 11 <http://www.perseus.tufts.edu/hopper/text?doc=Perseus%3Atext%3A1999.02.0011%3Atext%3DMil.%3Asection%3D11> accessed 31 July 2022; translation: 'For laws are silent when arms are raised' (Charles Duke Yonge (ed), 'The Orations of Marcus Tullius Cicero, literally translated by CD Yonge' (1891) para 11 <http://www.perseus.tufts.edu/hopper/text?doc=Perseus%3Atext%3A1999.02.0020%3Atext%3DMil.%3Asection%3D11> accessed 31 July 2022)

[3] Cambridge University Press, 'Crisis', *Cambridge Dictionary* (2022) <https://dictionary.cambridge.org/dictionary/english/crisis> accessed 31 July 2022

[4] WHO, 'Virtual press conference on COVID-19: Director-General's opening remarks' (2020) <https://www.who.int/docs/default-source/coronaviruse/transcripts/who-audio-emergencies-coronavirus-press-conference-full-and-final-11mar2020.pdf> accessed 31 July 2022

[5] See further: Frédéric Jenny, 'Competition Law Enforcement and the COVID-19 Crisis: Business As (Un)usual?' (2020) SSRN <https://ssrn.com/abstract=3606214> accessed 31 July 2022.

difficulties of firms in providing information about their business in a timely manner, but also state aid for firms in difficulties. Here, only the first questions, falling under the heads of antitrust and merger control, will be treated, while the last question concerning the very specific category of state aid will not be targeted.

The aim is to present a template of possible actions in antitrust and merger control, the branches of competition law which target undertakings, facing the Covid crisis. Thereby the focus does not lie on one specific regime, jurisdiction or authority. Methods of comparative and global[6] law are used to discern common patterns with the help of which national approaches can be demonstrated. Conceptions of and approaches to crisis response can be found in substantive law (I), as well as in procedure (II).

I. Responses in substantive law

There are several substantive issues related to Covid. The most significant one, from the antitrust and mergers perspective, are the interest of firms to cooperate in difficult times (A) and the problem of increasing prices (B)[7].

A. Reenforced need for cooperation between firms

The material content of competition law provides various possibilities in order to interpret, potentially or prima facie, anticompetitive practices in the light of exceptional circumstances. 'Cooperation' lato sensu includes, for this purpose, a variety of conduct: from the most informal cooperation (collusion, targeted by antitrust) to formal cooperation (mergers and acquisitions, targeted by merger control). A first reflex would be to mobilize all ordinarily available possibilities in order to assess such practices arising during the pandemic (1). However, some competition authorities might want to go beyond business as usual and develop a specific framework in times of crisis (2).

---

[6] Understood as the identification of common patterns or issues, matched with (sometimes) converging solutions.
[7] OECD 'Exploitative pricing in the time of COVID-19' (2020) 2; OECD 'Co-operation between competitors in the time of COVID-19' (2020).

1. Answers in the general framework

In times of crisis, there might be reenforced need for cooperation between firms. This cooperation is legally possible via the exceptions, exemptions or defences available under the general framework in antirust and mergers law:

Concerning agreements between undertakings, EU law contains express provisions which allow for exemptions of agreements. US law has a rule of reason approach instead. Mauritian law distinguishes between 'collusive' and 'other restrictive agreements'. Concerning collusive agreements, like US law, it does not ask expressly wether an anticompetitive behaviour is offset by consumer welfare gains. While a rule of reason approach seems thinkable at first sight, Mauritian law is closer to the EU approach than to the US approach. A provision serving a similar purpose as art 101(3) TFEU, s 50(2) of the Competition Act (Mauritius), contains the possibility to consider 'public benefits' when determining remedies. This possibility is not extended to 'collusive agreements' and expressis verbis limited to 'other restrictive agreements', monopoly situations and merger situations: if an exemption of 'collusive agreements', even via a rule of reason approach, were possible, why is it then not included in s 50(2) of the Act which targets this specific question? In EU law, agreements between undertakings can be justified via art 101(3) TFEU generally and the Vertical Block Exemption Regulation (VBER) specifically concerning vertical agreements[8]. Among other conditions of art 101(3) TFEU, the agreement has to contribute 'to improving the production or distribution of goods or to promoting technical or economic progress, while allowing consumers a fair share of the resulting benefit'.

---

[8] Commission Regulation (EU) No 330/2010 of 20 April 2010 on the application of Article 101(3) of the Treaty on the Functioning of the European Union to categories of vertical agreements and concerted practices [2010] OJ L 102/1 (VBER); Commission Regulation (EU) 2022/720 of 10 May 2022 on the application of Article 101(3) of the Treaty on the Functioning of the European Union to categories of vertical agreements and concerted practices (C/2022/3015), [2022] OJ L 134/4 (VBER 2022). As the issues covered here mainly occurred in 2020 as elements of the Covid crisis, the VBER (2010) will primarily be treated for our purposes. For extensive information on (horizontal) cooperation under EU law, see: European Commission, 'Guidelines on the applicability of Article 101 of the Treaty on the Functioning of the European Union to horizontal co-operation agreements' (2011/C 11/01), [2011] OJ C 11/1.

Art 2 VBER grants, under certain conditions, block exemptions for vertical agreements.

The Mauritian category of 'collusive agreements' (ss 41–43 Competition Act (Mauritius)), which, as seen above, cannot be justified, is a functional equivalent of hardcore cartels under EU law (although the concept of 'collusive agreements' under the Competition Act (Mauritius) is not limited to vertical agreements): 'fixing the selling or purchase prices', 'sharing markets or sources of the supply of the goods or services' or 'restricting the supply of the goods or services to, or the acquisition of them from, any person'. Hardcore cartels are listed in art 4 VBER which excludes block exemptions, where the vertical agreement has as its object, for example, '(a) the restriction of the buyer's ability to determine its sale price […]; (b) the restriction of the territory into which, or of the customers to whom, a buyer party to the agreement […] may sell the contract goods or services […]; (c) the restriction of active or passive sales to end users by members of a selective distribution system operating at the retail level of trade, […]; (d) the restriction of cross-supplies between distributors within a selective distribution system, including between distributors operating at different level of trade'. It is impossible or difficult to justify either collusive agreements or hardcore restrictions under their respective competition regimes[9].

A common rationale of art 103(3) TFEU (positive requirement: cooperation 'while allowing consumers a fair share of the resulting benefit') and art 4(a)–(d) VBER is that consumers or business partners (and in fine also their consumers) should, directly or indirectly, benefit from the cooperation, that undertakings are engaged in. This could be seen as a

---

[9] Concerning Mauritian law, the CCM states that it does not have the possibility to consider 'offsetting public benefit' in this category (e.g. Competition Commission Mauritius, 'Horizontal agreements' <https://competitioncommission.mu/horizontal-agreements/#1564978239220-ddc5821c-500d> accessed 31 July 2022); as seen above, a rule of reason approach is thinkable but, given the clear statement of the CCM, unlikely: 'the Competition Act 2007 does not allow the Commission to exempt or otherwise authorize a collusive agreement, on any ground whatsoever'. While EU does not exclude the applicability of art 101(3) TFEU to vertical hardcore restrictions falling under art 4 VBER 2010/2022 (Case C-230/16 *Coty Germany GmbH v Parfümerie Akzente GmbH* EU:C:2017:603, Opinion of AG Wahl, paras 119–121), it is considered to be 'unlikely' that such an agreement fulfils the conditions of art 101(3) TFEU (European Commission, 'Guidelines on vertical restraints' (2022/C 248/01), [2022] OJ C 248/1 para 180; see also: VBER, recital 10; VBER 2022, recital 15).

consumer-oriented approach: either consumers benefit directly from the cooperation (i.e. it does fall under art 101(3) TFEU) or the cooperation is not regarded to be dangerous from an economic perspective and therefore does not harm consumers (i.e. it does not fall under art 4 VBER)[10].

In merger control, a defence seldom succeeding is the failing firm defence (FFD). For example, paras 89–91 of the EC Horizontal Merger Guidelines[11] provide a legal regime for FFD and define it referring to three conditions (para 90):

(i) the allegedly failing firm would in the near future be forced out of the market because of financial difficulties if not taken over by another undertaking,

(ii) there is no less anti-competitive alternative purchase than the notified merger, in the absence of a merger,

(iii) the assets of the failing firm would inevitably exit the market[12].

The availability of FFD under Mauritian law has been confirmed by the Competition Competition Mauritius (CCM) during the Covid crisis[13]. Generally, this defence is interpreted very narrowly: competition authorities tend to have a strict approach towards FFD[14]. With the Covid crisis, the question was whether there would be an increase of successful FFD cases. In the UK, the Competition and Markets Authority (CMA) has provisionally approved a merger in the context of the Covid crisis

---

[10] The VBER has a consumer protection perspective, s recital 10: 'This Regulation should not exempt vertical agreements containing restrictions which are likely to restrict competition and harm consumers or which are not indispensable to the attainment of the efficiency-enhancing effects. In particular, vertical agreements containing certain types of severe restrictions of competition such as minimum and fixed resale-prices, as well as certain types of territorial protection, should be excluded from the benefit of the block exemption established by this Regulation irrespective of the market share of the undertakings concerned.'

[11] European Commission, 'Guidelines on the assessment of horizontal mergers under the Council Regulation on the control of concentrations between undertakings' (2004/C 31/03), [2004] OJ C 31/5 (EC Horizontal Merger Guidelines)

[12] See also: OECD, 'Merger control in the time of COVID-19' (2002) 8.

[13] Competition Commission Mauritius, 'Guidelines on mergers (CC5)' (2009) paras 3.19, 3.20.

[14] OECD, 'Merger control in the time of COVID-19' (n 11) 8: 'the number of cases in which the FFD has been invoked and accepted is very limited over the years'. A case where FFD was successfully invoked: *Aegean/Olympic II* (Case COMP/M.6796) C(2013) 6561.

in 2020 in *Amazon/Deliveroo*, but did in fact not consider Deliveroo a failing firm[15]. And subsequently, the anticipated change of approach of competition authorities towards FFD has not materialized: like the endogenous financial[16] crisis, the exogenous Covid crisis has, so far, not changed the general attitude regarding FFD.

A common point of these provisions discussed above is that efficiency gains are made because of, or despite, the potential or prima facie anticompetitive practice, or the merger, and these gains are transferred to consumers[17]. While consumer welfare might be an element of public interest, this approach is based on economic considerations[18]. It is thinkable that Covid related antitrust infringements could be justified or exempted, and some problematic mergers exceptionally allowed, using the possibilities of the general legal framework, as long as the envisaged cooperation provides some positive effect concerning consumer welfare.

---

[15] *Amazon/Deliveroo (Provisional findings report)* (2020 CMA) paras 4.23 ss <https://assets.publishing.service.gov.uk/media/60b8e10fd3bf7f4bcc06520a/Provisional_Findings_Report_2.pdf> accessed 31 July 2022; *Amazon/Deliveroo (Final report)* (2020 CMA) paras 6.11 s <https://assets.publishing.service.gov.uk/media/5f297aa18fa8f57ac287c118/Final_report_pdf_a_version_-----.pdf>, accessed 31 July 2022; Competition and Markets Authority, 'Merger assessments during the Coronavirus (COVID-19) pandemic' (2020) <https://assets.publishing.service.gov.uk/government/uploads/system/uploads/attachment_data/file/880570/Merger_assessments_during_the_Coronavirus__COVID-19__pandemic_.pdf>, accessed 31 July 2022; Competition and Markets Authority, 'Annex A Summary of CMA's position on mergers involving "failing firms"' (2020) <https://assets.publishing.service.gov.uk/government/uploads/system/uploads/attachment_data/file/880565/Summary_of_CMA_s_position_on_mergers_involving__failing_firms_.pdf>, accessed 31 July 2022

[16] OECD, 'Merger control in the time of COVID-19' (n 11) 9: 'In previous discussions at the OECD in the aftermath of the 2008 financial crisis, competition authorities found no justification for relaxing the standards of the FFD and argued that there are other policy instruments available (e.g. bankruptcy law and State interventions such as subsidies) to help failing firms'; Jurgita Malinauskaite, 'The failing firm defence in EU merger control: the story of Sisyphus?' (2012) 9 International Company and Commercial Law Review 314.

[17] See e.g.: Council Regulation (EC) No 139/2004 of 20 January 2004 on the control of concentrations between undertakings [2004] OJ L 24/1 (EC Merger Regulation), art 2(1)(b); EC Horizontal Merger Guidelines (n 10), paras 76–88; *Aegean/Olympic II* (n 13) paras 633 ss.

[18] EC Horizontal Merger Guidelines (n 10): 'deterioration of the competitive structure that follows the merger cannot be said to be caused by the merger' (para 89), 'no less anti-competitive alternative purchase than the notified merger' (para 90).

2. Specific possibilities in times of crisis

Apart from these general approaches, some authorities have targeted Covid with specific measures.

A common approach among competition authorities was to encourage cooperation in vulnerable sectors which are particularly important for crisis management (e.g. healthcare antirust). For example, in EU and US competition law, authorities have 'made it clear that collaborative activities between manufacturers, distributors, or purchasers (such as research and development, technical know-how or asset-sharing arrangements, information exchanges, joint production, transportation, storage, or purchasing agreements) may be compatible with competition rules where: the firms are working to benefit consumers by increasing output, or overcoming shortfalls, of vital products and services (such as medication, medical equipment, transport, food, energy, and broadband); and the arrangements are limited in scope and duration to that which is required during the period of the epidemic.'[19]

The underlying rationale could be public interest, but the approach could also be framed in economic terms: it is somehow also the result of a consideration of the possible costs of an interdiction of cooperation under general competition law, estimated to be higher than the costs of temporary and limited cooperation in a crisis framework. The question is which aspect prevails.

It is therefore of interest to know whether these statements are mere political declarations reminding firms of their available possibilities under the general framework or whether they constitute a suspension or relaxation of competition law. Historically, concerning other crises, e.g. after World Wars I and II[20] or during the Great

---

[19] Alison Jones, 'Cartels in the time of COVID-19' (2020) 8(2) Journal of Antitrust Enforcement 287 <https://doi.org/10.1093/jaenfo/jnaa013>, accessed 31 July 2022; on EU and US approaches: European Commission, 'Temporary Framework for assessing antitrust issues related to business cooperation in response to situations of urgency stemming from the current COVID-19 outbreak' (2020/C 116 I/02), [2020] OJ C 116 I/7 (Temporary Framework Communication); Department of Justice and Federal Trade Commission, 'Joint FTC-DOJ Antitrust Statement Regarding COVID-19' (2020).

[20] Nicolo Banks, 'Competition policy during pandemics: how to urgently produce healthcare goods and services while avoiding economic disaster' (2021) 9(3) Journal

Depression[21], competition law has indeed been relaxed. Nowadays, in general, there is reluctance with regard to so called crisis cartels, i.e. agreements 'between firms that a government body sanctions during a period of economic distress'[22], and reliance on self-assessment by undertakings: accordingly, one view regarding Covid crisis management in the US and EU is that there is no intention to suspend or relax competition law[23]. In contrast to this, South Africa has adopted block exemption regulations in certain sectors: healthcare[24], banking[25], retail property[26] and hotel industry[27]. Some authors have been sceptic about the statements made by competition authorities and express concern: the dangers of relaxation lie in the fact that 'even after the relaxing of competition rules ceases, there will still be an increased ability to continue colluding tacitly'[28]. But authorities also know about this risk: while having stressed the legal possibilities of cooperation in essential or Covid-related sectors, they have issued warnings to firms not to abuse of this possibility[29].

---

of Antitrust Enforcement 413, 415–418 <https://doi.org/10.1093/jaenfo/jnab005>, accessed 31 July 2022.

[21] Jones (n 18) 288.

[22] OECD, 'Crisis Cartels' (2009) 9.

[23] Jones (n 18) 288: 'the purpose of the announcements is not to relax antitrust law's traditional concern for some competitor collaborations and provide a general licence to cooperation or cooperation spilling over beyond COVID-related issues into non-COVID-related ones'.

[24] Covid-19 Block Exemption for the Healthcare Sector 2020 (GN R349 of 19 March 2020) (South Africa).

[25] Covid-19 Block Exemption for the Banking Sector 2020 (GN R355 of 23 March 2020) (South Africa).

[26] Covid-19 Block Exemption for the Retail Property Sector 2020 (GN R358 of 24 March 2020) (South Africa).

[27] Covid-19 Block Exemption for the Hotel Industry 2020 (GN R422 of 27 March 2020) (South Africa).

[20] Peter Ormosi, Andreas Stephan, 'The dangers of allowing greater coordination between competitors during the COVID-19 crisis' (2020) 8(2) Journal of Antitrust Enforcement 299, 301 <https://doi.org/10.1093/jaenfo/jnaa028>, accessed 31 July 2022: a sceptic view on the CMA statement. This critique could be transposed to the general practice of providing such statements.

[29] European Competition Network, 'Antitrust: Joint statement by the European Competition Network (ECN) on application of competition law during the Corona crisis' (2020) <https://ec.europa.eu/competition/ecn/202003_joint-statement_ecn_corona-crisis.pdf>, accessed 31 July 2022: 'At the same time, it is of utmost importance to ensure that products considered essential to protect the health of consumers in the current situation (e.g. face masks and sanitising gel) remain available at competitive prices. The ECN will therefore not hesitate to take action against companies

Especially, undertakings were also warned by competition authorities not to use the Covid-crisis as a pretext for charging excessively high prices for essential goods[30]. Also concerning excessive pricing, the competition law of South Africa has proven to be a source of interesting concepts and approaches towards Covid.

B. Increasing prices

There is a risk that in times of crisis and economic turmoil prices might rise excessively, i.e. beyond what is economically justified. From a theoretical point of view, this issue is however difficult to treat as a matter of antirust[31]. There is a doctrinal conflict whether excessive prices are to be targeted by competition policy, or whether this should not be regarded as a consumer protection, i.e. public interest, tool. In the general framework of antitrust, one could target increasing prices as excessive prices under the category of dominance, where that is possible. This would entail a two-step examination, firstly establishing a dominant position (1) before, secondly, targeting a conduct, here excessive pricing, which constitutes an abuse of this position (2).

1. Dominance

As outlined above, there are other possibilities, apart from competition law, in order to tackle excessive pricing: anti price gouging laws

---

taking advantage of the current situation by cartelising or abusing their dominant position.'; Competition Commission Mauritius, 'Communiqué in the wake of the COVID-19 sanitary crisis' (2020) <https://competitioncommission.mu/wp-content/uploads/2020/04/Communique-Covid.pdf>, accessed 31 July 2022: 'But at the same time, the Competition Commission is making it clear that it will not tolerate commercial conducts on part of dominant suppliers which opportunistically seeks to exploit the crisis to the detriment of consumers. Anticompetitive agreements endangering public interest and harming consumer welfare, together with unilateral anticompetitive practices by dominant companies which seeks to exclude competitors or exploit consumers will be dealt with by the Competition Commission to the full might of the law.'

[30] OCDE, 'Exploitative pricing in the time of Covid-19' (n 6) 9.
[31] See further: David Gilo, 'Excess prices' in Institut de droit de la concurrence (ed), *Global Dictionary of Competition Law* (Concurrences) Art N° 85402 <https://www.concurrences.com/en/dictionary/excess-prices/>, accessed 31 July 2022; Initiative on Global Markets (IGM) Forum, 'Price gouging' (2012) <https://www.igmchicago.org/surveys/price-gouging/>, accessed 31 July 2022.

pursue a public interest approach of consumer protection[32]. Price gouging laws or consumer protection in general do not require neither the definition of a relevant market nor the finding of dominance. US law has specific anti price gouging laws which cover certain essential goods and are only applicable in exceptional circumstances[33]. While US antitrust law is generally not interested in excessive prices, EU law has art 102 TFEU which may target excessive prices[34]. However a complex and time consuming market definition and finding of dominance is needed for this purpose. There are three aspects which could make the exercise of finding dominance easier:

Firstly, dominance could be established in a different way than it is usually conceived, i.e. dominance not primarily based on market shares but based on other factors. An interesting approach is that of South Africa. The Competition Act 89 of 1998 (South Africa) lists excessive pricing 'to the detriment of consumers or customers' as an express example of abuse (s 8(1)(a) Competition Act 89 of 1998 (South Africa)). However, dominance is needed, is it not? While this is de jure true, the Covid-related case law of South Africa shows a de facto relaxation of market definition in general and therefore also a relaxation of the requirement of dominance on a given market[35]. Instead, dominance is defined via behavioural criteria: the ability of excessive pricing. The point of entry is s 7(c) Competition Act 89 of 1998 (South Africa) which states that a firm with a low market share ('less than 35 % of that market') can nevertheless be dominant if it has market power. Market power under the South African Act is 'the power of a firm to control prices, to exclude

---

[32] OCDE, 'Exploitative pricing in the time of Covid-19' (n 6) 8 ss, 11.

[33] Matt Zwolinski, 'The Ethics of Price Gouging' (2008) 18(3) Business Ethics Quarterly 347 <https://ssrn.com/abstract=1099567>, accessed 31 July 2022

[34] OCDE, 'Exploitative pricing in the time of Covid 19' (n 6) 3; *Verizon Communications Inc v Law Offices of Curtis v Trinko* LLP 540 US 398, 407, 124 S Ct 872 (2004): 'the mere possession of monopoly power, and the concomitant charging of monopoly prices, is not only not unlawful; it is an important element of the free market system'; Gilo (n 30).

[35] *Competition Commission v Babelegi Workwear Overall Manufacturers & Industrial Supplies CC* CR003Apr20; *Competition Commission of South Africa v Dis-Chem Pharmacies Limited* CR008Apr20; critique: John Oxenham, Michael-James Currie and Charl van der Merwe, 'COVID-19 Price Gouging Cases in South Africa: Short-term Market Dynamics with Long-term Implications for Excessive Pricing Cases' (2020) 11(9) Journal of European Competition Law & Practice 524, 528 ss <https://doi.org/10.1093/jeclap/lpaa070>, accessed 31 July 2022.

competition, or to behave to an appreciable extent independently of its competitors, customers, or suppliers' (s1(1)(xviii) Competition Act 89 of 1998 (South Africa)). The way in which the Competition Act is applied with regard to increasing prices in times of Covid crisis, in *Babelegi* and *Dis-Chem*, i.e. dominance based on the exercise of market power in the form of excessive pricing, results in a de facto inclusion of price gouging into competition law: the requirement of dominance is relaxed because dominance is established via a potential abuse.

Secondly, another aspect which enables to establish dominance more easily than under normal circumstances is the geographic dimension of the relevant market[36]. While small businesses are usually not dominant in big geographic markets, they can become dominant in circumstances where freedom of movement and mobility of consumers is severely restricted, resulting in much smaller geographic markets.

Thirdly, the temporal dimension of the relevant market could be used to establish temporary dominance[37]. In EU law, the concept of temporary dominance was used by the European Commission in *ABG/Oil*, however the decision was annulled by the Court[38].

Having determined dominance, the practice envisaged, a potentially excessive pricing, must constitute an abuse of this market position.

2. Abuse of dominance

It is not easy to define and prove excessive pricing[39]. Under EU law, excessive prices are defined as prices disproportionate to the economic value of the priced good or service[40]. Under South African law, this very same definition was abandoned (s 1(b) Competition Amendment Act 18 of 2018 (South Africa)) and replaced by a new definition: the new criteria are wether the 'price is higher than a competitive price and whether such difference is unreasonable, determined by taking into account all relevant

---

[36] OCDE 'Exploitative pricing in the time of Covid-19' (n 6) 5; Dis-Chem (n 34).

[37] OCDE 'Exploitative pricing in the time of Covid-19' (n 6) 5.

[38] *ABG/Oil* (Case IV/28.841) Commission Decision 77/327/EEC [1977] OJ L 117/1; Case 77/77 *Benzine en Petroleum Handelsmaatschappij BV and others v Commission of the European Communities* [1978] ECR 1513, [ECLI:EU:C:1978:141].

[39] OCDE 'Exploitative pricing in the time of Covid-19' (n 6) 6 ss.

[40] Case 26/75 *General Motors Continental NV v Commission of the European Communities* [1975] ECR 1367, 1379, [ECLI:EU:C:1975:150].

factors' (s 8(3) Competition Act 89 of 1998 (South Africa)). The new definition under the Act stresses the comparative method of determining excessive prices, i.e. the assessed price is compared to a hypothetical price which would exist in a competitive market. This is, among other methods, also possible under the broader definition of excessive prices in EU law[41].

However, South Africa went further. Covid-specific Regulations[42] contain presumptions of excessive pricing in competition law and consumer protection law: concerning specifically listed goods, a price increase which 'does not correspond to or is not equivalent to the increase in the cost of providing that good or service' (para 4.2.1) or 'increases the net margin or markup on that good or service above its average margin or markup in the three-month period prior to 1 March 2020' (para 4.2.2) is presumed to be excessive under s 8(1)(a) Competition Act 89 of 1998 (South Africa)[43].

Presumptions can facilitate the assessment of facts. They are situated between substantive law and procedure. The responses to Covid are not limited to substantive competition law. Indeed, the statements of authorities with regard to cooperation in healthcare, seen above, have been combined with procedural tools of guidance.

II. Responses in procedural law

In EU law, before Regulation 1/2003[44], agreements could be approved by authorities ex ante: this was the way the exceptions, exemptions or defenses seen above were applied. While this notification system has been

---

[41] For a variety of different methods, among them, the comparative method, see: Andreas Fuchs, 'AEUV Art 102' in Torsten Körber, Heike Schweitzer and Daniel Zimmer (eds), *Immenga/Mestmäcker, Wettbewerbsrecht, Band 1: EU, Kommentar zum Europäischen Kartellrecht* (CH Beck 2019) paras 180 ss.

[42] Consumer and Customer Protection Regulations and National Disaster Management Regulations and Directions (GN R350 of 19 March 2020) (South Africa).

[43] Oxenham, Currie and van der Merwe (n 34) 525; Hardin Ratshisusu and Liberty Mncube, 'Addressing excessive pricing concerns in time of the COVID-19 pandemic – a view from South Africa' (2020) 8(2) Journal of Antitrust Enforcement 256 <https://doi.org/10.1093/jaenfo/jnaa030>, accessed 31 July 2022.

[44] Council Regulation (EC) No 1/2003 of 16 December 2002 on the implementation of the rules on competition laid down in Articles 81 and 82 of the Treaty [2002] OJ L 1/1 (Regulation 1/2003).

abolished, authorities still have possibilities to provide guidance (A) and some countries also have, due to the Covid crisis, decided to additionally change some procedural rules (B).

A. Guidance provided by competition authorities

Before the questions of when and how guidance has been given concerning Covid related issues will be answered (2), it is insightful to distinguish between the two main types of procedure concerning guidance: self-assessment and notification (1).

1. Self-assessment and notification

In EU law, the previous notification system was abandoned and has been replaced by a self-assessment system giving the firms the possibility to act more flexibly but also displacing the burden and responsibility on them[45]. With the Covid crisis and the various forms of guidance which have been used in this time, the question has been whether this can be considered a comeback of notification.

As a matter of principle, the European Commission decided not to return to the notification system. Apart from the usual, informal oral guidance and guidance letters, there are also comfort letters which have experienced a comeback. Nevertheless, while these Covid-related comfort letters come close to the notification system, they are seen as exceptional guidance in order to enable companies to do better self-assessment. They may have a similar effect to notification in giving reassurance to undertakings, however it is not mandatory to apply for such an instrument in order to proceed with certain practices and it is at the discretion of the European Commission to provide it or not[46].

In contrast, the COVID-19 Block Exemption for the Healthcare Sector (South Africa) provides for a notification system concerning agreements in the healthcare sector 'if undertaken at the request of, and in coordination with, the Department of Health for the sole purpose of

---

[45] Regulation 1/2003 (n 43), recital 5; Temporary Framework Communication (n 18), para 6.
[46] Regulation 1/2003 (n 43), recital 14; Temporary Framework Communication (n 18), paras 17 s: the European Commission does mention 'ad hoc "comfort" letters' as exceptional means at the discretion of the Commission.

responding to the COVID-19 pandemic national disaster' (para 3). This is in line with the general approach under South African competition law where an undertaking has to apply to the Competition Commission South Africa (CCSA) in order to be exempted (s 10 Competition Act 89 of 1998 (South Africa)).

2. Instruments of guidance

Various jurisdictions have provided schemes, frameworks and more or less formalized guidance. For example, US authorities, as well as the European Commission, 'have stated that, exceptionally, they will offer rapid guidance to businesses seeking clarification as to the compatibility of COVID-19-related business cooperation with competition law'[47]. There are various types of guidance, from formal comfort letters to informal guidance; competition authorities also have expanded means of communication, especially via internet and email[48].

In EU law, various comfort letters, the most formal type of guidance, have been issued, especially in the pharmaceutical sector[49]. The French Autorité de la concurrence has not issued comfort letters but has provided for informal guidance[50].

In the crisis response frameworks, professional associations, public or other representing bodies are given a specific role. In its Covid communication, the European Commission recognizes that professional associations could play some role in a healthcare context[51]. In Mauritius, apart

---

[47] Jones (n 18) 287.

[48] Temporary Framework Communication (n 18), para 7: the European Commission has provided for a specific website (https://ec.europa.eu/competition/antitrust/coronavirus.html), as well as an email address (COMP-COVID-ANTITRUST@ec.europa.eu) for questions relating to covid antitrust.

[49] For example: European Commission (DG Comp), 'Comfort letter: coordination in the pharmaceutical industry to increase production and to improve supply of urgently needed critical hospital medicines to treat COVID-19 patients' (2020) COMP/OG – D(2020/044003); European Commission (DG Comp), 'Comfort letter: cooperation at a Matchmaking Event – Towards COVID-19 vaccines upscale production' (2020) COMP/E-1/GV/BV/nb (2021/034137).

[50] For example: Autorité de la concurrence, 'L'Autorité éclaire une association professionnelle sur ses possibilités d'action concernant les loyers de ses adhérents dans le cadre de la pandémie actuelle de COVID-19' (2020) <https://www.autoritedelaconcurrence.fr/fr/communiques-de-presse/lautorite-eclaire-une-association-professionnelle-sur-ses-possibilites> accessed 31 July 2022.

[51] Temporary Framework Communication (n 18), paras 12 s.

from the possibility of undertakings to apply for guidance concerning mergers under s 7 Competition Commission Rules of Procedure 2009 (Mauritius), the Competition Commission of Mauritius (CCM) has issued general frameworks on Covid-related agreements: for enterprises[52], as well as for trade associations[53] whose potential role in overcoming the crisis has been recognized. In France, there is a formal *procédure d'avis* on specific questions concerning the application of competition law posed by professional associations (art L 462-1 ss, R 462-1 ss Ccom (France)): while not constituting a decision on a specific practice, the Autorité de la concurrence can give guidelines[54] saying what measures would be taken if a concrete hypothetic situation/practice arose.

The guidance has been provided by authorities in directly Covid-related contexts, as well as in fields indirectly related to Covid. The Bundeskartellamt (BKartA) approved a scheme for cooperation provided by the German Association of the Automotive Industry (*Verband der Automobilindustrie*, VDA) which intends to minimize economic consequences of Covid[55]. Thereby, the BKartA went beyond the pure healthcare antitrust context which has otherwise surrounded competition law in times of Covid crisis. Similarly, the French authority provided for an advisory opinion concerning the possibilities of cooperation in the cinema sector which has been asked for by the *Médiateur du cinéma* in order to preserve cultural diversity[56].

---

[52] Competition Commission Mauritius, 'Guidance to business on proposed Covid19-related collaboration' (2020) <https://competitioncommission.mu/wp-content/uploads/2020/06/Guidance-Competitior-Collaboration-290620.pdf>, accessed 31 July 2022.

[53] Competition Commission Mauritius, 'Trade associations: Caution and Best practices' (2020) <https://competitioncommission.mu/wp-content/uploads/2020/06/Covid19-Trade-Association-caution-and-best-practices.pdf>, accessed 31 July 2022.

[54] Autorité de la concurrence, *Avis n° 21-A-03 du 16 avril 2021 relatif à une demande d'avis du Médiateur du cinéma sur les modalités de sortie des films en salle* (2021) <https://www.autoritedelaconcurrence.fr/sites/default/files/integral_texts/2021-04/21a03.pdf>, accessed 31 July 2022.

[55] Bundeskartellamt, 'Maßnahmen zur Krisenbewältigung in der Automobilindustrie – Bundeskartellamt unterstützt VDA bei der Erarbeitung der kartellrechtlichen Rahmenbedingungen' (2020) < https://www.bundeskartellamt.de/SharedDocs/Publikation/DE/Pressemitteilungen/2020/09_06_2020_VDA.pdf?__blob=publicationFile&v=3 (2) >, accessed 31 July 2022.

[56] See: Autorité de la concurrence, *Avis n° 21-A-03 du 16 avril 2021* (n 53).

Hand in hand with the guidance provided by authorities in order to allow easier self-assessment for undertakings, many jurisdictions also have changed procedural rules.

B. Adaptation of procedural rules

The reenforced difficulties firms face with regards to business administration have repercussions on their ability to fulfil certain procedural obligations, e.g. to provide certain documents, and authorities were willing to make concessions (1). However, this does mainly concern ex ante administrative procedures like merger control or, more generally, the approval of cooperation. Of course, unilateral anticompetitive conduct, such as price fixing, needs to be targeted with stricter procedural rules (2).

1. Alleviations concerning cooperation

In times of crisis, alleviations concerning procedural rules in the category of ex ante procedures (merger control and, to some extent, Covid-cooperation) make life for both firms and authorities easier. Mergers or proposed cooperations cannot be duly examined by authorities when firms face difficulties in providing necessary information.

In France, procedural deadlines have been adapted[57]: for instance, this does concern merger cases, filing of observations and briefs, leniency applications, transmission of procedural documents prescription, appeals, execution of commitments and injunctions. As for mergers, the regular time limits of art L 430-5 and L 430-7 Ccom (France) were suspended[58]. Similarly, Germany also has adapted previously existing laws in the economic sphere to the Covid crisis[59]. Concerning mergers, more flexible time limits for mergers notified between 1 March and 31 May

---

[57] Loi n° 2020-290 du 23 mars 2020 d'urgence pour faire face à l'épidémie de covid-19 (1) (France), art 11; Ordonnance n° 2020-306 du 25 mars 2020 relative à la prorogation des délais échus pendant la période d'urgence sanitaire et à l'adaptation des procédures pendant cette même période (France), art 7.

[58] Ordonnance n° 2020-306 du 25 mars 2020 (France), art 1 I; Autorité de la concurrence, 'Adaptation of the time limits and procedures of the Autorité de la concurrence in times of health emergency' (2020).

[59] Gesetz zur Abmilderung der Folgen der COVID-19-Pandemie im Wettbewerbsrecht und für den Bereich der Selbstverwaltungsorganisationen der gewerblichen Wirtschaft (BGBl 2020 I 1067) (Germany).

2020 are applicable (s 186(7) Gesetz gegen Wettbewerbsbeschränkungen (GWB) (Germany)).

A second aspect of the German law with regard to competition policy is that, where payment of fines has been deferred, payment of interest on fines is waved until 31 June 2021 (s 186(8) GWB (Germany)).

2. Aggravations concerning excessive pricing

As seen above, excessive pricing cases under normal antitrust are time consuming: they are 'extremely data intensive and unavoidably fact-specific, operate ex-post, are subject to high error risks, and rarely provide bright-line guidance on how to set lawful prices. More importantly, such cases are hard to build and often difficult to prosecute, leading to delays and to risks of the case failing to succeed at court.'[60]. The risk is that a possible outcome of such a case, reached after a long period of investigation and hearings, could become irrelevant, especially for the consumer.

A policy goal could be to respond to excessive pricing in a quick manner. There are several possibilities: apart from interim measures, the use of other tools such as consumer protection and market monitoring, a quick response could be achieved by the aggravation of certain procedural rules, e.g. with regard to time limits[61]. In South Africa, specific procedural rules constitute a supplement to the substantive law on excessive pricing[62]. There are rules concerning urgent complaint referral procedures (Tribunal Directives, para 5.9: a respondent has a time limit of 72 hours after a complaint referral has been filed against its pricing practice, in order to reply by filing an answering affidavit; para 5.10: the complainant may in turn reply to the findings of the respondent within 24 hours), as well as urgent hearings (Tribunal Directives, para 6) and specific remedies (Tribunal Directives, para 7.1: pricing order)[63].

---

[60] OECD 'Exploitative pricing in the time of COVID-19' (n 6) 8; OECD, 'Excessive Pricing in Pharmaceuticals' (2018) DAF/COMP(2018)12 30.
[61] OECD 'Exploitative pricing in the time of COVID-19' (n 6) 9.
[62] Tribunal Directives for Covid-19 excessive pricing complaint referrals (GN R448 of 3 April 2020) (South Africa) (Tribunal Directives).
[63] Tribunal Directives (n 61); Ratshisusu and Mncube (n 42) 259; Oxenham, Currie and van der Merwe (n 34) 525.

Conclusion

The Covid crisis has been a global challenge. Concerning competition law, the general framework is not silent in times of crisis. However, every crisis being specific as to its origins and its effect, law cannot foresee all issues which might possibly arise. Therefore, the general competition regime needs to be supplemented with new rules targeting specific issues: this has clearly been seen in South Africa concerning excessive pricing, but also cooperation between undertakings has required some reassurance on the part of competition authorities and finely balanced procedural tools. Covid being a global issue, a comparative assessment of possible solutions is justified: facing the same questions and uncertainties, competition regimes around the world have developed different, but to some extent converging, approaches.

The impact of COVID-19 on the public debt of countries in Sub-Saharan Africa

Essohanam PELENGUEI[1], Benoit KAFANDO[2],
Kokouvi Kunalè MAWUENA[3], Joseph Essèmou-
Abalè Kossi ASSOGBAVI[4], Abdoulaziz
ALHASSANE GARBA[5], Soumaïla WONI[6] and
Rajendra Parsad GUNPUTH[7]

Based on the harmful effects of the health crisis in the world, this article analyses the impact of COVID-19 on the public debt of the countries of Sub-Saharan Africa. After a presentation of the changes in terms of public finance, a comparative analysis of the impact of COVID-19 on the budgetary balance and public debt of these countries was carried out. The analysis method is based on paired data comparison tests and analysis of variance (ANOVA). The results show that the current sanitary crisis has contributed significantly to the increase in budget deficits in these countries. There is also an increase in the level of public debt, but the effect of the crisis remains statistically insignificant. In order

---

[1] Research Assistant at the Centre of Research and Training in Economics and Management of the Faculty of Economics and Management at the University of Lomé-Togo.
[2] Research Advisor, Observatoire de la Francophonie économique, University of Montreal.
[3] Research Assistant at the Centre of Research and Training in Economics and Management of the Faculty of Economics and Management at the University of Lomé-Togo.
[4] MPhil/PhD Student at the Faculty of Law and Management, University of Mauritius, Mauritius.
[5] Laboratory of Finance for Development (LAFIDEV) at Cheikh Anta Diop University, Dakar, Senegal.
[6] Temporary Teaching and Research Assistant at the Training and Research Unit in Economic and Management Sciences, Thomas Sankara University, Burkina Faso.
[7] Professor, Dean of Faculty of Law & Management, University of Mauritius.

to give countries in Sub-Saharan Africa some budget space for post-COVID-19 resilience, immediate debt relief is needed.

Partant des effets néfastes de la crise sanitaire dans le monde, cet article analyse l'impact de COVID-19 sur la dette publique des pays d'Afrique subsaharienne. Après une présentation des changements en matière de finances publiques, une analyse comparative de l'impact de COVID-19 sur le solde budgétaire et la dette publique de ces pays a été réalisée. La méthode d'analyse est basée sur des tests de comparaison de données appariées et des analyses de variance (ANOVA). Les résultats montrent que la crise sanitaire actuelle a contribué de manière significative à l'augmentation des déficits budgétaires dans ces pays. On observe également une augmentation du niveau de la dette publique, mais l'effet de la crise reste statistiquement non significatif. Un allègement immédiat de la dette est nécessaire pour donner aux pays d'Afrique subsaharienne une certaine marge de manœuvre budgétaire afin de leur permettre de résister à la crise de l'après-COVID-19.

Introduction

Considered one of the greatest crises since the end of the Second World War, the COVID-19 pandemic led to instability in the social and economic environment in several countries of the world, particularly in those whose main economic indicators (level of per capita income, public deficit, level of intra- and inter-national inequalities, etc.) were already fragile (Flahault, 2009; Nicola et al., 2020). The greater weight of COVID-induced expenditure compared to the low level of wealth creation led to increased budget deficits, forcing many governments to resort to borrowing to cope with the socio-economic consequences of the crisis.

Major crises have negative impacts on the budget stability of the world's economies. They lead to large budget deficits and unprecedented levels of debt (Abuselidze and Mamaladze, 2020; Abuselidze and Slobodianyk, 2021). Like other crises in the past, the COVID-19 pandemic has led to a deterioration of public finances. The situation is and will remain even more problematic in the countries of sub-Saharan Africa given the undiversified structure of their economies. Depending largely on commodity exports and tourism revenues, these countries have experienced a sharp decline in revenues as a result of the border closures. Other health measures such as the closure of shops, public places and lockdowns have not been economically beneficial, especially as almost the entire population in the countries of sub-Saharan Africa is dependent on the informal sector.

Faced with rising levels of expenditure to care for the most vulnerable and limited opportunities for revenue mobilisation, countries in sub-Saharan Africa have seen their budget deficits widen and their debt levels increase. Indeed, in this region, the budget deficit increased from 0.2 % on average in 2019 to 3 % in 2020. Debt levels rose from 52.7 % of GDP in 2019 to 59.5 % in 2020 (IMF, 2021b). According to the same IMF data, the debt level is expected to remain above 59 % in 2021. In view of the evolution of these indicators over the last few years, one wonders about the effect of the COVID-19 pandemic on the public debt of Sub-Saharan African countries.

The objective of this study is to analyse the effects of the COVID-19 pandemic on public debt in sub-Saharan African countries. We use an analytical methodology and a comparative analysis to show that the COVID-19 pandemic has led to a widening of budget deficits and an increase in debt. This study contributes to the literature in two ways. On the one hand, it enriches previous work on the impacts of global crises on the level of public debt and, to our knowledge, it is one of the first to focus on exclusively countries in sub-Saharan Africa. In order to give the governments of these countries room for maneuver, a suspension of the repayment of all external debts, whether interest payments or the debt itself, is necessary for the short term.

The rest of the paper is organized into four sections. The second section (II) presents the literature review on the relationship between the global 'COVID-19 pandemic' crises and debt levels. The third section (III) focuses on the stylized facts on public finance in countries in Sub-Saharan Africa. In section (IV), we present a comparative analysis of the impact of COVID-19 on the budget balance and indebtedness of countries in Sub-Saharan Africa. Section (V) lists research recommendations and proposes new avenues for research. These sections are followed by a conclusion to the paper.

I. Literature review

Over the past two years, the COVID-19 pandemic has been the subject of several theoretical and empirical studies. This pandemic has allowed several researchers to revive, through their studies, analyses of the impact of health crises such as COVID-19 on a certain number of macroeconomic aggregates (Brinca et al., 2020; Eichenbaum et al., 2020; Baker et al., 2020; Morsy et al., 2020; Baldwin, 2020).

Among these studies, some have focused on the specific case of Africa. For example, the study conducted by Morsy et al. (2020) takes into account the economic structure of African countries. The authors analyse the impact of the pandemic on economic activity using a DSGE model in which the informal sector is emphasized. However, although it is difficult to identify a critical threshold of debt that impacts growth and to make it a single empirical law, the evidence from the empirical literature generally shows that high public debt tends to hamper growth by increasing uncertainty about future taxation. These accumulated debts crowd out private investment and weaken a country's resilience to external shocks (Schilirò, 2019). The increase in public debt due to the COVID-19 pandemic is a good example. Although they have justified the increase in debt, Burriel et al. (2020) warn that once the crisis is over and the recovery is firmly in place, economies will still be vulnerable with debt ratios maintained at high levels over the medium term. They find that in the euro area, for example, highly indebted countries are ill-equipped to cope with possible future supply and demand shocks (Baldwin, 2020; Kuikeu, 2021).

For those countries whose production may be severely affected in the event of a crisis, they are likely to carry with them not only in the short term, but also in the long term, the negative effects of the COVID-19 pandemic on supply (Burriel et al., 2020). Indeed, these countries face a crowding out of private debt in the short term and will be negatively affected in terms of potential output in the long term. In the same logic, some works argue that a long-term trend of debt accumulation seems incompatible with theories of optimal public debt policies (Yared, 2019). This public spending is directed at strengthening public affairs, rather than encouraging the economy to change its structure and improve its productivity to guard against potential future crises (Persson and Tabellini, 2000; Bignon and Garnier, 2020). It should be noted that before the COVID-19 pandemic, countries were already recording historical records of high public debt levels (Presbitero and Wiriadinata, 2020). Thus, the adoption of budgetary expansions in most countries to effectively respond to the new expenditures brought about by the COVID-19 pandemic carries several risks, which are either to add to the already excessive debt burden or to face a huge public deficit.

The COVID-19 pandemic as experienced today is leading economies to enter a recession and at the same time, they are witnessing an increase in the level of debt incurred as a result of the multiple expenses incurred (Moulin, 2020). The evolution of these indicators leads countries into situations of vulnerability to possible future shocks (Kemajou, 2021). This will then lead the economies in question to have a longer refinancing period and higher interest rate levels to cover what has already been contracted, thus impeding long-term sustainability.

The review of the literature on the COVID-19 pandemic noted some conclusions about its possible effects in developed countries and in some developing countries such as middle and low-income countries. Focusing specifically on the context of countries in sub-Saharan Africa, our paper complements previous work by exploring the relationship between the current health crisis and the evolution of public debt.

II. Stylized facts about public finances in countries of Sub-Saharan Africa

This section analyses the state of public finances in sub-Saharan African countries at the start of the pandemic in 2019 to the present day. The aim is to present the state of budgetary balances and public debts contracted over the period.

A. Overview of budget balances

The contraction of the economy and the economic measures taken in response to the crisis have led to increased budget deficits and debt burdens. In its Fiscal Monitor report, the IMF (2021a) estimates that by 2020, overall deficits averaged 9.8 % in emerging market countries and 5.5 % in low-income developing countries. The widening of deficits in these countries is due to the collapse of revenues caused by the economic slowdown. African countries in the South of the Sahara, which are mainly composed of middle-income and low-income countries, have experienced a heterogeneous variation in the state of public finances. Several countries that were in surplus in 2019 saw their budget balances move into contractionary territory, while others that were in deficit in 2019 saw their budget positions deteriorate further.

Graph 1 below shows the budget balances in 2019 and 2020 for countries in Sub-Saharan Africa. The budget deficit increased in 2020 in almost all of these countries, with the exception of a few countries that recorded an improvement in their balance. These are Mauritania (3.9 % of GDP in 2020 compared with 3.5 % of GDP in 2019), Chad (2.5 % compared with 0.8 % in 2019), the Democratic Republic of Congo (-1.3 % compared with -1.7 % in 2019), Comoros (0.1 % compared with -2.9 % in 2019) and Rwanda (-3.7 % compared with -3.9 % in 2019).

Countries in sub-Saharan Africa are mainly dependent on revenues from the export of raw materials. With the implementation of sanitary measures (e.g., border closures) to curb the spread of the pandemic, international trade has contracted sharply, leading to a sharp drop in trade earnings. The contraction in export earnings, combined with the economic measures taken in response to the crisis, has led to increased budget deficits and debt burdens for countries. With little scope for raising funds on the markets, financing these deficits will remain difficult in this part of the world.

As can be seen in Graph 1, the pandemic has led to a deterioration in the budget balance in several countries in Sub-Saharan Africa. In effect, the number of countries with a budget surplus has fallen from eleven (11) in 2019 to six (6) in 2020. Among the countries that have improved their budget balance is Mauritania. The Mauritanian economy seems to have been less severely affected by the crisis. In addition to enhancing its budget balance by 0.4 percentage points, it has maintained the highest budget surplus (3.9 %). In contrast, the situation has deteriorated significantly in countries such as Seychelles, whose budget deficit as a percentage of GDP has increased from 3.4 % in 2019 to -14.1 % in 2020.

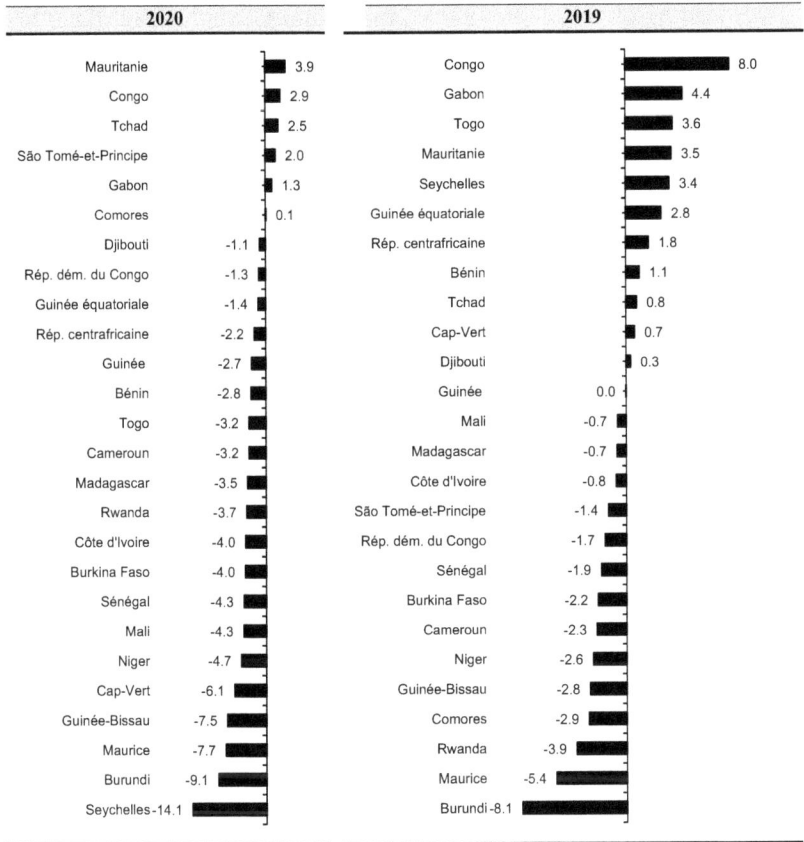

Graph 1: Budget balance in 2019 and 2020 in sub-Saharan African countries (as a percentage of GDP)
Sources: IMF (2021b) and IOF (2021).

The Tab. 1 presents some statistics on budget deficits in 2019 and 2020 in four regions of sub-Saharan Africa. These are countries from Southern Africa, from Central Africa, East Africa and West Africa. The median, mean, and standard deviation in this table are calculated from the data for the countries in each region. For example, in the case of Southern Africa, which is made up of countries such as Madagascar, Mauritius and Comoros, the average for the year 2020 is obtained from the budgetary balances recorded for the three (3) countries in 2020.

A reading of Tab. 1 shows that, apart from Central Africa, the other three regions recorded budget deficits for the years 2019 and 2020. In these three regions, there was also a deterioration in the budget deficit between 2019 and 2020: a deficit of 3.7 % of GDP in 2020 compared to 3 % of GDP in 2019 in Southern Africa, 7 % of GDP in 2020 compared to 2.1 % of GDP in 2019 in East Africa and 3.6 % of GDP in 2020 compared to 0.2 % of GDP in 2019 in West Africa.

Table 1: Descriptive statistics for budget balances in 2019 and 2020 in sub-Saharan Africa (as a percentage of GDP)

Year 2020			
Regions	Median	Mean	Standard Deviation
Southern Africa	– 3,5	– 3,7	3,9
Central Africa	0	0,1	2,4
Eastern Africa	– 6,4	– 7	5,8
West Africa	– 4	– 3,6	2,9

Year 2019			
Regions	Median	Mean	Standard Deviation
Southern Africa	– 2,9	– 3	2,4
Central Africa	1,3	1,6	3,5
Eastern Africa	– 1,8	– 2,1	5
West Africa	– 0,7	– 0,2	2,3

Sources: Authors' calculations based on IMF data (2021b).

Graph 2 shows the evolution of the budget balance in four regions of sub-Saharan Africa (Southern Africa, East Africa, Central Africa and West Africa). The budget balance for a region is obtained by averaging the budget balances of the countries in that region in a given year. For example, the budget balance for Southern Africa in 2020 is obtained from the average of the 2020 budget balances of Mauritius, Comoros and Madagascar. An analysis of Graph 2 shows that, overall, Africa in the south of the Sahara had a deficit between 2014 and 2020. A more detailed analysis shows that the West African region remained in deficit over the period 2009–2020 and that Central Africa recorded a surplus budget balance between 2017 and 2020.

Apart from Southern Africa, where the budget balance started to deteriorate significantly in 2018, the other regions have maintained a good budget deficit momentum by gradually reducing its level between 2016 and 2019. From 2019 onwards, a widening of budget deficits is observed in all four regions of Sub-Saharan Africa. This result could be attributed to the COVID-19 effect, as countries had to face additional expenditures to mitigate the disastrous consequences of the pandemic on their populations.

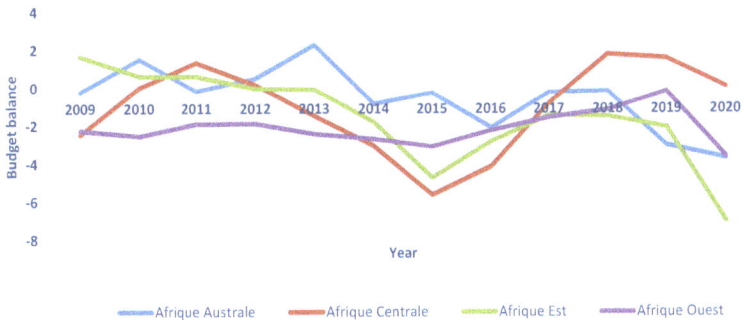

Graph 2: Evolution of the budget balance in the regions of Africa in the south of the Sahara
Source: Authors based on IMF data (2021b).

B. Overview of public debt

The COVID-19 pandemic has greatly exacerbated debt risks in developing countries, as sluggish growth, characterized by a slow recovery, is likely to further increase debt burdens and erode the ability to borrow countries to service them. In its October 2020 'Public Finance Monitor report', the IMF estimates average public debt as a percentage of GDP in emerging and low-income countries at 54.1 % in 2019. This estimate of the debt level was around 63.4 % in 2020, reflecting an increase of 9.3 percentage points (IMF, 2021a).

For the specific case of countries in Sub-Saharan Africa, the median public debt increased from 45.7 % of GDP in 2019 to 48.4 % in 2020, while the average public debt was around 59.5 %, up from 52.5 % of GDP in 2019. The level of public debt in these countries is expected to continue to rise in the short to medium term due to widening budget deficits, slower growth, higher interest costs and depreciation of some currencies (Habarurema et al., 2021).

As it can be seen in Graph 3, among the countries in sub-Saharan Africa, public debt has increased in Cape Verde from 125 % of GDP in 2019 to 139 % in 2020, Congo (from 83.7 % to 101.7 %), Seychelles (from 57.7 % to 98.4 %) and Mauritius (from 84.2 % to 87.7 %). On the other hand, it has decreased in countries such as the Democratic Republic of Congo (from 15.5 % in 2019 to 15.2 % in 2020), Chad (from 44.3 % to 43 %), the Central African Republic (from 47.2 % to 44.9 %).

In both emerging and low-income countries, accumulated public debt is at levels not seen since the debt crisis of the 1980s. Consisting mainly of low-income countries, the part of Africa at the south of the Sahara is at high risk of debt distress, i.e. an inability to service public debt, which could severely disrupt economic activity and employment, especially in a context of declining tax revenues and rising expenditures due to the implementation of health crisis response strategies.

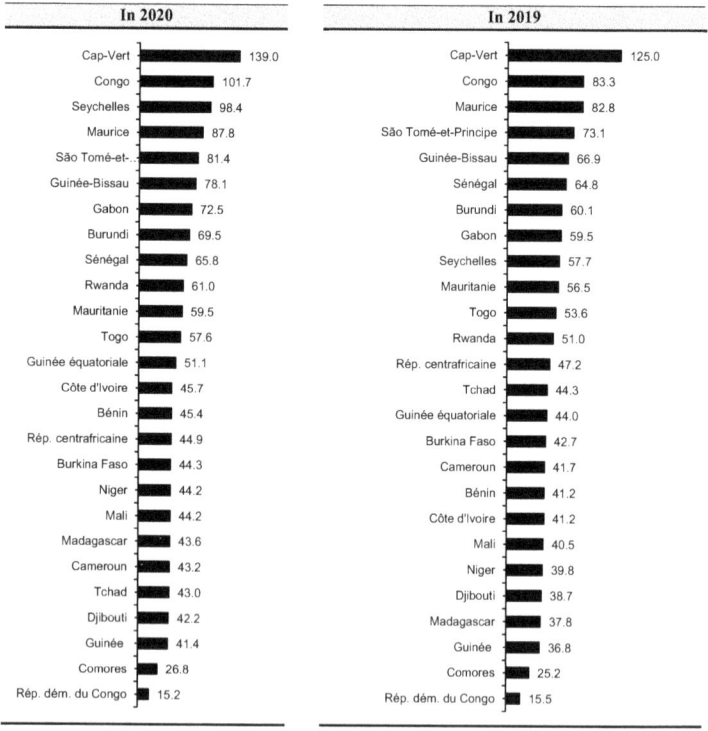

Graph 3: Gross debt in 2019 and 2020 in sub-Saharan African countries (as a percentage of GDP)

Sources: IMF (2021b) and IOF (2021).

The information in Tab. 2 is obtained using the methodology applied in Tab. 1. A reading of Tab. 2 shows that, on average, the level of gross debt increased in 2020 relative to its level in 2019 in all four regions of sub-Saharan Africa. More specifically, gross debt was estimated to average 48.8 % of GDP in 2019 in Southern Africa. In 2020, this average increased to 52.7 % of GDP. There is also a shift from 51.1 % of GDP in 2019 to 56.6 % of GDP in 2020 for Central Africa, from 51.9 % of GDP to 67.8 % of GDP for East Africa and from 55.4 % of GDP to 60.5 % of GDP for West Africa.

Table 2: Descriptive statistics on gross debt in 2019 and 2020 in sub-Saharan Africa (as a percentage of GDP)

	Year 2020		
Regions	Median	Mean	Standard deviation
Southern Africa	43,6	52,7	22,64
Central Africa	48	56,6	24,1
Eastern Africa	65,2	67,8	18,1
West Africa	45,7	60,5	23,3

	Year 2019		
Regions	Median	Mean	Standard deviation
Southern Africa	37,8	48,6	21,9
Central Africa	45,7	51,1	18,5
Eastern Africa	54,4	51,9	7,5
West Africa	42,7	55,4	23,4

Sources: Authors' calculations based on IMF (2021b) and IOF (2021) data.

Like Graphs 2 and 4 present the evolution of gross debt in four regions of sub-Saharan Africa over the period 2009–2020. Overall, there is an increasing trend in the level of debt in the four regions. From 2019 onwards, an increase in debt is observed, reflecting the countries' recourse to domestic or external borrowing to finance expenditure related to the COVID-19.

Graph 4: Evolution of gross debt in the regions of Sub-Sahara Africa (as a percentage of GDP)
Sources: Authors' construction based on IMF data (2021b).

C. Limited budgetary room for manoeuvre

In sub-Saharan Africa, the coronavirus emerged at a time when countries were highly indebted and had virtually no budget space to deal with the pandemic and the re-emerging economic and social expenditures. In this part of the world, pandemic-related budget measures remained marginal compared to those implemented in advanced countries (Habarurema et al., 2021). Public debt in Sub-Saharan Africa has increased to over 59.5 % of GDP in 2020, its highest level in almost two decades, largely due to a decline in government output and revenues.

According to the IMF, four challenges are behind this lack of space. The first is the high and unsustainable debt-to-GDP ratio. The second challenge is that high budget deficits will push countries to explore other alternatives for financing development projects. In doing so, these countries will resort more to borrowing, which is likely to lead to an increase in their debt burden. The third challenge is due to the high cost of borrowing, with interest rates ranging from 5 to 16 % on 10-year government bonds, while these same rates are close to zero (0) or even negative in Europe and America. Finally, the fourth challenge is that the depreciation of many African currencies against major international currencies has triggered inflation.

In order to address these challenges, reducing inequalities based on income, gender and race, and providing financial support to low-income countries would be plausible avenues to explore.

III. Comparative analysis of the effect of COVID-19 on the variables such as gross debt and budget balance

Comparative analysis allows us to check whether the difference between parametric and non-parametric values is significant. A number of statistical tests is available to objectively assess these differences, including the Student's t-test, which is applied according to the particularity of the given decision-making context (Réau and Chauvat, 2006). This test is therefore used in the context of this study to compare the dynamics of the gross debt and the budget balance of countries in Sub-Saharan Africa, before and during the coronavirus pandemic.

The parametric test of comparison of means of two matched samples fits perfectly to our expectations, as it is adapted to our data which describe a situation before and after a given phenomenon. Table 3 presents the correlations between the matched samples of gross debt and budget balance. It can be seen that the paired samples are related to each other, hence a good match. The table shows very high correlation values, ranging from 0.92 to 0.98 for gross debt and from 0.43 to 0.80 for the budget balance.

Table 3: Correlations of matched samples: Gross Debt and Budget Balance

		Gross debts		
		N	Correlation	Sig.
Paired 1	2018–2019	26	0,967	0,000
Paired 2	2019–2020	26	0,957	0,000
Paired 3	2019–2021	26	0,917	0,000
Paired 4	2020–2021	26	0,984	0,000
		Budget balances		
Paired 1	2018–2019	26	0,800	0,000
Paired 2	2019–2020	26	0,432	0,027
Paired 3	2019–2021	26	0,532	0,005
Paired 4	2020–2021	26	0,789	0,000

Source: Authors' calculations based on IMF (2021b) and IOF (2021) data.
Note: N (number of observations), Sig (test probability)

Following the presentation of the correlations, the paired samples test is performed for the case of gross debt and the budget balance. The results are presented in Tab. 4. A significant difference emerges, first between the gross debt series of countries in 2019 and 2020 (P-value = 0.000) and in 2019 and 2021 (P-value = 0.004). This reflects the effect of the COVID-19 pandemic on the debt of countries in sub-Saharan Africa, as the end of 2019 marks the beginning of the health crisis in many countries in Africa. On the other hand, the results show that there is no statistically significant difference at the 5 % level between the debt of countries in 2018 and 2019 (P-value = 0.314) or in 2020 and 2021 (P-value = 0.955). These results confirm what is said above for the simple reason that the pandemic had not yet taken hold in the 2018–2019 period. In the case of the budget balance, there is actually a significant difference between the budget deficits at a 5 % threshold for the years 2019 and 2020 or 2019 and 2021. This result also reflects the effect of the COVID-19 pandemic on the budget balance. This pandemic has caused budgetary gaps, with significant public spending in the countries of sub-Saharan Africa, in order to cope with the socio-economic consequences.

Table 4: Test of matched samples of gross debt and budget balance

Gross debt			Paired differencies			t	ddl	Sig (bilateral)
			Mean	Standard Deviation	Mean Standard error			
	Paired 1	2018–2019	−1,12	5,56	1,09	−1,027	25	n0,314
	Paired 2	2019–2020	−6,78	8,46	1,66	−4,087	25	0,000
	Paired 3	2019–2021	−6,73	10,79	2,12	−3,181	25	0,004
	Paired 4	2020–2021	0,05	4,66	0,91	0,057	25	0,955
Budget balances	Paired 1	2018–2019	−0,05	2,04	0,40	−0,136	25	0,893
	Paired 2	2019–2020	2,73	3,96	0,78	3,518	25	0,002
	Paired 3	2019–2021	2,20	3,06	0,60	3,672	25	0,001
	Paired 4	2020–2021	−0,53	2,46	0,48	−1,096	25	0,283

Source: Authors' calculations based on IMF (2021b) and IOF (2021) data.
Note: N (number of observations), Sig (test probability)

With the significant differences observed in the comparisons of the variables (budget balance or gross debt) for the periods 2019 and 2020 and 2019 and 2021, we used the analysis of variance (ANOVA) to measure the degree of contribution of the pandemic on the variation of the debt or budget balance. ANOVA, as a reminder, is a method of analysis that allows us to study the behaviour of a quantitative variable to be explained as a function of one or more qualitative variables, also known as categorical nominals. In our case, the categorical explanatory variable is represented by the variable COVID-19, which has the modalities 'Absence and Presence' of the pandemic.

In light of Tab. 5, which presents the results of the analysis of variance, it appears that, overall, there is a positive variation in the gross debt and the budget deficit. The budget balance, which averaged -0.268 in 2019, was -3.00 in 2020. Also, the countries' gross debt increased on average from 52.731 of GDP to 59.515 between 2019 and 2020. This implies a considerable part of the pandemic in explaining the variation of the two macroeconomic indicators.

Using ANOVA, we find that the pandemic contributed significantly to the variation in the budget balance, accounting for 12.43 % (P-value = 0.010). This contribution is statistically significant at the 5 % level. On the other hand, there is no significant difference in the contribution of the pandemic to the variation in gross debt (P-value = 0.316). This situation could be explained by the fact that countries in sub-Saharan Africa remain dependent on debt for the financing of public expenditure, regardless of the period (crisis or not). However, according to Burriel et al. (2020), there are drawbacks to increasing debt. For them, fragile economies may have difficulty coping with future supply and demand shocks in the post-pandemic period.

Table 5: Analysis of variance of gross debt and budget balance variables

	Cov19/20	N	Mean	Standard-deviation	F	Sig.	Eta squared (%)
Gross debt	Absence	26	52,731	21,692	1,026	0,316	2,01
	Presence	26	59,515	26,368			
	Total	52	56,123	24,149			
	Cov19/21						
	Absence	26	52,731	21,692	1,010	0,320	1,98
	Presence	26	59,463	26,371			
	Total	52	56,097	24,148			
Budget balances	Cov19/20						
	Absence	26	– 0,268	3,386	7,097	0,010	12,43
	Presence	26	– 3,000	3,986			
	Total	52	– 1,634	3,913			
	Cov19/21						
	Absence	26	– 0,268	3,386	6,401	0,015	11,35
	Presence	26	– 2,735	3,450			
	Total	52	– 1,913	3,602			

Source: Authors' calculations based on IMF (2021b) and IOF (2021) data.
Note: N (number of observations), F (Fischer's value measuring the validity of the ANOVA), Sig (probability of test), Eta squared (measure of the percentage contribution to the variation of the dependent variable).

IV. Recommendations

Among the assessment elements used by potential lenders to evaluate a country's capacity to fulfil its commitments, creditworthiness is one of the most important. Creditworthiness is therefore a fundamental determinant of a country's development, as it allows it to borrow more to finance its growth and development. In other words, a creditworthy debtor country is able to borrow funds to refinance its debt. In the previous section, it is clearly stated that the COVID-19 pandemic has contributed to the widening of budget deficits in countries in Sub-Saharan Africa. As the majority of these countries are structurally deficit countries and dependent on external financing, it goes without saying that the non-solvency and unsustainability of the debt will reduce the financing possibilities of the economy and thus slow down economic growth. The decline in real per capita income combined with high population growth will push a significant number of people into extreme poverty.

In order to give the countries of sub-Saharan Africa some budget space to deal with the pandemic and its economic and social consequences, immediate debt relief seems necessary. It is all the more necessary because the collapse of commodity prices, trade and tourism flows have led to a rapid drop in government revenues and countries are looking for rescue measures to deal with the current crisis. In the same vein, eight (8) leading African political and economic figures believe that a two-year suspension of all external debt repayments, whether interest payments or the debt itself, is necessary. They also call for comparable relief on private and commercial debts, which now account for a substantial share of the money owed by many African countries to lenders. All of these measures will not only make debt sustainable, but also allow for the possibility of restructuring it.

For example, with debt relief, governments in the Sub-Saharan Africa could better mobilize their efforts to protect the most vulnerable populations and strengthen social protection systems. The additional room for manoeuvre created by debt relief could also allow governments in this part of the world to support the private sector, particularly small and medium-sized enterprises, and thus save jobs. Without these measures, there is a risk that the living conditions of the population will deteriorate, with even more serious consequences in terms of political and social instability.

Conclusion

COVID-19 has caused economic disruption in developing countries, especially in the African region at the south of the Sahara. In these countries of Africa at the south of the Sahara, the informal sector plays a major role. It is the main source of income for many households. With the containment measures, curfews, border closures and business closures, there has been a slowdown in economic activity, resulting in job losses and an increase in the poverty rate. In order to address the urgency of the response to the COVID-19 pandemic and its economic and social consequences, the governments of these countries have put in place mitigation, support and recovery measures. The financing of these measures required recourse to borrowing. This alternative way of financing COVID-19-related expenditure has contributed to increasing the level of indebtedness and widening the budget deficit in Sub-Saharan Africa. It is with this in mind that this research is conducted to analyse the effects of the COVID-19 pandemic on the debt of the countries concerned. The results show that the pandemic has led to an increase in the level of debt, but also to a widening of budget deficits in the countries of sub-Saharan Africa. This research also highlighted the importance of reducing the debt burden in these countries to allow not only for future refinancing, but also for long-term solvency.

Bibliography

Abuselidze, G. and Mamaladze, L. (2020). The impact of the COVID-19 outbreak on the socio-economic issues of the Black Sea region countries. In International conference on computational science and its applications, pp. 453–467.

Abuselidze, G. and Slobodianyk, A. (2021). Pandeconomic crisis and its impact on small open economies: A case study of COVID-19. In Advances in intelligent systems and computing, 1258, 718–728. Cham: Springer, vol. 10, p. 978

Africa Renewal (2021). External debt complicates Africa's post-COVID-19 recovery. https://www.un.org/africarenewal/fr/magazine/juillet-2020/la-dette-extérieure-complique-le-redressement-post-covid-19-de-lafrique.

Baker, S. R., Bloom, N., Davis, S. J. and Terry, S. J. (2020). COVID-induced economic uncertainty. NBER Working Paper Series 26983.

Baldwin, R. and di Mauro, B. W. (2020). Economics in the time of COVID-19. CEPR Press.

Bignon, V. and Garnier, O. (2020). Measuring the impact of the Covid-19 crisis. Revue de l'OFCE, 166(2), 45–57.

Brinca, P., Duarte, J. B. and Castro, M. F. (2020). Is the covid-19 pandemic a supply or a demand shock? Economic Synopses – St Louis FED, 31, 2486–2495.

Burriel, P., Checherita-Westphal, C., Jacquinot, P., Schön, M. and Stähler, N. (2020). Economic consequences of high public debt: Evidence from three large-scale DSGE models. ECB Working Paper 2450.

Eichenbaum, M. S., Rebelo, S. and Trabandt, M. (2020). The macroeconomics of epidemics. CEPR Working Paper.

Flahault, A. (2009). Managing a health crisis: The example of chikungunya. Les Tribunes de la santé, 22, 53–66.

Habarurema, J.-D., Boudarbat, B. and Kafando, B. (2021). COVID-19: Bilan de la pandémie de COVID-19 dans les pays francophones, in La Francophonie économique 4. COVID-19: Impacts économiques et sociaux, politiques de riposte et stratégies de résilience, edited by B. Boudarbat, H. Guermazi and M. B. Ndiaye. Montreal, QC, Canada: Observatoire de la Francophonie économique de l'Université de Montréal, pp. 19–54.

IMF (2020). Public Finance Monitor, October. Online. https://www.imf.org/fr/Publications/FM/Issues/2020/09/30/october-2020-fiscal-monitor.

IMF (2021a). Public Finance Monitor, April. Online. https://www.imf.org/fr/Publications/FM/Issues/2021/03/29/fiscal-monitor-april

IMF (2021b). World economic outlook database. Online. https://www.imf.org/en/Publications/WEO/weo-database/2021/April

Jeune Afrique (2021). African debt relief needed to fight the coronavirus. Online. https://www.jeuneafrique.com/925491/economie/tribune-il-faut-alleger-la-dette-africaine-pour-combattre-le-coronavirus/

Kemajou Njatang, D. (2021). Economic impact of COVID-19 in Cameroon: Results from the SIR-macro model. African Development Review, 33, S126–S138.

Kuikeu, Oscar, 2020. "L'impact économique du COVID-19 au Cameroun: une approche par la Modélisation VAR [Economic impact of COVID-19 in Cameroon: an empirical assessment with the VAR

Methodology]," MPRA Paper 99727, University Library of Munich, Germany.

Morsy, H., Balma, L. and Mukasa, A. N. (2020). Not a good time: Economic impact of COVID-19 in Africa. African Development Bank. Published online 2021 May 18. doi: 10.1111/1467-8268.12526, https://www.ncbi.nlm.nih.gov/pmc/articles/PMC8207119/

Moulin, E. (2020). State indebtedness and the Covid-19 crisis. Revue d'économie financière, 3, 235–243.

Nicola, M., Alsafi, Z, Sohrabi, C., Kerwan, A., Al-Jabir, A., Agha, M. and Agha, R. (2020). The socio-economic implications of the coronavirus pandemic (COVID-19): A review. International Journal of Surgery, 185–193.

Organisation for Economic Co-operation and Development. (2016), Fragility states 2015, https://www.ncbi.nlm.nih.gov/pmc/articles/PMC7162753/

Organisation Internationale de la Francophonie (2021). Watch on the economic impact of Covid-19 in the 54 OIF member states and governments. Online. https://www.francophonie.org/veille-covid19.

Persson, T. and Tabellini, G. (2000). Political economics: Explaining economic policy. Cambridge, MA: MIT Press.

Réau, J.-P. and Chauvat, G. (2006). 'Probabilités & Statistiques' Résumé des cours – Exercices et problèmes corrigés – QCM. ARMAND COLIN. 4th Edition.

Schilirò, D. (2019). Public debt and growth in Italy: Analysis and policy proposals. International Journal of Business Management and Economic Research, 10(5), 1695–1702.

PART III

COVID-19 AND ECONOMIC AND SOCIAL LAW

COVID-19 ET LE DROIT ÉCONOMIQUE ET SOCIAL

In most countries, COVID-19 management was geared more towards dealing with health problems than economic ones. Curfews were used almost everywhere, sometimes for long periods of several months. The social and economic consequences were particularly severe. The contributions in this part try to analyse the pandemic's impact on economic factors, labour law, social rights and the environment. The protective measures against the COVID-19 mainly had consequences for economic and working life and social legislation had to be adapted to the new situation.

Dans la plupart des pays, la gestion de COVID-19 a été axée sur la résolution des problèmes de santé plutôt que sur les problèmes économiques. Presque partout, des couvre-feux ont été appliqués, parfois sur de longues périodes de plusieurs mois. Les conséquences sociales et économiques ont été particulièrement lourdes. Les contributions de cette partie tentent d'analyser l'impact de la pandémie sur les facteurs économiques, le droit du travail, les droits sociaux et l'environnement. Les mesures de protection contre le Covid ont surtout eu des conséquences sur la vie économique et professionnelle et la législation sociale a dû être adaptée à la nouvelle situation.

The effects of COVID-19 on quality auditor's report

Mootooganagen RAMEN and Aslam R. SAIB[1]

This paper aims to discuss the effects of COVID-19 on the auditor's report. The study therefore focuses on investigating the factors that are currently being affected in the COVID-19 crisis at different stages on the audit engagement namely audit planning, audit risk, audit evidence. Additionally, during the pandemic more emphasis should be placed on the assessment on going concern as well as the key audit matter. Primary data was collected by issuing questionnaires to auditors resulting in 102 respondents. The investigation was then carried out through the descriptive profile analysis, Cronbach's Alpha reliability tests, descriptive statistics, exploratory factor analysis and Pearson's correlation coefficients. The nature and the degree of relationship was then analysed before deriving a conclusion and provide recommendations.

Ce document a pour objectif d'examiner les effets de la directive COVID-19 sur le rapport de l'auditeur. L'étude s'est donc concentrée sur l'examen des facteurs qui sont actuellement affectés par la crise COVID-19 à différents stades de la mission d'audit, à savoir la planification de l'audit, le risque d'audit et les preuves d'audit. En outre, pendant la pandémie, il convient de mettre davantage l'accent sur l'évaluation de la continuité de l'exploitation ainsi que sur les questions clés de l'audit. Les données primaires ont été collectées en envoyant des questionnaires aux auditeurs, ce qui a permis d'obtenir 102 réponses. L'enquête a ensuite été menée au moyen d'une analyse descriptive du profil, de tests de fiabilité Alpha de Cronbach, de statistiques descriptives, d'une analyse factorielle exploratoire et de coefficients de corrélation de Pearson. La nature et le degré de relation ont ensuite été analysés avant de tirer une conclusion et de formuler des recommandations.

---

[1] Faculty of Law and Management, University of Mauritius.

Introduction

The World Health Organisation declared COVID-19 as a global pandemic on 11th March 2020. The rapid spread of the disease globally had already infected more than 60 million people and almost 1.5 million deaths. The COVID-19 is a highly contagious respiratory disease that was first reported in China. As a means to prevent the spread of COVID-19, many countries have implemented lockdown. Consequently, audit firms have been forced to move their operations and interactions online and undertake the challenge of remote working while focusing on the quality of the auditor's report.

The unprecedented circumstance of the COVID-19 crisis has presented the auditing profession with uncertainties and challenging risks. Auditors should ensure to maintain quality in the audit report during the pandemic. The audit of a firm should be in accordance with ISAs to provide consistency in the audit report. Audit report gives credibility to the financial statement (SAS 100) and it must be relevant and reliable. Furthermore, the users of account make use of the audit report for decision making (Robertson, 1998) and they confidently trust auditors for issuing a good report after scrutinizing the financial statement. In consequence of COVID-19, to sustain the confidence of the public, auditors are required to continue improving the quality of the auditor's report by making extensive efforts when conducting the audit.

During this turbulent time, the audit report highlights major areas that required auditor's attention (ACCA, 2020). The types of audit report issued depend on the quality audit procedures at different stages of the audit process. Additionally, business risks are increased leading to a greater uncertainty concerning the entity's ability to continue as a going concern and this risk must be included in the audit report. Therefore, this study aimed to discuss the effects of the pandemic on the audit report with regards to the of audit planning, audit risk, audit evidence, assessment on going concern and key audit matter as these factors were influenced in a significant way during the crisis.

I. Statement of the problem

The unprecedented circumstance of the COVID-19 pandemic has interrupted most professions worldwide with auditing being no exception. Auditors are facing unique challenges in determining the accurate and good quality of the audit report. Entities have been affected by this unforeseen situation thus, a greater emphasis on the possible impacts on the audit report must be placed. There are numerous factors in the audit report that have been affected by the COVID-19. Therefore, this paper analyses the effects that COVID-19 is generating towards the quality of the auditor's report.

II. Research objectives

The goal of this paper is to conduct an insightful research regarding the effects of COVID-19 on the quality auditor's report. To have a good grasp on how the auditor's report is being influenced, this research is broken down into five factors that were highly affected. After analysing these factors, recommendations are suggested on how to maintain the quality in the auditor's report during the COVID-19 crisis.

III. Literature review

The auditor should state in the auditor's report whether the FS is in accordance with the GAAP. The auditor's report is essential as banks, creditors and regulators request for an audit of an entity's FS before proceeding with any transactions. Whether to issue an unmodified audit report or a modified audit report depends on the findings of the auditor (Kenton, 2021).

More emphasis has been laid on the auditor's report since and even before the Enron and World.com scandal in 2001. The case was cited as the 'biggest audit failure' caused by multiple parties as there was conflict of interest of the auditors and the engagement. As a result, investment was reduced due to loss of the public confidence. Consequently, the reliability and reputation of auditor's report was lessened. According to Commonwealth of Australia (2009), the GFC in 2007 presented the auditing profession with challenging risks and uncertainties due to uncertain economic environment. IAASB (2015) stated that the prevalence of GFC and complexity in financial reporting has triggered the attention of users of FS to demand more informative auditor's report.

The Coronavirus was declared as a global pandemic by World Health Organization due to the rapid outbreak across the world. Financial institutions have to monitor and deal with consequences of this pandemic. As stated by Goodell (2020), the COVID-19 pandemic presents an alarming effect on the economic and financial that the world is grappling with. As per KPMG (2020), these economic turbulences are combined together with market uncertainties, influence the confidence of investors further to company's financial performance leading to financial distress. Reduction in investor's confidence leads to an unstable and decreasing pattern in the earnings during the economic turbulence period (Arthur et al., 2015). Auditors are faced up to these exceptional challenges accordingly and many companies may bankrupt or manipulate their earnings figures during this unprecedented circumstance (Gerged et al., 2020).

ISA 700 *'forming an opinion and reporting on the financial statement'* is issued by IFAC to serve as a guideline on the auditor's responsibility in order to form an opinion in the FS. It also includes the form and content of an audit report issued in result of an audit of financial statements (IFAC, 2009). In 2015, the IAASB had issued new and revised auditor reporting standards for auditors to come up with more instructive and transparent reports on the audited firms. In addition, IAASB introduced the new auditor's report to improve the usefulness and relevance of the report to shareholders and other related parties. According to Cagiran and Varici (2019), IAASB has issued a new auditor's report to make the audit report more reliable, information is provided more easily to users and entities and also, to issue a more transparent report for the users of the information.

It is essential to have quality audit report to promote trust, to secure the confidence and interest of investors, shareholders and stakeholders (Gray et al., 2011). As stated by EY (2020), consistent audit processes and innovative technologies are used to deliver audit quality and auditors are required to act with integrity, objectivity and professional skepticism. In addition, it is known as a key consideration for auditors across the globe (Francis, 2004). As per FRC (2008), in determining the audit quality it is critical to have a reliable and relevant audit report. A formal audit report guaranteed that a company is viable, and solvent as reported by Slamen (2009). As per Abdullah et al. (2015), the audit report improves the financial statement along with an increase in reliability and transparency of information. It is therefore certified that companies make available accurate information (Lennox, 1999). The judgements of source of reliability are considered important in the audit process because inferential value of evidence should continuously refer in the light of its source

(Hirst, 1994). Moreover, having a quality audit report is important as per IFAC (2021) audit report provides investors, shareholders and stakeholders with reasonable assurance whether the financial statement are prepared in accordance with financial reporting framework as a whole and are free from material misstatement.

The content of an auditor's report should be accurate and clear by giving sufficient verification to validate the auditor's estimation and users of the report need to be capable of understanding and identifying any unusual circumstances when occurred. As per ISA 700 *Forming an Opinion and Reporting on Financial Statements*, the auditor's report should incorporate the following contents.

IV. Methodology

Research methodology comprises of the detailed research methods used for the collection of data as well as the general philosophies upon which the data collection and data analysis is based. According to Zikmund (2003), a research design is a well-designed framework that represents the actions for the research that is being conducted. For the purpose of this study, a descriptive research design was used. In order to gather quantitative research based of the problem at hand, structured questionnaire was designed. A descriptive research design put emphasis on the accuracy of the problem, and it gives a description on what the study is concerned with. As per Adcock (1998), a descriptive research design includes various methods and procedures that describe variables by answering to questions like who, what, why and how. An explanatory research refers to research that were not well investigated previously. Boyd (1998) revealed that explanatory research is defined as the collection of information in an informal and unstructured manner. It is conducted to grasp more about the nature, the scope of the problem and to have a clearer understanding to find out the likely solutions. Hence, it was used to determine the relationship between the COVID-19 and the quality auditor's report. Quantitative approach attempts to explain phenomena or relationships (Frankel and Devers, 2000). To explain the relationships between the quality auditor's report and COVID-19, the quantitative approach seemed a better fit. Moreover, these phenomena have been explained by collecting and analysing numerical data with mathematical techniques. The Statistical Package for Social Science (SPSS) software were used to analysed the quantitative data.

Questionnaires were sent to the targeted population for this study, particularly, the auditors. The questionnaire focuses on five main aspects of an audit engagement, namely, audit planning, audit risk, audit evidence, going concern and key audit matters, that would impact on the audit report.

The following hypotheses were tested by using the Pearson correlation coefficient:

Hypothesis 1 COVID-19 has influenced audit planning.

Hypothesis 2: COVID-19 has influenced audit risk.

Hypothesis 3: COVID-19 has influenced audit evidence.

Hypothesis 4: COVID-19 has influenced the assessment on going concern.

Hypothesis 5: COVID-19 has influenced the key audit matter.

A. Analysis

The reliability test measures to what extent the test has consistency and stability when being used as an instrument (Salkind, 2015). In this study the reliability test was performed for each section in the survey. Additionally, the Cronbach's Alpha test is used to test the reliability and internal consistency of the survey. The acceptable value of Alpha is ranged from 0.70 to 0.95 (Tavacol and Dennick, 2011).

The descriptive statistics is carried out to assess the importance of the main factors in an audit engagement and the results is as follows:

Table 1: Descriptive statistics

Factors	Mean	Standard Deviation
Quality Auditor report	3.68	0.41
Audit planning	2.479	0.489
Audit risk	1.775	0.428
Audit evidence	2.345	0.525
Going concern	1.928	0.433
Key audit matters	2.029	0.477

For factor quality auditor's report, the mean of 3.68 indicates that the respondents tend to agree to the aspect of having a quality auditor's report. With the low standard deviation, it can be said that the majority of the means are close to this value. This represents that there is prevailing quality in auditor's report in the survey. As indicated above, most respondents agreed in this section that COVID-19 has an impact on audit planning as the mean is 2.479. The low standard deviation denotes that the majority of the responses were close to the mean. Judging from this and the general agreement percentages in the Tab. 1, it can be said that the respondents agreed that the COVID-19 has affected the audit plan. Audit risk brought more agreement with a mean of 1.775 and a standard deviation of 0.428. The low standard deviation denotes that the majority of the responses were close to the mean This shows that the majority of the respondents have agreed that COVID-19 has brought additional risk in the audit firms than usual which need to be identified properly. The respondents reveal that the effects of COVID-19 have caused difficulties in obtaining audit evidence by the overall agreement percentage of this factor. This is shown by the mean of 2.345 and standard deviation of 0.525 and the overall agreement percentages for this factor. The low standard deviation denotes that the majority of the responses were close to the mean. There is an overall agreement percentage. The mean of 1.928 indicates that majority of the respondents have agreed on this factor. The low standard deviation shows that most of the mean are close to this value. Judging from this, it can be generalized that in times of COVID-19 the assessment of going concern needs to be performed more than usual.

The overall agreement percentages for KAM indicates that the during the unprecedented situation, it is important to put emphasis on the key aspects as it increases in the pandemic. This is shown by a mean of 2.029 and standard deviation of 0.477. The low standard deviation denotes that many of the responses were close to the mean.

V. Factor analysis

Factor analysis aimed at shortening a large group of variables into a smaller, more controllable and concise set of 'components' (William et al., 2012).

Component	Rotated Component Matrix – Audit Planning	Factor Loadings
Higher Risk	Audit plan has altered in times of COVID-19 thus, reassessing the risk is paramount	0.825
	Audit plan has changed leading to the possibility of fraud and error and the control environment of the client needs to be reassessed	0.714
	Due to the pandemic the audit process has changed whereby the risk of fraud arises.	0.698
	Due to the COVID-19 outbreak, the existing audit plans are no longer represent the risk profile of an entity	0.668
Readjustment of Audit Plan	Auditors are required to plan the audit of the financial statement and make any modification such as recreate the audit plan due to remote working	0.977

Table 2: Rotated component matrix (audit planning)

This section contained 10 statements with the KMO of 0.720 (>0.5) and for Bartlett Test, the significant value is 0.000. For audit planning two constructs are required as Table 15 shows there were two components with eigenvalues greater than 1. They were then rotated by the Varimax method which are displayed in Table 15 and 16.

Using Kaiser's (1960) criterion, two factors with a total variance explained was accounted for 48.786 % as shown in Table 15. It implies that the factors account for 48.786 % of the variance in the data with the possibilities to forecast the data.

The extraction of factors resulted in two factors as shown in Table 16 the different statements had to be classified into two distinct factors. The Rotated Component Matrix was used to rotate the variables in order to know which statements were loading onto which factor. Due to factor loading less than 0.5, five statements were disregarded. The end results proposed the two factors namely which are higher risk and readjustment of audit plan.

Component	Items (Statements)	Factor Loadings
Additional Risk of material Misstatement	Additional risks of material misstatement that were not recognized by the auditor previously have arisen due to the pandemic	0.797
	To identify and assess the risks of additional material misstatement affected by the pandemic, auditors need to understand the company's performance measure	0.769
	To identify and assess the risks of additional material misstatement affected by COVID-19, auditors need to read publicly available information about the expected risks of the client's firm	0.64
Reassessment of Risk	Auditors are required to identify and reassess the risks of material misstatement in the pandemic.	0.899
	Auditors are required to revisit their risk assessment and the proposed response to identified risks due to the impact of the COVID-19	0.845

Table 3: Rotated component matrix (audit risk)

Audit risk section comprises of 10 statements with KMO 0.853 (>0.5) and the Bartlett's Test has a value of 0.000 statistical significance. There are two components whose eigenvalues are greater than 1 as shown in Table 17 which means for audit risk two constructs were required. Then, the Varimax method was used for rotation and the results are shown in the Tabs. 2 and 3.

For this section, 5 out of 10 statements have been extracted by the EFA and classified into two distinct factors. According to Kaiser (1960), two factors have to be retained with a total variance explained of 65.989 % as shown in Table 17. Thus, implying that 65.989 % of the data can be forecasted by using the factors. The five statements were allocated to its specific factor by subjecting variables to a rotation as demonstrated in Table 18. Moreover, it should be noted that five statements were dropped due to factor loading less than 0.5 which leads to two factors namely: Additional risk of material misstatement and Reassessment of risk.

Rotated Component Matrix – Audit Evidence		
Component	Items (Statements)	Factor Loadings
Stocktakes	In this unforeseen situation, one of the most concerning issue that is impairing auditor's report has been stocktakes	0.757
	Many companies have been unable to hold the end of year stock counts	0.863
	Auditors cannot attend the stocktakes due to lockdown as required by auditing standard	0.79
	The opinion of auditor is influenced by the evolving and challenging environment of COVID-19	0.7
	The gathering of sufficient and appropriate audit evidence need to change and alternative procedures need to develop	0.561
Remote Working	Due to the COVID-19 pandemic, the reliability of the auditor's report is reduced due to lack of audit evidences	0.93
	The sufficiency and reliability of audit evidences are affected as audit works are fully remote	0.872

Table 4: Rotated component matrix (audit evidence)

This section contained 10 statements with the KMO of 0.770 (>0.5) and the Bartlett Test, the significant value is 0.000. For audit planning two constructs are required as Table 19 shows there were two components with eigenvalues greater than 1. Then, they were rotated by the Varimax method. The results are shown in the Tab. 4.

For audit evidence, 7 out of 10 statements have been extracted by the EFA. As per Kaiser (1960), the two underlying factors must be retained with a total variance of 64.345 % in the data with the first order factors explaining more of the variance than the others.

The section has more than one component therefore, the rotated variance matrix was used to classify the statements according to their respective components. While running the EFA, some statements had to be disregarded as their loading factor was less than 0.5 thereby, leading to two factors namely stock takes and remote working.

Rotated Component Matrix – Assessment on Going Concern		
Component	Items (Statements)	Factor Loadings
Business Risks	Business risks are having an impact on the completion of the going concern assessment significantly	0.814
	The audit reports are being issued with uncertainties during the COVID-19 crisis as the continuity of company are in doubt due to the economic crisis for audit clients	0.75
	Due to the COVID-19 crisis, companies are facing many business risks such as liquidity crunch	0.677
Requirement of Sufficient Evidence	In times of COVID-19, when conducting the ongoing concern assessment, auditors must be more sceptical as well as the working documents are required to show evidence of scepticism	0.856
	Due to the pandemic, auditors are required to reassess the entity's ability to continue as a going concern and perform the evaluation again by collecting sufficient evidences and it is expected to be more extensive	0.795

Table 5: Rotated component matrix (assessment on going concern)

Assessment on going concern section, has 10 statements with the KMO of 0.729 (>0.5) and the Bartlett's Test has a value of 0.000 statistical significance. This section required two constructs as demonstrated in Table 20 and it shows there were two components with eigenvalues greater than 1. Then, they were rotated using the Varimax method. The results are shown in the Tab. 5.

For this section, 5 out of 10 statements have been extracted by the EFA. As per Kaiser (1960), the two factors account for 63.113 % variance in the data and hence can be used to predict 63.113 % of the data. The total variance explained table showed a result of more than 1 component therefore, the rotated component variance matrix classified the statements according to each appropriate factor. To show which statement were loading onto which factor, it was necessary for the variables to be rotated. In addition, some statements were dropped due to their loading factor were less than 0.5 and the other statements were categorized into two factors namely business risk and requirement of sufficient evidence.

Rotated Component Matrix – Key Audit Matter		
Components	Items (Statements)	Factor Loadings
Identify Key Aspects	Auditors need to reassess the key aspects in the audit due to the fast changing situation	0.868
	Recognising the key aspects will take place right up to the point of signing the auditor's report	0.689
	In times of COVID-19 outbreak, more focus is necessary to determine the KAM reported in the auditor's report as the situations have altered and difficulties have arisen	0.798
Specific Events	KAM is being affected by the inability to obtain sufficient appropriate audit evidence due to unusual events.	0.895
	KAM is being affected by specific events for example events that affect the financial statements differently that is new, unusual or once-off transactions	0.798

Table 6: Rotated component matrix (key audit matter)

This section has 10 statements with the KMO of 0.765 (>0.5) and for Bartlett's Test, the significant value is 0.00. For KAM two constructs are required because there are two components with eigenvalues greater than 1 as shown in table 23. They were then rotated using the Varimax method. The results obtained are displayed in table 23 and table 24.

As per Kaiser (1960), the total variance of the two factors retained is 69.811 % as detailed in table 21. It implies that the factors account for 69.811 % of the variance in the data hence forecasting 69.111 % of the data. The total variance explained table showed a result of two components thus, the rotated component variance matrix was used to classify the statements according to each appropriate factor as shown in table 24 whereby, five statements were classified into two distinct factors. It must be noted that, the other five statements were disregarded as their factor loading were less than 0.5. The end results proposed two factors namely: Identify key aspects and specific Events.

VI. Hypothesis testing

H_0: COVID-19 has not influenced audit planning.
H_1: COVID-19 has influenced audit planning.

There is a weak positive correlation between COVID-19 and audit planning as the p-value is less than 0.5 (P < 0.5) which rejects H_0 and accept H_1. Thus, indicates that COVID-19 has a positive influenced on audit planning. It can be said that audit plans are increased during the current pandemic due to the possibilities of fraud, the level of risk is paramount and even fail to operate as planned. This finding supports the study of IFAC (2020).

H_0: COVID-19 has not influenced audit risk.
H_1: COVID-19 has influenced audit risk.

This finding supports H_1 showing that COVID-19 has a weak positive influenced the audit risk as the p-value is less than 0.5. There is a positive correlation between the two variables exist as entities must revisit the risk assessment and risk of material misstatements in times of COVID-19. The audit risk is therefore increased in this unprecedented situation. This finding is in favour of the study conducted by FRC (2020).

H_0: COVID-19 has not influenced audit evidence.
H_1: COVID-19 has influenced audit evidence.

The analysis reveals a weak negative correlation between COVID-19 and audit evidence as the p-value is less than 0.05. This rejects H_0 and accepts H_1. This implies that COVID-19 has a negative impact on the audit evidence. It is justified by the fact that stocktakes cannot be carried out due to COVID-19. Thus, the gathering of sufficient appropriate audit evidence is unable to obtained due to lockdown which shows a negative correlation between the two variables. This finding goes in line with the study of PWC (2020a).

H_0: COVID-19 has not influenced the assessment on going concern.
H_1: COVID-19 has influenced the assessment on going concern.

In the table above, the p-value is less than 0.5 (P< 0.5) indicating that there is a weak positive relationship between the two variables. This finding accepts H_1 whereby the COVID-19 influences the assessment on going concern. As shown in the hypothesis, it has been affected the most. This can be explained that, in times of COVID-19 entities face difficulties to continue as a going concern due business risks and usual events are occurred. Therefore, the assessment of going concern is predominant and this finding supports KPMG (2020).

H_0: COVID-19 has not influenced the key audit matter

H_1: COVID-19 has influenced the key audit matter.

In this finding, there is no correlation between COVID-19 and KAM as the p-value exceeds 0.05 (0.558). This rejects H_1 and supports H_0 that is, COVID-19 has not influenced the KAM. In the study, it was found that KAMs are expected to rise due to the unprecedented situations of COVID-19. However, the finding suggests KAM was not found to be a significant factor that has been affected by the COVID-19 contradicting PWC (2020a). This may be explained as per ICAEW (2021), that the pandemic is not expected to be widespread in the auditor's report because this will occur only when the matter is said to be 'fundamental'. Otherwise, the widespread use of the emphasis of matter paragraph might decrease the efficacy and usefulness of the auditor's communication regarding essential matter.

Conclusions

The effect of COVID-19 is the current toughest challenge being faced by the auditors since the GFC. Following this exogenous shock, this paper attempts to explicate the effects of COVID-19 on the quality of auditor's report. As a result of this pandemic, it is expected to see failure or amendments of the audit plan, increase of the audit risk, unable to gather the necessary audit evidence, inability of the firms to continue as a going concern and the number of key audit matter is expected to rise which in turn influences the quality of the auditor's report.

As a result of the findings, the descriptive statistics indicates that the respondents have overall agreed that the pandemic has affected the audit report. To make the analysis more precise, the EFA was then conducted. The findings in the EFA revealed the multidimensional character of all the variables by extracting the dimensions that were in accordance with the literature. The hypotheses were used to conclude which factor has been influenced the most and it was found that the assessment on going concern required the most attention in the pandemic and follows by audit risk, audit evidence and audit planning.

Additionally, the findings of this research are a reflection of what has been postulated in the literature review. First and foremost, it was mentioned in the literature that audit planning has affected due to the unprecedented situation of COVID-19 because, audit plan does not represent the risk profile of an entity (Movchanc, 2020). It must be reviewed and modified (Divilly, 2020) and it is unable to carry out effectively. This was shown in the findings as it had a significant positive relationship with COVID-19. During the pandemic, more audit plan must be implemented. As extracted by the EFA, higher risks and adjustments of the audit plan are required. Moreover, audit risk has affected in times of COVID-19 as the degree of uncertainties are heightened in terms of business performance and economic conditions are more complex to determine (ACCA, 2020). It was supported in the finding as audit risk and COVID-19 has a positive significant relationship. During the pandemic audit risks are higher. The factor extracted by the EFA are additional risk of material misstatement and reassessment of risk. In addition, in the literature it was also mentioned that another issue facing by the auditors is the inability to gather sufficient appropriate audit evidence. The major issue in the pandemic has been stocktakes (PWC, 2020a) which reduces the reliability of the auditor's report (Baskan, 2020). In the findings, audit evidence has a significant negative correlation with COVID-19 as the level of audit evidence is affected during the pandemic and are unable to obtain. Thus, this finding again supports the study. The two important factors are stocktakes and remote working as extracted by the EFA. Furthermore, the assessment of going concern has been discussed in the literature. Auditors must reassess the entity's ability to continue as a going concern in times of COVID-19 (IAASB, 2020). In the pandemic, sales have reduced drastically for most businesses which cause doubt about the company's ability to proceed as a going concern (KPMG, 2020) and there is lack of audit evidences (IRBA, 2020). The finding supports this study as the assessment on going concern has a significant positive relationship with COVID-19 as the pandemic has affected the going concern basis. The two significant factors extracted from the EFA business risk and requirement of sufficient evidence. Any events or conditions exist that can cause significant doubt on the entity's ability to continue as a going concern, the auditors should consider whether to include a separate section known as the '*Material Uncertainty Related to Going Concern*' in the auditor's report. However, the KAM was not found to be a significant factor that has been affected by the COVID-19 which contradicts PWC (2020a) which stated the number of KAM are increased. This is reasonable as the unprecedented situation caused in times of COVID-19 is not expected to be widespread in the auditor's report because this will occur only when the matter is said to be 'fundamental'. Otherwise, the widespread use of the emphasis of matter paragraph might decrease the efficacy and usefulness of the auditor's communication regarding essential matter (ICAEW, 2021).

A. Limitations of the study

The principal limitation of this study was the gathering of data as it was performed only electronically due to lockdown. It was difficult to find willing respondents to fill in the questionnaire. The participants have busy schedules which means that time constraint was also an issue. Unfortunately, the sample size was restricted and less representative which brings out concerns toward the generalizability of the findings. Due to quantitative research, the research restricts the respondent's point of view and certain information are omitted.

B. Scope for future research

The COVID-19 is a major concerning issue that is affecting the quality of the auditor's report. Therefore, a full empirical study can be conducted on the effects of COVID-19 on each of the factors mentioned in this research which are audit planning, audit risk, audit evidence, assessment on going concern and KAM as each factor is vast. Investigating in each factor individually would be more specific and precise. The research could examine how and why the outbreak is being affected in the COVID-19 crisis in further details. These questions have to be investigated in detail in the future due to their practical implications.

Bibliography

Abdullah et al. 2015. 'Transparency and reliability in financial statement: Do they exist? Evidence from Malaysia.' Open Journal of Accounting, [online], 4(04), 49 Available from: https://file.scirp.org/pdf/OJAcct_201511270 9585892.pdf

Arthur et al. 2015. 'Corporate accruals quality during the 2008–2010 Global Financial Crisis.' Journal of International Accounting, Auditing and Taxation, 25, 1–15.

Baskan. 2020. 'Analysing the going concern uncertainty during the period of COVID-19 pandemic in terms of independent auditor's reports'. ISPEC International Journal of Social Sciences & Humanities, 4(2), 28–42.

Çagiran and Varci. 2019. 'Key audit matters within the framework of Isa 701: An analysis on audit reports of companies listed in Bist Manufacturing Industry.' International Journal of Economics and Administrative Studies, 22, 193–208.

Divilly. 2020. 'Potential impact of Covid-19 on auditor reporting'. Accountancy Plus.

EY. 2015. 'Key audit matters: What they are and why they are important. [online] EY Building a better working world'. Available at: [Accessed 13 April 2021].

EY. 2020. 'Our commitment to audit quality Information for audit committees, investors and other stakeholders'. [online] assets.ey.com. Available at: https://assets.ey.com/content/dam/ey-sites/ey-com/en_us/topics/assurance/ey-2020-commitment-to-aqr-brochure.pdf

Financial Reporting Council. 2020. 'Guidance on audit issues arising from the Covid-19 (Coronavirus) pandemic'. Available at https://www.frc.org.uk/news-and-events/news/2020/03/guidance-on-audit-issues-arising-from-the-covid-19-coronavirus-pandemic/.

Gerged et al. 2020. 'Did corporate governance compliance have an impact on auditor selection and quality? Evidence from FTSE 350'. International Journal of Disclosure and Governance, 17(2), 15–60.

Goodell, W. J. (2020). 'COVID-19 and finance: Agendas for future research.' Finance Research Letters.

Gray et al. 2011. 'Perceptions and misperceptions regarding the unqualified auditor's report by financial statement preparers, users, and auditors.' Accounting Horizons, 25(4), 659–684.

Guiral et al. 2011. 'To what extent are auditors' attitudes toward the evidence influenced by the self-fulfilling prophecy?' Auditing: A Journal of Practice & Theory 30(1), 173–190.

IAASB. 2017. Handbook of International Quality Control, Auditing, Review, Other Assurance, and Related Services Pronouncements, 2016–2017 Edition, Volume I, available at https://www.ifac.org/system/files/publications/files/2016-2017-IAASB-Handbook-Volume-1.pdf

IAASB. 2020. 'Auditor reporting in the current evolving environment due to COVID-19.' Staff Audit Practice Alert May 2020, 32.

ICAEW (2021). How to report an emphasis of matter under COVID-19: A guide for auditors? [online] Available at: https://www.icaew.com/technical/audit-and-assurance/audit/reporting-and-completion/covid-19-how-to-report-anemphasis-of-matter-a-guide-for-auditors.

ICAP. 2020. 'The impact of COVID 19 on audit a guidance for auditors.' The Institute of Chartered Accountants of Pakistan. 34.

IFAC (2009). International Standards on Auditing (ISA) 7(Redrafted), 'Forming an Opinion and Audit Reporting on Financial Statements' (pp 1–30), Retrieved from http://www.ifac.org/sites/default/files/meetings/files/4075.pdf

KPMG. 2020. COVID-19: 'Potential impact on financial reporting.' Available from: https://home.kpmg/xx/en/home/insights/2020/03/covid-19-financial-reporting-resource-centre.html

PWC. 2020a. 'Likely impact of COVID-19 on audit reports.' The New Zealand member firm: PricewaterhouseCoopers (PWC).

PWC. 2020b. COVID-19: Responding to the business impacts of Coronavirus. Available from: https://www.pwc.com/gx/en/issues/crisis-solutions/covid-19.html

Salehi et al. 2020. 'A meta-analysis approach for determinants of effective factors on audit quality'. Journal of Accounting in Emerging Economies, 9(2), 287–312.

COVID-19 and new working conditions as the new normal: The domino effect – The Mauritian and African human rights comparative case study

Rajendra Parsad GUNPUTH[1] and Ambareen BEEBEEJAUN[2]

The COVID-19 pandemic disease has an impact on, inter alia, workers' rights to a fair remuneration. There were also risks of unemployment and workers becoming redundant provoking gender inequality in the labour market especially when the Mauritian legislator came up with new legislations and regulations. The Mauritian government and the Mauritian legislator started to pass new legislations as from 2019 to cater for new working conditions such as work from home with a 'domino effect' with infringements to the basic fundamental rights have been detected and reported on the media[3]. Indeed, individuals started to suffer from lockdown following the curfew and its spread among the population. Most human and fundamental rights were restricted like in most countries, worldwide.

La pandémie de COVID-19 a un impact, entre autres, sur les droits des travailleurs à une rémunération équitable. Il existe également des risques de chômage et de licenciements qui provoquent des inégalités entre les hommes et les femmes sur le marché du travail, en particulier lorsque le législateur mauricien propose de nouvelles législations et réglementations. Le gouvernement mauricien et le législateur mauricien ont commencé à adopter de nouvelles lois à partir de 2019 pour répondre aux nouvelles conditions de travail telles que le travail à domicile, avec un 'effet domino' et des violations des droits fondamentaux de base qui ont été détectées et rapportées dans les médias. En effet, les individus ont commencé à souffrir de l'enfermement à la suite du couvre-feu et

---

[1] Professor, University of Mauritius.
[2] Dr. Senior Lecturer, Department of Law, University of Mauritius.
[3] Mardemootoo, S., Balgobin-Bhoyrul, P., Kissoon, G., Guttoo, H., Tung, S. and Desai, J., 2020. The COVID-19 (Miscellaneous Provisions) Act of 2020 introduced by the Parliament of Mauritius – Amendments and their implications.

de sa propagation au sein de la population. La plupart des droits de l'homme et des droits fondamentaux ont été restreints comme dans la plupart des pays du monde.

Introduction

This contextualized paper deals with the actual situation in the small Republic of Mauritius with its approximately 1.3 million inhabitants. It also allows to better understand the latest trend in the development of new legislations and regulations (*infra*, Tab. 2) to protect workers, and it has signed and ratified practically most international and regional covenants to enhance human rights of all its individuals. However, the COVID-19 pandemic disease also started to impose new conditions of live and various limitations to human rights against the will of most individuals of the island.

As an illustration, like many countries, the small Republic of Mauritius, as a member of the United Nations Development Program (UNDP) is committed to the 17 Sustainable Development Goals (SDGs) which have been set up by the UNDP in order to 'protect the planet, to eradicate poverty and ensure that all people enjoy peace and prosperity' to be achieved by 2030.

To achieve these SDGs, the Mauritian legislator passed *The Equal Opportunities Act 2008*, The *Employment Relations Act 2008 (Act 32/2008)* and the recent *Workers' Rights Act 2019 (Act 20/2019)* to reduce inequality, to protect all workers against victimisation and discrimination[4] on the workplace[5]. The new *Workers' Rights Act 2019 (Act 20/2019)*[6] came into force and it also provides sufficient provisions to promote decent work and economic growth through sustained economic growth, higher levels of productivity and technological innovations as per the SDG 8. The Preamble of the *Equal Opportunities Act 2008* enacts that that act was passed to: 'Promote equal opportunity between persons,

---

[4] Section 31 of the Employment Relations Act 32 (Act 32/2008) provides for protection against discrimination and victimisation.

[5] Part II of The Workers' Rights Act 2019 (Act 20/2019) (sections 4–7) provides for "Measure against discrimination in employment and occupation".

[6] The Preamble of The Workers' Rights Act 2019 (Act 20/2019) provides that: "To provide a modern and comprehensive legislative framework for the protection of worker, and to provide for matters related thereto".

prohibit discrimination on the ground of status and by victimisation, establish a Commission and an Equal Opportunities Tribunal and for related matters'.

Chapter II of the Mauritian Constitution[7] (1968) provides for fundamental rights and most of these rights are inspired from the *Universal Declaration of Human Rights*, 1948 and the European Convention on Human Rights, 1950 and they are very useful to protect the constitutional rights of all individuals in Mauritius without exception (Tab. 1).

Table 1

		Constitution: Chapter II on Fundamental Rights (Sections 3–16)	
	Sections	Human Rights	Precedents
3	Section 3	Right to life and Right to personal liberty	
4	Section 4	Right to life	
5	Section 5	Right to personal liberty, right to be informed of the reasons for one's arrest or detention (5(2)); right, after arrest or upon being detained, to be afforded reasonable time facilities to consult a legal representative of one's own choice (section 5(3)); right, after being arrested or detained, to be brought without undue delay before a Court of law (section 5(3))	
6	Section 6	*Protection from slavery and forced labour*	
7	Section 7	*Protection from inhuman treatment*	
8	Section 8	*Protection from deprivation of property*	
9	Section 9	Right to privacy of home and other property	Retreaders Ltd v Marie 1989 MR 272
10	Section 10	Right to a fair hearing (section 10(1)), right to be tried by an independent and impartial court (section 10(1)), right to be tried by a court established by law (section 10(1)),	

Continued

---

[7] Chapter II of the Mauritian Constitution 1968 (sections 3–16) provides for fundamental rights to all individuals in Mauritius.

Table 1 Continued

right to be considered innocent until proved guilty (section 10(2)(a)), right to be informed, as soon as reasonably practicable, in a language which he understands and in detail, of the nature of the offence(section 10(2)(b)), right to be given adequate time and facilities for the preparation of his defense (section 10(2)(c)), right of the person charged to defend himself in person (section 10(2)(d)), right to defend himself at his own expense, by a legal representative of his own choice (section 10(2)(d)), right to defend himself, where so prescribed, by a legal representative provided at the public expense (section 10(2)(d)); right to be afforded facilities to examine, in person or by his legal representative, the witnesses called by the prosecution before nay court (section 10(2)(e)); right to obtain the attendance and carry out the examination of witnesses to testify on his behalf before the court on the same conditions as those applying to witnesses called by the prosecution (section 10(2)); right to have without payment the assistance of an interpreter if he cannot understand the language used at the trial of the offence (section 10(2)(f)); right to be present at his trial (section 10(2)); right to obtain within a reasonable time after judgement, upon payment of any reasonable fee prescribed by legislation, a copy of the court record (section 10(3)), right to be judged only in accordance with the substantive criminal law in force at the time of the offence (section 10(4)), right after a conviction or acquittal not to be tried a second time for the same offence except where a re-trial is ordered by a court of appeal or review; right not to be tried for a criminal offence where a pardon has been granted, by the competent authority, for that offence (section 10(6)); right not to be compelled to give evidence at the trial (section 10(7))	P. Boolell v The state 2006 UKPC 46 (PC Appeal no 39 of 2005)- appeal was allowed because the accused was not tried within a reasonable time Babet v The Queen 1979 MR 222-right to a fair hearing. François v The Queen 1975 MR 236-right to be given adequate time and facilities for the preparation of his defence. R v Boyjoo 1991 MR 84-right to defend himself

Table 1 Continued

11	Section 11	Protection of freedom of conscience	
12	Section 12	Freedom of expression	Cie de Beau Vallon Ltd v Nilkomol 1979 MR 254
13	Section 13	Freedom of association and assembly	Young, James and Webster v UK 1981 IRLR 408 Wilson v UK and Palmer v UK 2002 35 EHRR 20
14	Section 14	Protection of freedom to establish schools	
15	Section 15	Protection of freedom of movement	
16	Section 16	Right not to be discriminated against a person on account of race, caste, place of origin, political opinion, colour, creed or sex	Singh v Rowntree Mackintosh 1979 IRLR 199 Kaur v Butcher & Baker Foods Ltd 1997 1304563/97

Soon, trade unions[8] were created with political parties and some federations as well. And all Mauritians enjoy a free and fair election explaining the political stability of the island, foreign investors started to invest in Mauritius coupled with foreign direct investments from India, China, South Africa, UK and other great nations of the world through the Double Taxation Avoidance Agreement (DTAA). The sugar price fell down and Sir Aneerood Jugnauth started to build a new nation more focused on modern technology and the island became a republic on the 12th March 1992. It remains very active in terms of regional development and became a member of regional blocks (COMESA, SADC of the IORA) and also became a steppingstone for China and India to invest in Africa. Because of its sudden socio-economic development, the Mauritian legislator started to pass Bills and Acts of Parliament, based on the Westminster Model, for the welfare of all workers in Mauritius and they saw the promulgation of the *Workmen's Compensation Act 1931*, *Labour Act 1975*, *Industrial Relations Act 1976*, *Export Processing Zone Act* or the *Industrial Expansion Act*. Some of them were repealed and replaced by new legislations to cope

---

[8] The Industrial Relations Act 1976 was repealed, and *The Employment Relations Act 2008* came into force.

with a more modern island with the passing of the *Employment Rights Act 2008 (Act 38/2008)*, the *Employment Relations Act 2008 (Act 32/2008), OSHA 2005* and these legislations are constantly amended to be in line with the requirements and needs of the population as Mauritius became a centre for export, import, doing business, commerce and trade attracting foreign workers to work in its industries and factories with export of textile to the USA under the African Growth and Opportunity Act (AGOA).

However, though the COVID-19 pandemic disease is under control in Mauritius, it has, nevertheless, impacted very negatively on the workers' rights in various ways through quarantine, lockdowns, restrictions on movement, personal liberty, and freedom of expression and freedom of association and assembly just to name a few[9]. For the first time and inadvertently workers started to discover new legislations and regulations such as *The Prevention and Mitigation of Infectious Disease Coronavirus Regulations 2020*, which imposed a curfew order of 21 days to contain the spread of the Coronavirus-19 pandemic disease in Mauritius, and any breach would entail any person to a term of imprisonment of a maximum term of 6 months and a fine (Rs 500,000).

At the very outset, it is important to know that the COVID-19 pandemic disease is certainly not an Act of God[10] (*cas de force majeure*[11]), and that their various obligations and implied duties[12] on both an employee and an employer irrespective of whether workers are working on their workplace or at home. Both should be of good faith, that any worker is fit to work and the employer must provide work and remuneration to them though he/she may be facing financial difficulties especially during lockdown and confinement[13], the Supreme Court held in the case of *Ismael v Jay Fashions Co. Ltd v 1988 SCJ 497*, where it was held that: 'The issue arose as to whether an employer who claimed that he could not

---

[9] Sutherland, E., 2020. Coronavirus Overview of the impacts of the lockdown, Publications – Eversheds Sutherland.

[10] Potayya, S., 2021. An analysis of force majeure in the context of Mauritian banking law.

[11] Richard, N. and Ribet, A., 2020. COVID-19 and its impact on contractual performance in Mauritius – Force Majeure, DLA Piper Africa, Mauritius, Juristconsult Chambers.

[12] Mauritius has still retained the English Common Law and its procedure also follows the English law of Evidence as *per* section 162 of the Courts Act 1945.

[13] Dentons.com. 2020. "Force Majeure" and Coronavirus (COVID-19) under the Laws of Mauritius –What is Force Majeure?

provide to his workers on the ground of financial difficulties leading to the closing of the company, albeit temporarily, could avail himself of this ground to justify the termination of his worker's employment. It was held that the dismissal of workers in the above circumstances was unjustified'.

The author would rely on new legislations and regulations passed recently by the Mauritian legislator to demonstrate that the spreading of the COVID-19 pandemic disease has a 'domino effect' on all sectors of the socio-economic development of the small island of Mauritius but the article is more focused on human right issues in a comparative approach. In order to demonstrate the same, the structure of this paper is to understand how the Republic of Mauritius reacted when new legislations and regulations were passed: after an Introduction (I), there is a literature review of the subject matter (II), COVID-19 and The New Working Conditions Under New Legislations: The Mauritian Legal and Institutional Framework (III), The Impact of The COVID-19 on The Workers' Rights To Health and Safety Measures (IV), the Impact of The COVID-19 on The Workers' Rights: The Socio-Economic Impact (V) and this article will close with a list of references (IV) to enhance further research in this emerging field of the law.

I. Literature review

As far as literature review is concerned on the impact of the COVID-19 on the Mauritius economy and the impact of new legislations and regulations, there are already a very wide and important data which have been reported by, *inter alia*, the Wealth Health Organization (WHO), the World Bank Household Survey Report, the Socio-Economic Impact Assessment of COVID-19 in Mauritius, the International Labour Organisation (ILO[14]) has also published its ILO Standards and COVID-19 (Coronavirus), Business Mauritius Report[15], Afrasiabank[16], KPMG and Rogers Capital[17], and Central Statistics Mauritius, and therefore it is

---

[14] *International Labour Organisation.* (n.d.). Retrieved from https://www.ilo.org/global/about-the-ilo/newsroom/news/WCMS_742203/lang--en/index.htm

[15] PLCJ. 2020. *COVID-19(Mauritius): Can companies suspend the payment of commercial rents?.*

[16] *Afrasia Bank.* (2020, April 17).

[17] *Rogers Capital.* (n.d.). Retrieved from https://www.rogerscapital.mu/9135/key-measures-by-the-government-to-sustain-the-mauritian-economy-amidst-covid-19

important to make a study to know how some legislations and covenants in the small Republic of Mauritius have played an important role in their participation by giving a legal blow to contain the COVID-19 pandemic disease. Various firms, local and international, have also published research they have undertaken to better understand the impact of the COVID-19 disease on workers' rights in small and medium enterprises, large enterprises and companies: the British firm Burges and Salmon have published the COVID-19 Burges And Salmon's Commitments to Client Service (burges-salmon.com), and in practically the same lien the University of Cambridge Press on its article on COVID-19: Resting the limits of Human Rights. However, the aims and objectives of this paper are to fulfil in some loopholes with regard to legislations and regulations, and its implementation and to what extent human rights are affected at their workplace.

II. COVID-19 and the new working conditions under new legislations: The Mauritian legal and institutional framework

This paper, on the Mauritian legislations and regulations with a view to deal a legal blow against the propagation of the COVID-19 pandemic disease on the small island, reflects to what extent the COVID-19 pandemic disease had exacerbated unemployment and various forms of crisis and abuses, as explained, on the small island State when the Mauritian government passed various legislations and regulations such as, *inter alia*, *The COVID-19 (Miscellaneous Provisions) Act 2020, The Prevention and Mitigation of Infectious Disease Coronavirus Regulations 2020, The Public Health (COVID-19 Vaccines for Emergency Use) Regulations 2021, The Quarantine Act 2020, The Quarantine (COVID-19) Amendment Regulations 2021, The Work from Home Regulations 2020, The Worker's Rights (Additional Remuneration) 2021 Regulations 2021, The Worker's Rights (Payment of Special Allowance 2021) Regulations 2021 or The Workers' Rights (Extension of Time During COVID-19 Period) Regulations 2020* coupled with various schemes and communiqués sent by the government in place such as The Government Wage Assistance Scheme or The Self-Employed Assistance Scheme.

Table 2

The Mauritian Legislations and Its Adaptability on Some Human Rights Issues

1	The COVID-19 (Miscellaneous Provisions) Act 2020	16	The Government Wage Assistance Scheme
2	The Prevention and Mitigation of Infectious Disease Coronavirus Regulations 2020	17	The Self-Employed Assistance Scheme.
3	The Public Health (COVID-19 Vaccines for Emergency Use) Regulations 2021	18	The Additional Remuneration and Other Allowances (2019) Regulations 2019
4	The Quarantine Act 2020	19	Constitution of Mauritius 1968
5	The Quarantine (COVID-19) Amendment Regulations 2021	20	The Employment Relations Act 2008 (Act 32/2008)
6	The Work from Home Regulations 2020	21	The Employment Relations (Amendment) Act 2019
7	The Worker's Rights (Additional Remuneration) 2021 Regulations 2021	22	The Equal Opportunities Act 2008
8	The Workers' Rights (Extension of Time During COVID-19 Period) Regulations 2020	23	The Industrial Relations Act 1973 (repealed)
9	The Industrial Court Act 1973	24	The Workers' Rights 2019 (Act 20/2019)
10	The Occupational Safety Health and Welfare Act 1988	25	The Occupational Safety and Health Act 2005
11	The End of Year Gratuity Act 2001	26	Public Bodies Appeal Tribunal Act 2010
12	Public Service Commission (PSC) Act	27	The Protection of Human Rights Act
13	The Registration of Association Act 1979	28	The Workers' Rights (Payment of Special Allowance 2021) Regulations 2020
14	The Public Health Act 1925	29	The Workers' Rights (Extension of Time during COVID-19 Period) Regulations 2020
15	The Code Civil Mauricien, The Code de Commerce Mauricien and the Code Pénal	30	The Public Gathering Act

In addition, the Republic of Mauritius has signed and ratified most international conventions, treaties and protocols on human rights and with a view to protect its citizens against forced labour (*Forced Labour Convention 1930*), and other international covenants such as, *inter alia, The Universal Declaration of Human Rights 1948, The International Covenants on Civil and Political Rights* or *The International Covenant on Economic, Social and Political Rights*. It is also a member of the International Labour Organisation. However, most citizens in Mauritius, just like all citizens in Africa or elsewhere found themselves face to face with a new pandemic disease and new working conditions when *The Quarantine Act 2020* and *The Work from Home Regulations 2020* were passed causing certain disruptions, chaos, frictions and disorder among workers and employees because these new conditions and modalities on working conditions were imposed suddenly to enhance health and precautionary measures on one side and socio-economic effects on the other side.

Table 3

The Mauritian International Covenants and Its Adaptability on Some Human Rights Issues			
1	*The Universal Declaration on Human Rights 1948*	4	*The International Covenants on Economic, Social and Cultural Rights (ICESR)*
2	*The International Covenant on Economic, Social and Political Rights (ICCPR)*	5	ILO Conventions
3	*Forced Labour Convention, 1930 (No. 29) and its 2014 Protocol*	6	*European Convention on Human Rights 1950*

Indeed, the Mauritian written Constitution 1968 (*supra*) is colonial law, as the supreme law of the island, which Mauritius inherited during the British colonisation (1810–1968) but it has also a very strong hybrid law with English Common Law and French Civil Law when, again, Mauritius was under French colonisation (1715–1810) where the French Code Napoléon 1804 was imposed on the inhabitants of the small island coupled with the French Code de Commerce and the French Code Pénal such that, actually, the Mauritian legislator is still borrowing and inspiring from legislations and precedents from England, and France from the French *Cour de Cassation*. Therefore, in addition to legislations passed by Parliament, there are *The Workers' Rights 2019 (Act 20/2019)* and *The Employment Relations Act 2008 (Act 32/2008)* which have been inspired from English law, legislations and regulations among which important employment legislations such as *The Equal Opportunities Act 2008, The Occupational Safety Health and Welfare Act 1988* was repealed and replaced actually by *The Occupational Safety and Health Act 2005* or *The End of Year Gratuity Act 2001* to be in line with the government policies to combat the COVID-19 pandemic disease. *The COVID-19 (Miscellaneous Provisions) Act 2020* amended a broad array of 56 existing public health parameters in order to be line with the government policies.

And when Mauritius has signed and ratified The International Labour Convention it has also implemented various conventions, collective agreements, Remuneration Orders and trade union law inspired from the English Employment law with various courts in case of violation of worker's rights in all its forms such that any citizen living in Mauritius may have recourse to various instances; ranging from appeals, injunctions and judicial review (based on UK injunctions and UK Order 53); with its relevant jurisdiction, such as the Industrial Court (*The Industrial Court Act 1973*), the Employment Relations Tribunal (*The Employment Relations Act 2008*) to hear industrial disputes, the Public Bodies Appeal Tribunal (*Public Bodies Appeal Tribunal Act 2010*) to hear grievances from public officers, and the Supreme Court (*The Constitution, 1968*) as the highest court with unlimited jurisdictions in both civil and criminal proceedings. In addition, there are various boards and commissions to cater for any violation of human rights on the workplace and they comprise of, *inter alia*, the Commission, Conciliation and Mediation (CCM), the Public Service Commission (PSC) which is empowered to impose disciplinary measures against public officers as *The Public Service Commission Act*, the National Remuneration Board (NRB), the Human Rights Commission (HRC) or the Equal Opportunity Commission and they empowered to advise, guide or protect workers and employees as per the different legislations and regulations in place in case of abuses in all its forms and strong violations of workers' rights on the workplace.

And when the *Workers' Rights Act 2019* came into force recently, the aims and objectives of the Mauritian legislator were to protect all workers and employees in Mauritius against discrimination, to provide equal remuneration for equal work; protection against unjustified, wrongful, unfair, constructive dismissal including redundancy, right to be heard before a disciplinary committee, right to be represented by any legal representative of one's choice and a member of one's trade union, right to leaves[18], various forms of agreements or right to a workfare

---

[18] Sections 45–53 of *The Workers' Rights 2019 (Act 2019) for* different types of leaves ranging from annual leave, sick leave, vacation leave, special leave, juror's leave, leave to participate in international sport event and leave to attend Court.

programme[19]. All these rights are of course in string compliance with Chapter II of the Constitution 1968, which contains various provisions on fundamental rights, and which have been inspired from *The Universal Declaration on Human Rights 1948*.

When the World Health Organisation (WHO) proclaimed a public international health emergency worldwide the Government of Mauritius, just like most countries of the world, imposed a lockdown period but the citizens in Mauritius had face to several restrictions related to, inter alia, human rights and freedom of movement and liberty, sanitary confinement or work from home (WFH) but in the overall economic and employment activities on the small island got a severe legal blow with the sudden and unexpected closure of all activities and important sectors of the country (public hospitals, airports, education or the tourism sector) save for some essential services in case of a national acute crisis where COVID-19 cases were reported.

There were several confinement, deconfinement; several lockdown and resumption of activities were allowed with new regulations imposed by the Mauritian government to restrictions of liberty of the individuals on the small island despite The Temporary Restriction of Movement Order and consequently these new legislations, regulations, 'communiqués' and orders heavily impacted on the worker's rights; restrictions and limitations to access to workplace and information, limitations on their right to work, right to health and safety, right to entitlement to leaves, labour gender inequality, discrimination, unfair treatment, risk to redundancy without any compensation such that all these pertinent issues compromise directly on all fundamental and constitutional rights of all individuals in Mauritius when all local courts were closed, legal advisors were not available due to confinement, and over and above other important rights such as, *inter alia*, right to privacy, right to the security of the individual, right to life, freedom of movement, freedom of association and assembly, right to be tried before an impartial court within a reasonable time, or right to protection from discrimination were jeopardized. Therefore, workers and employees in Mauritius found themselves in new conditions of work when *The Work from Home Regulations 2020* was passed coupled with various 'communiques' and workplace preparedness plan were both

---

[19] Part VII of *The Workers' Rights 2019 (Act 2019)* provides for a workfare programme fund where an employment may join for financial assistance and social aid from the government.

set up and passed promptly to stop the propagation of the COVID-19 pandemic disease on the island.

Nevertheless, there were complaints from civil societies, front liners and other human rights fighters who advocated for the protection of workers, and that their rights should be maintained because all human beings are born free and equal in dignity and rights, and second during the curfew workers and employees became redundant especially in the tourism and airport sectors despite the Republic of Mauritius has signed and ratified the ILO Conventions on workers' rights, which in turn set the ILO Declarations on Fundamental Principles and Rights at Work and which consists of eight fundamental conventions (Tab. 4).

Table 4

	ILO Declarations on Fundamental Principles and Rights at Work		
1	Forced Labour Convention, 1930 (No. 29) and its 2014 Protocol	5	Abolition of Forced Labour Convention, 1957 (No.105)
2	Freedom of Association and Protection of the Right to Organise Convention, 1948 (No.87)	6	Discrimination (Employment and Occupation) Convention, 1958 (No.111)
3	Right to Organise and Collective Bargaining Convention, 1949 (No.98)	7	Minimum Age Convention, 1973 (No.138)
4	Equal Remuneration Convention, 1951 (No.100)	8	Worst Forms of Child Labour Convention, 1999 (No.182)

In addition to legislations, which are very often amended, repealed or both; these new legislation and regulations (*supra*) were passed by the Mauritian legislation before Parliament, some loopholes were felt in our system because for any employment relationship it is crucial for a worker to enter into an agreement but the Mauritian law is not clear at all when a contract of employment is in issue, and there is no enactment about the definition of a 'contract of employment' *per se*, and our law and legislations provide for 'workers' save for some few exceptions such as *The National Pensions Act 1976* and *The Occupational Safety and Health Act 2005*, which provide for the term 'employee'. As explained (*supra*), Mauritian is a hybrid law and based on French civil law, there is no proper definition of a contract of employment. Section 2 of *The Worker's Rights Act 2019 (Act 20/2019)* enacts that an agreement is a contract of employment which may be oral or verbal, expressed or implied, and based on French Civil law it is *un 'acte consensuel'* which may be agreed upon even orally. As a result, in the absence of any definition of a contract of employment, our courts follow relevant and pertinent definition which emanates, in fact, from the French *Cour de cassation*, and in the same line of thought, Mauritius has retained the various forms of contract which exist in France, various forms of *fautes* which prevail in France, and English forms of dismissal.

However, as explained (*supra*), in Mauritius our legislations and regulations provide for 'workers', and there is a distinction between workers and employees as per section 2 of *The Labour Act 1975* (repealed), *The Employment Right Act 2008 (Act 33/ 2008)* (repealed), and now recently when the Mauritian Legislator passed *The Workers' Rights Act 2019 (Act 20/2019)*. If *The Workers' Rights Act 2019 (Act 20/2019)* innovated in enacting various forms of new forms of agreements, which never existed before, there is still no definition of a contract of employment, and which has very often been deplored, in our Mauritian law, legislations and various regulations which have been passed. Very aware of this lacuna in our law, the Employment Relations Tribunal in the case of *Balakrishna Kuppan v Central Electricity Board ERT/RN 32/2019* stated that: 'The employment contract does not exist in a vacuum. It is subject to the various employment laws that have been enacted by the legislator, which have the objectives of *inter alia* safeguarding the rights of the worker and to protect the worker from any abuse by the employer'.

Table 5

Convention	Ratification date	Status
C2 Unemployment Convention 1919	02.12.1969	ratified
C5 Minimum Age (Industry) Convention 1919	02.12.1969	denounced on 30.07.1990
C7 Minimum Age (Sea) Convention 1920	02.12.1969	denounced on 30.07.1990
C8 Unemployment Indemnity (Shipwreck) Convention 1920	02.12.1969	ratified
C11 Right of Association (Agriculture) Convention 1921	02.12.1969	ratified
C12 Workmen's Compensation (Agriculture) Convention, 1921	02.21.1969	ratified

Table 5 Continued

Convention	Ratification date	Status
C14 Weekly Rest (Industry) Convention, 1921	02.12.1969	ratified
C15 Minimum Age (Trimmers and Stockers) Convention, 1921	02.12.1969	denounced on 30.07.1990
C16 Medical Examination of Young Persons (Sea) Convention 1921	02.12.1969	ratified
C17 Workmen's Compensation (Accidents) Convention, 1925	02.12.1969	ratified
C19 Equality of Treatment (Accident Compensation) Convention, 1925	02.12.1969	ratified
C26 Minimum Wage-Fixing Machinery Convention (Revised), 1934	02.12.1969	ratified
C42 Workmen's Compensation (Occupational Diseases) Convention (Revised), 1934	020.12.1969	ratified
C50 Recruiting of Indigenous Workers Convention, 1976	02.12.1969	denounced on 02.03.2000
C58 Minimum Age (Sea) Convention (Revised) 1936	02.12.1969	denounced on 30.07.1990
C 59 Minimum Age (Industry) Convention (Revised), 1937		Denounced on 30.07.1990
C63 Convention concerning Statistics of wages and Hours of Work, 1939	02.12.1969	denounced on 14.06.1994
C64 Contracts of Employment (Indigenous Workers) Convention, 1939	02.12.1969	denounced on 08.07.1999
C65 Penal Sanctions (Indigenous Workers) Convention, 1939	02.12.1969	denounced on 08.07.1999
C74 Certification of Able SeamenConvention,1946	02.12.1969	ratified
C81 Freedom of Association and Protection of the Right to Organise Convention, 1948	01.02.2005	ratified
C81 Labour Inspection Convention, 1947	02.12.1969	ratified
C86 Contracts of Employment (Indigenous Workers) Convention, 1947	02.12.1969	ratified
C87 Freedom of Association and Protection of the Right to Organise Convention, 1948	01.04.2005	ratified
C88 Employment Service Convention, 1948	03.09.2004	ratified
C94 Labour Clauses (Public Contracts) Convention, 1949	02.12.1969	ratified

Continued

Table 5 Continued

Convention	Ratification date	Status
C95 Protection of Wages Convention, 1949	02.12.1969	ratified
C97 Migration for Employment Convention (Revised), 1949	02.12.1969	ratified
C98 Right to Organise and Collective Bargaining Convention, 1949	02.12.1969	ratified
C99 Minimum Wage Fixing Machinery (Agriculture) Convention, 1951	02.12.1969	ratified
C100 Equal Remuneration Convention, 1951	18.12.2002	ratified
C105 Abolition of Forced Labour Convention, 1957	02.12.1969	ratified
C108 Seafarers' Identity Documents Convention, 1958	02.12.1969	ratified
C111 Discrimination (Employment and Occupation) Convention, 1958	18.03.2003	ratified
C137 Dock Work Convention, 1973	30.07.1990	ratified
C144 Tripartite Consultation (International Labour Standards) Convention, 1976	14.06.1994	ratified
C150 Labour Administration Convention, 1978	05.04.2004	ratified
C156 Workers with Family Responsibilities Convention, 1981	05.04.2004	ratified
C159 Vocational Rehabilitation and Employment (Disabled Persons) Convention, 1983	09.06.2004	ratified
C160 Labour Statistics Convention, 1985	14.06.1994	ratified
C175 Part-Time Work Convention, 1994	14.06.1994	ratified
C182 Worst Forms of Child Labour Convention, 1999	08.06.2000	ratified

III. The impact of the COVID-19 on the workers' rights to health and safety measures

As soon as the COVID-19 pandemic disease started to spread on the small island of the Republic of Mauritius, the Mauritian government started to pass new legislations and regulations with scheme and various forms of 'communiqués' (Tabs. 2 and 3) in addition to international legal instruments which the Mauritian government has already signed and ratified (Tab. 4) which were also communicated to all citizens and individuals in the country but they also adversely impacted on human rights of all individuals. As explained (*supra*), since the disease is foreseeable, the

COVID-19 pandemic disease is not an Act of God (*cas de force majeure*), that all obligations and implied duties on both the worker or employer are maintained. In the case of *Hosseny v Maico 1970 SCJ 163*, the Supreme Court of Mauritius stated that: 'in the absence of any agreement, or of any law to the contrary, the obligation of the employer to provide work must be subject to the exception that is contained in the general principle of the Code Civil regarding force majeure'.

As explained *(supra)*, the Mauritian Constitution 1968, in its Chapter II, provides for the most basic of fundamental rights to all its individuals without exception, and they are also in line with international covenants such as *The International Covenant on Civil and Political Rights (ICCPR)* and *The International Covenant on Economic, Social and Cultural Rights (ICESR)*. The *Employment Relations Act 2008 (Act 32/2008)* has been amended by the *Employment Relations (Amendment) Act 2019* and it provides for freedom of association and assembly and protection against discrimination and victimisation with rights a worker may enjoy in terms of trade unions and collective bargaining provided the worker is found fit to work because in the presence of the COVID-19 pandemic disease any worker may be found unfit to work.

Following French and English relevant precedents, the Supreme Court of Mauritius in some relevant cases on unfitness to work explained in the case of *New Mauritius Docks Co. Ltd v PAS Ministry of Labour on behalf of Perrine1974 MR 50* held that: 'An employer I bound to provide work to a workman who presents himself for work and is found fit to work, and if the employer does not fulfill his obligation on any day, the workman is nevertheless deemed to have worked and to have earned his wages for a full day'.

In Mauritius, *The Occupational Safety and Health Act 2005* provides in its section 5 that 'Every employer shall so far as is reasonably practicable, ensure the safety, health and welfare at work of all his employees'. And with a view that workers are not contaminated they were also encouraged to work from home (WFH) when the legislator passed *The Work from Home Regulations 2020*. In the absence of any relevant case as whether a worker may refuse to resume work in case of any apprehension of health and safety risk at work reference may be made to the case of *Rodgers v Leeds Laser Cutting Limited ET 1803829/2020* where the Employment Tribunal found that in case it would be reasonable for the employee to refuse that part of the work which expose him to higher risks or to raise the issue with the employer to find appropriate solutions for a safer working environment but that a mere circulation of COVID-19 virus in society is not a 'good and justifiable cause' for being absent at work. In Mauritius, just like in most countries worldwide, employers are providing face masks, sanitiser and encourage social distancing at the workplace to encourage preventive measures in addition to self-isolation and enforcement of *The Quarantine Act 2020* and other legislations and regulations relating to the workplace.

True that various legislations and regulations were passed by the Mauritian legislator which took all precautionary measures to protect all its citizens provided they are compatible with Article 4(1) of the ICCPR, which provides for derogations from international human rights obligations in time of public emergency provided that these new measures do not 'threaten the life of the nation to the extent strictly required by the exigencies of the situation, provided that such measures are not inconsistent with their other obligations under international law and do not involve discrimination solely on the ground of race, colour, sex, language, religion or social origin'. However these new measures, as to measures which were imposed by the Mauritian government, shall not affect, however, the inherent right to life (Article ICCPR), the prohibition of torture and inhumane treatment (Article 7 ICCPR), prohibition of slavery (Article 8 ICCPR), freedom of imprisonment on ground of inability to fulfil a contractual obligation (Article 11), right not to be subjected to retroactive application of criminal law (Article 15 ICCPR), right to recognition as a person before the law (Article 16 ICCPR), right to freedom of thought, conscience and religion (Article 18 ICCPR). It is trite law that no State party to the ICCPR shall not have recourse to public emergency in an abusive manner.

In Mauritius, *The Quarantine Act 1954* was repealed, and *The Quarantine Act 2020* came into force, and the purpose for the Act was: 'to provide appropriate measures for the prevention and spread of communicable diseases in Mauritius'. However, *The Quarantine Act 2020* was much criticized as it imposes a fine of Rs 500,000 and a term of imprisonment not exceeding five years for criminal offenders, and its sections are also infringing most fundamental rights of the individuals in Mauritius. As an illustration, section 3 of *The Quarantine Act 2020* imposes restrictions of entry by aircrafts and ships in Mauritian borders and imposition of confinement at home and closure of business premises. Section 7 of the same Act enacts confinement of persons in Quarantine facilities and self-isolation, section 19 of the same Act imposes a duty to provide information, section 10 of the same Act provides for the duty to disclose communicable diseases and section 11 of the same Act provides for police powers to enter premises without a warrant and arrest without a warrant. *The Quarantine Act 2020* was passed to protect Mauritian citizens from the COVID-19 pandemic disease otherwise contaminated workers will jeopardise the life and health of other fellow workers and employees in a sane environment place. In contrast, many professionals, such as dentists, private medical practitioners or barristers; had no access to their workplace and it was deplored that it constitutes an abuse of access to workplace.

When the *Employment Rights Act 2008 (Act 33/2008)* was repealed, and the *Workers' Rights Act 2019 (Act 20/2019)* came into force the main aim and objectives of the Mauritian legislator were to provide equal remuneration for equal work as a matter of fairness without gender distinction. Most provisions of the International Covenant on Economic, Social and Cultural Rights (ICESCR); which the Republic of Mauritius has signed but not ratified, are also covered by *The Workers' Rights Act 2019 (Act 20/2019)*; provides for State parties to recognize the right of every individual to favourable and just condition of work, to ensure a minimum and fair and equal remuneration for equal work without gender distinction, it also provides for a safe and healthy working conditions, the need to recognize seniority and competence as benchmarks for equal opportunity for promotion at work, reasonable limitation of working hours and holidays and leisure for every worker and that State must meet certain conditions such as condition of strict necessity, non-discrimination, international notification and of consistency with other legal obligations under international law.

The Prevention and Mitigation of Infectious Disease Coronavirus Regulations 2020 came into force with strict criminal penalties (*supra*) in case of breach of the regulation and any contaminated person was immediately quarantined as *per The Quarantine Act 2020*, and as highlighted, the Mauritian government priority was to ensure public health to one and all after the country has suffered one lockdown (19th March 2020 to 1st June 2020) and a second lockdown (10th March 2021 to 25th March 2021) with regular red zones in different rural and urban constituencies to avoid any risk of resurgence of the COVID-19 pandemic disease otherwise it would definitely impact on the country's health service and economy, and its socio economic developments as most keys sectors (tourism, hotels, importation and exportation of goods to the SADC countries, or foreign direct investment (FDI) were also affected) but there were very often partial lift of lockdowns in order for the country to breathe economically and financially and to resume economic activities but international transport in the tourism sector remains close. As per *The Quarantine Act 2020* only 10 persons may meet at any time and 50 persons in exceptional cases (wedding or important social gatherings).

Actually, most countries; such as France, Italy, USA or China; are under the influence of Article 4 ICCPR which provides for legitimate derogations (supra) and limitations in case of national security and/or in case of emergency in the interest of the nation and its people. In Mauritian law and legislations, there are similar derogations which are available under the Constitution, 1968. Article 4 ICCPR is in line with section 18 of the Constitution 1968 which provides that: 'the law authorizes the taking of measures that are reasonably justifiable for dealing with the situation that exists in Mauritius during that period'. Section 5(g) of the Constitution 1968 enacts that: 'for the purpose of preserving the spread of an infectious or contagious disease'. Section 15 of the Constitution, 1968 enacts that: 'No person shall be deprived of his freedom of movement', as highlighted by the Supreme Court in the case of *Coorbanally v The Queen*, where the Commissioner of Police may impose an objection to departure to any individual who may have committed or is suspected of committing a criminal offence as per section 15(3)(a) of the Constitution, 1968 imposes restrictions within Mauritius which is in the interest of defense, public safety, public order, public morality or public health or of securing compliance with any international obligation which shall not be held inconsistent with or in contravention of this section.

There were serious concerns about vaccination in Mauritius though *The Public Health (COVID-19 Vaccines for Emergency Use) Regulations 2021* was passed to circumvent the pandemic disease and there will be a vaccination program around the island. People complained that they suffered from allergies, some people died when they were vaccinated, other suffered from headache and workers needed a Work Access Permit and a Vaccination Card to have access to their workplace. The media reported that some workers refused to be vaccinated because there were risks to health and safety. Therefore, questions arose to mandatory vaccination, and should it be imposed by any employer? In Mauritius, just like in the UK, Italy, vaccination is imperative and compulsory as *per* the various legislations and regulations in force especially for front liners and people who are regularly in touch with COVID-19 pandemic patients and other healthcare workers. However, there is a pertinent legal issue as Isra Black, a law lecturer at the University of York, pointed out that: 'any public authority, whether the State or individual NHS trust, that mandates vaccination will need to comply with human rights and equality law. Mandatory vaccination interferes with the right to private life protected by article 8 of the *European Convention on Human Rights 1950*, so the relevant authorities will need to show that the interference is justified in its pursuit of a legitimate aim and its proportionality. The human rights and equality dimension of mandatory vaccination cannot be avoided by the use of health and safety law'.

IV. The impact of the COVID-19 on the workers' rights: The socio-economic impact

The ravages and havocs of the COVID-19 pandemic disease remain unprecedented in human history affecting all sectors of the socio-economic development of a country affecting furthermore to the rate of unemployment (it raised from 1.1 % to 6.5 % according to the International Labour Organisation) with, *inter alia*, a sharp increase in poverty, inequalities, loss of labour income or infringement of human rights especially on the workplace.

The Government of the small Republic of Mauritius reacted promptly to the COVID-19 pandemic disease with the promulgation of new legislations and regulations, to control its spread and to cater for its socio-economic development in key sectors such a textile, manufacturing sectors, food, tourism, retail, wholesale and agriculture with a direct impact of Mauritian economy and finance, and, consequently, on its GDP, which contracted by 11 % in 2020 according to the International Monetary Fund.

However, these new government policies have a direct bearing and impact on the life of its citizens with tourism and closure of borders, trade across border and closure of most local businesses, production, supply chains, movement and freedom of citizens have been suddenly disrupted during curfew, quarantine, imposition of red zones which were prevailing at a time provoking, unfortunately, loss of jobs and an increase of unemployment rate coupled with infringement of most fundamental human rights including freedom of movement, freedom of expression and speech including the workers' rights in terms of unemployment and other social crisis but which no other country was ready to such unexpected impact on inequality, discrimination, dismissal and other abuses.

The psychological and philosophical impact had finally a last say because most Mauritians believe that they will have to live under the 'new normal' that is, henceforth, they will have to live with the COVID-19 pandemic disease. Indeed, the COVID-19 pandemic disease came and infringed the right to life and the right to health with repercussions on various human rights, *inter alia*, right to vaccination, right to access to workplace, freedom of expression and speech, freedom of association and assembly in a democratic country like the Republic of Mauritius where courts were closed, and disputes were delayed until deconfinement, but '*justice delayed is justice denied*'.

Therefore, it is important to know and understand how the legislator is operating in other African countries in passing relevant legislations and regulations with a view to contain the pandemic disease to spread, and how people find them as a threat to their freedom to life and dignity. To prevent any redundancy, the Mauritian government implemented several measures to prevent massive redundancy especially among low-skilled workers and those working in small and medium enterprises due to the lockdown.

Section 72 A (1) of the *Workers' Rights Act 2019 (Act 20/2019)* was amended so that an employer cannot during the prescribed period starting '1st June 2020 and ending on 31 December 2020 (was extended to 30 June 2021) reduce the number of workers in his employment either temporarily or permanently or terminate the employment of any of his worker', but save and except in cases where an agreement has been reached in relation to the termination of employment for economic, financial, structural, and technological or any other similar reasons, an employer is not allowed to reduce its workforce during the prescribed period. In the case of *Les Frais de l'Artigiano Ltd RB/RN/38/2020*, and the Redundancy Board found that the employer did not comply with the relevant section (Section 72 A (1) of the *Workers' Rights Act 2019 (Act 20/2019))* and the termination of the workers' employment on ground of redundancy was unjustified. Relying on the precedent of *H. Nunkoo Mauritius Biscuit Making Company Ltd 2015 IND 54*, the Industrial Court Magistrate stated that: 'It is not enough for an employer to claim that his business is facing economic or financial downturn. He has to adduce sufficient objective proof of economic difficulties to such an extent that it could no longer keep a particular employee or employees without affecting its competitiveness. Therefore, statement of accounts and expert evidence has to be adduced. The mere fact that the plaintiff has conceded that the company was facing economic difficulties is not in itself sufficient proof that it was facing economic difficulties that the post occupied by the plaintiff should be made redundant'.

Conclusion and recommendations

It can be concluded that the COVID-19 pandemic disease has a domino effect spreading on all sectors affecting by the same time the socio-economic development of a country. In addition, it also affected the most basic fundamental rights of all its citizens without any exception when new legislations and regulations were passed with a view to provide social protection relief to all households and individuals especially to those workers in the private sector with the Government Wage Assistance Scheme (GWAS) and the Self-Employed Assistance Scheme (SEAS) during the COVID-19 period. Despite the Mauritian government was facing financial constraints due to the COVID-19 all workers in the public sector received the same monthly salaries without any cut except for overtime. Since Mauritius is a welfare State with free education at all levels, free health care and free transport for elderly persons and tertiary students the Mauritian government immediately implemented a Government Wage Assistance Scheme (GWAS) and a Self-Employed Assistance Scheme (SEAS) during the COVID-19 to assist workers in the private sector as a wage of subsidy. And this effort was highly recommended.

Bibliography

PLCJ. 2020. *COVID-19(Mauritius): Can companies suspend the payment of commercial rents?*

Potayya, S. 2021. *An analysis of force majeure in the context of Mauritian banking law.* [online] Ibanet.org.

Richard, N. and Ribet, A. 2020. *COVID-19 and its impact on contractual performance in Mauritius – Force Majeure | DLA Piper Africa, Mauritius | Juristconsult Chambers.* [online] DLA Piper Africa.

Sutherland, E. 2020. *Coronavirus overview of the impacts of the lockdown in Publications – Eversheds Sutherland.* [online] Eversheds-sutherland.com.

L'avenir du travail et le contrat de travail face au COVID-19 – l'expérience mauricienne

Goran GEORGIJEVIC[1]

Le Workers Rights Act de 2019, entrée en vigueur quelques temps avant la première épidémie du COVID-19 à Maurice, a introduit une nouveauté remarquable dans la législation mauricienne, rendue nécessaire par les changements de la configuration économique et technologique dans le pays, comme dans le monde entier. Cette nouveauté figurait à la section 17 de la loi : il s'agissait de travailleur atypique réunissant toutes les formes de travailleurs autres que ceux employés sur un contrat de travail traditionnel à durée indéterminée. La section 3 (2) (d) de la loi esquissait les premiers contours du nouveau régime juridique applicable à ce groupe hétérogène englobant, entre autres, les travailleurs qui travaillent depuis leur domicile (home workers), les travailleurs travaillant sur une plateforme (online plateform workers) et les travailleurs à temps partiel travaillant simultanément pour plusieurs employeurs.

L'élaboration du régime juridique du travailleur atypique à Maurice a été précipitée par l'épidémie du COVID-19 à partir de Mars 2020, et deux Règlements, nommément le Workers' Rights (Atypical Workers) Regulations de 2019 et le Workers' Rights (Working from Home) Regulations de 2020 ont grandement contribué à ce que la position juridique du travailleur atypique soit la plus complète possible. Ces règlements ont été pris dans le sillage de l'ajout de la nouvelle section 17A du Workers' Rights Act prévoyant la possibilité d'organiser le travail depuis le domicile (work from home) même pour les travailleurs traditionnels qui exécutent normalement leurs tâches dans les locaux de leur employeur. Néanmoins, malgré la qualité incontestable des textes mentionnés dans les développements qui précèdent, des réflexions académiques sur l'avenir du travail et le contrat de travail de ces travailleurs atypiques, dans le contexte du COVID-19, sont permises.

---

[1] Dr., *Lecturer*, Département de Droit, Faculté de Droit et Gestion, Université de Maurice.

Après avoir esquissé le régime juridique actuel des travailleurs atypiques en droit mauricien, nous nous poserons les questions sur d'éventuelles améliorations qui pourraient être apportées à ce régime. Par ailleurs, certains travailleurs atypiques, demandés dans le contexte du COVID-19, tels que les travailleurs zéro heures (zero hours workers), les travailleurs sur appel (on-call workers) et les travailleurs temporaires ne sont pas mentionnés dans les textes actuels, alors qu'une réflexion académique peut contribuer à ce qu'on améliore leur position juridique.

The Workers Rights Act of 2019, came into force some time before the first COVID-19 epidemy in Mauritius, has introduced in its Section 17 a new category of workers, namely atypical worker. This new category encompasses all the forms of work, except the traditional full-time work. Section 3 (2) (d) of the Act gave the basis of the new legal regime of atypical workers.

The elaboration of the legal regime of atypical workers has been accelerated by the outbreak of the COVID-19 epidemy in Mauritius starting from March 2020. Two Regulations, namely the Workers' Rights (Atypical Workers) Regulations of 2019 and the Workers' Rights (Working from Home) Regulations of 2020 have considerably completed the legal regime of atypical workers in Mauritius. However, in spite of the great quality of the above mentioned laws and regulations, there are certainly some points pertaining to the atypical worker's legal regime that still might be improved. In this paper those possible improvements to the legal regime of atypical worker will be addressed, after the legal regime of atypical worker, as per the current legislation, has been set out.

Introduction
A. La primauté du contrat de travail à durée indéterminée à partir de la seconde moitié du XXème siècle

Les circonstances économiques (la reconstruction et l'essor économique) dans le monde et à Maurice après la 2ème Guerre mondiale ont mené à l'installation, à partir des années 1970, du modèle traditionnel de contrat de travail, à savoir *le contrat à durée indéterminée*[2]. Ce modèle

---

[2] Sur le droit du travail à Maurice, axé autour du contrat de travail traditionnel à durée indéterminée voir notamment : GUNPUTH R. P., *Labour and Industrial Relations Law : Study Guide*, Réduit: University of Mauritius, 2020; FOKKAN D., *Introduction au droit du travail mauricien : les relations individuelles de travail*, Aix-Marseilles III : Faculté de Droit et des Sciences Politiques, 1995. – Voir aussi : SCHOUKENS P., BARRIO A., « The changing concept of work: When does typical work become atypical? », *European Labour Law Journal*, 2017, Vol 8(4),

semble s'appuyer sur la théorie dite « du bien commun », selon laquelle « l'entreprise est comprise non commun un lieu de luttes mais comme une institution pérenne où les différents organes œuvres dans un même but »[3]. En parallèle se produisent des changements au sein des entreprises favorables aux employés (délégués du personnel). La sécurité sociale est créée[4]. Un salaire minimum est prévu dans la législation. La stabilité de l'emploi est préservée en cas de grève, à l'exception d'une faute lourde du salarié[5]. L'accent est aussi mis sur l'éducation des travailleurs[6].

B. Le changement dans le monde du travail de ces dernières décennies

Depuis quelques décennies, à Maurice, comme dans le monde entier, on peut observer quelques facteurs qui ont contribué à ce que le modèle classique de contrat à durée indéterminée, exécuté dans les locaux de l'employeur ou sur un site déterminé par ce dernier, soit de plus en plus remis en question[7]. Il s'agit d'abord des changements économiques où les employeurs ont moins besoins d'une force de travail durable et ont de plus en plus besoins d'une force de travail « disposable » travaillant pour eux sur un ou plusieurs projets bien spécifiques (« *gig economy* »). La mondialisation économique et le développement technologique (internet, logiciels, ordinateurs)[8] ont aussi contribué à ce phénomène de précarisation

---

p. 307–308 ; ENGLAND G., *Part-Time, Casual and Other Atypical Workers: A Legal View*, Industrial Relations Centre, Queen's University, Kingston, Ontario, Canada, 1987, p. 1.
[3] WOLMARK C., PESKINE E., *Droit du travail 2022*, Dalloz, 2021, $15^{\text{ème}}$ éd., p. 12, n° 27.
[4] DOCKES E., AUZERO G., BAUGARD D., *Droit du travail 2022*, Dalloz, 2021, $35^{\text{ème}}$ éd., p. 17, n° 18.
[5] DOCKES E., AUZERO G., BAUGARD D., *op. cit.*, p. 17, n° 19.
[6] DOCKES E., AUZERO G., BAUGARD D., *op. cit.*, p. 18, n° 21.
[7] KNIFFIN, "Covid 19 and the Workplace: Implications, Issues and Insights for Future Research and Action", *American Psychologist*, 2020, p. 6.
[8] LALIVE R., OESCH D., *AI & The Future of Work* [Online] Zurich, Credit Suisse, p. 5, disponible depuis: https://www.credit-suisse.com/media/assets/corporate/docs/about-us/research/publications/ai-the-future-of-work.pdf [dernière visite 13 July 2022]; SCHULTE P., HOWARD J., *The Impact of Technology on Work and the Workforce*, 2019, p. 2, [Online] disponible depuis: https://www.ilo.org/safework/events/safeday/33thinkpieces/WCMS_681603/lang--en/index.htm [dernière visite le 13 juillet 2022].

des accords de travail, car grâce à l'*outsorcing* il est devenu assez facile de trouver la force de travail de bonne qualité pour un ou plusieurs projets, payée moins cher que si la force de travail local était utilisée.

Les employeurs à Maurice et dans le monde recourent donc aux contrats de travail moins sûrs que le contrat de travail à durée indéterminée. Il s'agit des accords de travail atypiques.

C. L'apparition du concept de travailleur atypique dans le *Workers' Rights Act* de 2019

Le *Workers Rights Act* de 2019, entrée en vigueur quelques temps avant la première épidémie de COVID-19 à Maurice, a introduit une nouveauté remarquable dans la législation mauricienne. Cette nouveauté a été rendue nécessaire par les changements de la configuration économique et technologique à Maurice, comme dans le monde entier et figurait à la section 17 de la loi. Il s'agissait de travailleur atypique, réunissant toutes les formes de travailleurs autres que ceux employés sur un contrat de travail traditionnel à durée indéterminée. La section 3 (2) (d) de la loi esquissait les premiers contours du nouveau régime juridique applicable à ce groupe hétérogène englobant, entre autres, les travailleurs qui travaillent depuis leur domicile (*home workers*), les travailleurs travaillant sur une plateforme (*online plateform workers*) et les travailleurs à temps partiel travaillant simultanément pour plusieurs employeurs.

L'élaboration du régime juridique du travailleur atypique a été précipitée, à partir de mars 2020[9], par l'épidémie du COVID-19. Deux règlements, nommément le *Workers' Rights (Atypical Workers) Regulations* de 2019 et le *Workers' Rights (Working from Home) Regulations* de 2020 ont grandement contribué à ce que la position juridique du travailleur atypique soit la plus complète possible en droit mauricien. Ces règlements

---

[9] Sur l'augmentation du nombre de travailleurs travaillant depuis la maison: RAMAMURTI B., 2020. *The Shift toward Remote Work Could Leave Blue-Collar Workers behind* [Online] disponible depuis: https://edition.cnn.com/2020/09/16/perspectives/remote-work-blue-collar/index.html [dernière visite le 22 septembre 2020].

ont été pris dans le sillage de l'ajout de la nouvelle section 17A du *Workers' Rights Act*[10].

Définition du travailleur atypique. Le travailleur atypique peut être défini en droit mauricien négativement, comme étant *le travailleur dont le contrat de travail n'est pas le contrat standard à durée indéterminée*[11]. Du côté des textes mauriciens, la section 2 des *Workers' Rights (Atypical Workers) Regulations* de 2019 définit le travailleur atypique comme une personne âgée de 18 ans ou plus, qui ne travaille pas en vertu d'un contrat standard à durée indéterminée. La section 2 des Règlements reprend ensuite l'essentiel de la section 17 du *Workers' Rights Act* de 2019 en précisant que la notion de travailleur atypique englobe, entre autres le télétravailleur, le travailleur travaillant sur une plateforme, le travailleur travaillant depuis la maison et le travailleur qui travaille simultanément à temps partiel pour plusieurs employeurs[12].

D. Formes principales de travailleurs atypiques

En droit mauricien, le travailleur à temps partiel est défini comme celui qui travaille moins d'heures pour son employeur qu'un travailleur à temps plein, mais qui travaille pour son employeur sur une base régulière. Cette définition a été confirmée à la section 2 des *Atypical Workers Regulations* de 2019. Les travailleurs travaillant depuis la maison font leur travail à la maison et depuis la maison. Cette catégorie qui est très large et hétérogène, englobe ceux dont le travail demande un

---

[10] La section 17 A du *Workers' Rights Act* de 2019 prévoit que l'employeur peut demander à son employé de travailler depuis la maison, à condition de lui laisser un préavis d'au moins 48 heures.

[11] TAYLOR D., 2017. *Ain't that typical? Everyday challenges for an atypical workforce*, ACAS Discussion Papers, p. 4 disponible depuis: https://www.acas.org.uk/aint-that-typical (dernière visite le 13 juillet 2022); STAVROU-COSTEA E., KABST R. ISIDOR R., "The utilization of atypical employment – One size does not fit all", *Personal Quarterly*, 2014, Vol. 66, n° 4, pp. 6–8.

[12] SCHOUKENS P., BARRIO A., MONTEBOVI S., *"The EU social pillar: An answer to the challenge of the social protection of platform workers?"*, European Journal of Social Security, 2018, Vol. 20 (3), p. 223 s.; GYULAVARI T., "Collective rights of platform workers: The role of EU law", *Maastricht Journal of European and Comparative Law*, 2020, Vol. 27 (4), p. 406; DOCKES E., AUZERO G., BAUGARD D., *op. cit.*, p. 281, n° 209; WOLMARK C., PESKINE, *op. cit.*, p. 27–28, n° 34–35.

haut degré de connaissances et de compétences (conseillers financiers, informaticiens, etc.) ainsi que ceux dont le travail manuel repose sur un savoir-faire relativement simple (les fabricants d'objets divers)[13]. Ces travailleurs peuvent être temporaires ou permanents, à temps partiel ou à temps plein. Il existe aussi des travailleurs temporaires qui concluent avec leurs employeurs les contrats de travailleur de courte durée, afin de répondre aux besoins saisonniers de leurs employeurs. Ces travailleurs sont souvent engagés par l'intermédiaire d'une agence[14]. Les travailleurs dits « zéro heures » n'ont pas le droit à un nombre minimal d'heures de travail, leur nombre d'heures de travail dépendra des besoins de leur employeur[15]. Ce type de travail est très favorable à l'employeur qui en a le contrôle absolu, économiquement et psychologiquement. Enfin, les travailleurs sur appel (*on-call*) travaillent pour leur employeur lorsqu'il les appelle, en fonction de ses besoins, et sont parfois les travailleurs zéro heures, mais ce n'est pas toujours le cas, et peuvent même être les travailleurs à temps plein (certains médecins par exemple).

Dans ce papier, en se basant sur la méthode analytique puis synthétique, nous allons esquisser, analyser et apprécier le régime juridique du travailleur atypique dans les textes actuels en droit du travail (Première partie) mais aussi la partie qui n'est pas couverte dans la législation en droit du travail, dans le but de suggérer de possibles améliorations dans le cadre légal de notre pays (Seconde partie).

---

[13] AMMONS K. S., MARKHAM W. T., "Working at Home: Experiences of Skilled White Collar Workers, *Sociological Spectrum*, 2004, 24, p. 193; STONE K. V. W, "Legal Protections for Atypical Employees: Employment Law for Workers without Workplaces and Employees without Employers", *Berkeley Journal of Employment and Labor Law*, 2006, 27, n° 2, p. 270.

[14] SCHIEK D., "Agency Work – from Marginalisation towards Acceptance? Agency work in EU Social and Employment Policy and the "implementation" of the draft Directive on Agency work into German law", *German Law Journal*, 2004, 5 (10), p. 1234; STONE, *art. précit.*, p. 255.

[15] LANG C., SCHOMANN I. & CLAUWAERT S., *Atypical Forms of Employment Contracts in Times of Crisis*, European Trade Union Institute, 2013, Working Paper 2013.03, pp. 18–19.

I. Le régime juridique du travailleur atypique dans les textes en droit mauricien du travail

La section 3 (2) (d) du *Workers' Rights Act* de 2019 prévoit avec précision les sections et parties de cette loi applicables au travailleur atypique. Ainsi, sont applicables au travailleur atypique les sections 5, 26, 31 et 33 de la loi ainsi que les Parties VI, VII, VIII, XI, XII et XIII de la Loi. Ce renvoie permet, d'une part, d'ébaucher un certain régime juridique du travailleur atypique (A) complété par des textes réglementaires (B).

A. Le régime juridique du travailleur atypique selon le *Workers' Rights Act* de 2019

Une lecture attentive du *Workers' Rights Act* de 2019 permet de constater que le législateur y a déjà ébauché le régime juridique du travailleur atypique dans une certaine mesure (1), mais que des aspects importants de ce régime ont été laissés en dehors de ce texte législatif (2).

1. Les éléments du régime juridique des travailleurs atypiques établis dans le Workers' Rights Act de 2019

L'application de la section 3 (2) (d) du *Workers' Rights Act* de 2019 procure aux travailleurs atypiques une certaine protection légale.

Ainsi, les travailleurs atypiques sont protégés contre toute forme de discrimination injustifiée[16] (section 5 de la loi), qui serait basée sur la race, le genre, l'âge, la couleur, l'origine, etc. Toute discrimination des travailleurs atypiques relative à leur salaire est également interdite. La protection agit non seulement contre la discrimination des travailleurs atypiques déjà engagés mais aussi contre la discrimination dans l'accès à l'emploi. Cette règle louable assure le traitement digne et égalitaire de cette nouvelle catégorie de travailleurs qui sont les travailleurs atypiques.

La loi (section 31) protège également les travailleurs atypiques contre le non-paiement des rémunérations dues au moment de la fin du contrat

---

[16] *Rodrigues Government Employees Association & Ors v. The Government of Mauritius* 2000 SCJ 375.

(salaire et autres compensations)[17]. Cette protection vise à assurer aux travailleurs atypiques le paiement des sommes dont dépend sa survie ainsi que cette de sa famille tout en empêchant d'éventuels abus que l'employeur pourrait être tenté de commettre à la fin du contrat. Du point de vue du droit civil mauricien, la protection contre le non-paiement des rémunérations dues au moment de la fin du contrat évite un enrichissement sans cause de l'employeur[18].

Le travailleur atypique n'est pas dénué de toute protection légale en cas de fautes commises par l'employeur. La loi lui garantit le droit d'intenter une action en justice contre son employeur fautif à l'égard du travailleur atypique concerné (section 61 de la loi).

Le *Workers' Rights Act* de 2019 protège le travailleur atypique contre la rupture abusive du contrat de travail, c'est-à-dire contre le licenciement abusif (section 64 de la loi)[19]. L'employé atypique ne peut être renvoyé sans juste cause, et même si une telle cause existe, une procédure, décrite dans la loi, doit être respectée, afin d'éviter des abus à l'égard de l'employé atypique fautif. Le travailleur atypique étant la partie faible dans le contrat de travail, la loi interdit à l'employeur de produire en tant que preuve, dans une procédure disciplinaire ou judiciaire, la reconnaissance écrite de la faute émanant de l'employé (section 64 (9) de la loi).

Les revenus professionnels d'une personne étant le pilier de sa vie privée et familiale, le *Workers' Rights Act* de 2019 assure également une protection du travailleur atypique contre les conséquences financières négatives d'une éventuelle suspension. Le travailleur atypique suspendu recevra ses salaires pendant la période de suspension (section 66 de la loi)[20].

---

[17] H. Nunkoo v. Mauritius Biscuit Making Company Ltd (In Receivership) 2015 IND 54; Mukerjee Subrata v The Habitat Development Co. Ltd. 2017 IND 4.

[18] PORCHY-SIMON S., *Droit des obligations 2022*, Dalloz, 13ème éd., 2021, p. 523 s. n° 1038 s.; TRANCHANT L. EGEA V., *Droit des obligations 2021*, Dalloz, 24ème Ed., 2021, p. 172 s.; ANCEL P., *Droit des obligations en 12 thèmes*, Dalloz, 12ème éd. p. 507 s.; CABRILLAC R., *Droit des obligations*, Dalloz, 2020, 14ème éd. p. 210 s., n° 208 s.; CHENEDE F., *Le nouveau droit des obligations et des contrats 2019/2020*, Dalloz, 2ème éd. 2018, p. 179 s. n° 134. 00 s.

[19] *Madelen Clothing Co. Ltd. v. Termination of Contracts of Service Board and Ors.* 1981 MR 284 1981 SCJ 264; *Pierre Louis J.R. & anor v Pointe Cotton Resort Hotel Co. Ltd.* 2021 SCJ 27.

[20] *L.S. Lascarie v. Gas Transport Ltd.* 2014 IND 61; *Trubohun A.N. v. S & T Three Eights Co. Ltd.* 2010 SCJ 330.

Il faut aussi noter que le *transitional unemployment benefit* (section 84 de la loi), qui aide un travailleur à surmonter les difficultés financières liées au chômage, est applicable aux travailleurs atypiques. Ils peuvent aussi bénéficier du *Portable Retirement Gratuity Fund* en cas de retraite (sections 88 et suivantes de la loi).

En dépit de l'existence d'une ébauche du régime juridique du travailleur atypique dans le *Workers' Rights Act* de 2019, on peut noter un certain nombre de lacune dans ce texte législatif.

2. Les éléments du régime juridique du travailleur atypique laissés en dehors du Workers' Rights Act de 2019

Certains éléments du régime juridique des travailleurs atypique sont laissés en dehors du *Workers' Rights Act* de 2019, ce qui signifie qu'il y a des sections de la loi qui ne s'appliquent pas au travailleur atypique. Il en va ainsi d'abord du principe de priorité donné au travailleur à temps partiel lorsque son employeur est en train de recruter à temps plein[21] (section 6 de la loi), des principes gouvernant la promotion, nommément les qualifications, expérience et mérite[22] (section 7 de la loi).

La loi n'a pas explicitement étendu les interdictions d'embauche, concernant les très jeunes mineurs, âgés de moins de 16 ans ni les restrictions à l'embauche applicables aux mineurs âgés entre 16 et 18ans aux travailleurs atypiques[23] (section 10 de la loi). Ceci est fort regrettable car la protection d'un travailleur mineur dans sa santé physique et mentale fait partie de l'ordre public de direction, que le travail soit atypique ou non[24].

La loi passe aussi sous silence le droit de l'employé atypique de demander un exemplaire écrit du contrat de travail un mois et demi après le début de l'exécution du contrat[25] (section 11 de la loi), ce qui

---

[21] *Gokool Soomatee and Others v. Permanent Secretary of the Ministry of Health and Quality of Life and Public Service Commission* 2007 PRV 84 2008 MR 350.
[22] *Chittoo, Dr. H. B. v. The University of Technology, Mauritius* 2021 SCJ 264; *Dussoye R.A.A. & Ors v. State Investment Corporation Ltd. & anor* 2016 SCJ 141 I.
[23] *Bantu Motors Africa Co Ltd v. Mauritian Eagle Leasing Company Ltd.* 2016 SCJ 61.
[24] DOCKES E., AUZERO G., BAUGARD D., *op. cit.*, p. 239, n° 168.
[25] *Kauroo-Rugbur P. v. Tropic Knits Ltd* 2020 IND 7; *Medine S.E. Co. Ltd. v. P.A.S. Ministry of Labour* 1967 MR 163.

peut être pénalisant pour le travailleur atypique en cas de litige avec son employeur.

En dépit de l'importance des revenus professionnels d'un travailleur pour sa vie personnelle et familiale[26], l'application de l'interdiction de payer l'employée dans les intervalles plus longs qu'un mois n'a pas été étendue au travailleur atypique (section 18 de la loi).

Les règles du *Workers' Rights Act* de 2019 relatives aux heures de travail normales[27] (section 20 de la loi), aux heures de travail compressées (section 21 de la loi) et aux heures de travail supplémentaires[28] (section 24 de la loi) ne s'appliquent pas aux travailleurs atypiques. Il en va de même des interdictions et des restrictions liées aux prélèvements sur le salaire du travailleur (pas plus d'une moitié du salaire, l'exigence d'un consentement écrit de l'employé lorsque les déductions sont autorisées par la loi)[29] (section 34 de la loi), des congés annuels, des congés maladie, des congés maternité et paternité (sections 45 et suivantes de la loi), du bonus de fin d'année (section 54 de la loi), etc.

Le législateur mauricien de 2019 n'a pas voulu étendre l'application de toutes les sections du *Workers' Rights Act* aux travailleurs atypiques car il souhaitait donner du temps aux pouvoirs réglementaires pour réfléchir à la façon de compléter et organiser le régime juridique des travailleurs atypiques. Le COVID-19 a accéléré les choses et cela a été fait dans les deux règlements *Atypical Workers Regulations* de 2019 et *Working from Home Regulations* de 2020 qui ont complété le régime juridique des travailleurs atypiques à Maurice.

B. Le régime juridique du travailleur atypique dans les Règlements

Les deux règlements mentionnés plus haut ont complété le régime juridique des travailleurs atypiques esquissé dans le *Workers' Rights Act*

---

[26] PORCHY-SIMON S., *op. cit.*, p. 152; TRANCHANT L., EGEA V., *op. cit.*, pp. 44–45; ANCEL P., *op. cit.*, p. 57 s.

[27] *Rungee B. v Employment Relations Tribunal* 2013 SCJ 388; *Fooraballly Golap & ors v Ministry of Health and Wellness & anor* 2021 INT 80.

[28] *Meerah S.J.F.S. v. Omnicane Milling Operations Limited* 2020 IND 12; *The Medical Records Staff Power Union v.The Ministry of Health and Wellness* 2020 SCJ 200.

[29] *Safety Construction Company Limited v State* 2020 INT 102.

de 2019. Ainsi, l'employé atypique a désormais le droit d'obtenir en écrit son contrat de travail, a le droit de demander le retour au travail dans les locaux de son employeur, a le droit d'obtenir les fiches de paye.

Par ailleurs, le travailleur atypique a l'obligation au rapport, à la demande de l'employeur.

L'*Atypical Workers Regulations* de 2019 et le *Working from Home Regulations* de 2020 énoncent aussi des règles sur les heures de travail normales de travailleurs atypiques, les heures de travail compressées et les heures de travail supplémentaires, sur les congés annuels, les congés maladie et les congés maternité et paternité. Enfin, les Règlement se prononcent aussi sur le bonus de fin d'année du travailleur atypique et sur le remboursement des dépenses raisonnables liées au travail.

Les deux règlements encadrent très strictement le droit de l'employeur d'entrer dans la résidence de son employé où le travail se fait. Ainsi, les causes permettant une telle entrée sont la livraison de matériels, la collecte de produits finis, l'installation et la réparation d'outils de travail et l'inspection liée à la sécurité au travail.

Les règlements prévoient explicitement la protection du travailleur atypique contre des blessures au travail, mais aussi contre des risques à la santé et à la sécurité au travail.

Sans surprise, les deux règlements sont d'ordre public, ce qui signifie que l'employé ne peut renoncer aux droits qui lui sont conférés.

Il est indéniable que le *Workers' Rights Act* de 2019 ainsi que les deux règlements l'accompagnant esquissent un régime juridique de travailleur atypique passablement complet. Néanmoins, quelques améliorations restent possibles à notre avis.

II. Possibles améliorations du régime juridique du travailleur atypique

Des améliorations qui peuvent être apportées, à notre avis, au régime juridique du travailleur atypique à Maurice concernent, d'une part, les catégories traitées dans les textes existants (A) et, d'autre part, les catégories qui n'y sont pas spécifiquement visées (B).

Possibles améliorations du régime juridique des catégories existantes de travailleurs atypique.

Parmi les améliorations à suggérer certaines concernent tout travailleur atypique, tel qu'il est défini dans les textes actuels (1) et les autres sont relatives à des catégories existantes de travailleurs atypiques bien précises (2).

A. Possibles améliorations relatives à tout travailleur atypique

Dans le but d'assurer l'égalité de tous les travailleurs, il serait opportun, à notre sens, d'affirmer dans la loi ou les règlements que le principe de priorité dans le recrutement s'applique aussi aux travailleurs atypiques à temps partiel (sect. 6 (1) de la loi). Pour la même raison, il nous semble opportun que le principe de promotion basé sur les qualifications, l'expérience et le mérite s'applique aussi aux travailleurs atypiques (sect. 7 (1) de la loi).

L'interdiction d'employer les mineurs de moins de 16 ans doit aussi s'appliquer aux travailleurs atypiques (sect. 8(1) de la loi), le mineur devant plutôt se consacrer à l'éducation et l'acquisition de compétences qu'au travail rémunéré. Des restrictions telles que l'interdiction du travail nocturne ou du travail nuisible à la santé et au développement doit aussi s'appliquer aux travailleurs atypiques âgés entre 16 et 18 ans (sect. 9 de la Loi). La protection de la santé et de la minorité d'un mineur âgé entre 16 et 18 ans doit être assurée quelle que soit la forme de travail à laquelle il a eu recours.

La règle qu'aucun travailleur ne travaillera plus de 12 heures consécutives doit aussi s'appliquer aux travailleurs atypiques, sous réserve de celui qui travaille selon les heures compressées où la limite passe à 13 heures (sect. 20 (3) de la loi). La santé physique et mentale de tout travailleur à Maurice est une valeur fondamentale faisant partie de l'ordre public de direction. Pour la même raison, la règle que tout travailleur aura au moins 24 heures de repos consécutif au cours d'une semaine doit aussi s'appliquer aux travailleurs atypiques (sect. 20 (5) de la loi).

Nous sommes aussi d'avis qu'aucune raison plausible ne peut expliquer le refus d'application du congé connus sous le nom de *vacation leave* (section 47 (1) de la loi) et du congé spécial (*special leave*) (section 47 (1) de la loi) aux travailleurs atypiques.

Les règles sur les interdictions et les restrictions relatives aux déductions sur le salaire de l'employé doivent aussi s'appliquer aux travailleurs atypiques (section 34 de la loi). Eux aussi ont besoin d'être protégés contre leur propre brusquerie et contre des abus que leur employeur pourrait être tenté de commettre en recourant facilement aux prélèvements sur le salaire.

Finalement, la règle que l'employé a droit à un congé pour prendre part dans un procès judiciaire en tant que partie ou en tant que témoin et que ce congé sera payé doit aussi s'appliquer aux travailleurs atypiques (section 51 de la loi).

Outre ses améliorations relatives au régime juridique de tout travailleur atypique, en voici quelques-unes concernant les catégories existantes de travailleur atypique.

B. Possibles améliorations relatives aux catégories spécifiques de travailleur atypique

Pour ce qui est du travailleur à temps partiel, il nous semble injuste qu'un travailleur à temps partiel, travaillant moins de 24 heures par semaine pour le même employeur n'a pas droit au *transitional unemplyment benefit*. Par ailleurs, il pourrait être explicitement prévu dans la loi que les clauses de non-concurrence ne s'appliquent pas aux travailleurs à temps partiel. Les clauses de non-concurrence sont bien connues dans la jurisprudence de la Cour suprême de Maurice, ce dont témoignent les arrêts *Hardy Henry and Cie Ltée vs. Kaloo* 1986 MR 173 and 1986 SCJ 269, *L'Acropole Ltd. vs Gerbe d'or Ltd. and Anor* 1982 MR 153 and SCJ 169, *Lenoir Ducray Ltd v. Ramdhany B. & Anor* 2004 SCJ 35 et *Nabridas Ltd vs Coombes M.* 2019 SCJ 142. La validité des clauses de non-concurrence dépend essentiellement de l'existence des intérêts légitimes de l'employeur qu'il faut protéger (protection des secrets commerciaux) et de la limitation de l'obligation de non-concurrence dans le temps et dans l'espace. Néanmoins, nous sommes d'avis, en conformité avec la position de notre Cour suprême, que la clause de non-concurrence ne doit pas s'appliquer à l'employé à temps partiel, même si les critères exposés plus haut seraient satisfaits. Comme il n'est pas complètement intégré dans la structure de son employeur, et travaille pour lui un nombre d'heures limité, interdire au travailleur à temps partiel de chercher des heures de travail supplémentaires serait contraire à sa dignité ainsi qu'à celle de sa famille. Cela l'empêcherait de gagner correctement sa vie.

Possibles améliorations du régime juridique des catégories de travailleurs atypiques laissées en dehors des textes actuels

Il y a trois catégories de travail atypique, laissées en dehors des textes actuels à Maurice, dont le régime juridique pourrait être amélioré, nommément le travailleur temporaire (1), le travailleur sur appel (2) et le travailleur zéro heures (3).

1. Possibles améliorations relatives au travailleur temporaire

Il nous semble injuste que le travailleur temporaire, resté dans l'emploi auprès d'un même employeur pour une période de moins de 6 mois, soit privé du droit à tous les congés reconnus aux autres catégories de travailleurs (section 45 (4) de la loi). Il devrait avoir droit aux congés sur une base *pro rata*. De plus, il nous semble inique qu'un travailleur temporaire de sexe masculin, ayant travaillé pour un même employeur moins de 12 mois consécutif ne soit pas éligible au congé paternité (section 53 de la loi). Nous sommes d'avis qu'il devrait avoir droit à ce congé sur une base *pro rata*. Finalement, il nous semble inéquitable qu'un travailleur temporaire, ayant travaillé pour un même employeur moins de 180 jours n'a pas le droit au *transitional unemployment benefit* (section 84 de la loi). A notre avis, il n'y a pas de raison qu'un tel bénéfice ne lui est pas accordé sur une base *pro rata*.

2. Possibles améliorations relatives au travailleur sur appel

Un travailleur sur appel, qui n'est pas employé sur un contrat à durée déterminée, a besoin d'une solide protection contre des abus que son employeur pourrait être tenté de commettre. Nous sommes d'avis qu'un travailleur sur appel, qui attend chez pour être appelé et faire le travail pour son employeur, doit être rémunéré pour le temps qu'il a passé en attendant *si le temps d'attente a été passé principalement dans l'intérêt de l'employeur et de son entreprise*[30]. C'est un critère flexible qui sera appliqué

---

[30] STONE K. V. W, *art. précit.*, 2006, p. 5–6; *California Employees Should be Paid While "On call"*, disponible depuis: https://www.asmlawyers.com/california-employees-should-be-paid-while-on-call/ (dernière visite le 14 juillet 2022).

au cas par cas et d'après les circonstances de l'espèce. Les indices à prendre en compte sont les contraintes géographiques et temporelles, l'impossibilité de se livrer à des activités personnelles et familiales et l'imminence de l'appel de l'employeur[31]. Le travailleur sur appel doit, bien sûr être rémunéré pour les heures effectives de travail, mais aussi pour le temps passé dans les transports alors qu'ils se déplacer pour exécuter sa mission[32].

En revanche, il ne semble opportun, à notre avis, d'imposer un nombre minimum d'heures de travail par jour. La rémunération du travailleur sur appel est calculée d'après le même mode que pour les autres travailleurs. Autant que possible, il faut faire une notification en laissant un délai raisonnable au travailleur sur appel pour se préparer pour le travail. Cependant, ce ne sera pas toujours possible. Autant que possible, le travailleur sur appel devrait être impliqué dans l'organisation de son travail.

3. Possibles améliorations relatives au travailleur zéro heures

Le travailleur atypique zéro heure, de même que le travailleur sur appel se trouve dans une position de précarité et de dépendance économique et psychologique face à son employeur[33]. Même si ce type de travailleur atypique est très approprié du point de vue de la « *gig economy* », qui s'est imposée de plus en plus à Maurice comme dans le monde, il faut protéger ce type de travailleur atypique. La responsabilité délictuelle et les articles 1382 et 1383 sont les fondements applicables contre les

---

[31] *On call working – what is working time and what remuneration should you receive?*, disponible depuis: https://www.the-pda.org/wp-content/uploads/On call working-detailed-legal-advice-FINAL.pdf (dernière visite le 14 juillet 2022); MCCLELLAND N., *When are On-Call Shifts considered working time?*, disponible depuis: https://www.thorntons-law.co.uk/knowledge/when-are-on-call-shifts-con sidered-working-time (dernière visite le 14 juillet 2022).

[32] *Working Time Directive – On Call and Sleeping In*, Unison Bargaining Support, disponible depuis: https://www.unison.org.uk/content/uploads/2013/06/Briefi ngs-and-CircularsWorking-Time-Directive-On-call-and-Sleeping-in-ver12.pdf (dernière visite le 14 juillet 2022).

[33] *Zero-Hours Contracts, Understanding the Law*, 2021, disponible depuis: https:// www.cipd.co.uk/Images/zero-hours-contracts-guide-web-2021_tcm18-10706.pdf (dernière visite le 14 juillet 2022), p. 10.

employeurs qui abuseraient de ce type de travail atypique. Concrètement, au cas où un employeur refuserait à son travailleur atypique zéro heure la possibilité de refuser une offre cela constituerait une faute délictuelle (un comportement contraire à ce qu'aurait fait un employeur prudent raisonnable)[34] entrainant l'obligation pour l'employeur de réparer le préjudice subi par le travailleur atypique.

Conclusion

L'analyse faite dans ce papier nous amène à une double conclusion. D'une part, le régime juridique du travailleur atypique dans les textes mauriciens actuels semble être un édifice solide, qui n'a pas besoin d'un remaniement radical. D'autre part, certaines améliorations législatives sont tout de même envisageables, afin d'améliorer davantage le statut juridique des travailleurs atypiques déjà mentionnés dans les textes actuels, notamment les travailleurs travaillant depuis la maison et les travailleurs à temps partiel, mais aussi dans le but d'éclairer le statut juridique des travailleurs qui sont laissés en dehors des textes actuels, tels que les travailleurs temporaires, les travailleurs sur appel et les travailleurs zéro heures.

Bibliographie

Ammons K. S. & Markham W. T., 'Working at home: Experiences of skilled white collar workers', *Sociological Spectrum*, 2004, 24, pp. 191–238.

Ancel P., *Droit des obligations en 12 thèmes*. Dalloz, 12ème éd., 2020.

Cabrillac R., *Droit des obligations*. Dalloz, 14ème éd., 2020.

California employees should be paid while 'On call', disponible depuis: https://www.asmlawyers.com/california-employees-should-be-paid-while-on-call/ (dernière visite le 14 juillet 2022).

Chenede F., *Le nouveau droit des obligations et des contrats 2019/2020*. Dalloz, 2ème éd., 2018.

---

[34] GEORGIJEVIC G., "Mauritian Tort Law", *Belgrade Law Review (Annals of the Faculty of Law in Belgrade)*, n° 4/2020, p. 191–194.

England G., *Part-time, casual and other atypical workers: A legal view*. Kingston, ON, Canada: Industrial Relations Centre, Queen's University, 1987.

Georgijevic G., 'Mauritian Tort Law', *Belgrade Law Review (Annals of the Faculty of Law in Belgrade)*, 2020, n° 4, pp. 184–203.

Gunputh R. P., *Labour and industrial relations law: Study guide*. Réduit: University of Mauritius, 2020.

Gyulavari T., 'Collective rights of platform workers: The role of EU law', *Maastricht Journal of European and Comparative Law*, 2020, 27, n°4, pp. 406–424.

Kniffin, 'Covid 19 and the workplace: Implications, issues and insights for future research and action', *American Psychologist*, 2020, pp. 1–15.

Lalive R. & Oesch D., *AI & The future of work* [Online] Zurich, Credit Suisse, disponible depuis: https://www.credit-suisse.com/media/assets/corporate/docs/about-us/research/publications/ai-the-future-of-work.pdf [dernière visite 13 juillet 2022].

Lang C., Schomann I. & Clauwaert S., *Atypical forms of employment contracts in times of crisis*. European Trade Union Institute, 2013, Working Paper 2013.03.

Mcclelland N., *When are on-call shifts considered working time?*, disponible depuis: https://www.thorntons-law.co.uk/knowledge/when-are-on-call-shifts-considered-working-time (dernière visite le 14 juillet 2022).

On call working – What is working time and what remuneration should you receive?, disponible depuis: https://www.the-pda.org/wp-content/uploads/On-call-working-detailed-legal-advice-FINAL.pdf (dernière visite le 14 juillet 2022).

Okkan D., *Introduction au droit du travail mauricien : les relations individuelles de travail*. Aix-Marseilles III : Faculté de Droit et des Sciences Politiques, 1995.

Porchy-Simon S., *Droit des obligations 2022*. Dalloz, 13ème éd., 2021.

Ramamurti B., *The shift toward remote work could leave blue-collar workers behind*, 2020. [Online] disponible depuis: https://edition.cnn.com/2020/09/16/perspectives/remote-work-blue-collar/index.html [dernière visite le 22 septembre 2020].

Schiek D., 'Agency work – From marginalisation towards acceptance? Agency work in EU social and employment policy and the 'implementation' of the draft directive on agency work into German law', *German Law Journal*, 2004, 5, n° 10, pp. 1233–1257.

Schoukens P. & Barrio A., 'The changing concept of work: When does typical work become atypical?', *European Labour Law Journal*, 2017, 8, n°4, pp. 306–322.

Schoukens P., Barrio A. & Montebovi S., *'The EU social pillar: An answer to the challenge of the social protection of platform workers?'*, European Journal of Social Security, 2018, 20, n° 3, pp. 219–241.

Schulte P. & Howard J., *The impact of technology on work and the workforce*, 2019, [Online] disponible depuis: https://www.ilo.org/safework/events/safeday/33thinkpieces/WCMS_681603/lang--en/index.htm [dernière visite le 13 juillet 2022].

Stavrou-Costea E., Kabst R. & Isidor R., 'The utilization of atypical employment – One size does not fit all', *Personal Quarterly*, 2014, 66, n° 4, pp. 6–8.

Stone K. V. W., 'Legal protections for atypical employees: Employment law for workers without workplaces and employees without employers', *Berkeley Journal of Employment and Labor Law*, 2006, 27, n° 2, pp. 252–286.

Taylor D., *Ain't that typical? Everyday challenges for an atypical workforce*, 2017, ACAS Discussion Papers, disponible depuis: https://www.acas.org.uk/aint-that-typical (dernière visite le 13 juillet 2022).

Tranchant L. & Egea V., *Droit des obligations 2021*. Dalloz, 24ème ed., 2021.

Wolmark C. & Peskine E., *Droit du travail 2022*. Dalloz, 15ème éd., 2021.

Working time directive – On call and sleeping in, Unison Bargaining Support, disponible depuis: https://www.unison.org.uk/content/uploads/2013/06/Briefings-and-CircularsWorking-Time-Directive-On-call-and-Sleeping-in-ver12.pdf (dernière visite le 14 juillet 2022).

Zero-hours contracts, understanding the law, 2021, disponible depuis: https://www.cipd.co.uk/Images/zero-hours-contracts-guide-web-2021_tcm18-10706.pdf (dernière visite le 14 juillet 2022), p. 10.

An Empirical Study on Socio Economic Status of Indians in turbulent times of COVID-19

Sid CHOUDARY[1]

By the end of 2019, the world witnessed unusual hues and cries for saving human lives from the unknown disease namely the novel COVID-19 or SARS-CoV-2. The situation was alarming as this life-threatening virus was spreading its tentacles over neighbouring areas of the infected region at an unprecedented rate, hence most of the nations opted for the obvious crisis-driven solution; the lockdown. These lockdowns which were imposed and observed for immediate relief brought the socio-cultural and economic life of the world to a standstill. Around 100 countries of the world were strictly observing the lockdown which led to the temporary shutdown of formal and informal businesses. This directly or indirectly had ramifications over roughly 60 million into the extreme poverty reversing the positive steps in the direction of the eradication of the poverty [1]. This was for the first time in knowing the human history that such a large number of people were subjected to restricted movement. A long-term crisis is caused in the International economy, health, politics, and socio-cultural environment after various concomitant outbreaks like polio, plague, and Spanish flu. The testing times as more than 195 countries, including the world's most advanced and developed nations around the globe at the same time were suffering from SARS-CoV-2. The restricted national and international mobilities as well as economic activities in agriculture, manufacturing, and the service sector of the economy pushed every nation into the gallows of economic slowdown and recession. This situation was further worsened by the disruption of the global supply chain. The scary scenes of the mass exodus of migrants on foot during the nationwide lockdown and their related concerns about the daily ration availability, health care facilities, loss of jobs, and absence of social security at large. All this made think tanks of India make necessary customized adjustments in policymaking and its implementation by making it more inclusive and secular. This opens the door to preparing India to stand tall and play a crucial role in a resilient and sustainable global supply chain.

---

[1] PhD student University Paris Nanterre.

À la fin de l'année 2019, le monde a été témoin de manifestations inhabituelles pour sauver des vies humaines de la maladie inconnue qu'est le nouveau COVID-19 ou SRAS-CoV-2. La situation était alarmante, car ce virus mortel étendait ses tentacules sur les zones voisines de la région infectée à un rythme sans précédent, si bien que la plupart des pays ont opté pour la solution de crise la plus évidente: le confinement. Ces fermetures, imposées et observées en vue d'un soulagement immédiat, ont paralysé la vie socioculturelle et économique du monde. Une centaine de pays ont observé strictement le lockdown, ce qui a entraîné la fermeture temporaire des entreprises formelles et informelles. Cette situation a eu des répercussions directes ou indirectes sur environ 60 millions de personnes qui se sont retrouvées dans une situation d'extrême pauvreté, ce qui a inversé les progrès accomplis dans l'éradication de la pauvreté [1]. C'était la première fois dans l'histoire de l'humanité qu'un si grand nombre de personnes étaient soumises à des restrictions de mouvement. Une crise à long terme est provoquée dans l'économie internationale, la santé, la politique et l'environnement socioculturel après diverses épidémies concomitantes telles que la polio, la peste et la grippe espagnole. La période d'essai, alors que plus de 195 pays, y compris les nations les plus avancées et les plus développées du monde, souffraient en même temps du SRAS-CoV-2. La restriction des mobilités nationales et internationales ainsi que des activités économiques dans l'agriculture, l'industrie manufacturière et le secteur des services de l'économie a poussé tous les pays dans le gouffre du ralentissement économique et de la récession. Cette situation a encore été aggravée par la perturbation de la chaîne d'approvisionnement mondiale. Les scènes effrayantes de l'exode massif des migrants à pied pendant le bouclage de l'ensemble du pays et leurs inquiétudes quant à la disponibilité des rations quotidiennes, aux soins de santé, à la perte d'emplois et à l'absence de sécurité sociale dans l'ensemble du pays. Tout cela a incité les groupes de réflexion indiens à procéder aux ajustements personnalisés nécessaires dans l'élaboration et la mise en œuvre des politiques en les rendant plus inclusives et laïques. Cela ouvre la voie à la préparation de l'Inde pour qu'elle puisse se tenir debout et jouer un rôle crucial dans une chaîne d'approvisionnement mondiale résiliente et durable.

Introduction

A family of viruses known as CoV (Coronaviruses) is the reason behind most diseases starting from the mild common cold to the severe MERS (Middle East respiratory syndrome) or SARS-CoV (severe acute respiratory syndrome). The first patient of SARS-CoV-2 who was reported by China to the WHO was from the Wuhan city of Hubei province, on 31 December 2019. While the first patient in India was identified in Kerala on 27 January 2020. Considering its impact on human lives worldwide, this disease was aptly declared a global pandemic by the WHO on 11 March 2020.

With coughing and sneezing, shortness of breath, and fever as its main symptoms, this virus initially acts like influenza. Being a communicable disease transmitted by touching the contaminated surface or inhaling infected particles present in the air. This virus usually remains alive in the body of the host for 5 days. Sometimes it can remain in a state of dormancy in the body of an infected person for 14 days in a row before beginning to show any visible symptoms of this. Many nations diverted and concentrated a considerable amount of their resources on the R&D of their vaccines to tackle this pandemic. For reference, many nations like the UK [2] and the USA [3] aggressively took conscious decisions to suspend non-crucial research and related funding for the time being and focus all that energy on the research of COVID-19. For the contentment of this virus, not only nationwide lockdowns but also travel restrictions and entry bans from the infected regions were duly imposed. During this time, pharmaceutical products imported from China stumbled to 13 % from 34 %, while European Union India stood at merely 26 % and 18 % respectively [4]. Several countries meticulously planned and conducted the evacuation of their citizens, especially students struck on foreign land. They were brought back to their homeland by prolonged, well-coordinated, and sincere multi-nation efforts. Uncensored and unedited spread of misinformation and disinformation on various available social media platforms regarding COVID-19 not only hindered the government's efforts in its curtailment but also was disturbing to many individuals. There are far-hitting multi-sectoral consequences across various strata of society. Check on social events like clubbing, kitty parties, marriages, or religious as well as cultural functions or gatherings. Increasing unemployment further added to the woes of individuals and marred the basic fabric of society. All this not only affected economical or mental health of the individual, but also the social health. This pandemic has changed forever the behaviour and dynamics of the engagements of the individual in the private and public levels or nations at the regional and international levels. In a nutshell, rightfully it is labeled as the worst global recession post the Great depression of 1930.

However, induced lockdowns were also the reason behind a reduced carbon footprint. This helped in reducing the otherwise ever-increasing menace of air and water pollution levels. Such an unanticipated positive impact of COVID-19 induced lockdowns on the environment and the ecosystem finds special mention [5]. Now with this unlock, the economy has started to open up, the industries gearing up for a fresh reboot in this new scenario and migrant workers have again started to hunt a suitable job for themselves, with a gradually improving business conditions, manufacturing sector getting back on its feet is anticipated to have a pragmatic impact on the rupee, international trade, and unemployment rates.

This paper tries to analyse the pandemic's impact on socio-cultural and economic factors and further delving into the remedial governmental policies enacted or extended to keep in check the disruptions and eventually improve the ease of living and ease of doing business, particularly in India.

There are various compelling reasons for choosing India as a subject of interest as follows:

1. The emergence of India in the global arena in recent times because of this growing soft power and strong presence of the Indian diaspora worldwide.
2. Being the largest democracy in the world and home to approximately 138 million people belonging to vivid ethnicities and religions thriving on 2.4 % of the total earth's surface.
3. Over the last decade, India riding on its accelerated economic growth managed to become the 5th largest economy based on the nominal GDP and a 3rd largest as per the GDP-based PPP[15] (purchasing power parity) out of the 195 countries as noticed by the IMF. Even institutions like the world bank see her as a potential economic giant and hub of global economic activities shortly.
4. India is one of the oldest and greatest surviving civilizations on this planet and is a hot spot of rich cultural heritage. Currently, India stands on the 6th position globally, having 40 World Heritage Sites: 32 cultural, 7 natural, and 1 mixed type of site.
5. As per the IMF, the repercussions of the various covid waves, Russian-Ukraine war's impact, global food shortage, energy crisis, stressed monetary conditions and shooting inflation (inflation above target) will try to slowdown India 29. Under section 45ZA of the RBI Act, 1934, the Central government has fixed the target CPI inflation at 4 % with a +/-2 % tolerance band for the next 5 years i.e., 2021–2026.

These are some of the most prominent factors behind the visible fault lines on the road ahead. The economic crisis in recent times in India adversely affects GDP per capita and supply chains at intra-national along with international ones. Owing to the robustness and resilience of India's economy, she has managed to bounce back and emerge again as one of the fastest-growing nations in the world[16]. After extrapolating these economic parameters, one expects her to enter the top three leading global economies within the following 15 years[16] timescale.

This study, observes and analyses the divergences in the economic health of India in the three phases i.e., before, during and after impositions of lockdowns, between 2019 to 2022. In the last two years, India has faced three waves. For the empirical analysis purposes, data from pre-lockdown (till 24 March 2020), lockdown (25-March 2020 to 31-May 2021) and unlocking phase (01-April 2022 to 31-December 2022) are taken into consideration. Different socioeconomic factors' impact on Indian economy, including the following, examined in detail: High unemployment rate; High inflationary pressure; Deceleration in growth; Shrink in various sectors of economy or window of new opportunities; FDI fluctuations; Reduction of the Foreign exchange rates; Price increase of gold and silver; and GDP.

Additionally, thorough investigation of remedial policies rolled out by different institutions and how the rebound of the Indian economy post unlocks happening.

I. Unemployment rate fluctuations with lockdown

Around 122 million Indians were thrown out of their jobs in April 2020 [6] after first lockdown and around 10.1 million in the second wave in 2022. Out of them, more than 75 % were found to be small traders including hawkers and daily-wagers. Though it might be comparatively easy to bring back the wagers and hawkers into the ambit of employment than the salaried ones.

In 2019–20 there were approximately 77 million entrepreneurs which fell to around 61 million in April 2020–21. Out of 63 million mushrooming MSMEs, around 97 % are found to be micro enterprises by February 2022. Amongst them, roughly 100,100 enterprises were having revenue of more than US$ 1 million. Only a minuscule 5.2 % approx. of these enterprises were earning revenue in excess of US$ 3 million.

Tamil Nadu top the list of the worst hit states with its minimum labour participation and highest unemployment rate. Massive fall can be determined from the various statistical charts shared in the paper. While an estimated 404 million people were employed in the year 2019–20, were reduced to 396 million by March 2020. This number further took a nosedive when it stood at 282 million in April 2020. It is worth mentioning that when jobs were evaporating in the other sectors rest were facing the heat of salary cut. Then farming came to the rescue of most of the aggrieved.

Unemployment shot up dramatically from 6.68 % on 15 March 2020 to 25.9 % on 19 April 2020 with the declaration of 21 days complete lockdown on 24 March 2020. And it again went back to pre-lockdown levels by mid-June of 2020.

This lockdown began from 25 March for 21 days, discontinued most of the non-essential products. Though detailed lockdown was imposed in four phases in 2020, and it took several months even after its relaxations to bring down the rate to somewhat pre-lockdown levels. This had an impact over approximately 28.1 million informal labourers working particularly in the urban areas. As observed from the various charts in Fig. unemployment rate for urban areas increased from an average value of 7.3 % during pre-lockdown period to 27.1 % during the lockdown, whereas for rural region this rate for rural areas before lockdown was around 6.19 % which rose to 23.42 % in the months of March, April, and May. This adversely affected about 93 % of urban informal workers in who were associated with the non-agricultural sector owing to restrictions in financial activities of cities inclusive of business startups and industrial ventures. Major chunk of these informal labours is engaged in manufacturing, tourism sector, hotel industry, Food & Beverages industry, logistics, supply chain and real estate. Amongst them, Real estate sector especially the Constructions was badly hurt because of the unreliable nature of work conditions and environment. The troubled reimbursement of the daily wagers was the real pain. Gradually, depletion and depreciation of the resources crippled the micro or small-scale businesses. They were pushed to the verge of shutdown with virtually no capital for their subsistence.

It continued its surge and peaked at 8.3 % at one-year high rate in August 2022. After reaching this point it reduced to 6.43 % in the next month, which was the lowest level in the last four years, since August 2018 [7].

An empirical study on socio economic status of Indians 247

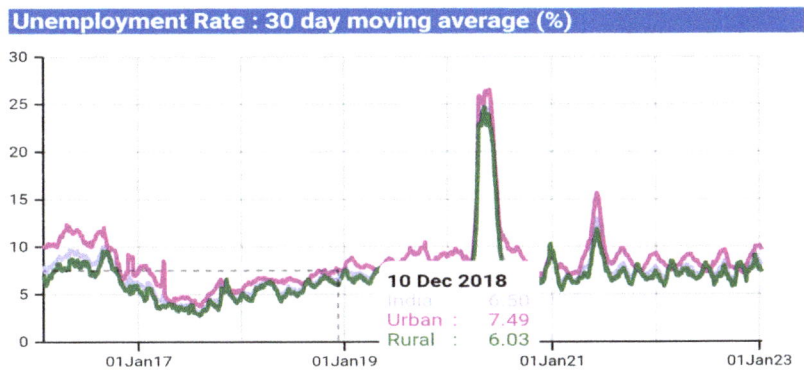

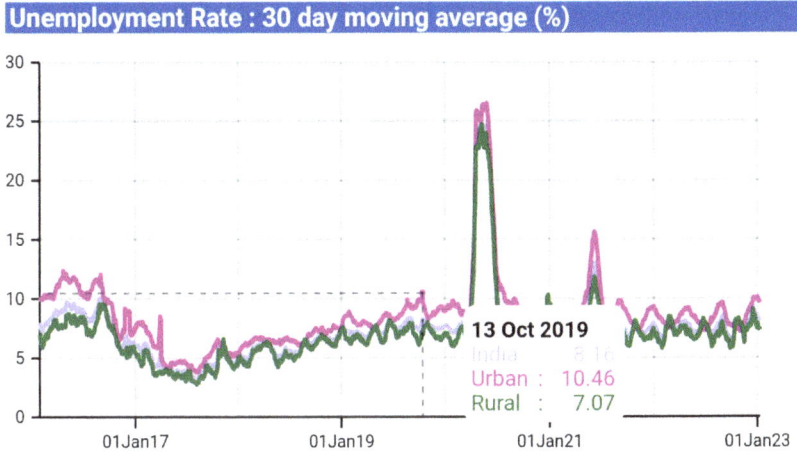

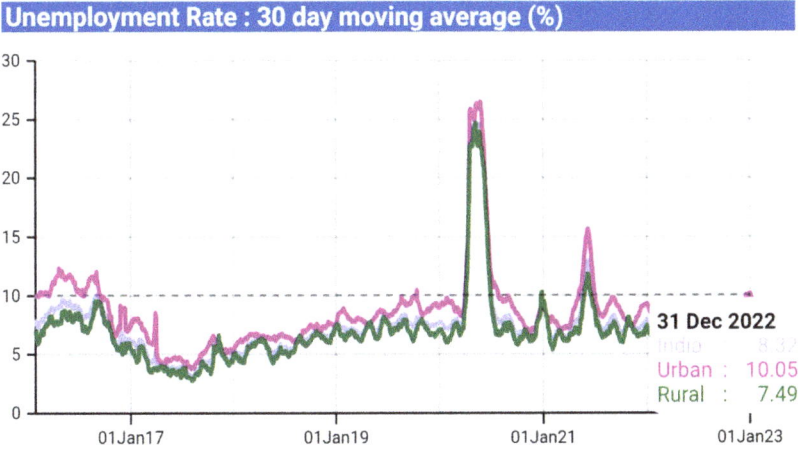

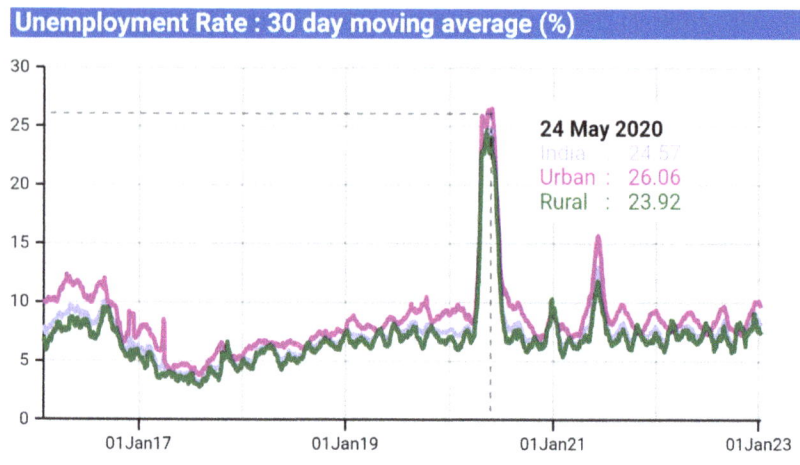

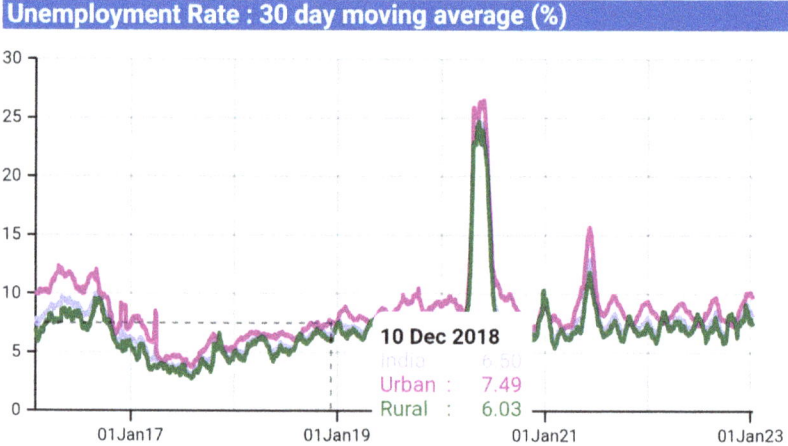

Fig. 1: Variation of Estimated Unemployment Rate (%) with Lockdowns in Urban and Rural areas. (Source: CMIE, Centre for Monitoring Indian Economy)

A. *Unemployment rate variations amongst different states*

Every state has specialized in certain sector like that of agriculture to manufacturing to services. Some states have earned their name in providing skilled to manual workforce. For reference, states like Bihar (46.6) and Jharkhand (59.2) which are home to most of labourers working in other states witnessed the highest unemployment rates of about 47 % and 59 % respectively. This surge was the effect of their mass exodus from their respective workplaces to their home states.

There was a wide spectrum of the rates for example in April 2020–21, Puducherry's unemployment rate stood tall at approximately 76 % in comparison to hilly states. For one of the Himalayan states Himachal Pradesh, it was hovering around 2 %. In the month of May 2020, this rate worsened further in some cases like in that of Delhi, Maharashtra, Jharkhand, and Punjab while it improved for many including the likes of Odisha, Tamil Nadu and Puducherry with reference to previous month level.

Figure 2 depicts the worst-hit Indian states due to nationwide lockdown. The lockdown also made the lives of economically exposed people such as daily-wage earners, industrial workers, and informal labourers much more difficult.

As inferred from Fig. 3, high levels of unemployment were reported from the major states including Delhi (44), Tamil Nadu (50), and Haryana (43) with a strong industrial presence. The primary reasons include a halt in the production and manufacturing of goods in the month of April and May. The same pattern can be drawn from the chart for the other manufacturing hubs like that of Karnataka (30), Maharashtra (21) or Gujrat (19) for reporting surge in an unemployment rate of over three times rise over the previous ones. This rise in the rate was duly reinforced by unchecked layoffs of the industrial labourers at large.

Debt traps, increasing rate of interest, inflation, untimely or no payments of wages, mass layoffs, mass exodus, cost of treatments, emergency expenses not only worsened financial condition of almost every single house but broke the spine micro startups. This was recipe of disaster which triggered vicious cycle pushing the higher middle-income groups to middle or lower middle while lower middle to below poverty line. Coming out of and providing relief to them in time was a daunting task for every concerned organisations. In this hour of human catastrophe, respective Governments swung into action and tried to provide the necessary aid through schemes like Pradhan Mantri Garib Kalyan Anna Yojana (Food scheme), PM-KISAN scheme (minimum income support scheme), the government aims to support the vulnerable people in these testing times.

II. FDI (Foreign Direct Investment)

This refers to foreign investments with the lasting interest in the economy. This is considered relatively a stable source of foreign exchange reserves. FII (Foreign Institutional Investment); primarily go to the secondary market and debt-funds, i.e., shares and other financial instruments. This is considered quite volatile.

FDIs are of two kinds, namely Greenfield and Brownfield. FDI that directly increases the production capacity of an economy is termed as Greenfield for example new ventures and Brownfield doesn't directly increase the capacity like the ones related to mergers and acquisitions. In India FDI is allowed through two routes:1. Autonomous route, directly allows FDI by RBI basically in new ventures or old venture augmenting capital base except the cases which are restricted by sectoral policies. And all others requiring Government based approval based on recommendations of FIPB (Foreign Investment Promotion Board) and the final decision of CCEA (Cabinet Committee on Economic Affairs). Pros of FDI ranges from additional investable resources, increased access to modern technologies, improving technological capacity, enhanced domestic productions, increasing exports to improving both quantity and quality of foreign reserves. All this comes with a certain cost like MNCs' flexing financial muscles to manipulate domestic policies, destruction of domestic productions and reduced employment opportunities, issues like transfer pricing, asset price bubble or regional inequalities as FDI especially private capital tends to go to developed regions.

Thus, FDI had both merits or demerits and whether it still be beneficial to a country, it largely depends on the fact how this is utilized for the humanitarian crisis

Despite the 'Make in India' shot in the arm of manufacturing sector, the recent India Ratings and Research's (Ind-Ra) Corporates Group shows biased behaviour of majority of the foreign investors realising their fortune in the services [8]. As per the Fitch Ratings, Services are preferred choice for their better ease of doing business than that of manufacturing. The bulk of it pumped in manufacturing as a brownfield investment.

FDI attracted by Services sector in the period of April 2000 to March 2014 was US$ 80.51 billion and US$ 153.01 billion for April 2014 to March 2022. Although, in case of manufacturing lesser hike of US$ 77.11 billion with respect to US$ 94.32 billion was observed. It is worth mentioning that in 2014, 'Make in India' was introduced to facilitate the investments across sectors in order to cash its untapped potential and turn it into a manufacturing hub. It was followed up by the Production-Linked Incentive (PLI) scheme to further scale up domestic manufacturing capability, accompanied by higher import substitution and employment generation as concentrates more on labour-intensive sectors. Under the PLI schemes for 13 manufacturing sectors central government allocated Rs 1.970 trillion and in Budget 2022–23, an additional amount of Rs 195 billion was set aside for solar PV modules manufacturing.

Between 2000 and 2014, majority of services sector FDI was directed towards banking/insurance, hotels/tourism, telecommunications, trading and IT/business outsourcing. And auto, chemicals, drugs and pharmaceuticals, metallurgical and food processing were the favourites from the manufacturing sector side.

Computer hardware and software industries were a star performer as its FDI picked up from US$ 12.8 billion during April 2000 to March 2014 to whopping US$ 72.7 billion during April 2014 to March 2022 [9]. PLI scheme rolled out red carpet for major MNCs. Conducive environment grabbed the eyes of Apple, Samsung, Flextronics, and Nokia, all announcing large investments in the various parts of India.

Till 2020, India riding on the tide of series of successful reforms, turned out to be more preferred destination FDI especially amongst the group of emerging market economies. This increase settled at 6.65 % in 2020 before getting obstructed by Covid. It stumbled down to 2.83 % in 2021.

Beginning from October 2019 to March 2022, an estimated 83 % of FDI was welcomed by four states due to prevalent enabling conditions, are Maharashtra (27.5 %), Karnataka (23.9 %), Gujarat (19.1 %) and (Delhi 12.4 %) [9]. This has led to the emergence FDI corridors namely Maharashtra-Gujarat in the west, NCR of Delhi in the north and Karnataka-Tamil Nadu-Andhra Pradesh-Telangana in the South. Its noticeable skewed pattern will not be of much help to the national cause of the broad-based development.

III. ForEx (Foreign reserves)

Since the global recession in 2008, the forex saw its biggest weekly fall of US$ 11.98 in March 2020 due to COVID [10].

Unscheduled capital flight from emerging markets to safe havens was crippling the Indian currency which also had fallen to a record low. To arrest its slump any further, the central bank reluctantly sold some of its forexes.

In October 2021, the forex kitty touched its all-time high of US$ 645 billion [12]. It further slipped to $597.72 billion by April 2022. These reserves are deployed to defend the rupee against evolving global pressure owing to capital outflows and the strengthening dollar amid corona. The Ukraine-Russia war led to a spike in oil and commodity prices. This also was crucial in keeping the demand for dollars high. Therefore, they are depleting and after registering a drop of US$ 1.268 billion, reached the mark of US$ 561.583 billion for the week ended 6 January 2023 (as per RBI) [11]. After this week, RBI's special drawing rights (SDR) and reserve position in the International Monetary Fund was US$ 18.217 billion and US$ 5.141 billion. And US$ 41.784 billions of gold reserves was held by RBI in this period.

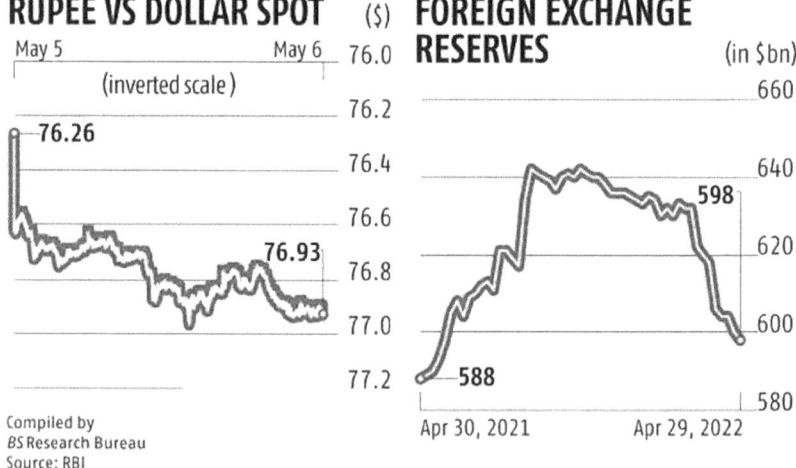

Fig. 3: Fluctuations in the value of Rupee (INR) against Dollar (USD) and its effect on the India's Foreign Exchange Reserves. (Source: RBI, GoI)

Now it is interesting time ahead as if this trend continues what will be the strategy of the RBI (Reserve Bank of India)? Whether it will sacrifice the rupee to sustain forex or vice-versa on the horizon.

IV. Impact of COVID-19 on gold and silver prices

In the period of global crisis, change in the consumer demand, decline in consumer spending, industrial production, and foreign trading was seen. Restricted economic activities crippled most of the companies, as they failed to generate revenue as before. Therefore, low turnovers kick-start a fall in their share prices respectively. This volatility of the stock market disinterested its investors, so they were forced to look for alternatives. Even real estate sector was also suffering from uncertainties. Then Gold and Silver stood out as most promising investment amongst the available alternatives. With surge in demand and limited supply of these precious metals due to disrupted global supply chain pushed its price on the higher side not only in the domestic but also in the international markets. The yellow metal on 31 March 2020 was Rs. 48651 which was priced at Rs. 48720 on 31 March 2021 which rose to Rs. 51484 on 31 March 2022 rupees per 10 grams (standard 24 carats). This shows steady hike in the price due to its strengthening demand in the market [13].

On the other hand, silver was proved to be a more volatile asset. Initial rise in the price of silver was less in comparison to that of the yellow metal, as it was priced at Rs. 40600 on 31 March 3019 while for Rs. 40500 on 31 March 2020 rupees per kilogram. Post lockdown with increasing economic activities, the liquidity crunch started to ease. The sharp surge in the prices of silver was observed when it was Rs 65400 on 31 March 2021. A marginal hike was observed in its prices. A trend was determined as these metals became preferred choice for the investors because of their assured and better returns.

V. GDP

A. Growth rate in times of ongoing global turbulence

On account of the global developments owing to corona, the real GDP suffered a shrinkage of 7.3 % in 2020–21. It was the worst performance in any year post-independence. This shrinkage could be comfortably above 8 % if the informal sectors are taken into the ambit of consideration. During this period, the informal sectors unarguably were the worst hit. The two biggest engines of India's economic growth are expected to be private consumption and investments. Agriculture was the sole saviour when the performances of the remaining sectors were shabby and poor. The economy was already reeling under tremendous pressure as its fault lines were exposed and worsened by an ongoing humanitarian crisis much before the arrival of the second wave. Corona instigated recession seemed inevitable with the continuing economic shrinkage for the next four quarters. Its dampening rate was accentuated by shooting unemployment and shutting MSMEs. The Indian economy was struggling and stumbling and set to miss its anticipated deadline on the way of becoming a US$ 5 trillion one. It was desperately in want of billions of dollars in injection. It was one of the most effective solutions implemented by the government. The need for time to consolidate the acceleration of the economic recovery and tackle the health-related issues. GDP growth hit the rock bottom and it consequently shrank to the lowest ever.

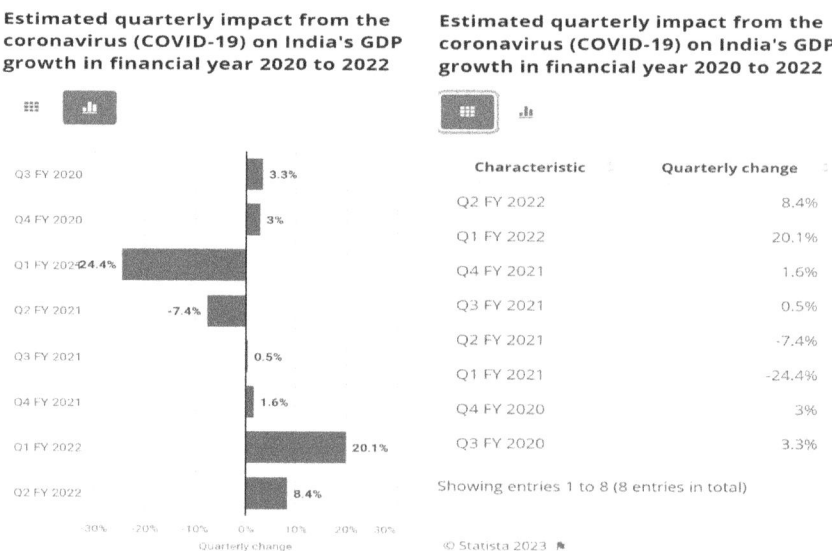

Fig. 4: Corona Impact on GDP analysed quarterly for financial year 2020–22. (Source: World Bank)

Despite the drags from these spillovers, it marched on the road to recovery with 8.7 % growth in the next year i.e. 2021–22. It was exactly 1.5 % higher than the real GDP of 2019–20. By mid of 2022, economy begins to rebound after easing out of the covid restrictions [14]. War since February 2022, fervors the inflationary pressure forcing government to pullback the loose monetary policy invoked around pandemic. In May 2022, key interest rates were raised to the three-year highest mark of 6.25 % by 225 basis points. Another hike is around the corner. To revive consumption and keep a check on rising inflation, Government reduced the Central Excise duty on petrol and diesel in August 2022.

Now pandemic induced distortions are gradually levelling out. For the passing 2022–23, it is expected to stick around 7 %, making it second fastest growing nation. Although the rate is pulled down a little against the previous year because of the weakening exports and crimping purchasing power. Still, it remains a 'bright spot' in the global economy.

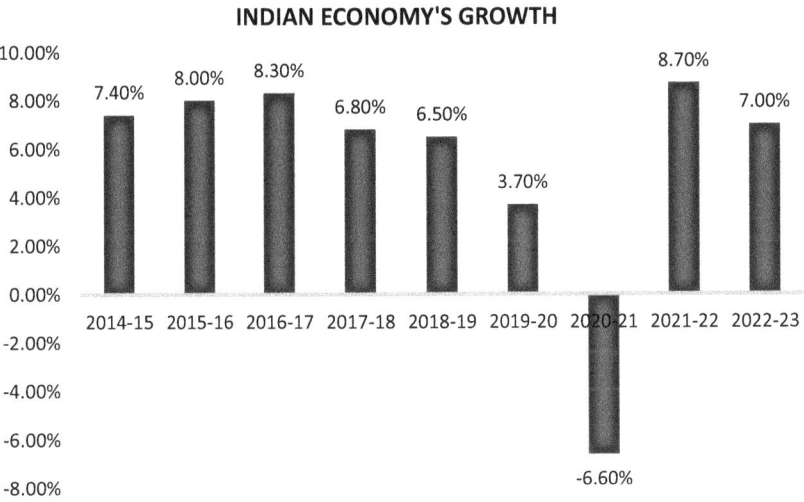

Fig. 5: For 2022–23, India is anticipating 7 % of economic expansion against the previous year. (Source: MoSPI, GoI)

B. Transition into an export-led

In most of the developed Asian economies including Japan, Singapore, South Korea, Taiwan and likes, export has greater say in their development. Till date, India has been missing from the elite club of such export-led economies. Chatterjee and Subramanian (2020) overruled this prevalent notion and reinstated their faith in the belief highlighting India as the paragon of the growth model dictated by the export. Stalled growth of exports for some time have been substantiated by the delayed or diluted legislative policies.

After the merchandise exports were knocked out by the corona, it bounced back to an astounding $421 billion with a growth of 44.6 % in 2022–23. Spike in the exports of agricultural products, engineering and electronic goods played a pivotal role in its record growth. To provide a high-octane boost to competitiveness and exportability of sectors and their global scale, a smooth acceleration and sustainability of its growth wired with employment opportunities generation in the near future, the Centre implemented the schemes like Pradhan Mantri Gati Shakti, National Master Plan and PLI. Moreover, narrow tailoring of policies for providing a conducive environment led to many innovative and globalized initiatives such as that of the 'one district one product' (ODOP) and state-specific products and services for turning it into an exporting hub. This finds special support of the 'team India' with co-operative federalism in its spirit where all state machineries and administrative units work in synergy. Export Preparedness Index 2021 by NITI Aayog, underlines the incredible potential and odds of becoming an export-led economy [15].

For the furtherance of such economic aspirations, India is extensively exploring the possibilities of having free trade agreements (FTAs) with various friendly and like-minded democracies including those with Canada, the European Union and United Kingdom. In this course, she is already occupied in expanding her 7 existing ones and negotiating 16 new ones. India signed CEPA with UAE on 18th February 2022 with a vision of expansion in their bilateral trade to $100 billion against $60 billion in 5 years. Amidst ongoing global macroeconomics headwinds, India-UAE CEPA has started to bear fruit. Between June-August 2022 (Year on year) India's non-petroleum exports to UAE grew in excess of 5 folds against her non-petroleum exports to the rest of the world [16]. India and Australia entered into an Economic Cooperation and Trade Agreement on 29 December 2022 [17], covering almost all the tariff lines dealt in respective nations. India will benefit from Australia providing preferential market access on 100 % of its tariff lines while India offering 70 % of its tariff lines for preferential access to each other. Before Australia, Japan and South Korea are other two OECD (Organization for Economic Co-operation and Development) countries with which India has signed a Free Trade Agreement (FTA).

A correct mix and match of various reforms enabling better EODB (ease of doing business), signing of

FTAs, and world class export infrastructure is indispensable for the swift transition of India into an export-oriented economy. It is necessary to lay the strong foundation for her secular and sustainable growth of 7 %-8 % over the following 25 years.

C. A global bright spot; destined for more accelerated growth

India aspires to be a $5 trillion economy by 2022–26, and later a $10 trillion by the mid of 2030. But, the drag of global and domestic economic situations as mentioned in this chapter, muted the prospects. In May 2022, RBI reluctantly shifted to off-cycle monetary policy by increasing its the repo rate and subsequently increasing it periodically to total 90 basis points by June 2022. This is recorded as a major shift in the stance of the central bank in the last 2 years concentrating on the growth and accommodative monetary policy.

The resultant debt and money market dynamics is all set to cast aspersions on the costs and finances besides EODB in various sectors in the coming fiscal year. Economic activities may anticipate tough times ahead since inflation is projected to soar high at 6.7 % for FY2023. Thus, inflationary pressure presents all around, will keep on pulling interests to uncomfortably higher rates. So, growth prospects will feel the pinch in a continuously deteriorating environment at regional and global levels.

For instance, it is worth noting that RBI in its April resolution for FY2023, downsized from its pre-war projection by a 60 basis points to lower 7.2 % of economic growth [18].

The growth aspirations can still be realized despite all these odds by creating an enabling start-up ecosystem for proper nurturing of the emerging as well as the upcoming startups. Along with, a series of successive comprehensive reforms and customized liberalisation in industries (with an eye on manufacturing), services, agriculture, and export sectors to achieve their developmental and business goals set for the FY2023 as they survived through the last 2 difficult years.

Bibliography

Annual Report Publications 2021–22, Department of Foreign Affairs and Trade, Australian-India ECTA, [cited (2022). May 27]. [Internet].

Available from: https://www.rbi.org.in/Scripts/AnnualReportPublicati ons.aspx?year=2022

Australian Government, Department of Foreign Affairs and Trade, Australian-India ECTA, [Internet]. Available from: https://www.dfat.gov. au/trade/agreements/in-force/australia-india-ecta/outcomes

Chaudhary, A., Gupta, V., Jain, N., & Santosh, K. C. (2021). COVID-19 on air quality index (AQI): A necessary evil?. In *COVID-19: Prediction, decision-making, and its impacts* (pp. 127–137). Singapore: Springer.

Covid effect: Biggest weekly fall in forex reserve since 2008, [cited (2020). Mar 27]. [Internet]. Available from: https://economictimes.indiatimes. com/markets/forex/covid-effect-forex-reserve-posts-biggest-weekly-fall-in-12-years/articleshow/74850984.cms?utm_source=contentofinter est&utm_medium=text&utm_campaign=cppst

Data | An estimated 12.2 crore Indians lost their jobs during the coronavirus lockdown in April: CMI, [cited (2020). May 07]. [Internet]. Available from: https://www.thehindu.com/data/data-over-12-crore-indians-lost-their-jobs-during-the-coronavirus-lockdown-in-april/article61660110.ece

Export Preparedness Index 2021, [cited (2022). Mar 25]. [Internet]. Available from: https://www.niti.gov.in/sites/default/files/2022-03/ Final_EPI_Report_25032022.pdf

India Ratings and Research (Ind-Ra). Available from: https://www.indiarati ngs.co.in/

India's August unemployment highest in last one year at 8.3%, [cited (2022). Sept 02]. [Internet]. Available from: https://timesofindia.indiatimes.com/ business/india-business/indias-august-unemployment-highest-in-last-one-year-at-8-3/articleshow/93940438.cms

India's forex reserves drop by USD 1.268 bn in first week of year, [cited (2023). Jan 13]. [Internet]. Available from: https://www.hindustantimes. com/business/indias-forex-reserves-drop-by-usd-1-268-bn-in-first-week-of-year-101673617112783.html

More FDI in services than manufacturing despite govt's Make in India push: Report, [cited (2022). Dec 28]. [Internet]. Available from: https:// www.livemint.com/news/india/more-fdi-in-services-than-manufacturing-despite-govt-s-make-in-india-push-report-11672228609302.html

Press Releases, [cited (2020). May 08]. [Internet]. Available from: https:// www.rbi.org.in/Scripts/BS_PressReleaseDisplay.aspx?prid=49794

Press Releases, [cited (2022). Aug 01]. [Internet]. Available from: https://pib.gov.in/PressReleaseIframePage.aspx?PRID=1847122

Press Releases, [cited (2022). Sep 25]. [Internet]. Available from: https://pib.gov.in/PressReleasePage.aspx?PRID=1862136

Reserve Bank of India, Available from: https://www.rbi.org.in/

World Bank Group: 100 countries get support in response to COVID-19 (Coronavirus), [cited (2020). May 19]. [Internet]. Available from: https://www.worldbank.org/en/news/press-release/2020/05/19/world-bank-group-100-countries-get-support-in-response-to-covid-19-coronavirus

PART IV

COVID-19, MEDIA, TECHNOLOGY AND DIGITISATION
COVID-19 MEDIEN, TECHNOLOGIE ET DIGITALISTION

The aim of this part is to study the coverage of the epidemic crisis by the media, including social networks, and their role over time on public opinion and public authorities, as well as the role of digitalisation. During the COVID-19 period, as social and professional life came to a halt, the use of digital media in all aspects of life boomed. Not only online learning, but also family gatherings and aperitifs were organized online. This has raised issues such as the protection of the digital data collected (V. Roux) and the risks of misinformation in social media (R. P. Gunputh, A. Beebeejaune). The increased use of digital media has also strengthened GAFAM's position of power and dependence on them (D. J. Boutoille).

L'objectif de cette partie est d'étudier la couverture de la crise épidémique par les médias, y compris les réseaux sociaux, et leur rôle dans le temps sur l'opinion publique et les pouvoirs publics, ainsi que le rôle de la numérisation. Pendant la période COVID-19, alors que la vie sociale et professionnelle s'arrêtait, l'utilisation des médias numériques dans tous les aspects de la vie a explosé. Non seulement l'apprentissage en ligne, mais aussi les réunions de famille et les apéritifs ont été organisés en ligne. Cette évolution a soulevé des questions telles que la protection des données numériques collectées (V. Roux) et les risques de désinformation dans les médias sociaux (R. P. Gunputh, A. Beebeejaune). L'utilisation accrue des médias numériques a également renforcé la position de pouvoir du GAFAM et sa dépendance à leur égard (D. J. Boutoille).

The protection of employee personal data in times of COVID-19 health crisis

Victoria ROUX[1]

Since the COVID-19 pandemic, many companies have been proposing or even preferring to oblige their employees to be tested or even vaccinated among others, in order to limit the spread of the virus within their company. However, the use of tests automatically generates the processing and storage of sensitive personal data, which is particularly protected by the General Data Protection Regulation (GDPR) in the European Union and European Economic Area (EEA). This creates a conflict between the duty incumbent on employers to protect their employees' health and respect for employees' informational self-determination. The aim of this presentation will therefore be to examine the legal framework for protecting employee data in times of health crisis.

Depuis la pandémie de COVID-19, de nombreuses entreprises proposent ou préféreraient même parfois obliger leurs salariés à se faire tester ou même vacciner entre autres, afin de limiter la propagation du virus au sein de leur entreprise. L'utilisation de tests génère cependant automatiquement le traitement et stockage de données personnelles sensibles qui sont particulièrement protégées par le règlement général sur la protection des données (RGPD) au sein de l'Union Européenne (UE) et dans l'Espace Économique Européen (EEE). Il en découle un conflit entre le devoir incombant aux employeurs de protéger la santé de leurs salariés et le respect de l'autodétermination informationnelle des salariés. Cette présentation aura ainsi pour objet d'étudier le cadre juridique de protection des données des salariés en temps de crise sanitaire.

---

[1] Dr. Postdoc Université Paris Nanterre.

Introduction

The World Health Organization (WHO) named the coronavirus disease, which began at the end of the year 2019 'COVID-19'[2]. This paper will hence use the term 'COVID-19' but also 'Corona' in this contribution. With the pandemic came especially the obligation for employees in companies to test themselves or let themselves be tested by their employers. The same problem continued when the vaccination status had to be controlled by employers. Sensible data is in this case being transmitted and stored.

In Europe, the General Data Protection Regulation (GDPR), which is a Regulation in European Union (EU) law on data protection and privacy, not only in the EU but also in the European Economic Area (EEA), is relevant for the protection of the personal data of people as well as employees.

Employers have to protect their employees while also having to respect their right to informational self-determination ('Recht auf informationelle Selbstbestimmung' in Germany). Hence, the right for employers or anyone to process any kind of data is directly opposed to the people's right to informational self-determination.

This article addresses the legal framework of data protection for employees during this sanitary crisis.

I. Employer's obligation and the employees right to informational self-determination in light of the GDPR

The article 4 of the GDPR contains in its paragraph 1 the definition of what a 'personal data' is. According to Art. 4 para. 1 GDPR, '*"personal data" means any information relating to an identified or identifiable natural person ("data subject")*'. An identifiable natural person is a person who can be '*identified, directly or indirectly, in particular by reference to an identifier such as a name, an identification number, location data, an online identifier*

---

[2] World Health Organization, *Naming the coronavirus disease (COVID-19) and the virus that causes it*, https://www.who.int/emergencies/diseases/novel-coronavirus-2019/technical-guidance/naming-the-coronavirus-disease-(covid-2019)-and-the-virus-that-causes-it#:~:text=WHO%20announced%20"COVID%2D19",the%20United%20Nations%20(FAO).

or to one or more factors specific to the physical, physiological, genetic, mental, economic, cultural or social identity of that natural person'. It is especially important to protect natural persons from data breaches, through which personal data could be as listed in art. 4 para. 12 GDPR unlawfully destroyed, lost, altered, disclosed to unauthorized persons or otherwise processed.

The right to informational self-determination[3] is derived from the general personal right pursuant to Article 2 (1) in conjunction with Article 1 (1) of the German constitutional law ('Grundgesetz'), which contains fundamental rights placed at the very beginning, symbolizing their primacy.

It grants individual people the right to decide for themselves when and within what limits, personal facts of life are to be disclosed[4]. An encroachment on the fundamental right will be present in any case, if the individual is obliged to disclose his or her data by government action for example.

No interference will however on the other hand occur, if the individual decides to voluntarily disclose his or her data. This applies, for example, to the German 'Corona-Warn-App' which was in use until the 1st June 2023[5].

An infringement will also happen in the event of a mandatory introduction of proof of immunity[6]. One example of an interference with the fundamental right that has already actually been carried out was the obligation to keep 'contact lists', which was provided for in the Corona ordinances of the federal states for innkeepers as well as operators of other businesses in the fall of 2020[7].

---

[3]   https://www.bundestag.de/resource/blob/842618/658988ef97f601229d6d37afd8bae8d9/WD-3-047-21-pdf-data.pdf
[4]   BVerfGE 103, 21 (33).
[5]   Ausarbeitung der Wissenschaftlichen Dienste des Deutschen Bundestages, Handytracking in Deutschland, WD 3 – 3000 – 097/20, S. 6 f; Die Bundesregierung, *Corona-Warn-App im Ruhemodus*, https://www.bundesregierung.de/breg-de/aktuelles/corona-warn-app-ruhemodus-2182638
[6]   Siehe dazu die Ausarbeitung der Wissenschaftlichen Dienste des Deutschen Bundestages, *Fragen zur Einführung einer Immunitätsdokumentation*, WD 3 – 3000 – 123/20.
[7]   The state used here private parties to collect data. See the Sachstand der Wissenschaftlichen Dienste des Deutschen Bundestages, *Verpflichtung zur*

Furthermore, not all personal data is equal. For example, the name, address, e-mail address and telephone number which are protected in Europe by the GDPR, can be processed if one of the legal bases in Article 6 of the GDPR permits it: this is known as a prohibition with reservation of permission.

Indeed, according to art 6 para 1 GDPR, *'the processing shall be lawful only if and to the extent that at least one of the following applies.'*

Either the data subject has given its consent for one or more purposes which need to be specified; or the processing of the personal data is necessary in order to perform a contract to which the subject is a party or to take steps at the data subjects' request prior the entering into a contract; or the processing of the data is necessary in order to comply with a legal obligation to which the controller is subjected to; or the processing is necessary to protect the vital interests of the data subject or another natural person; or the processing is necessary for the performance of a task carried out in the public interest or exercise of official authority which has been vested in the controller; or the processing is necessary for the purposes of the legitimate interests pursued by the controller or a third party, with an exception in the case that such interests are overridden by the interests or fundamental rights and freedoms of the data subject which require the protection of personal data, especially if the data subject concerned is a child.

Aside from these 'usual' everyday life personal data, sensible data is however even more protected in the EU (and EEA), with article 9 para. 1 GDPR prohibiting the processing of sensible data: The *'Processing of personal data revealing racial or ethnic origin, political opinions, religious or philosophical beliefs, or trade union membership, and the processing of genetic data, biometric data for the purpose of uniquely identifying a natural person, data concerning health or data concerning a natural person's sex life or sexual orientation shall be prohibited.'* In the second paragraph are found the only exemptions of this prohibition.

Datenerhebung zum Zwecke der Kontaktverfolgung nach den Corona-Verordnungen der Länder, WD 3 – 3000 – 087/21.

II. New obligations for employees in time of Corona as well as data processing through voluntary vaccination

At the beginning of the pandemic, the biggest question concerned the covid test(s) and the obligation or not for employees to test themselves. Since then, a lot changed with the marketing of different vaccinations, which is why this article will also review the processing of employee data in the event of a vaccination and not only through obligatory testing. Especially since vaccination was and is still encouraged in Germany.

Aside from the vaccination, enterprises were working towards ensuring the security of their employees at the workplace, wanting them to come back to the office. For this, several hygiene measures needed to be implemented. An example would be devices which measure the temperature. In this regard, Germany would see this chosen measure very critically, since a rise in temperature does not really prove, that someone has COVID-19 and accordingly, the German data protection supervisory authorities have spoken strongly against the use of such devices[8]. Apart from the technicalities of for example whether the device chosen records or documents and for how long the temperature and if a personal reference can be made, a legal obligation is needed in order to use such a device. In Europe, the employees but also broadly speaking all data subjects whose temperature is being recorded have to be informed by the controller, in this case the employer, to what purpose or purposes this data is necessary. This information should also contain the contact detail of the controller processing the data and especially important is the notice about how long this data will be processed and saved. In Germany also, an employer had for a long time a legal obligation to document the 3G status of its employees, meaning whether the employee had recovered from a corona infection or if he is vaccinated or if he is testing himself regularly.

According to the GDPR principle of data minimisation[9], only a few persons should be allowed to process and have access to this very sensible

---

[8] Konferenz der unabhängigen Datenschutzaufsichtsbehörden des Bundes und der Länder (DSK), 10. September 2020, Beschluss zum „Einsatz von Wärmebildkameras beziehungsweise elektronischer Temperaturerfassung im Rahmen der Corona-Pandemie"; Die Landesbeauftragte für den Datenschutz Niedersachsen, 26. Tätigkeitsbericht 2020, S. 122.
[9] Art. 5 para. 1 c) GDPR.

health information. The vaccination should therefore not be openly laid out at the workplace for every employee or guests to see, especially given that data protection fines can even go up to 20 million euros or 4 % of annual turnover of the previous year, whichever is higher according to art. 83 para. 5 GDPR.

The aim of the GDPR is to protect people's data, encompassing employee data. Therefore, even though vaccinations against the Corona virus could normalize working life, there was much discussion about whether and how companies can require or at least encourage vaccination of employees in order to achieve this goal more quickly once sufficient vaccine is available for all.

Companies often do not understand why they cannot take all measures for employee protection against corona. Even though vaccination is seen as enabling normal life, the documentation of the vaccination status is indeed linked to the collection of personal and especially sensible data, which cannot be ignored.

This is also very important regarding employees who do not wish to be vaccinated. In companies, where employees work closely together, if it gets known, that one person is not vaccinated but all others are, this employee could get under pressure if the colleagues learn of it. This goes of course also for a vaccinated person in a non-vaccinated group.

A. Is the processing of health data therefore inadmissible in principle?

Article 9 para. 2 of the GDPR and § 26 (3) of the German data protection law ('Bundesdatenschutzgesetz', BDSG) specifies when such sensible data can be processed as an exception. During especially the beginning period of COVID-19, there was for a long time no real applicable legal basis to process the vaccination status.

Problematic points were especially the following: it is not certain that individuals who have been vaccinated against COVID-19 no longer transmit the virus. In addition, it has not been clarified whether the vaccination provides reliable long-term protection against new cases, especially new mutations. And the employer's duty of care with regard to the health protection of its employees, could be also fulfiled through other suitable measures. This opinion was also held by the State Commissioner for Data Protection and Information Security of North Rhine-Westphalia in its statement of March 18, 2021:

> "The necessity of the query of the Corona vaccination status by the employer is based on § 26 para. 3 of the German data protection law BDSG, Art. 9 para. 2 lit. b) GDPR[10], as far as no special norm (such as § 23 a Infection Protection Act) ("Infektionsschutzgesetz", IfSG) applies. This is currently to be negated in principle. There is currently no legal basis for the collection of vaccination status by employers who are not covered by special standards. Accordingly, vaccination certificates may not be included in the personnel file!
>
> The necessity depends on the specific purposes. Employers often state that they can better protect themselves, their employees (duty of care and protection, § 613 German Civil Code BGB, § 3 German occupational safety and health act ArbSchG) and customers (who may demand this) from potential risks of infection by requesting the vaccination status. In view of the encroachment on the fundamental rights of the individual, the legal situation still does not provide for a vaccination obligation to protect against COVID-19. But Social pressure does build up in the case of inquiries about vaccination status by the employer. [...]
>
> Article 9 para. 2 lit. g) of the GDPR cannot be invoked either, which legitimizes processing for reasons of public interest, because the employer ostensibly has an operational and not a public interest in the disclosure.

B. Is the processing of health data permissible by way of exception?

There were exceptions until the end of 2021, in which it was and is permissible to query the vaccination status in situations in which the exception in § 23 a Infection Protection Act (IfSG)[11] applies. Such

---

[10] Art. 9 para. 2 lit. b) GDPR foresees that *"processing is necessary for the purposes of carrying out the obligations and exercising specific rights of the controller or of the data subject in the field of employment and social security and social protection law in so far as it is authorised by Union or Member State law or a collective agreement pursuant to Member State law providing for appropriate safeguards for the fundamental rights and the interests of the data subject;"*

[11] § 23 a IfSG: „*Soweit es zur Erfüllung von Verpflichtungen aus § 23 Absatz 3 in Bezug auf übertragbare Krankheiten erforderlich ist, darf der Arbeitgeber personenbezogene Daten eines Beschäftigten über dessen Impf- und Serostatus verarbeiten, um über die Begründung eines Beschäftigungsverhältnisses oder über die Art und Weise einer Beschäftigung zu entscheiden. Dies gilt nicht in Bezug auf übertragbare Krankheiten, die im Rahmen einer leitliniengerechten Behandlung nach dem Stand der medizinischen Wissenschaft nicht mehr übertragen werden können. Im Übrigen gelten die Bestimmungen des allgemeinen Datenschutzrechts.*" Translation by the author of this article: "*To the extent necessary*

examples were for employees in medical practices or hospitals. Here, the employer of such a facility was and is allowed to query and process the vaccination status.

In addition, employers who do not belong to such a facility could request the vaccination status of their employees if they linked this to a vaccination bonus. Possible options here include a one-time bonus payment, gifts in kind, or even an additional day of vacation. It should be noted here, that employees may not be disadvantaged without a reason. If the employee wishes to receive a bonus, proof of vaccination may be required. However, within the framework of data minimization and storage limitation, it is not possible to store a copy of the vaccination certificate for example. It would be conceivable to have the proof shown and to check this off in a list where, in order to limit the processed data, the first name and surname of the employee should be checked off on a list on the respective day of the check without any more information on whether the proof shown was a vaccination or test or recovery certificate. The documentation should be kept in a locked cabinet or otherwise protected from access in the case of paper-based documentation. In the case of electronic documentation, files should be encrypted. Access rights should be documented and restrictively assigned, and those authorized to access should be advised of their particular confidentiality. Furthermore, all data must be deleted no later than the end of the sixth month after it was collected and this information do not belong in the personal file of the employees. In addition, and in accordance with Article 13 DSGVO, the employer has the obligation under data protection law to inform his employees about the data processing associated with the control of the vaccination, recovery and test certificates. This information about the manner of data processing should be made available to all employees, in any case at the time of the control of the relevant evidence.

Furthermore, the question was raised whether an employer could invoke consent as in Article 9 para. 2 a) GDPR and request the vaccination status if the employee had consented to answering the question.

---

to fulfill obligations under § 23 (3) with respect to communicable diseases, the employer may process personal data of an employee on his or her vaccination and serostatus in order to decide on the establishment of an employment relationship or on the manner of employment. This does not apply with regard to communicable diseases that can no longer be transmitted within the framework of guideline-based treatment according to the state of medical science. In all other respects, the provisions of general data protection law apply."

Such a voluntary answer is not ruled out, but is associated with high hurdles, which should always be discussed with a data protection officer, especially given the employees relationship with its employer and the resulting relationship of superiority/subordination between them. For this reason alone, a given consent would mostly be not freely given and such a legal basis should not be used.

It is sometimes argued that the employer's right to ask about a stay in a risk area, for example, can be seen as a parallel to the question about vaccination and that a right to ask can therefore also be affirmed here. This view is not followed in the present case. A distinction must be made between the employer's need to know whether an employee is (possibly) infected in order to protect the other employees and the question about the vaccination status, which (at least at present) does not play a decisive role for the colleagues of the vaccinated person. This was also represented in the Press Release of the German Conference of the Independent Data Protection Supervisors (DSK) from March 13, 2020 with the consideration that only the following measures are legitimate under data protection law: '*collection and processing of personal data (including health data) of employees by employers in order to best prevent or contain the spread of the virus among employees. This includes, in particular, information on cases in which an infection has been detected or there has been contact with a demonstrably infected person or in which there has been a stay in an area classified as a risk area by the Robert Koch Institute (RKI) during the relevant period.*'[12].

As a summary for this part, with no compulsory vaccination against COVID-19 in Germany, it is and should stay the personal and private matter of an employee whether or not to be vaccinated.

III. Change with 3G at work in line with data protection requirements

On November 19, 2021, the German Federal Council (Bundesrat) approved the amendment to the Infection Protection Act (IfSG) passed by the German Federal Parliament (Bundestag) on November 18, 2021. This provided for various far-reaching measures to combat the corona pandemic. Most of the issued measures were introduced with an expiry

---

[12] https://www.datenschutzkonferenz-online.de/media/pm/20200325_Informationen_zu_Corona_und_Arbeitgeber.pdf, page 1.

date scheduled for the end of September 23, 2022, as laid out in § 28a para. 10 IfSG.

The revised § 28 a et seq. IfSG stipulates among others, that workplaces may only be entered into, if the employer and employees have been vaccinated, have recovered or have been tested. In addition, they must carry proof of vaccination, proof of recovery or official proof of testing in accordance with the COVID-19 Protective Measures Exemption Ordinance (test centre, test under the supervision of the employer or by trained personnel). If a PCR test is presented, it must be no more than 48 hours old. Entering the workplace without carrying proof was now only permitted as an exception in the following cases: Either a test offer from the employer is taken immediately prior to starting work or a vaccination offer is taken up at the workplace.

This was the first time that the so-called '3G regulation' applied at the workplace. The regulation went into application in November 24, 2021, regardless of the activity performed, to all workplaces where physical contact between employers and employees or with third parties cannot be ruled out. It is irrelevant whether employees actually encounter other persons – the mere possibility is sufficient.

The German Federal Ministry of Labour and Social Affairs (BMAS[13]) stated that '*The possibility of physical contact exists if an encounter with other persons cannot be ruled out in the workplace, even if there is no direct physical contact.*' The requirement for 3G in the workplace became therefore the rule. Workplaces in home offices, on the other hand, are not workplaces in the sense of the regulation, so the aforementioned regulations do not apply there.

Conclusion

Since corona appeared, data protection authorities had to adjust a lot. Especially since sensible health data is involved. Companies were also going a little overboard, checking the temperature of their employees and guests, having special cameras, on top of all the new apps coming to the market and promising to follow COVID-19 at every turn. Then came the will to test the employees or to have the employees test themselves. The rigidity of controls had also to be differentiated. For example, for

---

[13] Bundesministerium für Arbeit und Soziales.

employees of a hospital it was indeed important to ensure that they were tested regularly and negative. However, in a more 'regular' company, the tests which had to be paid for by the company were less obligatory and relying more on a trust basis.

With the vaccination, many companies tried to find ways to bring the vaccination to their employees. However, with it came the problem that the employer got to know who did not want to be vaccinated. In all these new developments coming with a sanitary crisis on a global scale, the data protection supervisory authorities adjusted their guidelines in order to ensure that the health data, which by the end of 2021 could be documented under specific conditions, should not fall in the wrong hands.

The technology acceptance model post COVID-19

Rajendra Parsad GUNPUTH[1] and Ashwin Michael Claudius THODDA[2]

In 1986, the Technology Acceptance Model was introduced, and it continues to be applied as theoretical model in the in the field of Information Systems. This study briefly traces its history and examines the impact of the COVID-19 Pandemic on its future trajectory.

En 1986, le modèle d'acceptation des technologies a été introduit et continue d'être appliqué comme modèle théorique dans le domaine des systèmes d'information. Cette étude retrace brièvement son histoire et examine l'impact de la pandémie du virus COVID-19 sur sa trajectoire future.

Introduction

Several models have been proposed over the years to explain the acceptance of new technologies. In this paper, we make an overview of models regarding user acceptance of new technology and focus on the potential impact of COVID-19 on the Technology Acceptance Model.

I. Literature review

Technology Acceptance Model is the most employed theory to describe acceptance of information systems. It is an adaptation of the Theory of Reasoned Action (Ajzen and Fishbein, 1980). The Theory of Reasoned Action was developed by Fishbein and Azjen's for psychological research, it then became a foundation to investigate IS usage behaviour (Ajzen,

---

[1] Professor, Dean of Faculty of Law & Management, University of Mauritius.
[2] PhD Candidate at the Open University of Mauritius.

1985). According to them behaviour of individuals could be explained by attitudes, social influence, and intentions. Behaviour should be systematic, rational and volitional. Three boundary factors were used to test the Theory of Reasoned Action; intention stability over time, volitional control and measurement of intention with elements such as target, context and generality. For Taherdoost (2018) the main disadvantage of the Theory of Reasoned Action is its inability to take into consideration factors such as cognitive deliberation, the role of habit and moral factors.

The Theory of Planned Behaviour added perceived behavioural control as a new variable to extend the Theory of Reasoned Action. At its base, this theory is determined by the availability of opportunities, skills and resources to achieve an outcome (White, 2015). While both the Theory of Reasoned Action and Theory of Planned Behaviour assumed that behavioural intention affects behaviour, the Theory of Planned Behaviour use perceived behavioural control for actions which are not under volitional control. For Taherdoost (2018), this increased the efficacy of the model and made it more realistic. For Taherdoost et al. (2011) and Taherdoost et al. (2011) the Theory of Planned Behaviour model would not be relevant if a computer system was not accessible, as one's attitude to it would be irrelevant.

The Theory of Interpersonal Behaviour investigates the complexity of behaviour by digging in social and emotional factors. It contains the aspects of both the Theory of Reasoned Action and the Theory of Planned Behaviour while adding facilitation conditions and habits to improve predictability. For Taherdoost (2018) under this model individuals are neither completely autonomous nor completely social and neither fully automatic nor fully deliberative. In this model, emotions, social factors, and habits are the main factors which will lead an individual to form an intention. The Theory of Interpersonal Behaviour argues that there are three levels to decide the behaviour; in the first level social factors, beliefs and attitudes interact with the previous experiences and characteristics of the person. The second level explains the effect of social determinants, cognition and personal normative belief on the formation of intention and finally situational conditions and behavioural intentions together with experience will determine the possibility of performing a behaviour. For Taherdoost (2018) lack of parsimony is the main disadvantage of this model.

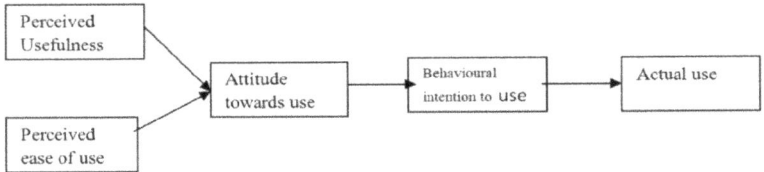

Fig. 1: Technology Acceptance Model originates from Davis (1986). It assumes that the degree of acceptance of Information System is originally based on two variables as illustrated in the figure below.
Source: Based on Davis (1989)

Articles published over the past decades reveals that the IS community considers Technology Acceptance Model as a powerful theory (Venkatesh and Davis, 2000; Lucas and Spitler, 1999). Venkatesh and Davis (2000) found that 424 journal citations were received by the two papers published by Davis (1989) and Davis et al. (1989) in the Social Science Citation Index. In 2003 this was extended to 698 by Lee et al. (2003). To test its robustness, Technology Acceptance Model was applied to various forms taken by technology ranging from Hospital Information Systems to Emails; under different circumstances such as cultural influences and different control factors such as gender and with different subjects from undergraduate students to knowledge workers (Lee et al. 2003).

Using meta-analysis, Lee et al. (2003) traced the Technology Acceptance Model trajectory from 1986 to 2003. Meta-analysis had been successfully applied in the research of IS (Dennis and Gallupe, 1993; Farhoomand and Drury, 1999). Meta-analysis is useful to combine the results of independent studies (Glass, 1981; Hwang, 1996; Mahmood et al., 2001) and to effectively analyse data to resolve inconsistencies in their findings (Hwang, 1996; Hwang and Wu, 1990). They found that Technology Acceptance Model did not remain static and evolved like an organic being. They classified the progress of Technology Acceptance Model in four periods namely introduction, validation, extension, and elaboration which outcome was very efficient.

After its introduction in organisations Information Systems received attention from researchers (Rogers, 1983; Kwon and Zmud, 1987; Swanson, 1988) who endeavoured to identify the factors which led individuals to accept or resist IS (Lucas et al., 1990). As previously stated, TAM organically evolved from Ajzen and Fishbein's (1980) Theory of

Reasoned Action to '*provide an explanation of the determinants of computer acceptance that is general, capable of explaining user behavior across a broad range of end-user computing technologies and user populations, while at the same time being both parsimonious and theoretically justified*' (Davis et al., 1989, p. 985).

After the introduction period, Lee et al. (2003) noted that studies focused mainly on attempting to replicate TAM with longitudinal situations, different forms of technologies, and settings to verify whether it was a parsimonious model and also to situate TAM vis-à-vis the theory of Reasoned Action, that is assessing whether it could be differentiated or superior to the Theory of Reasoned Action.

Adams et al. (1992) assessed Technology Acceptance Model in five applications namely word processors, spreadsheets, graphics, e-mail, and v-mail. They found that TAM maintained its consistency in explaining the users' acceptance behaviour. Davis (1993) replicated his experience of 1989 by this time using a text editor and e-mail with 112 knowledge workers and found that Technology Acceptance Model was successful to explain the adoption of both the text editor and e-mail. Sambamurthy and Chin (1994) found that the ratio Perceived Utility/Perceived Ease of Use was successful in predicting group attitude to GDSS use.

In the other stream of research, Davis et al. (1989) compared the Theory of Reasoned Action with Technology Acceptance Model in how they measure student's relative facility with a word processor and found that Technology Acceptance Model better explained the acceptance intention of the users than the Theory of Reasoned Action. Hubona and Cheney (1994) compared both the Theory of Reasoned Action and Technology Acceptance Model and found that Technology Acceptance Model offered a more powerful model to explain the acceptance of technology. During this period, it was found that TAM was a much simpler and more powerful model of the determinant of user acceptance of computer technology than the Theory of Reasoned Action (Igbaria et al., 1997).

Following Bejar's (1928) perspective that robust instruments increased the value of research, the norms of Technology Acceptance Model researchers at this stage (Jarvenpaa et al., 1985; Moore and Benbasat, 1991; Straub, 1989) were to rigorously test the validation of their measurement instruments under different circumstances. Adams et al. (1992) replicated the study of Davis (1989) and confirmed the reliability of measurement of Perceived Usefulness and Perceived Ease of Use for different Information Systems and under different settings. Hendrickson et al. (1993, 1996) examined and confirmed the test-retest reliability of Perceived Usefulness and Perceived Ease of Use. Segars and Grover (1993) proposed to add a third variable in the modelling by including effectiveness. This study earned both support and objections. For Barki and Hartwick (1994) Perceived Usefulness was made of distinctive features which could be independently measured. However, for Chin and Todd (1995), a single factor Perceived Usefulness has enough psychometric properties. There was no rationale therefore to segregate Perceived Usefulness in two parts (Perceived Usefulness and effectiveness). Szajna (1994) concentrated her research to measure the accuracy of Technology Acceptance Model to predict future behaviour and found good predictive validity. Finally, Davis and Venkatesh (1996) found that item grouping vs. item intermixing had no significant effect on bias.

After the model validation, Technology Acceptance Model evolved to reach the Model Extension Period. In this phase, the measurement instruments started to include new variables to identify boundary conditions. Agarwal and Prasad (1999) added five types of external variables namely role with regard to technology, prior experiences, level of education, tenure in workplace, and prior experience as external variables of Perceived Usefulness and Perceived Ease of Use. They found that the outcomes were predicted successfully. Igbaria et al. (1995) found that managerial support, training and computing support significantly affected Perceived Usefulness/Perceived Ease of Use. Karahanna and Limayem (2000) conducted a study on email and voicemail and found that the usage of email was not influenced by PU but by social influence. On the other hand, voicemail was not influenced by social influence but by Perceived Usefulness. Efforts in this phase were also directed to investigate Technology Acceptance Model's boundary conditions. Adams et al. (1995) suggested that the impact of task, gender and culture on the IS type need to be examined. Straub (1994) found that culture played a decisive role in the choice of communication media after applied Technology Acceptance Model in two different countries, he found that Japanese preferred fax while U.S. preferred email. Another effort in this phase was to identify Technology Acceptance Model's boundary conditions, Gefen and Straub (1997) found that gender had an impact on Perceived Usefulness, Perceived Ease of Use and social presence; men were more influenced by Perceived Usefulness and women by subjective norms and Perceived Ease of Use. Gefen and Straub (2000) also found that Perceived Ease of Use was influenced by task type. Perceived Ease of Use significantly predicted the use of WWW for purchasing tasks but not for inquiry tasks. Moon and Kimo (2001) investigated in the same direction and found that PU was pivotal for work related task on the internet and perceived playfulness was pivotal for entertainment task. Ridings and Gefen (2000) used Technology Acceptance Model to investigate on a situation were old Information System and new Information System were used in parallel. They found that the Perceived Usefulness of the new Information System was pivotal in its acceptance while that of the old Information System decreased its usage.

The period of the Model Elaboration Period can be characterized by the development of the next generation of Technology Acceptance Model by resolving the limitations of the existing studies. This period can be characterized as the elaboration of TAM in two keyways: to develop the next generation TAM that synthesizes the previous effects and to resolve the limitations raised by previous studies. Venkatesh (2000) and Venkatesh and Davis (2000) introduced TAM II, with clear definitions of PU and PEOU they proposed a concrete way towards a multi-level model. Venkatesh (2000) developed externals variables of PEOU such as computer anxiety, self-efficacy, external control and computer playfulness and adjustments such as perceived enjoyment as anchor. Venkatesh and Davis (2000) defined subjective norms (such as social influence) and cognitive instruments (such as image and job relevance) as external variables of Perceived Usefulness.

Lee et al. (2003) investigated the different studies which were made since inception. After the examination of 101 research on the Technology Acceptance Model, they found that most researchers used a one-shot cross-sectional method after exposing the research subjects with the new IS through training or hands-on sessions and only three studies used qualitative data, such as content analysis and participatory observations. Most research were questionnaire based and data analysed using regression with software such as SAS and SPSS. They observed that the studies were made on two groups: knowledge workers in their early 30's and students in their early 20's. They identified the four pillars of TAM as being Perceived Usefulness (PU), Perceived Ease of Use (PEOU), Behavioral Intention (BI), and Behavior (B). PU is both a dependent and independent variable as it is predicted by PEOU and predicts BI and B. The relationship between PU and BI was found to be strong. On the contrary, they found that PEOU was not stable in predicting BI or B, this observation was also made by Gefen and Straub (2000) and Keil et al. (1995) who concluded that 'no amount of PEOU will compensate for low usefulness.' Many studies tried to discover the reason of that non-significance. For Subramanian [1994] systems used in studies were relatively easy to use, therefore PEOU had less impact on the IS acceptance decision. For Igbaria et al. (1995a) organizations put priority on the usefulness of IS and not on the pleasure brought by them. Davis et al. (1992) also observed that PEOU was a significant antecedent of PU rather than existing in parallel. It therefore impacted on acceptance through PU.

For Lee et al. (2003) Technology Acceptance Model added value to the Information System field by conceptualizing usefulness and ease of use as as determinant factors for the adoption of new systems. Before the Technology Acceptance Model, the field of Information System did not contain many foundations for its research. They identified the shortcomings of research on Technology Acceptance Model as the researchers themselves. For Lee et al. (2003) researchers have fallen in the trap of replicating previous studies with minor amendments, this 'cumulative tradition' was carried too far. Technology Acceptance Model's ease of operationalizability have led many researchers into conducting fast and simple studies by merely adding a relationship or variable to Technology Acceptance Model and then move to compare the modified versions of Technology Acceptance Model with its original form.

After their meta-analysis for Lee et al. (2003) concluded that a deeper understanding of factors influencing the ease of use and usefulness was required. One important aspect which was overlooked by researchers is the impact of the environmental setting on IS. While research investigated the effects of different environments and differences (e.g., cultural difference) (Chau, 1996; Straub et al., 1997) and also gender (Gefen and Straub, 1997), more study was required to include environmental factors such as emotion, personality difference, technology change, habit. Research should explore beyond individual acceptance to societal acceptance (Taylor and Todd, 1995) and additional mandatory settings should trigger further study (Davis et al., 1992; Davis, 1993; Venkatesh, 2000).

According to scholars, social influence is crucial to determine decision and human (Azjen, 1991; Barki and Hartwick, 1994; Taylor and Todd, 1995b). Results of TAM studies were mixed in its attempt to uncover the impact of social influence on the acceptance of new technology technology (Davis, 1989). For Barki and Hartwick (1994), and Mathieson

(1991) there is a weak relation between variables and subjective norms while for Taylor and Todd (1995), and Thompson et al. (1991) there is a strong relationship. Venkatesh and Davis (2000), Venkatesh and Morris (2000), Barki and Hartwick (1994) found that subjective norm has the greatest importance at the earliest stage of the IS development and for Taylor and Todd (1995) subjective norm is an importance predictor of intention with inexperienced research subjects. For Doll and Ahmed (1983) longitudinal study was important as user's expectations may change as people become more familiar with technology and for Lee et al. (2003) qualitative study is another extension method which would be more useful to determine richer information with a small number of research subjects.

For Maillet (2015) the Extension of the Technology Acceptance Model (ETAM) new factors were added to the Technology Acceptance Model to improve its explanatory power. ETAM's proposal was focused firstly by adding social influence (such as image and voluntariness) and cognitive factors (such as output quality) to the Technology Acceptance Model to improve prediction capabilities regarding perceived usefulness. Another study focused on Perceived Ease of Use which was adjusted into anchors (objective usability) and adjustments (computer anxiety and playfulness) as illustrated below.

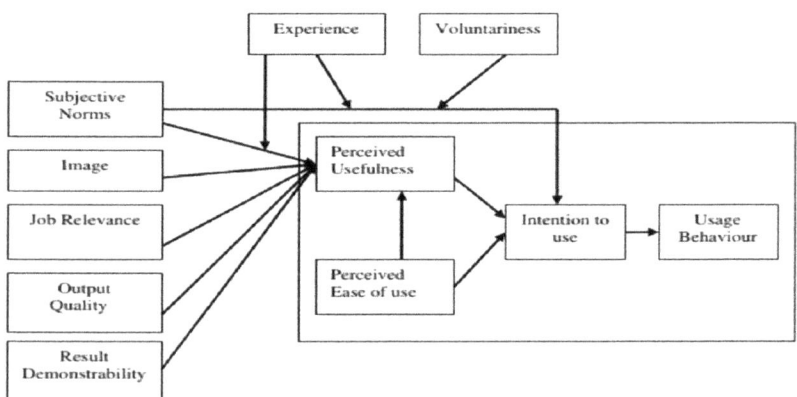

Fig. 2 : Extension of the Technology Acceptance Model (ETAM)
Source: Based on Khater (2016)

The Igbaria Model examines both extrinsic and intrinsic motivators and their impact on the acceptance of new technologies (Igabaria, 1994). For Igbaria perceived usefulness is an extrinsic motivator and perceived fun is an intrinsic motivator. Both have a direct and indirect (through satisfaction) impact on acceptance. Apart from these two factors, computer anxiety has a negative impact on both motivators while satisfaction has a direct influence on usage.

For Rana et al. (2015) The Social Cognitive Theory Model was designed from social psychology and founded on the following factors: behavioural, personal, and environmental. They interact bi-directionally to predict group and individual behaviour. Behaviour focuses on performance and adoption problems. Personal factors are any aspect which serve to characterize a person such as personality and environmental factors include both social and physical aspects which could be external to the person. The three factors are inseparable and determine each other. This model is used to investigate the use of technology by including factors such as anxiety, outcome expectations and self-efficacy.

For Sila (2015) the Diffusion of Innovations Theory examines diversity by introducing factors which have an impact on the spread of a new idea. These factors are time, channels of communication, social system and innovation. This model can be used at global, organisational, and individual level. It consolidates adopter characteristics, innovation decision progress and the characteristics of an innovation. In the innovation decision step, there are five elements; confirmation, knowledge, implementation, decision, and persuasion which operate through a communication channel between people in an identical social system over a given period. The innovation step is also composed of five main elements which are advantage, compatibility, complexity, trialability, and observability as triggering the acceptance of innovation. The adopter characteristic is also composed of five elements which are early adopters, innovators, laggards, late majority, and early majority. For Taherdoost (2018) this model has less explanatory power than other models.

The Perceived Characteristics of Innovating Theory expanded the Diffusion of Innovations Theory by adding three variables: Image, voluntariness, and behaviour. The latter is impacted by the perception of voluntariness. For Hameed (2012) voluntariness has an influence on user's acceptance and rejection of an innovation. For Taherdoost (2018) adoption rate and demonstrability are related to each other. Demonstrability accelerates adoption rate.

The motivational model uses two motivators, one intrinsic and one extrinsic. For Bagozzi et al. (1991) perceived usefulness is an extrinsic motivation and perceived enjoyment is an intrinsic motivation. Perceived ease of use has an impact on both perceived usefulness and perceived enjoyment. The quality of output has an impact on usefulness. Both output quality and perceived ease of use have an impact on perceived usefulness and perceived enjoyment. Behavioural intention is therefore indirectly influenced by perceived enjoyment and perceived usefulness. In this model, intrinsic motivation is the willingness to perform an activity for no reason other than performing it while external motivation is the perception that users want to perform an activity to obtain a desired outcome.

For Grellhesl (2010) the Uses and Gratification Theory attempts to investigate the participation of individuals in certain medium of communication compared to others. It explores the social and psychological depths of users in their search for motivation and satisfaction. It is composed of three elements; motivations, behavioural usage and satisfaction. For Chen (2015) motivation represents the overall disposition which influence the actions of individuals. Behavioural usage is the pattern of use such as type and duration of use. It is useful to assess media in a work or play process.

The Model of PC Utilization was designed to predict acceptance and the utilisation of Personal Computers. As it was designed to assess actual usage, therefore actual behaviour, it excluded behavioural intention. As habits would have a tautological relationship with the actual usage of personal computers, habits were excluded as well. For Chang (2015) this model specifically evaluates facilitating conditions, job fit, long term of use and complexity of the usage of Personal Computers. Results show that except for facilitating conditions, all these factors have a strong impact on the usage of Personal Computers.

Venkatesh et al. (2003) assessed all the models mentioned above to develop the Unified Theory of Acceptance and Use of Technology. They integrated the constructs of all these models such as performance expectancy, effort expectancy, facilitating conditions and social influence. In addition, they identified four main moderating variables; experience, gender, age and voluntariness of us. Bouten (2008) integrated compatibility beliefs in the Unified Theory of Acceptance and Use of Technology model to test new boundary conditions. As the aim was to investigate the behavioural perceptions with the compatibility beliefs, actual usage behaviour was irrelevant. For Taherdoost (2018) however as the study was cross sectional and did not test different time periods, the relationships as initially proposed by Venkatesh et al. (2003) could not be exactly replicated.

Singh (2015) noticed a gap between technology used in the engineering industry and technology advancement. He therefore investigated technology acceptance in the engineering sector. He confirmed Rogers (1995) on the notion that technology diffusion includes innovators, early adopters, the early majority and the late majority and the laggards. Innovators being the ones who take risks, early adopters being the opinion leaders, early majority is constituted of the pragmatist and the remaining part is constituted of the sceptics. This could be represented in the pyramid below.

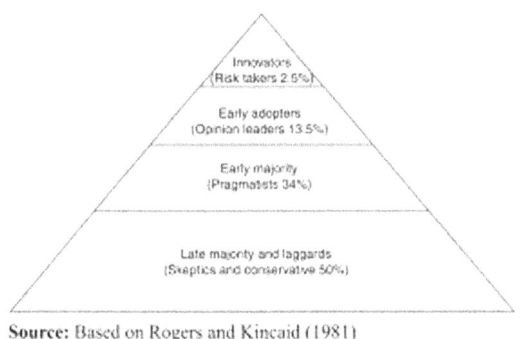

Source: Based on Rogers and Kincaid (1981)

Fig. 3: Rogers and Kincaid 1981 Communication networks.

Singh (2015) observed that the behaviour of the actors was congruent with Maslow's (1943) hierarchy of needs. He would keep the pyramid simple in his research and focus only on the assumption that needs have a hierarchical structure which is arranged by a preferential order. He will distinguish primary needs as financial security and secondary needs as innovation. In the figure, most of the actors who represent the sceptics are at the bottom of the pyramid, he explains that their concern for their security and primary needs explains their position. The early majority feels, the pragmatists, feel confident enough to risk innovation. The opinion leaders are always looking for an opportunity to lead and be recognized, they are thus drawn to creativity. Based on this observation, Singh would use Maslow's hierarchy of needs as framework for his research in technology acceptance decisions. He found a consensus across research subjects that despite the perceived utility and related systemic innovations, the priority remained on ongoing projects which prioritized risk mitigation and were revenue centred. Long terms benefits were overlooked, and short-term goals remained the priority.

He however observed that evidence suggests that perturbations in the environment could foster or willingness to adopt innovation. This observation was in line with Meyer's (1982) findings on the importance of 'environmental jolt' in the adoption of innovation. Singh's findings also suggest that under environmental pressure, actors involved in the innovation chain also acquire new roles which change their usual status under 'business as usual' framework. He asserts that innovation-related needs could therefore be explained by the stable or excited states of actors. For innovators, the stable state would trigger needs for upper state of minds like creativity, while for the sceptics the stable state would make them focus only on earning their livelihoods. Environmental factors can however redistribute the cards and push routine actors to become creative for search for innovation.

II. Maslow hierarchy of needs

Contrary to the classical management approach that 'human is a passive element that does what he is told,' in the 21st century human, it is generally considered that human is an active element. It is widely accepted today that for any business to be successful employees should be passionate and cooperate to achieve results (Gignac and Palmer, 2011). Empirical evidence demonstrate that motivation is a key determinant of success (Hunter and Schmidt, 1996). Humans are affected and influenced by many factors, they are sensitive to behaviours and attitudes. To obtain productivity, it is therefore essential to motivate the labour force. Though motivation was known since ancient times, it was only developed in our age following the era of the classical management approach where people were only considered as machines. According to Buchbinder and Shanks motivation causes someone to get into action (Buchbinder and Shanks, 2007), for Cleveland and Murphy it is the creation means to an end (Cleveland and Murphy, 1992). For Clark it is the factor which will determine any increase in effort in occupational performance (Clark, 2003). Internal prizes are superior to external prizes in terms of job satisfaction. Intrinsic motivation has a long-term positive influence on workers because they are not imposed by the management (Uysal, Aydemir and Genc, 2017). Edrak confirmed that internal motivation leads to higher job satisfaction than external sources of motivation (Edrak et al., 2013).

The first theory of motivation was Maslow's hierarchy of needs in 1943. After Maslow, many theories emerged such as the double factor theory of Herzberg in 1959, the expectation theory of Vroom in 1964, the objective theory of Locke and the expectation theory of Locke and Lawler in 1968, the ERG theory of Alderfer in 1969 and the achievement need of McClelland in 1988 (Uysal, Aydemir and Genc, 2017). However nearly all motivational theories fall short of Maslow's hierarchy of needs because according to him humans are not motivated by external factors such as rewards and punishment but by internal factors (Adair, 2013). For Maslow (1943) human needs are unlimited. Therefore, following the satisfaction of one need, another will arise. However, no need can be considered independently of other needs as they are all interrelated, and a form of hierarchy emerge. The needs which are yet to be satisfied are the source of motivation for workers (Maslow, 1943, 1948). Maslow's hierarchy of needs is illustrated in the Fig. 4.

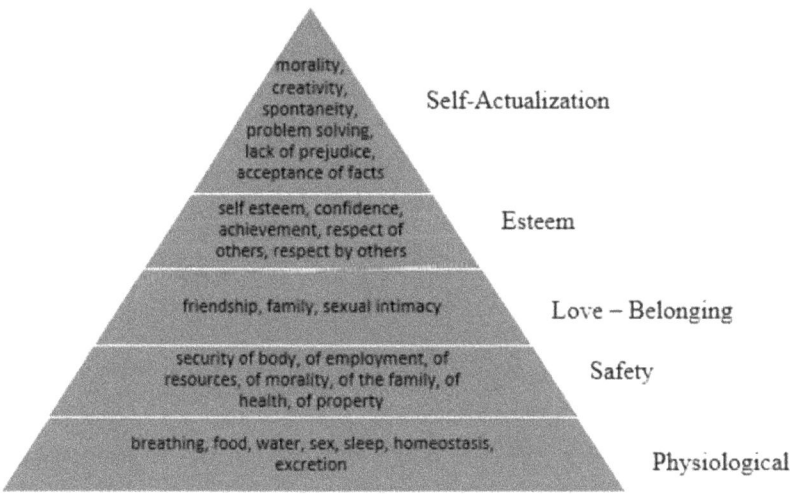

Fig. 4: Maslow's hierarchy of needs

Maslow's hierarchy can be divided in two categories namely deficiency needs and growth needs. While Physiological needs, Safety needs, love or belonging needs and esteem needs are considered as deficiency needs, self-actualisation is considered as growth or being needs. Deficiency needs increase the motivation of people the longer they are unmet, for example hunger will increase the longer a person lacks food. But however, motivation will decrease as needs are met. On the other hand, at the self-actualisation stage, motivation increases as needs are met. In 1943 Maslow's position was that all the deficiency needs must be met before progress towards higher needs, but he later clarified that deficiency needs need not be met at 100 % before progressing to the next need, it was not an all-or-none phenomenon. When a need has been adequately satisfied the activities of the person will automatically be directed to satisfy the next set of needs (Uysal, Aydemir and Genc, 2017).

Three motivational mechanisms to direct workers' behaviour in line with operational goals have been identified in the literature namely economic, psychosocial, and organizational-managerial. The economic motivational mechanism are benefits such as wages, private health insurance and coffee service. The psychosocial mechanisms are non-monetary and include independence at work and psychological assurance. Organizational-managerial mechanisms are focused on goal-congruence such as open management policy, fair and continuous disciple systems and career advancement opportunities (Gibbons, 1998; Gürüz and Gürel, 2006; Qasimov and Israyilova, 2016). Maslow and other authors extended the pyramid over time cognitive needs (need for understanding, curiosity, discovery, etc.) were added to the concept, aesthetic needs (beauty, shape, etc.) as well McLeod added the need for transcendence, which is the need to help others realize themselves, after the need for self-actualization (McLeod, 2016). For Koltko-Rivera (2006) 'self-transcendence' means achieving a state where one's personal interests are no longer considered.

Miller (2020) updated the channels of the hierarchy of needs to reflect the input of social media.

Fig. 5: Miller's updated channels of the hierarchy of needs
Source: Based on Miller (2020)

It is argued that connecting with people through social media is as vital to the man of the 21st century as basic needs such as food, shelter, and clothing. According to Lieberman (2013) '*a growing body of research shows that the need to connect socially with others is as basic as our need for food, water, and shelter*' and humans were now '*more connected to the social world and more dependent on the social world*' (Lieberman, 2013). He went further and through magnetic resonance imaging (MRIs) showed that social pain reacted in the human brain in the same way as physical pain. While it would seem ridiculous to equate lack of connection through social media and lack of water, the input of phenomenology helps us to understand the situation. Just like phenomenologist were persuaded that the world in which scientists believed, Cartesian dualism, was just one life world among many worlds (Unwin et al., 1975), We can conceive that existence in social media means existence in the world of social media which would not be possible without a good network, Wi-Fi, smart phones and power.

Maslow argued that a person would try to find security whenever they feel unsafe and extended the concept of safety to the establishment of routine and predictability. For Griffin, most children prefer routine events for they provided a secure and consistent environment (1991,

p. 127). According to a study cited by Smith (2015) and conducted by Pew Research in2015, '*65 percent of Americans now use social media platforms, and for many users, these sites offer a venue for highlighting professional accomplishments to prospective employers, finding jobs through one's networks and alerting friends to available employment opportunities.*' As businesses are now relying more heavily on social media for hiring processes, social media and Maslow's safety needs are becoming more and more strongly tied.

For Maslow '*love loses its pull when you've had enough*' and therefore classified love as a deficiency need (Griffin, 1991, p. 128). Before the technological advances of this age, couples and relationships could only connect face to face. Nowadays, relationships are started, maintained, and ended via social media. For Farrugia (2013), '*online social networking sites (SNS) have tried to re-create face-to-face interactions on the web by allowing people to interact publicly or privately.*' Long distance relationships for example can survive with the input of social media. For Maslow (1943) '*satisfaction of the self-esteem need leads to feelings of self-confidence, worth, strength, capability, and adequacy of being useful and necessary in the world.*' For David McClelland (1961) the need for achievement is a motivator alongside the need for affiliation and power. The platforms which emerged with the internet provide formidable space to boost esteem needs, for example ResearchGate allows scholars to publish their works and make them accessible worldwide. LinkedIn allows professional to connect and publish their professional achievements. According to Maslow (1943) the need for self-actualization is '*the desire to become more and more what one is, to become everything that one is capable of becoming.*' It can present itself in various forms such as the search for knowledge or life's meaning. According to Griffin (1991) such needs are linear and not hierarchically arranged (Griffin, 1991, p. 130). Self-actualisation is not a steady state, instead it is a cyclical and continued process to remain in a euphoric state.

III. COVID-19 pandemic

The COVID-19 caused a shift at the grassroots of society, for example a shift from the usual framework of offline education to emergency online teaching. Studies, for example Ferdig et al. (2020); Knig et al. (2020); Quezada et al. (2020) show that teachers were suddenly under unprecedented pressure to use technology. People were forced to use technology to keep their career alive. Ishaq et al. (2021) investigated the impact of reverse causality on the Technology Acceptance Model. Their theoretical model focused on beliefs influencing perceived usefulness and perceived ease of use following COVID-19. They suggested that the pandemic forced the usage of technology in such a way that it impacted mastery experience, computer efficacy and self-regulated learning of users which may in turn affect the latters' beliefs on technology usefulness and ease of use. Instead of an individual's attitude influencing his movement towards technology, COVID-19 stimulated unprecedently the use of technology. Ajzen and Fishbein (2005) already observed that performance of a specific behaviour updates expectations by providing new information and ultimately lead to the development of new beliefs. By being obliged to use technology users self-learning is compelled and their efficacy in using technology is elevated due to exposure. Reverse causality on the Technology Acceptance Model is therefore of valuable importance for business strategies. The model proposed by Ishaq et al. (2021) is illustrated below.

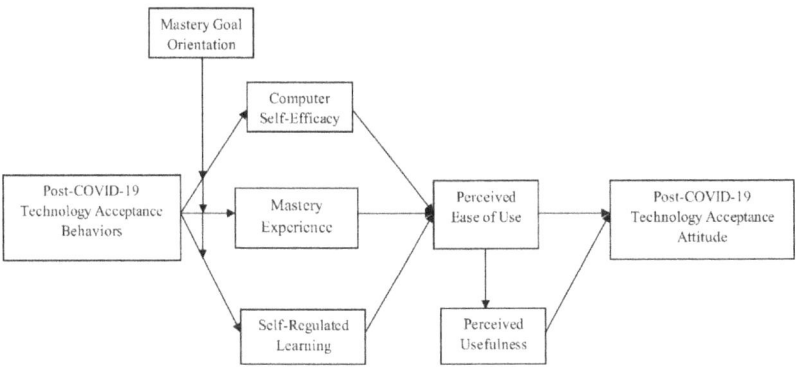

Fig. 6:

Ishaq et al. (2021) noted that since inception, the distinctive feature of research based on the Technology Acceptance Model has been to attempt to extend the model using external variables of Perceived Usefulness and Perceived Ease of Use. Venkatesh and Davis (2000) for example made use of subjective norms (such as social influence) and cognitive instruments (such as image) for Perceived Utility and anchors (such as computer anxiety) and adjustments (such as objective usability) for Perceived Ease of Use. Despite the rise of technology before the pandemic, its use was optional. Ishaq et al. (2021) tried to investigate the impact of the lack of option on the beliefs of users.

For Venkatesh (2000) control is a key predicator of Perceived Ease of Use. In the domain, control is conceptualized as computer self-efficacy which represent the person's ability to perform a specific task. For Joo et al. (2000) repetition of a task is most often the strongest factor which will influence the percept of efficacy of a person. Direct experience allows an individual to assess personally their skills and overcome any bias they may have. For Igbaria et al. (1995) this increases efficacy over time. For McLeod (2007) survival instincts force acceptance, performance of actions and adoption of behaviour unconditionally. Therefore, the forced dependency of Technology in the Post COVID-19 world will increase the general efficacy in the use of technology.

As people would have no other alternative, they will have to concentrate technology to perform their tasks, for Yesh et al (2019) as attention is focused on a specific activity, this will eventually lead to mastery experience. Mastery experience will improve the quality of judgement of users and reduce the possibility of unfounded bias judgement on the Perceived Ease of Usefulness. Bandura (1982) suggested that mastery experiences (personal attainments) were strong factors in the formation of controlled judgement. While for Gist and Mitchell (1992) judgements formed from mastery experience were more stable than those formed indirectly on modelling, arousal and persuasion. For Valentini and Rudisill (2006) Mastery-learning-oriented individuals are less likely to fail as their work is not driven by external reasons, effort rather that the way is the most significant factor. For Zumbrunn et al. (2011) such people are resilient under difficult learning conditions and will finally develop mastery and efficacy. Ishaq et al. (2021) proposed that mastery-oriented individuals will adjust their learning strategies toward using technology better than people with low mastery orientation.

IV. Facts and findings

The adoption models were developed from different sources, the Innovation Diffusion Theory emanates from the sphere of sociology. For Bouten (2008) the Theory of Reasoned Action comes from social psychology, For Gagnon (2006) the Theory of Interpersonal Behaviour, Theory of Planned Behaviour, and Social Cognitive are psychosocial. These theories managed to explain human behaviour under certain circumstances. For Carillo (2010) the Theory of Reasoned Action and the Theory of Planned Behaviour differ from the Diffusion of Innovation Theory as the former focus on investigating individual behaviour while the Diffusion of Innovation Theory concentrates on organized characteristics instead of individual characteristics. Social Cognitive Theory and the Theory of Planned Behaviour include perceived outcomes to predict behaviour while the Diffusion of Innovation Theory and the Technology Acceptance Model concentrate on beliefs about the new technology. Diffusion of Innovation Theory, Technology Acceptance Model and the Theory of Planned Behaviour use a unidirectional perspective when it comes to causal relationship in which cognitive beliefs are impacted by environmental constructs. The Social Cognitive Theory's perspective is bidirectional when it comes to the nature of causation. Factors such as emotions, environment and cognitive influences behaviour constantly and mutually.

For Thompson (1990) the Model of PC Utilization is grounded in the theory of human behaviour. For Limayem (2004) and Woon (2004) The Theory of Interpersonal Behaviour, Theory of Planned Behaviour and Social Cognitive Theory conceptually overlap but for Taherdoost (2018) the Theory of Interpersonal Behaviour has been less used than the other two. For Carter (2005) the Technology Acceptance Model and the Diffusion of Innovation Theory overlap when it comes to perceived usefulness and ease of use. In the same line, he found that Venkatesh et al. (2003) integrates the notions of Ajzen (1991) perceived behavioural control together with Thompson et al. (1991) facilitating conditions. They also included Moore et al. (1991) compatibility contract. Perlusz (2004) observed that though cognitive processes and emotions affect behaviour, theories of technology adoption are agnostic about emotions and feelings in general. Noting some exceptions like Venkatesh et al. (2000) technology acceptance models use exclusively cognitive predictors. Scholars like Perlusz (2004), Venkatesh (2000) and Loewenstein (2001) mostly classify emotions as negative to technology acceptance such as anxiety or even fear for Fishloff (1978) and worry for Sjoberg (1998). For Perlusz (2004) positive emotions like joy and enthusiasm were ignored by scholars. For Robinson (2009) a quantity of models did not provide a clear definition of the variables. The Unified Theory of Acceptance and Use of Technology, the Technology Acceptance Model and the Diffusion of Innovations Theory seems to be the most applied models for research in this field.

Technology plays a vital role in our day-to-day tasks but seems to have become unavoidable post COVID-19. This shift allowed Ishaq et al. (2021) to consider the probability of reverse causality. However, their study on reverse causality is focused on individuals and do not take into consideration the broader perspective which can be captured by Maslow's Hierarchy of Needs and the coercive force of the environment as noted by Singh (2015).

Discussions and recommendations

We attempt to contribute to existing literature by investigating the reverse-causality mechanism in the Technology Acceptance Model in the post-COVID-19 world. Despite appearing to have several strengths, we do acknowledge that the current study is limited in terms of empirical validation of its perspectives. However, we believe that we are opening avenues for technology-oriented researchers to understand past findings of the Technology Acceptance Model with a different perspective. We aim to adapt and test the reverse-causality model proposed by Ishaq et al. (2021) to develop propositions and conduct empirical studies to further investigate reverse-causality on the Technology Acceptance Model in relation to Maslow's Hierarchy of Needs.

Bibliography

Adair, J. (2013). Etkili Motivasyon. Çev. S. Uyan, İstanbul: Babıali Kültür Yayıncılığı, 4. Baskı.

Adams, D. A., R. R. Nelson, and P. A. Todd (1992). Perceived Usefulness, Ease of Use, and Usage of Information Technology: A Replication. MIS Quarterly 16(2), pp. 227–247.

Agarwal, R., and J. Prasad (1998). A Conceptual and Operational Definition of Personal Innovativeness in the Domain of Information Technology. Information Systems Research 9(2), pp. 204–215.

Agarwal, R., and J. Prasad (1999). Are Individual Differences Germane to the Acceptance of New Information Technologies? Decision Sciences 30(2), pp. 361–391.

Bagozzi, P. R. Warshaw (1989). User Acceptance of Computer Technology: A Comparison of two Theoretical models. Management Science 35(8), pp. 982–1003.

Bagozzi, P. R. Warshaw (1992). Extrinsic and Intrinsic Motivation to Use Computers in the Workplace. Journal of Applied Social Psychology 22, pp. 1111–1132.

Bandura, A. (1977). Self-efficacy: Toward a Unifying Theory of Behavioral Change. Psychol. Rev. 84, p. 191. doi: 10.1037/0033-295X.84.2.191.

Carillo (2010). Social Cognitive Theory in IS Research Literature Review, Criticism, and Research Agenda. In International Conference on Information Systems, Technology and Management (ICISTM 2010). Bangkok, Thailand.

Carter, F. Bélanger (2005). The Utilization of e-Government Services: Citizen Trust, Innovation and Acceptance Factors. Information Systems Journal 15(1), pp. 5–26.

Chang, et al. (2015). Exploration of Usage Behavioral Model Construction for University Library Electronic Resources. The Electronic Library 33(2), pp. 292–307.

Davis, F. D. (1986). Technology Acceptance Model for Empirically Testing New End-user Information Systems Theory and Results. Unpublished Doctoral Dissertation, Massachusetts Institute of Technology, Cambridge, MA.

Davis, F. D., and V. Venkatesh (1996). A Critical Assessment of Potential Measurement Biases in the Technology Acceptance Model: Three Experiments. International Journal of HumanComputer Studies 45(1), pp. 19–45.

Doll, W. J., A. Hendrickson, and X. Deng (1998). Using Davis's Perceived Usefulness and Easeof-use Instruments for Decision Making: A Confirmatory and Multigroup Invariance Analysis. Decision Sciences 29(4), pp. 839–869.

Edrak, B. C. Yin-Fah, B. Gharleghi and T. K. Seng (2013). The Effectiveness of Intrinsic and Extrinsic Motivations: A Study of Malaysian Amway Company's Direct Sales Forces. International Journal of Business and Social Science 4(9), pp. 96–103.

Gagnon, E. Sanchez (2006). J. M. V. Pons, from Recommendation to Action: Psychosocial Factors Influencing Physician Intention to Use Health Technology Assessment (HTA) Recommendations. Implement Science, pp. 1–8.

The COVID-19 crisis in the EU, France and Germany: Between data sovereignty and GAFAM dependency

Danielle-Josée BOUTOILLE[1]

The COVID-19 pandemic has necessitated adaptations from various entities to ensure the continuity of their operations amidst the virus' spread. Consequently, a significant number of individuals, professionals, and public institutions have intensified their utilization of digital resources, primarily sourced from abroad. This sudden and heightened reliance on external technical infrastructures located beyond the digital borders of the European Union raises concerns regarding the circumstances of the hosting of data belonging to millions of European citizens. Additionally, the regulation of end-use becomes questionable when it falls beyond the purview of European regulatory control.

La pandémie de COVID-19 a nécessité des adaptations de la part de diverses entités afin d'assurer la continuité de leurs opérations malgré la propagation du virus. Par conséquent, un nombre important de particuliers, de professionnels et d'institutions publiques ont intensifiés leur utilisation des ressources numériques, principalement en provenance de l'étranger. Ce recours soudain et accru à des infrastructures techniques externes situées au-delà des frontières numériques de l'Union européenne soulève des questions quant aux circonstances de l'hébergement de données appartenant à des millions de citoyens européens. En outre, la réglementation de l'utilisation finale peut-être remise en question lorsqu'elle échappe au contrôle réglementaire européen.

Introduction

During his speech, given last February 2021, the President of the European Council, Charles Michel mentioned: 'COVID has shone a brutal spotlight into every corner of our societies. It has revealed our

---

[1] PhD student Université Paris Nanterre.

strengths, but also our weaknesses. This is particularly true where our over-dependency makes us vulnerable.'[2]

As a matter of fact, we were and still are in a global health crisis which has repeatedly given us the opportunity to look at certain legal aspects from different perspectives.

With the omnipresence of the American GAFAMs on one hand (Google – Apple – Facebook – Amazon – Microsoft) and the forced arrival of the Chinese BATXs on the other hand (Baidu – Alibaba – Tencent – Xiaomi), Europe is today a territory where the challenge is not only limited to geographical or spatial areas, but also virtual. Additionally, this means redefining the terms 'territory' and 'space' could be a current necessity.

The Old Continent, with an estimated population of approximately 446.8 million as of January 1, 2022[3], presents a lucrative opportunity for these companies. Their primary objective appears to consist in acquiring an increasing amount of data, in order to analyse, exploit, and derive valuable insights from it. However, the growing presence of these companies in various aspects of our daily lives, across all societal strata, gives rise to a multitude of concerns. As a result, there is currently a public debate regarding the urge for European-level regulations to address these issues.

Both individually and collectively, the neighbouring countries France and Germany are collaborating to establish digital sovereignty not only for themselves but also for the European Union as a whole. While the General Data Protection Regulation (GDPR)[4] can be seen as an initial step towards achieving 'digital sovereignty,' it is evident that the GDPR

---

[2] Charles Michel, « La souveraineté numérique est au cœur de l'autonomie stratégique européenne – Discours du président Charles Michel lors de l'événement en ligne "Masters of Digital 2021" », consulté le 21 février 2022, https://www.consilium.europa.eu/fr/press/press-releases/2021/02/03/speech-by-president-charles-michel-at-the-digitaleurope-masters-of-digital-online-event/.

[3] European Commission, « EU population continues to decrease for a second year », consulté le 11 juillet 2022, https://ec.europa.eu/eurostat/web/products-eurostat-news/-/ddn-20220711-1.

[4] « Règlement (UE) 2016/679 du Parlement européen et du Conseil du 27 avril 2016 relatif à la protection des personnes physiques à l'égard du traitement des données à caractère personnel et à la libre circulation de ces données, et abrogeant la directive 95/46/CE (règlement général sur la protection des données) (Texte présentant de l'intérêt pour l'EEE) », Pub. L. No. 32016R0679, OJ L (2016), http://data.europa.eu/eli/reg/2016/679/oj/fra.

alone is insufficient in attaining this objective. Therefore, it becomes imperative to consider a more comprehensive regulatory framework that encompasses the activities of these companies, organizations, and individuals.

In general, '*sovereignty is defined, in law, as the possession of supreme authority, that is to say, absolute power (on which all depend) and unconditional power (which does not depend on anyone)*'[5]. In France and in Germany, numerous actors and organizations have endeavoured to establish a clear understanding of the term 'digital sovereignty'. BITKOM, the German Federal Association for Information Technology, puts forth the following definition: '*the ability to act autonomously and to be able to make decisions in a digital space*[6]'.

On the one hand, this implies that the State mentioned in this definition must be able to establish rules within its digital space and sanction individuals and organizations that do not respect them. However, the European Union and its Member States such as France and Germany still have little authority over the digital giants, even though European citizens and many actors use their services and are therefore exposed to given risks.

The question is, to what extent the need to establish digital sovereignty is amplified in times of health crisis? To address this inquiry, our initial focus will be on examining the challenges and opportunities regarding the establishment of digital sovereignty (I), followed by an exploration of the initiatives taken to reach a certain level of digital sovereignty (II).

---

[5] Ministère de l'Europe et des Affaires étrangères, « Deutsch-französische Initiative zur wirtschaftlichen Erholung Europas nach der Coronakrise (Mai 2020) », Frankreich Diplomatie – Ministerium für Europa und auswärtige Angelegenheiten, consulté le 26 octobre 2020, https://www.diplomatie.gouv.fr/de/frankreichs-beziehungen-zu-deutschland-osterreich-und-der-schweiz/bilaterale-beziehungen-mit-deutschland/neuigkeiten/article/deutsch-franzosische-initiative-zur-wirtschaftlichen-erholung-europas-nach-der.

[6] Olivia Andre-Vincens, « L'United States Cyber Command, Centre de documentation de l'École militaire », octobre 2019, https://www.dems.defense.gouv.fr/sites/default/files/2019-11/US-CYBERCOMMAND.pdf.

I. Challenges and opportunities regarding the establishment of digital sovereignty

A. The role of foreign legal models regarding the establishment of digital sovereignty

One of the functions of comparative law is to examine foreign legal systems in order to enhance domestic legislation[7].

Hence, it would be insightful for Europe to explore non-EU models and their interpretations and applications of digital sovereignty. In this study, we will briefly delve into the legal landscape of the United States of America (USA) and China.

Compared to the European Union, both the USA and China exhibit a high level of digital independence due to the presence of major digital players with significant shares in the global market and/or robust domestic markets.

Assessing the USA alongside other countries prompts us to consider the complexity involved in achieving an improved model of digital independence. In the United States, digital sovereignty relies on various private actors and extends the country's digital sphere beyond national borders[8].

On the regulatory front, numerous laws have been enacted in the United States to solidify the concept of digital sovereignty[9,10].

In contrast, China places less reliance on private actors and more on political entities. The concept of digital sovereignty in China is driven by the defense of the Chinese model and the protection of national

---

[7] « LA RECHERCHE JURIDIQUE – Sciences et pensées du droit, Boris Barraud – livre, ebook, epub », p. 7, s. d., consulté le 20 juillet 2022.

[8] M. Philippe LATOMBE M. Jean-Luc WARSMANN, « RAPPORT D'INFORMATION sur le thème « Bâtir et promouvoir une souveraineté numérique nationale et européenne » », consulté le 1 février 2022, https://www.assemblee-nationale.fr/dyn/15/rapports/souvnum/l15b4299-t1_rapport-information.

[9] « Policies and Regulations », Digital.gov, consulté le 12 février 2022, https://digital.gov/topics/policy/.

[10] National Conference of State Legislation, « 2022 Consumer Privacy Legislation », consulté le 1 août 2022, https://www.ncsl.org/research/telecommunications-and-information-technology/2022-consumer-privacy-legislation.aspx.

institutions[11]. It predominantly centres on national aspects and is closely tied to national infrastructures, equipment, and software, with a firm rejection of foreign digital tools, especially those of American origin[12].

B. The issue of digital dependency regarding the establishment of digital sovereignty

Both the American and Chinese models exhibit a shared political determination and the utilization of public authority to selectively choose and promote the development of digital actors.

Within this paper we will briefly discuss that digital sovereignty for the EU, means that we could work towards a compromise between digital autarchy and digital dependance. More precisely, the goal seems not to exclusively consist in attaining digital independence, but rather in establishing a legal framework that safeguards the digital aspects relevant to the European Union and its Member States, with a particular emphasis on protecting users and end users of the impacts of digital services within the digital space.

As mentioned earlier, the COVID-19 crisis has resulted in a significant increase in our reliance on digital tools[13]. In contrast to China and the United States, the EU presently finds itself in a state of pronounced digital dependency, although the situations may vary among its Member States. Certain countries, such as France, enjoy a more favourable position due to their available resources[14][15].

---

[11] The Economist, « China has become a laboratory for the regulation of digital technology », consulté le 27 juillet 2022, https://www.economist.com/china/2021/09/11/chIna-has-become-a-laboratory-for-the-regulation-of-digital-technology.

[12] Wanshu Cong, « The Spatial Expansion of China's Digital Sovereignty: Extraterritoriality and Geopolitics », SSRN Scholarly Paper (Rochester, NY, 2 september 2021), https://doi.org/10.2139/ssrn.4019797.

[13] OECD, « Digital Transformation in the Age of COVID-19: Building Resilience and Bridging Divides, Digital Economy Outlook 2020 Supplement, OECD, Paris », s. d, pp. 2–3.

[14] Annegret Bendiek, « Integrationspolitische Bedeutung des Digital Service Act (DSA) und Digital Markets Act (DMA) », s. d., p. 18.

[15] M. Jean-Luc WARSMANN, « RAPPORT D'INFORMATION sur le thème « Bâtir et promouvoir une souveraineté numérique nationale et européenne » ».

When we examine our own behaviours, we observe that European citizens often purchase devices manufactured by non-European companies, utilizing Asian components and operating on American systems[16].

This highlights a digital dependency primarily attributable to the absence of European players. Consequently, this prompts us to explore the evolving solutions for Europe's digital sovereignty. Moreover, steps have been taken and there are possibilities for both present and future actions to be undertaken.

II. Towards the establishment of digital sovereignty in the European Union

A. A need of regulation regarding the activities of the Big Tech amplified by the pandemic

In the Member State's battles against the pandemic, digital infrastructures have played a pivotal role, encompassing contact tracing and alert applications, online platforms, and Earth observation technologies[17].

However, currently, EU law does not allow for sufficiently effective regulation of digital companies. It is therefore essential to establish a legal framework that respects European values and that digital companies must comply with.

In terms of regulation of online content, the current proposals are based on the *Directive on electronical commerce* of June 8, 2000[18]. The main issue consists in the fact that, since the year 2000, many new digital services have emerged and contributed to the digital and societal transformation in the European Union. The conditions for the provision of digital services in the internal market must therefore guarantee

---

[16] Cristiano Codagnone et al., « Europe's Digital Decade and Autonomy », s. d., 85, p. 11.

[17] European Commission, « Digital Solutions during the Pandemic », Text, consulté le 30 juillet 2022, https://ec.europa.eu/info/live-work-travel-eu/coronavirus-response/digital-solutions-during-pandemic_en.

[18] « Directive 2000/31/EC of the European Parliament and of the Council of 8 June 2000 on Certain Legal Aspects of Information Society Services, in Particular Electronic Commerce, in the Internal Market ('Directive on Electronic Commerce') », 178 OJ L § (2000), http://data.europa.eu/eli/dir/2000/31/oj/eng.

online security, the protection of fundamental rights and the fight against disinformation.

It is indeed fundamental that what is illegal offline is also illegal online[19]. Therefore, it is imperative that the above-mentioned directive evolves[20].

Furthermore, we will look at the current evolutions regarding the regulation of the digital market within the European Union[21].

B. Legislative projects aiming to establish digital sovereignty at the European level

On December 15th 2020, the European Commission introduced two regulatory proposals: the Digital Services Act (DSA) and the Digital Market Act (DMA)[22][23]. These two texts are designed to establish a set of unified regulations that bolster Europe's position in the digital sphere.

The DSA primarily focuses on ensuring the smooth functioning of the internal digital market through standardized rules. On the other hand, the DMA follows a proactive approach, aiming to preemptively address potential problematic practices even before they come to light.

---

[19] Europäischer Rat der Europäischen Union, « Was außerhalb des Internets verboten ist, sollte auch im Internet illegal sein: Rat legt Standpunkt zum Gesetz über digitale Dienste fest », consulté le 28 juillet 2022, https://www.consilium.europa.eu/de/press/press-releases/2021/11/25/what-is-illegal-offline-should-be-illegal-online-council-agrees-on-position-on-the-digital-services-act/.

[20] M. Jean-Luc WARSMANN, « RAPPORT D'INFORMATION sur le thème « Bâtir et promouvoir une souveraineté numérique nationale et européenne » ».

[21] Frédéric Pourrière, « Dans la continuité du RGPD : vers une souveraineté numérique européenne. Par Frédéric Pourrière, Avocat. », Village de la Justice, 20 juillet 2021, https://www.village-justice.com/articles/dans-continuite-rgpd-vers-une-souveraineete-numerique-europeenne,39718.html.

[22] In this paper, we will refer to this proposal as DSA (digital services act) : « Proposition de RÈGLEMENT DU PARLEMENT EUROPÉEN ET DU CONSEIL relatif à un marché intérieur des services numériques (Législation sur les services numériques), COM(2020) 825 final du 15.12.2020. », consulté le 15 février 2022, https://eur-lex.europa.eu/legal-content/FR/TXT/HTML/?uri=CELEX:52020PC0825&from=en.

[23] In this paper, we will refer to this proposal as DMA (digital markets act): « Proposition de RÈGLEMENT DU PARLEMENT EUROPÉEN ET DU CONSEIL relatif aux marchés contestables et équitables dans le secteur numérique (législation sur les marchés numériques), COM(2020) 842 final du 15/12/2020. » (s. d.).

France and Germany, while expressing their enthusiasm and support for these new proposals, have underscored the necessity for further strengthening these two initiatives on various fronts to fully realize their shared objective[24][25].

As it is stated in its article 1, the DMA 'shall apply to core platform services provide or offered by gatekeepers to business users established in the union or end users established or located in the Union'. What business users and end users represent seems unproblematic, but when it comes to the definition of gatekeepers in Article 1 and Article 3, it appears that the number of global players designated is highly limited.

The criteria outlined in Article 3 of the DMA provide the definition of a gatekeeper. Moreover, one criterion refers to the gatekeeper as *'a provider of core platform services'* that has *'achieved an annual EEA turnover equal to or above EUR 6.5 billion in the last three financial years, or where the average market capitalization or the equivalent fair market value of the undertaking to which it belongs amounted to at least EUR 65 billion in the last financial year.* As we can observe, the figures stated in the DMA are extremely high. For instance, in Europe, only the German software developer SAP reaches that market size[26]. We can therefore presume that it is primarily the GAFAMs that are targeted by the DMA.

The examination of Article 1 of the DMA is equally noteworthy. It aims to ensure contestable and fair markets in the digital sector across the Union where gatekeepers are present. Indeed, one revolutionary point here is that it covers establishments located both inside and outside the European Union.

Article 6 explicitly states that platforms are prohibited from utilizing non-publicly data generated by business users. It also specifies that major

---

[24] Ministère de l'Europe et des Affaires étrangères, « Régulation des grandes plateformes numériques : la France se félicite du vote du Parlement européen sur le Digital Services Act (20.01.22) », France Diplomatie – Ministère de l'Europe et des Affaires étrangères, consulté le 31 juillet 2022, https://www.diplomatie.gouv.fr/fr/politique-etrangere-de-la-france/diplomatie-numerique/actualites-et-evenements/article/regulation-des-grandes-plateformes-numeriques-la-france-se-felicite-du-vote-du.

[25] Johannes Bahrke et Charles Manoury, « EU-Kommission begrüßt die Einigung auf Regeln für Online-Plattformen », European Commission, consulté le 31 juillet 2022, https://www.bundesregierung.de/breg-de/suche/eu-regeln-online-plattformen-1829232.

[26] Bendiek, « Integrationspolitische Bedeutung des Digital Service Act (DSA) und Digital Markets Act (DMA) ».

platforms, like Amazon, are forbidden from leveraging the confidential information of merchants on their marketplace to analyse high-demand products and subsequently promote their own versions at highly competitive prices[27]. This could be seen as an indirect follow up: In fact, in November 2020, the Commission sent a Statement of Objections to Amazon for the use of non-public independent seller data and opened a second investigation into its e-commerce business practices[28]. This emphasizes and redefines the meaning of article 6.

As we know, the EU is not limited to these proposals, as discussions are on-going on subjects such as the 'semiconductor chips'[29] or the proposed 'regulation on artificial intelligence'[30].

These recent developments highlight the necessity of addressing the existing gap in the legal framework of the EU. It is crucial to fill this void in order to mitigate the potential threat that online platforms and large technology companies represent to our collective democratic values.

Conclusion

As exposed earlier, a regulation based on digital sovereignty does not mean banning foreign services. This implies the necessity to instate adequate and fair rules, in order to give the Member States of the European Union a seat around the table regarding digital matters developing inside its digital territories. This could also represent an opportunity for the EU to decrease its digital dependence.

---

[27] Pourrière, « Dans la continuité du RGPD ».
[28] Arianna Podesta, « Antitrust: Commission Sends Statement of Objections to Amazon for the Use of Non-Public Independent Seller Data and Opens Second Investigation into Its e-Commerce Business Practices », Text, European Commission, consulté le 3 mars 2022, https://ec.europa.eu/commission/presscorner/detail/en/ip_20_2077.
[29] « Règlement européen sur les semi-conducteurs – Questions et réponses », Text, European Commission – European Commission, consulté le 1 mars 2022, https://ec.europa.eu/commission/presscorner/detail/fr/QANDA_22_730.
[30] « Regulatory Framework Proposal on Artificial Intelligence | Shaping Europe's Digital Future », consulté le 1 juillet 2022, https://digital-strategy.ec.europa.eu/en/policies/regulatory-framework-ai.

Bibliography

Andre-Vincens, Olivia. « L'United States Cyber Command, Centre de documentation de l'École militaire », octobre 2019. https://www.dems.defense.gouv.fr/sites/default/files/2019-11/US-CYBERCOMMAND.pdf.

Bahrke, Johannes, et Manoury, Charles. « EU-Kommission begrüßt die Einigung auf Regeln für Online-Plattformen ». European Commission. Consulté le 31 juillet 2022. https://www.bundesregierung.de/breg-de/suche/eu-regeln-online-plattformen-1829232.

Bendiek, Annegret. « Integrationspolitische Bedeutung des Digital Service Act (DSA) und Digital Markets Act (DMA) », s. d., 18.

Codagnone, Cristiano, Giovanni Liva, et Laura Gunderson, Emanuele Rebesco, Open Evidence, Gianluca Misuraca, et Inspiring Futures. « Europe's Digital Decade and Autonomy », s. d., 85.

Cong, Wanshu. « The Spatial Expansion of China's Digital Sovereignty: Extraterritoriality and Geopolitics ». SSRN Scholarly Paper. Rochester, NY, 2 septembre 2021. https://doi.org/10.2139/ssrn.4019797.

Digital.gov. « Policies and Regulations ». Consulté le 1 août 2022. https://digital.gov/topics/policy/.

Europäischer Rat der Europäischen Union. « Was außerhalb des Internets verboten ist, sollte auch im Internet illegal sein: Rat legt Standpunkt zum Gesetz über digitale Dienste fest ». Consulté le 28 juillet 2022. https://www.consilium.europa.eu/de/press/press-releases/2021/11/25/what-is-illegal-offline-should-be-illegal-online-council-agrees-on-position-on-the-digital-services-act/.

European Commission. Consulté le 31 juillet 2022. https://www.bundesregierung.de/breg-de/suche/eu-regeln-online-plattformen-1829232.

European Commission. « Digital Solutions during the Pandemic ». Text. Consulté le 30 juillet 2022. https://ec.europa.eu/info/live-work-travel-eu/coronavirus-response/digital-solutions-during-pandemic_en.

European Commission, « EU population continues to decrease for a second year ». Consulté le 11 juillet 2022. https://ec.europa.eu/eurostat/web/products-eurostat-news/-/ddn-20220711-1.

European Commission, « Règlement européen sur les semi-conducteurs – Questions et réponses ». Text. Consulté le 1 mars 2022. https://ec.europa.eu/commission/presscorner/detail/fr/QANDA_22_730.

« LA RECHERCHE JURIDIQUE – Sciences et pensées du droit, Boris Barraud – livre, ebook, epub », s. d. Consulté le 27 juillet 2022.

Michel, Charles. « La souveraineté numérique est au cœur de l'autonomie stratégique européenne – Discours du président Charles Michel lors de l'événement en ligne "Masters of Digital 2021" ». Consulté le 21 février 2022. https://www.consilium.europa.eu/fr/press/press-releases/2021/02/03/speech-by-president-charles-michel-at-the-digitaleurope-masters-of-digital-online-event/.

Ministère de l'Europe et des Affaires étrangères. « Deutsch-französische Initiative zur wirtschaftlichen Erholung Europas nach der Coronakrise (18. Mai 2020) ». Frankreich Diplomatie – Ministerium für Europa und auswärtige Angelegenheiten. Consulté le 26 octobre 2020. https://www.diplomatie.gouv.fr/de/frankreichs-beziehungen-zu-deutschland-osterreich-und-der-schweiz/bilaterale-beziehungen-mit-deutschland/neuigkeiten/article/deutsch-franzosische-initiative-zur-wirtschaftlichen-erholung-europas-nach-der.

Ministère de l'Europe et des Affaires étrangères, « Régulation des grandes plateformes numériques : la France se félicite du vote du Parlement européen sur le Digital Services Act (20.01.22) ». France Diplomatie – Ministère de l'Europe et des Affaires étrangères. Consulté le 31 juillet 2022. https://www.diplomatie.gouv.fr/fr/politique-etrangere-de-la-france/diplomatie-numerique/actualites-et-evenements/article/regulation-des-grandes-plateformes-numeriques-la-france-se-felicite-du-vote-du.

National Conference of State Legislation. « 2022 Consumer Privacy Legislation ». Consulté le 1 août 2022. https://www.ncsl.org/research/telecommunications-and-information-technology/2022-consumer-privacy-legislation.aspx.

OECD. « Digital Transformation in the Age of COVID-19: Building Resilience and Bridging Divides, Digital Economy Outlook 2020 Supplement, OECD, Paris », s. d.

Plöger, Iris. « Deutschland und Frankreich ebnen Weg für Europas digitale Souveränität », 4 juin 2020. https://bdi.eu/position/news/deutschland-und-frankreich-ebnen-weg-fuer-europas-digitale-souveraenitaet/.

Podesta, Arianna. « Antitrust: Commission Sends Statement of Objections to Amazon for the Use of Non-Public Independent Seller Data and Opens Second Investigation into Its e-Commerce Business Practices ». Text. European Commission. Consulté le 3 mars 2022. https://ec.europa.eu/commission/presscorner/detail/en/ip_20_2077.

Pourrière, Frédéric. « Dans la continuité du RGPD : vers une souveraineté numérique européenne. Par Frédéric Pourrière, Avocat. » Village de la Justice, 20 juillet 2021. https://www.village-justice.com/articles/dans-continuite-rgpd-vers-une-souverainete-numerique-europeenne,39718.html.

« Regulatory Framework Proposal on Artificial Intelligence | Shaping Europe's Digital Future ». Consulté le 30 juillet 2022. https://digital-strategy.ec.europa.eu/en/policies/regulatory-framework-ai.

The Economist. « China has become a laboratory for the regulation of digital technology ». Consulté le 27 juillet 2022. https://www.economist.com/china/2021/09/11/china-has-become-a-laboratory-for-the-regulation-of-digital-technology.

Warsmann, Jean-Luc, et Latombe, Philippe. « RAPPORT D'INFORMATION sur le thème « Bâtir et promouvoir une souveraineté numérique nationale et européenne » ». Consulté le 1 août 2022. https://www.assemblee-nationale.fr/dyn/15/rapports/souvnum/l15b4299-t1_rapport-information.

Freedom of expression and the spread of misinformation during COVID-19 in Mauritius

A. BEEBEEJAUN and R. P. GUNPUTH[1]

As COVID-19 continues to spread at a fast pace across the globe, it becomes more than ever imperative to regulate the content of information such that people have access to accurate information. Nevertheless, there is the fear that governments are abusing legislation to limit freedom of expression and that the pandemic is simply being used as an excuse to further obstruct expression. As such, it is through the lens of human rights that this research purports to critically examine the approaches undertaken by the Mauritian authorities to deal with misinformation during COVID-19 in the context of domestic laws and international conventions on expression. To achieve this research objective, a content analysis of international responses, the black letter research methodology will be adopted, and a comparative analysis will be made between Mauritian responses and those of other countries to uphold freedom of expression in the light of the COVID-19 pandemic.

Alors que le COVID-19 continue de se propager rapidement à travers le monde, il devient plus que jamais impératif de réglementer le contenu de l'information afin que les gens aient accès à des informations exactes. Néanmoins, il est à craindre que les gouvernements abusent de la législation pour limiter la liberté d'expression et que la pandémie serve simplement d'excuse pour entraver davantage l'expression. C'est donc sous l'angle des droits de l'homme que cette recherche vise à examiner de manière critique les approches adoptées par les autorités mauriciennes pour lutter contre la désinformation pendant la COVID-19, dans le contexte des lois nationales et des conventions internationales sur l'expression. Pour atteindre cet objectif de recherche, une analyse de contenu des réponses internationales, la méthodologie de recherche 'black letter' sera adoptée, et une analyse comparative sera faite entre les réponses mauriciennes et celles d'autres pays pour défendre la liberté d'expression à la lumière de la pandémie du COVID-19.

---

[1] Professor, Dean of Faculty of Law & Management, University of Mauritius.

Introduction

As COVID-19 continues to spread at a fast pace across the globe, it becomes more than ever imperative to regulate the content of information being shared with the view of ensuring that governments, companies, the medical community and the society in general have access to accurate and timely information (Agley and Xiao, 2021). In this regard, various international institutions like the World Wide Web Foundation, the UNESCO, the Association of Progressive Communications and the World Health Organisation have raised serious concerns over the massive information asymmetries being circulated in the society, which makes it difficult for civilians to rely on trustworthy sources.

Indeed, the purveyors of fake news are sharing information which has induced unnecessary panic among the public whilst simultaneously slowing the progress of the fight against the pandemic (Mian and Khan, 2020). For instance, there were rumours spread by the press that drinking whisky could kill the coronavirus (South China Morning Post, 2020) or that continue with virus affects only white people (Collier, 2020), or even racist news that larceny is being committed on Chinese shop owners in Nigeria (Premium Times, 2020). As such, there is a dire need to take the appropriate action plans to stop the spread of this incorrect information but primarily, it is imperative to highlight the various types of inaccurate news ranging from fake news, misinformation, disinformation and infodemic. In this regard, in its Handbook for Journalism Education and Training, the UNESCO has defined fake news to refer to non-factual information (UNESCO, 2018) but most experts are against the use of this term since it does not consider intentions of the purveyors but is rather used to undermine journalists (Web Foundation, 2021). In contrast, disinformation refers to the deliberate propaganda of misleading or biased information, manipulated narrative or facts while misinformation also refers to the spread of false information but without necessarily involving the mens rea to mislead (Dictionary.com, 2022). On the other hand, infodemic has been described by the WHO as an overabundance of information, whether accurate or not, that makes it hard for people to find trustworthy and reliable guidance when they need it (WHO, 2020).

Undoubtedly, the rise of disinformation, misinformation or infodemic adversely affects the reputation of a country and more specifically those targeted by this news but alongside, it is dangerous to rely on such information to protect public interest. Moreover, people's health may be at stake due to over-reliance on unverified or unreliable information which are made universally accessible via social media platforms and the internet in general. Consequently, to address information issues which are a frequent source of frustration (Pan American Health Organisation, 2021), governments across the world are adopting strict measures such as censorship, warning or arresting those who spread false news. In this context, Mauritius also has not been spared and has also fallen prey of false news being shared on social media since in the year 2020, immediately upon the announcement of the closure of supermarkets and shops, a civilian had falsely claimed the eruption of riots in one particular region of the island. This had mobilized police force and special quad teams to reach the area further to which it was found that the news was a fake one. Accordingly, to prevent the recurrence of such an event, the civilian was arrested under the Mauritius Information and Communication Technology Act (L'Express.mu, 2020).

Nevertheless, there is the fear that governments are abusing libel laws, defamation laws and internet restrictions to limit the freedom of expression of citizens and the media and that the pandemic is simply being used as an excuse to further obstruct freedom of expression (Tandoc et al., 2020). Hence, since the outbreak of COVID-19, some international agencies like the WHO and Human Rights Watch have established checklists to ensure the protection of human rights and this includes the protection of freedom of expression and the broadcasting or sharing of verified, scientific, fact-based news and analysis (Guterres, 2021). As such, it is through the lens of human rights that this research purports to critically examine the approaches undertaken by the Mauritian authorities to deal with misinformation during COVID-19 in the context of domestic laws and international conventions on freedom of expression. To achieve this research objective, a content analysis of international responses, the black letter research methodology will be adopted, and a comparative analysis will be made between Mauritian responses and those of other countries to uphold freedom of expression in the light of the COVID-19 pandemic.

At present, there are few literatures on the researched topic and this study will be amongst the first academic writings on the effectiveness of the Mauritian laws concerning freedom of expression. The study is carried out with the aim of combining a large amount of empirical, theoretical and factual information that can be of use to various stakeholders and not only to academics. While the first part of the paper has set out the context of the research including the research objectives and methods, the second part of the paper will discuss some existing literature highlighting the main sources of misinformation and its impact during COVID-19 as well as some governmental actions taken across the globe to counter misinformation spreading. Part 3 will critically analyse the main international conventions as well as the laws of Mauritius on freedom of expression in the context of misinformation during COVID-19 while Part 4 will examine some other countries' responses to deal with misinformation. Part 5 will critically assess the various approaches adopted by several countries and will conclude the paper.

I. Literature review

A. Sources of misinformation

Misinformation is not a new phenomenon although in today's digitalized era, the spread of misinformation is accelerated by firstly the social media and secondly, due to the diversification of actors that produce and disseminate misinformation (Association for Progressive Communications, 2021). Initially, media operators were mostly responsible for sharing disinformation but now a simple post or hash tagging relating to the personal opinion of an individual on social media platforms may become the subject of information which may not be necessarily true or accurate. It is apposite to note that misinformation propagates without constraints, does not entail any curation or peer-review and does not require any professional verifications.

Indeed, in support of the statement that misinformation is gaining popularity due to social media, Brennen et al. (2020) assessed the main types, sources and claims of COVID-19 misinformation in the Great Britain between January to March 2020 published by some randomly chosen social media platforms and traditional media institutions. The findings revealed that 59 % of misinformation emanated from three well-known social media platforms being YouTube, Facebook and Twitter and in terms of the nature of misinformation, it was found that misleading or false claims about actions or policies of public authorities such as the government, international bodies like the UN or WTO, are the first and largest category of misinformation. Along similar lines, Kouzy et al. (2020) sought to examine the extent of misinformation being spread on Twitter regarding COVID-19 on one particular day in February 2020. The study included some 673 tweets and the results showed that 153 tweets contained misinformation while 107 tweets shared some unverifiable information. Furthermore, the researchers analysed the Twitter accounts by user category and the results reveal that the diffusers of misinformation were informal personal/group accounts (33.8 %) followed by unverified Twitter accounts (31 %) while formal institutions like the government, press companies and healthcare providers had a lower rate of misinformation (6.1 %). Moreover, Twitter has been accused by Pulido et al. (2020) of promulgating information which may hinder efforts to combat COVID-19. Content analysis methodology was used by the researchers and the results demonstrated that out of the 1,000 Tweets selected, 92 % consisted of false information from which 63.3 % were retweeted.

Undoubtedly, the ease of access to internet facilities across the globe has turned online platforms an accessible and easy tool of communication but a lack of objective information shared on these platforms has resulted in an unprecedented surge of misinformation and unauthentic news. In this regard, Li et al. (2020) examined the sharing of misinformation during COVID-19 on YouTube on one particular day of March 2020. The researchers found that out of the 145 online videos, 64 % contained misinformation elaborating on myths, vaccination discovery and decontextualization while more than one-quarter of the most viewed YouTube videos contained misinformation which represented millions of viewers worldwide. Consequently, the sharing of videos containing false or unauthentic information may delay the elimination of the coronavirus. As such, to deal with this issue, it becomes imperative to understand the reasons as to why there is the rising presence of misinformation on social media. Accordingly, a study conducted by Laato et al. (2020) revealed that sharing online information has become a typical behaviour nowadays and the 294 respondents in Bangladesh affirmed that although they were aware that the information was unverified, they still shared it without considering the adverse outcomes of their action. In addition, to corroborate the findings of Laato et al. (2020), another study conducted by Pennycook et al. (2020) used a close-ended survey with 1,600 American participants and the findings indicated that more than 50 % of respondents prefer to share information without validation since for them, information sharing is essential to aware the masses.

B. Impact of misinformation

As the WHO warned about misinformation, people are finding it difficult to rely on trustworthy sources of information which is also acting as a barrier against response efforts to mitigate the pandemic. Consequently, several researchers analysed the potential impacts of misinformation and Arenas (2020) summarized all these effects into three categories namely, xenophobia, LGBT healthcare rights violation and psychological distress.

Primarily, rumours and misinformation have made people to believe that COVID-19 is a result of intentionality and personal interest of one particular country which when riddled with hate speech and racism, human societies have witnessed unprecedented disruptions (Arenas, 2020). For instance, a study conducted by Rzymski and Nowicki (2020) suggest that Asian medical students situated in Poland are facing discrimination and isolation due to their origin, which is affecting their career development. Likewise, xenophobia against Chinese people is prevalent in the US which is confirmed by Reny and Barreto (2020) who investigated some 4,311 Americans' perceptions towards the Chinese. The results revealed a strong association between COVID-19 misinformation and xenophobia towards the Chinese. In addition to xenophobia, several international institutions like the WHO and the UN have declared the LGBT community more vulnerable during COVID-19 due to the already prevailing stigmatization and discrimination against these individuals (Lopez, 2020). Basically, the LGBT community is facing issues with accessing healthcare services and they are falling prey of bullying at home and online which is making it more difficult to move easily due to lockdown and sanitary restriction measures (UNHR, 2020).

Apart from xenophobia against the Chinese and the increase in vulnerability of the LGBT community, it is believed that misinformation plays a vital role in undermining one's mental health by inducing fear, anxiety and stress (Arenas, 2020). This is because people living in isolation or quarantine often rely on the main source of information which is readily available, that is information shared on social media platforms. As mentioned earlier, these platforms entail the majority of misinformation which may severely cause risk to mental and physical health of the vulnerable groups (Brennen et al., 2020). In this regard, Rajkumar (2020) conducted a study to assess the psychological impacts of COVID-19 on people's mental health. The findings showed that anxiety, stress and depression are the most important psychological problems encountered during COVID-19 and that reducing or eliminating mental health issues can be carried out by counteracting misinformation and its potential resources.

Furthermore, more alarmingly, a study conducted by Islam et al. (2021) and another one carried out by the John Hopkins Centre for Communication Programs (2020) has proven that relying on misinformation relating to health matters can prove to be fatal and even deadly. Their findings suggest that during the first 3 months of 2020, nearly 6000 people were hospitalized and at least 800 people have died due to reliance on COVID-19 misinformation. Spreading like wildfire alongside the pandemic, false information is the underlying principle for uncertainty and distrust which in turn fuels an environment vulnerable to fear, anxiety and violent behaviours.

C. International instruments and Mauritian laws on freedom of expression

1. International conventions

Essentially, to curb the spectrum of negative impacts of misinformation during COVID-19, it is first and foremost imperative to control the source of this inaccurate information. In this regard, governments across the world have implemented various strategies to tackle the issue of distribution of false and misleading information such as the holding of sensitization campaigns or press conferences and strengthening existing or establishing new regulations on the subject matter. However, in this attempt, governments are having to balance the dichotomy between freedom of expression and people's right to be safe from the adverse effects of misinformation (Rodrigues and Xu, 2020).

Fundamentally, freedom of expression is guaranteed by several international instruments. For instance, Article 19 of the Universal Declaration of Human Rights (UDHR) empowers every person to have the right to freedom of opinion and expression and to receive and share information through any media and regardless of frontiers. This particular article is further replicated in Article 19(2) of the International Covenant on Civil and Political Rights (ICCPR) but with a more elaborated explanation on the methods of communication and some restrictions on the exercise of these rights. In particular, Article 19(2) of the ICCPR adds on the corresponding article of the UDHR by precising that communication channels may be either oral, in writing or print, in the form of art or any other media of the person's choice. Indeed, Article 19 of the ICCPR differs from Article 19 of the UDHR by mentioning that the right to freedom of expression shall be exercised by respecting the rights and reputations of others and for the protection of national security, public order or public health and morals.

Furthermore, under Article 10 of the European Convention of Human Rights (ECHR), any person is entitled to hold opinions, receive and disseminate ideas and information without interference. Essentially, 'ideas' and 'information' referred to in Article 10 of the ECHR not only encompass inoffensive or indifferent contents, but they also include stuff that may shock, offend or disturb the State or any sector of the population (Muller and Ors v. Switzerland, 1988). Similarly, Article 9 of the African Charter on Human and Peoples' Rights provides for the right to receive information, to express and disseminate opinions within the law. Nevertheless, this legal provision has been criticized by various scholars such as Kas (2021) and Fielden (2012) on the ground that it does not provide the freedom of expression as afforded by other international instruments such as the UDHR, the ICCPR or the ECHR. This is because firstly, there is no corresponding right to impart information and secondly, the right of expression and dissemination has been curtailed with the proviso 'within the law'.

Nevertheless, these rights are not absolute since Article 19(3) of the ICCPR outlines some permissible limitations on freedom of expression if these are required by the law or are necessary to respect the rights and reputation of others or to protect national security, public order, public health or morals (United Nations Human Rights Office of the High Commissioner, 2020a). Accordingly, these limitations have to be clearly spelt in terms of scope, meaning and effect in order to regulate individuals' behaviours to avoid violations. Also, Article 19(3) of the ICCPR highlights the necessity of domestic laws that any restriction on the exercise of free expression must be proportionate to the threat to national security, public order and health or morals. In other words, any restriction of freedom of expression has to be mandated by the exigencies of the situation and must meet the tests of necessity and proportionality with the view of achieving a legitimate objective whilst not undermining the right to expression itself (Pomeranz and Schwid, 2021).

Hence, from the above elaboration on international conventions, in the context of COVID-19, common consensus agrees that the onus is on the government who is seeking to limit expression to establish a direct and immediate link between freedom of expression and the threat and any restriction must be the 'least intrusive instrument' to protect national security and public health (United Nations Human Rights Office of the High Commissioner, 2020b). However, there is a gap in literature as to how countries have complied with their duties under the ICCPR during the pandemic in the light of the rising amount of misinformation, especially in the Mauritian context.

2. Mauritian laws on freedom of expression

Primarily, Mauritius being a sovereign democratic country, has embedded the fundamental right of expression in Article 12 of its constitution which is the sovereign law of the island. This particular Section 12 has been inspired from Article 10 of the ECHR and accordingly, the Supreme Court of Mauritius (SCM) relies on judgements rendered by the European Court of Human Rights when considering disputes regarding freedom of expression.

However, Section 12 of the Mauritian constitution sets out some limitations to the enjoyment of freedom of expression. In particular, it is a limited right and there is the need to strike a balance between the right to freedom of expression and the rights of others. This reasoning has been thoroughly applied by Mauritian courts since decades for instances in the cases of Cehl Meeah v. Commissioner of Police (2001), Armoogum v. La Sentinelle Ltée (2002), Soornack v. Le Matinale (2013). Essentially, the Supreme Court of Mauritius has highlighted in the landmark case of DPP v. Boodhoo (1992) that an abuse of freedom of expression can be a potential threat in a democratic society which may lead to a chaotic situation.

Moreover, apart from respecting the rights of others when expressing an opinion, Mauritian laws have criminalized the publication, diffusion or reproduction of false news with the aim of defaming another person or which will disturb public order or peace according to Section 299 of the Mauritian Criminal Code. For instance, a newspaper cannot publish inappropriate, malicious or illegal articles without the required facts or evidence and this principle was supported in the Mauritian case law of Joseph France Michel Favolle v. Advance Publications (Mauritius) Co. Ltd (2017). However, where the facts are true and relevant for public benefit, then the court will not prohibit the publication of an article despite being defamatory and this reasoning was upheld in the case of Fraser v. Evans (1969).

Additionally, freedom of expression is limited on the grounds of avoiding contempt of court's offense. In fact, any person who impedes the fair administration of justice will be guilty of this offense and even journalists may fall prey sometimes. For instance, the media was accused in the case of DPP v. Ahnee (1992) of making insulting remarks in respect of a judge that had casted some doubts regarding his independence and impartiality. The relevant media operator was thus sanctioned for having scandalized the court. Additionally, in the case of Procureur General v. Delaroche (1893), a media operator was found guilty of a contempt of court's offense for having influenced a pending trial that had interfered with the administration of justice in this particular case. The rationale behind these convictions is to avoid 'trial by media' which will negatively affect the right to a fair trial of an accused.

3. Misinformation in Mauritius during COVID-19

It follows that the Mauritian government has taken a proactive approach to discourage the spread of misinformation during COVID-19 at an early stage. This statement is evidenced by the first attempt to mislead the general population through the sharing of a post on Facebook by a Mauritian citizen just after the Prime Minister of the country announced the first national lockdown back in March 2020. His post read as follows:

> *"Rioting right now around the capital Port-Louis, Abercombie and Roche Bois Police Station under attack, […] Jumbo Riche Terre being looted as I write this…"*

According to the police officials, these words have disturbed public interest since this post was shared by 10,000 individuals which has in turn raised serious panic in the civil society for fear of being shortage of food materials (L'Express.mu, 2020). Additionally, the police force had to deploy special teams to reach the areas which were allegedly under attack and this has undoubtedly created unnecessary turmoil to the stakeholders concerned. This particular act has been sanctioned as an offense under Section 46(g)(a) of the Mauritius Information and Communications Technology Act of 2001 for having deliberating using a telecommunication equipment or service to send, transmit, transfer, post, publish, deliver or show a message which is obscene, indecent, offensive, abusive, threatening, menacing, false or misleading, which is likely to cause harm or causes harm to a person. Consequently, the Mauritian purveyor of false news was immediately imprisoned, a strong message passed by the authorities in Mauritius that they will not tolerate such kind of behaviour. If found guilty on conviction by a court of law, the offender will have to undergo a term of imprisonment not exceeding 10 years and will need to pay a fine not exceeding MUR 1 Million (USD 22,900).

In addition to the immediate arrest of the purveyor of fake news in Mauritius as a corrective and preventive mechanism, the country has left no stone unturned in upholding the diffusion of true and accurate information. Accordingly, the Cybercrime Unit of the police force in Mauritius is thoroughly scrutinising and monitoring any instance of misconduct like the spreading of false information on a rigorous basis either on social media platforms or live radio shows (UN Africa Renewal, 2020). Simultaneously, the government had instituted a national communication committee on COVID-19 which has the mandate of addressing rumours, misinformation and fake news and bringing forth clarifications. Moreover, this committee is the sole official authority recognized by the Mauritian government to communicate information regarding the prevalence of COVID-19 cases in the country, the number of deaths, shopping guidelines, precautionary measures as well as medical treatments and advice. Laudably, during the early stages of the pandemic, members of this national committee were punctually present at 6 p.m. sharp for a special communication which was broadcasted by the national television of Mauritius for at least three months on a daily basis and this regular and transparent communication has proven to be highly effective. Essentially, a decrease in rumours and fake news was observed among the population and on social media and no severe signs of panic were witnessed among the population who reacted responsibly and in discipline as evidenced by a study carried out by Musango et al. (2021), who collected data through participative observation of key stakeholders involved in the fight against COVID-19 in Mauritius including the WHO and Ministry of Health and Wellness.

Furthermore, coupled with corrective and punitive actions as well as clear and official communication channels, several media platforms were created to transmit information from decision-makers to the general public. In particular, a specific website, a Facebook page '*Coronavirus Moris*' dedicated to COVID-19 in Mauritius and a mobile application '*beSafeMoris*', all of which are still operational, were established.

Undeniably, considerable efforts have been undertaken by the Mauritian authorities in dealing with misinformation during COVID-19. However, in one particular instance, the Mauritian government was accused of acting illegitimately by the Centre for Law and Democracy (CLD) (2020) for having arrested a woman for having spread fake news regarding the Prime Minister.

In fact, the Mauritian woman was arrested under the Mauritius Information and Communications Technology Act of 2001 for having posted a humorous message although fake, about the Prime Minister of the country on Facebook to the effect that the latter will be holding live interview with several world leaders regarding the success story of Mauritius in dealing with COVID-19. Additionally, adding fire to fuel, this woman's barristers were charged for breaching curfew while travelling to visit her without the appropriate work permit and these actions had led to severe criticism against the Mauritian authorities. Thereafter, the woman was granted bail upon payment of a sum of money. In particular, the CLD advocated that the charge against the woman in question was unconstitutional and that the sharing of fake news that has no consequence of defamation or fraud, have no legitimacy whilst highlighting simultaneously that the humorous message against the Prime Minister was not a statement of fact. Ultimately, in September 2021, the court of Mauritius removed the provisional charge indicating that this charge was unconstitutional. To reiterate, international instruments like Article 19(2) of the ICCPR and the constitutional right of freedom of expression are subject to limitations if the rights or reputation of others are at stake or if there is a need to protect public order or interest. Accordingly, critical comments targeted towards political leaders or their positions regarding the COVID-19 must not in all instances be the target of breach of specific legislation on misinformation or the spread of fake news.

However, apart from these two cases, no other person was incriminated during the COVID-19 in Mauritius for having spread misinformation which is indeed a positive signal and this success may largely be attributed to both the punitive and correction actions by the Mauritian government and the vast range of communication campaigns undertaken by the latter for information on COVID-19. Nevertheless, it is still worth considering some other countries' approaches to deal with misinformation with the view of comparing the functioning of the Mauritian stakeholders' initiatives to models, benchmarks and examples from outside Mauritius.

4. Government intervention across the world

From an evaluation of government responses against misinformation during COVID-19, five main categories of actions were noted ranging from sensitization initiatives, increasing access to accurate information, addressing commercial fraud and criminalizing expression. Primarily, being concerned of the gravity of the consequences of misinformation, a subtle approach was endeavoured by the UK government, which in collaboration with the WHO, has come up with a series of sensitization campaigns, one of which is the '*Stop the Spread*' television programme broadcasted by the BBC World. The message being passed on is to shed light on the bulk of misinformation surrounding COVID-19 matters and the negative impacts therefrom. Moreover, this programme aims at encouraging people to check their source of information and only if this is trustworthy, they can share it. Additionally, as a corrective mechanism, the UK government again alongside the WHO had launched a digital series on '*Reporting Misinformation*' to explain to people how to report misinformation which they come across. This information was launched by WHO on its website and is shared in five international languages. It is purported to be the second most viewed COVID-19 related page by the WHO (2022) which implies that the caution behind the spread of false information is catching people's attention in general.

Moreover, with the view of attracting people's attention on the dangers of spreading misinformation, especially the young generation, an innovative online game under the name of '*Go Viral*' was developed by the UK Cabinet Office and the Cambridge University. This game highlights the importance of fact-checking and gives people an insight of the techniques used to share false information on social media. In particular, the players are put in the shoes of a purveyor of misinformation further to which they discover how real news gets distorted by the involvement of fake doctors, remedies and false rumours. Indeed, according to a study conducted by Maertens et al. (2021), it was found that a single play of this game can reduce the spread of false information for at least three months. Essentially, the success of the UK government's various initiatives was applauded by Islam et al. (2021) who believe that the common misconceptions on vaccines were wiped out and more people are now understanding the safety of approved COVID-19 vaccines in the UK.

In addition to sensitization campaigns, governments have also increased access to the general population to accurate information by sharing facts on a continuous basis. For instance, likewise Mauritius, the government of Taiwan held daily press conferences and issued newsletters on matters related to COVID-19 whilst at the same time, establishing the '*Taiwan FactCheck Center*' which is a social media application that can verify the accuracy of information provided online within 60 minutes. Any false news detected is then clarified to the public. Moreover, in Ethiopia, a simple gesture put forward by the governmental authority like the sending of an automatic message on COVID-19 prevention when someone placed a phone call, has helped to a large extent curb down misinformation on the pandemic. Similarly, stakeholders in South Africa and Nigeria worked with WhatsApp to provide users in these countries with information on the virus and the ways of prevention.

Indeed, misinformation about COVID-19 is also being spread through false advertisements and commercial fraud especially regarding preventions and cures. Accordingly, some countries are enforcing their consumer protection laws so that the public is not defrauded into purchasing ineffective, unsafe or harmful products (WHO, 2019). For example, the European Union's law enforcement agency Europol, identified and took down 2,500 online links related to COVID-19 websites, marketplaces and advertisements and seized 4.4 million units of fake pharmaceuticals (Pomeranz and Schwid, 2021). Along the same lines, with the view of protecting the public, governments have adopted a strict approach by making use of cyber misuse laws, penal codes and defamation legislation to prosecute people who share incorrect information on COVID-19. In this context, officials in the Philippines arrested people for allegedly spreading false rumours about COVID-19 in their local neighbourhoods; and Sri Lankan authorities arrested people for criticizing public officials' response to the pandemic. Journalists were similarly sanctioned. Similarly, Cambodian authorities arrested the director of a news site for accurately reporting the prime minister's statements made during a press conference. Also, Iraq's media regulator fined Reuters and suspended its license for reporting COVID-19 statistics in violation of its media broadcasting rules while in Serbia, police arrested a journalist for her article reporting on a lack of personal protective gear, sanitary materials, and medicine in a hospital (Pomeranz and Schwid, 2021).

Furthermore, to its merit, some countries took strong measures to criminalize the dissemination of misinformation through emergency laws. For instance, in April 2020, the country of Botswana issued the Emergency Powers (COVID-19) Regulations criminalizing the sharing of any information to the public about COVID-19 from a source other than the Director of Health Services while in Hungary, the Prime Minister was given additional powers to rule by decree and sanction people who share fake news about the pandemic. Correspondingly, Zimbabwe passes a new regulation entitling the government with the power to prosecute any person who publishes or communicates false news about officials during the lockdown. It is apposite to note that any breach of the new emergency laws may entail fines and imprisonment for up to 20 years.

Being aware of the gravity of the implications of misinformation, the EU Directive on Audiovisual Media Services 2018 emphasized the need to educate citizens of responsibly using information in its Recital 59. In particular, to achieve this objective, Recital 59 highlighted that the civil society needs to possess advanced media literacy skills, which is not only limited to tools and technologies, but it should aim to equip citizens with critical thinking skills required to exercise judgement and to recognize the distinction between opinion and fact. The EU Directive thus expects media service providers and video-sharing platform providers to cooperate with all relevant stakeholders to promote media literacy and progress in this regard shall be monitored continuously. In turn, this collaboration relies on a dire need to improve critical thinking which is an ever-changing process that requires constant reflection and adaptations. This raises the concern as to whether people are ready to adopt critical thinking since sharing and diffusing information without verifying its source has now become the norm.

However, the European Commission is optimistic of the desired change in mentality and this statement is demonstrated by the issuance of a Code of Practice on disinformation in May 2021. The Code was signed by online platforms like Facebook, Google, Twitter, Microsoft, Mozilla and some other marketing websites to set various commitments ranging from transparency in political advertising, closure of fake accounts and demonetization of purveyors of misinformation. To fasten its effort in dealing with misinformation, the European Commissioner further implemented an annual assessment of the signatories by investigating the efforts carried out by the latter to implement their commitments. The first assessment was published in 2020 covering the COVID-19 crisis and the online platforms have reported on various endeavours like development of tools to facilitate access to reliable information of public interest, removal of false or misleading information that will cause physical damage, prohibiting advertisements that either exploit the crisis or promote anti-vaccines behaviours. In addition, to bring about a more robust framework, the EU aims at transforming the Code of Practice as a co-regulatory instrument within the Digital Services Act 2020.

Discussion and conclusion

All the countries mentioned in this research including Mauritius have either ratified or signed the ICCPR which imply their commitment to protect free expression. However, several countries deviated from these commitments in the name of addressing COVID-19 misinformation. For instance, the use of existing or new laws to criminalize expression about the pandemic do not meet the requirements under Article 19(3) of the ICCPR which are basically to protect the rights and reputations of others or to protect public interest. Undeniably, governments act contrary to international law when they criminalize journalism or prosecute expressions that are truthful or that criticizes the government (United Nations Human Rights Committee, 2011). In fact, these approaches are not necessary to address the public health crisis and they are not proportionate to the public health threat which are two essential elements in seeking the restrictions of free expression under Article 19(3) of the ICCPR.

From the research conducted, it is noted that accurate and regular reporting by governmental bodies play an essential role in fostering the public's trust in accurate sources of information which can in turn reduce misinformation. However, one must not undermine the role and function of the press which has the mandate to expose government malfeasance and to share accurate information to the public. Consequently, establishing a law that provides the power to share information to only governmental authorities underestimate the role of the press and accordingly, it is suggested that governments should avoid any action that interfere with the press obligation towards the civil society.

Essentially, cases surrounding misinformation on COVID-19 are relatively lower in Mauritius than in other countries. This is largely attributed to the diffusion of official information on the pandemic by the Mauritian authorities either through the media or via mobile applications or official websites and also due to the strict application of the information technology laws on the purveyors of fake news that are likely to disturb public security. However, in one particular instance, it has been noted that the cyber misuse laws have been used to restrict freedom of expression of a woman who was humorously critical towards government response to COVID-19 in Mauritius. Fortunately, the judiciary in the country is independent and this charge was struck off by the court.

Nevertheless, the dangers of spreading misinformation are still looming around and this consequently calls for the much-appreciated initiative to sensitize civilians on media literacy. It is undisputed that people need to be equipped with the necessary critical thinking to use and create media content responsibly and safely especially in complex situations like the COVID-19 pandemic. In this effort, the role of the academia, consumer's associations, press bodies and social media platforms cannot be underpinned. For instance, the setting up of a new Media Education Chair at the Lille Graduate School of Journalism in collaboration with Facebook France has been seen as a laudable initiative to show Facebook's commitment to promote critical thinking and fight against false information.

On a concluding note, from the comparative study conducted in this paper, it is imperative to highlight firstly that there is a dire need for countries to strictly abide by the principles of necessity and proportionality to the threat being endangered in order to restrict freedom of expression or to resort to libel laws, defamation laws or cyber misuse laws to prosecute those who express their opinion. Secondly, although misinformation cannot be entirely eradicated, they can still be managed through campaigns and collaborations especially by showing people how to recognize and report misinformation and improve their media literacy. As such, media literacy is a matter of each and every one and through constant education and robust collaboration among various stakeholders, people's mindset is likely to be changed which will help in eradicating the issue of misinformation.

Bibliography

Agley, J. and Xiao, Y. (2021). Misinformation about Covid-19: Evidence for differential latent profiles and a strong association with trust in science. BMC Public Health, 21(8), 8–16. Available at https://bmcpublichealth.biomedcentral.com/articles/10.1186/s12889-020-10103-x [Accessed on 16 February 2022].

Ali, S. (2022). Combatting against Covid-19 & misinformation: A systematic review. Human Arenas, 2022(5), 337–352. Available at https://link.springer.com/article/10.1007/s42087-020-00139-1 [Accessed on 30 May 2022].

Armoogum v. La Sentinelle Ltée (2002) SCJ 341.

Association for Progressive Communications. (2021, April 5). 'Disinformation and freedom of expression' [Online]. Available at https://www.ohchr.org/Documents/Issues/Expression/disinformation/2-Civil-society-organisations/APC-Disinformation-Submission.pdf [Accessed on 22 February 2022].

Brennen, A., Scott, J., Simon, F., Howard, P. and Nielsen, K. (2020, December 5). 'Types, sources and claims of Covid-19 misinformation' [Online]. Oxford University Press. Available at https://reutersinstitute.politics.ox.ac.uk/types-sources-and-claims-covid-19-misinformation [Accessed on 22 February 2022].

Cehl Meeah v. Commissioner of Police (2001) SCJ 252.

Centre for Law and Democracy. (2020, April 9). 'Mauritius: Fake news arrest for political satire not legitimate' [Online]. Available at https://www.law-democracy.org/live/mauritius-fake-news-arrest-for-political-satire-not-legitimate/ [Accessed on 22 February 2022].

Collier, B. (2020, February 16). 'Why is Covid-19 killing so many Black Americans?' [Online]. Available at https://greatergood.berkeley.edu/article/item/why_covid_19_killing_black_americans [Accessed on 17 February 2022].

Dictionary.com. (2022, February 28). 'Disinformation' [Online]. Available at https://www.dictionary.com/browse/disinformation [Accessed on 16 February 2022].

Digital Services Act. (2020, May 23). 'Proposal for a REGULATION OF THE EUROPEAN PARLIAMENT AND OF THE COUNCIL on a Single Market For Digital Services (Digital Services Act) and amending Directive 2000/31/EC' [Online] COM/2020/825 final/ Available at https://eur-lex.europa.eu/legal-content/en/TXT/?uri=COM%3A2020%3A825%3AFIN [Accessed on 2 May 2022].

DPP v. Ahnee (1992). MR 184.

DPP v. Boodhoo (1992). MR 284.

EU Directive. (2018, January 23). 'Directive (EU) 2018/1808 of the European Parliament and of the Council of 14 November 2018 amending Directive 2010/13/EU on the coordination of certain provisions laid down by law, regulation or administrative action in Member States concerning the provision of audiovisual media services (Audiovisual Media Services Directive) in view of changing market realities' [Online]. PE/33/2018/REV/1 Available at https://eur-lex.europa.eu/eli/dir/2018/1808/oj [Accessed on 2 May 2022].

Fraser v. Evans (1969) 1 QB 349.

Guterres, A. (2021, April 6). 'Message by Antonio Guterres on World Press Freedom Day 2021' [Online]. Available at https://indonesia.un.org/en/125972-message-antonio-guterres-world-press-freedom-day-2021 [Accessed on 16 February 2022].

Islam, M., Sarkar, T., Khan, A., and Seale, M. (2021). Covid-19 related infodemic and its impact on public health: A global social media analysis. The American Journal of Tropical Medicine and Hygiene. 103(4), 1621–1629. Available at https://doi.org/10.4269/ajtmh.20-0812 [Accessed on 23 February 2022].

John Hopkins Centre for Communication Programs. (2020, February 23). 'How to convince the Covid-19 vaccine hesitant' [Online]. Available at https://ccp.jhu.edu/2021/01/21/covid-19-vaccine-hesitant/ [Accessed on 23 February 2022].

Joseph France Michel Favolle v. Advance Publications (Mauritius) Co. Ltd (2017) SCJ 94.

Kouzy, R., Jaoude, K., Kraitem, A. and Baddour, K. (2020). Coronavirus goes viral: Quantifying the Covid-19 misinformation epidemic on twitter. Cureus. 12(3), 55–72. Available at doi: 10.7759/cureus.7255 [Accessed on 22 February 2022].

Laato, S., Islam N. and Whelan, E. (2020). Why do people share misinformation during Covid-19 pandemic? European Journal of Information Systems. 2020(3), 26–36. Available at https://doi.org/10.1080/0960085X.2020.1770632 [Accessed on 22 February 2022].

L'Express.mu. (2020, June 25). 'Fake news: Jameel Peerally arrested' [Online]. Available at https://www.lexpress.mu/article/373277/fake-news-jahmeel-peerally-arrete [Accessed on 16 February 2022].

Li, H., Bailey, A. and Chan, J. (2020). YouTube as a source of information on Covid-19: A pandemic of misinformation? BMJ Global Health. 5(5), 15–35. Available at doi: 10.1136/bmjgh-2020-002604 [Accessed on 22 February 2022].

Lopez, O. (2020, July 21). 'LGBT + community at heightened risk of coronavirus' [Online]. Available at https://www.reuters.com/article/us-health-coronavirus-lgbt-trfn-idUSKBN20Y3JS [Accessed on 22 February 2022].

Maertens, R., Roozenbeek, J., Basol, J. and Van der Linden, S. (2021). Long-term effectiveness of inoculation against misinformation: Three longitudinal experiments. Journal of Experimental Psychology: Applied. 27(1), 1–16. Available at https://pubmed.ncbi.nlm.nih.gov/33017160/ [Accessed on 22 February 2022].

Mian, A. and Khan, S. (2020). Coronavirus: The spread of misinformation. BMC Medicine. 18(89), 11–26. Available at https://link.springer.com/article/10.1186/s12916-020-01556-3 [Accessed on 16 February 2022].

Musango, L., Veerapa, L. and Joomaye Z. (2021). Key success factors of Mauritius in the fight of Covid-19. BMJ Global Health. 6(53–72). Available at http://dx.doi.org/10.1136/bmjgh-2021-005372 [Accessed on 22 February 2022].

Pan American Health Organisation. (2021, September 18). 'Understanding the infodemic and misinformation in the fight against Covid-19' [Online]. Available at https://iris.paho.org/bitstream/handle/10665.2/52052/Factsheet-infodemic_eng.pdf [Accessed on 16 February 2022].

Pennycook, G., McPhetres, J. and Rand, D. (2020). Fighting Covid-19 misinformation on social media: Experimental evidence for a scalable accuracy nudge intervention. Psychological Science. 31(7), 44–56. Available at https://doi.org/10.1177/0956797620939054 [Accessed on 22 February 2022].

Pomeranz, J. and Schwid, A. (2021). Governmental actions to address Covid-19. Journal of Public Health Policy. 42(1), 201–210. Available at https://doi.org/10.1057/s41271-020-00270-x [Accessed on 23 February 2022].

Premium Times. (2020, March 29). 'Looting across Nigeria as arsonists, hoodlums, thieves take control' [Online]. Available at https://www.premiumtimesng.com/news/headlines/422994-looting-across-nigeria-as-arsonists-hoodlums-thieves-take-control.html [Accessed on 17 February 2022].

Procureur General v. Delaroche [1893] MR 13.

Pulido, C., Carballido, V. and Gomez, A. (2020). Covid-19 infodemic: More retweets for science-based information on Coronavirus than for false information. International Sociology. 3(4), 6–9. Available at doi: 10.1177/0268580920914755 [Accessed on 22 February 2022].

Rajkumar, R. (2020). Covid-19 and mental health a review of existing literature. Asian Journal of Psychiatry. 52(January). Available at doi: 10.1016/j.ajp.2020.102066 [Accessed on 22 February 2022].

Reny, T. and Barreto, M. (2020). Xenophobia in the time of pandemic. Politics, Groups and Identities. 1(24), 16–26. Available at 10.1080/21565503.2020.1769693 [Accessed on 22 February 2022].

Rodrigues, U. and Xu, J. (2020). Regulation of Covid-19 fake news infodemic in China and India. Media International Australia. 177(1), 125–131. Available at doi: 10.1177/1329878X20948202 [Accessed on 23 February 2022].

Rzymski, P. and Nowicki, M. (2020). Covid-19 related prejudice toward Asian medical students: A consequence of SARS-CoC-2 fears in Poland. Journal of Infection and Public Health. 13(6), 873–876. Available at doi: 10.1016/j.jiph.2020.04.013 [Accessed on 22 February 2022].

Soornack v. Le Matinale. (2013). SCJ 58.

South China Morning Post. (2020, March 26). 'Why whisky could kill the coronavirus' [Online]. Available at https://www.scmp.com/news/china/science/article/3075971/why-whisky-could-kill-coronavirus-drinking-it-wont-work [Accessed on 16 February 2022].

Tandoc, E., Wei, L. and Ling, R. (2020). Defining fake news: A typological of scholarly definitions. Digital Journalism. 6(2), 11–29.

UN Africa Renewal. (2020, September 26). 'Mauritius, Senegal and South Africa among the co-authors of cross-regional statement on Covid-19 infodemic' [Online]. Available at https://www.tralac.org/news/article/14700-mauritius-senegal-and-south-africa-among-co-authors-of-cross-regional-statement-on-covid-19-infodemic.html [Accessed on 22 February 2022].

UNESCO. (2018). Fake news and disinformation. In Handbook for Journalism Education and Training. France: United Nations Educational, Scientific and Cultural Organisation.

United Nations Human Rights. (2020, February 23). 'Covid-19 and the human rights of LGBT people' [Online]. Available at https://www.ohchr.org/Documents/Issues/LGBT/LGBTIpeople.pdf [Accessed on 22 February 2022].

United Nations Human Rights Office of the High Commissioner. (2020a, March 21). 'International Covenant on Civil and Political Rights' [Online]. Available at https://www.ohchr.org/en/professionalinterest/pages/ccpr.aspx [Accessed on 23 February 2022].

United Nations Human Rights Office of the High Commissioner. (2020b, March 21). 'General Comment No. 34, Article 19: Freedom of Opinion and Expression' [Online]. Available at https://www2.ohchr.org/english/bodies/hrc/docs/GC34.pdf [Accessed on 22 February 2022].

Web Foundation. (2021, April 20). 'Covid-19 policy brief: Misinformation and freedom of expression' [Online]. Available at http://webfoundation.org/docs/2020/04/Covid-Policy-Brief-Misinformation_Public.pdf [Accessed on 16 February 2022].

WHO. (2019, December 30). 'Novel Coronavirus – 2019-nCov situation report' [Online]. Available at https://www.who.int/docs/default-source/coronaviruse/situation-reports/20200202-sitrep-13-ncov-v3.pdf [Accessed on 26 February 2020].

WHO. (2020, January 13). 'Novel Coronavirus situation report – 13' [Online]. Available at https://www.who.int/docs/default-source/coronaviruse/situation-reports/20200202-sitrep-13-ncov-v3.pdf [Accessed on 16 February 2022].

WHO. (2022, July 15). 'Fighting misinformation in the time of Covid-19, one click at a time' [Online]. Available at https://www.who.int/news-room/feature-stories/detail/fighting-misinformation-in-the-time-of-covid-19-one-click-at-a-time [Accessed on 22 February 2022].

Part V

Health, End of Life and COVID-19/
Santé, fin de vie et COVID-19

The COVID-19 pandemic was above all a major challenge to the health system, which was not prepared for a crisis of this magnitude in any country in the world. Especially at the beginning of the pandemic, the health care system quickly reached its limits. Covid patients had to be shifted between different regions and even countries in order to be able to use bed capacities, and all other non-urgent medical interventions were postponed in order to keep the capacities for the covid crisis. The question for the future is therefore how to distribute insufficient treatment resources to too many people in need. In this context, there is also the question of the necessity of new laws or a reform of the health systems (S. Rohlfing Dijoux). In particular, the protection of vulnerables must be guaranteed in this context (C. Wallet). The sanitary crisis also exacerbated other independent health problems, such as psychological illness and illness linked to domestic violence (D. Devi Sookur, N. Devi Horill).

La pandémie COVID-19 a surtout constitué un défi majeur pour le système de santé, qui n'était préparé à une crise de cette ampleur dans aucun pays du monde. Au début de la pandémie en particulier, les soins de santé ont rapidement atteint leurs limites. Les patients atteints du Covid ont dû être déplacés d'une région à l'autre, voire d'un pays à l'autre, afin d'utiliser les capacités en lits, et toutes les autres interventions médicales non urgentes ont été reportées afin de conserver les capacités pour la crise du Covid. La question qui se pose pour l'avenir est donc de savoir comment distribuer des moyens de traitement insuffisants à un trop grand nombre de personnes dans le besoin. Dans ce contexte, la question de la nécessité de nouvelles lois ou d'une réforme des systèmes de santé se pose également (S. Rohlfing Dijoux). La protection des personnes vulnérables doit notamment être garantie dans ce contexte (C. Wallet). La crise sanitaire a également renforcé d'autres problèmes de santé indépendants, tels que les troubles psychologiques et les violences domestiques (D. Devi Sookur, N. Devi Horill).

The right to life and care in a crisis situation with limited resources

Stephanie ROHLFING-DIJOUX[1]

The present paper deals with the end-of-life legislation in a comparative way in different European countries pertaining to assistance in dying and guarantee the respect of the dignity of the patient until death. We analyse the rights of the patient, such as right to information, ban of unreasonable therapeutical obstinacy, the right to access to palliative care as well as the respect of the autonomy and will of a person, expressed as the right to appoint a person of confidence and to write advanced directives. The core subject is the problem of the respect of these rights in a situation of health crisis or pandemic such as COVID-19 where decisions are made in emergency and time for special procedure and decision making is not available. The paper depicts the fundamental rules and guidelines for physicians in such difficult situations where they do not dispose of enough medical resources.

Le présent document traite de la législation sur la fin de vie de manière comparative dans différents pays européens en ce qui concerne l'aide à mourir et la garantie du respect de la dignité du patient jusqu'à sa mort. Nous analysons les droits du patient, tels que le droit à l'information, l'interdiction de l'obstination thérapeutique déraisonnable, le droit d'accès aux soins palliatifs ainsi que le respect de l'autonomie et de la volonté d'une personne, exprimé par le droit de désigner une personne de confiance et de rédiger des directives anticipées. Le sujet central est le problème du respect de ces droits dans une situation de crise sanitaire ou de pandémie telle que COVID-19, où les décisions sont prises dans l'urgence et où l'on ne dispose pas du temps nécessaire à une procédure spéciale et à la prise de décision. Le document décrit les règles fondamentales et les lignes directrices pour les médecins dans ces situations difficiles où ils ne disposent pas de ressources médicales suffisantes.

---

[1] Professeur Université Paris Nanterre.

Introduction

The right to life is one of the most important human rights, but there is also a right to health, which has been developed as a second-generation human right. In a health crisis situation, the primary task of the state is to prevent imminent harm and protect the health and life of its citizens. In the Corona crisis, its action consists of reducing the risk of infection by restricting individual freedoms and organising the medical care of infected patients.

But one of the fundamental human rights is also that of self-determination of the human person over his or her body and life and individual freedom. Each human being has full power over their bodies, including the right to choose interventions on their bodies in all areas, i.e., mutilation, health and ultimately life.

At the same time, however, it must preserve the human dignity and freedom of action of every person. Respect for the patient's will may be incompatible with the protection of life. In order to reconcile these two constitutional values, a legislative system has been developed which, by means of procedures such as advance directives, trusted persons, etc., tries to take the hypothetical or real will of the patient into account as well as possible without betraying the fundamental principle of the protection of life.

This difficult balance between the obligation to protect every life and the self-determination of the person over his or her own body and life as a profound expression of constitutionally guaranteed human dignity and freedom is decided by the legislator in each country differently and reflects the prevailing religious and cultural values and influences.

In those states within the European Union that are influenced by Christianity, the law has historically been marked by the principle that the human body is intangible and not available, not even subject to the will of the person. The current strengthening of the right to self-determination in Europe changes this concept and opens up new perspectives for personal freedom[2].

---

[2] Renger/Rohlfing, *The strengthening of the rights of the patient by the reform of the « Claeys-Leonetti Act » in France and the liability of medical doctors*, in « Interactions between culture and law in India and Europe », Aracne Editrice 2019, p. 141.

In a first part, I will present the different legal rules in general end-of-life situations in European countries before examining the application of these rules in a sanitary crisis situation such as the COVID-19.

I. The comparative legislative situation

A. *The Claeys-Léonetti Act of 2016 in France*

On the 2nd of February 2016, France passed a reform of its end-of-life legislation (called Leonetti-Claeys Act) that integrates for the first time a ban of unreasonable therapeutical obstinacy and the possibility of terminal sedation. This new legislation, a reform of the Leonetti Act of 2005, improves patients' rights on the one hand, and increases physicians' obligations on the other hand[3].

The fundamental principles of the new legislation in France are the interdiction of unreasonable therapeutical obstinacy, the recognition of the patient's right to receive palliative care avoiding or reducing his suffering, legal rules are authorizing deep and continuous sedation until death with the aim of the respect of patients' dignity until his death.

The Claeys-Leonetti law of February 2016 provides in its Art L 1110-5 I 2° CSP (Public Health Act) « Every person has a right to have a peaceful end-of-life and to be accompanied with the best appeasement possible of suffering. » This support also includes a right to sedation, which is enshrined in art. L 1110-5-3. It is assumed that palliative medicine reaches its limits in certain exceptional cases. In these cases, sufficient pain management is not possible because the patients are refractory to painkillers. These cases require more extensive intervention to ensure the dignity of the patient at the end of life. The Act Claeys-Léonetti, which rendered France one of the first countries to enact legislation specifically introducing the right to deep and continuous sedation. Nevertheless, in April 2021, the proposal for a reform of the Claeys-Leonetti buy the law Falorni[4], aiming to legalize euthanasia, has failed because it couldn't find a majority on the French National Assembly.

---

[3] Renger/Rohlfing, *The strengthening of the rights of the patient by the reform of the « Claeys-Leonetti Act » in France and the liability of medical doctors*, in « Interactions between culture and law in India and Europe », Aracne Editrice 2019, p. 141.

[4] Proposition de loi n° 3755 visant à affirmer le libre choix de la fin de vie et à assurer un accès universel aux soins palliatifs en France du 19 janvier 2021.

The patients' right to autonomy allows their self-determination and to make informed choices after being fully informed about the state of health. The principle of Distributive justice aims to guarantee the same medical treatment for all patients in similar circumstances.

The new Léonetti-Claeys act emphasizes these principles. It assumes the respect of medical deontology (particularly Art. 35, 36, 37 and 38). Its core concept is the dignity of the patient[5]. But these principles can't be respected in a situation where not enough medical resources are available.

B. The evolution of end-of-life rules in England and Wales

In England and Wales, similar legislative projects have also been in preparation for several years but have not yet led to a law being passed. The legal situation there is therefore determined by isolated regulations and case law. For example, the Suicide Act 1961 and the Terminal Illness (Provisions of Palliative Care and Support for Carers) Bill 2017–2019 as well as the Access to Palliative Care Bill 2017–2019 partially determine end-of-life rules in England and Wales.

The situation in the UK, as a common law country, makes the comparison with continental law countries interesting. As the UK has left the EU but not the ECHR, there are significant decisions in the case law of the ECtHR concerning the UK (e.g., Diane Pretty[6]), particularly in relation to medical futility related to minors[7].

---

[5] Idem n°1.
[6] On English law: J. Keown, Cambridge: Cambridge University Press, 2018; C. Hobson, Medical Law Review 514–530; N. Richards, Medical Anthropology 348–362.; E. Wicks, 'Nicklinson and Lamb v UK: Medical Law Review 633–640; R. Heywood & A. Mullock, 'The Value of Life in English Law: Revered but not Sacred?' (2016) 36(4) Legal Studies 658–682; *Pretty ./. UK*, Nr. 2346/02 of 29.04.2002, ECHR 2002-III EuGRZ 2002, 234; NJW 2002, 2851; ÖJZ 2003, 311.
[7] Kartina A. Chong, *Re M (Declaration of Death of Child) [2020]: "No Best Interests to Consider"?*

in Rohlfing-Dijoux/Hellmann, Law and culture: Multidisciplinary crossfertilisation of views on the end of life, p. 104.

C. The diversity of end-of-life legislation in Germany

In Germany, in contrast to France and Italy, there is no single law that brings together all regulations relating to the end of life. Germany has opted for a system in which the relevant regulations are integrated into different laws according to their legal context: some provisions are integrated in the Criminal Code (StGB), the regulations on respecting the patient's wishes and the living will into the general Civil Code (Medical care contract of §§ 630 a ff. BGB; § 1901a, 1901b BGB) and the palliative case is subject to a specific Bill (Gesetz zur Verbesserung der Hospiz- und Palliativversorgung v. 5.11.2015). These various laws have also been the subject of reforms in recent years.

As part of these various reforms, a law of 10.12.2015 introduced a new provision on the criminalisation of the commodification of suicide into the German Criminal Code (§ 217 StGB). The image of Switzerland, where, indeed, a kind of death tourism has become established, led the German legislator to prevent the emergence of private facilities where terminally ill patients go to die. However, this provision was recently invalidated and declared unconstitutional in a highly controversial ruling by the Federal Constitutional Court (Bundesverfassungsgericht) on 26 February 2020.

With great clarity, the Bundesverfassungsgericht states in this decision that the right of a person to freely dispose of his or her life and to be responsible for it is covered by the general right of personality (Article 2.1 in conjunction with Article 1.1 of the Basic Law). 'The right to self-determined death as an expression of personal freedom is not limited to situations defined by others'. The right to self-determination, which touches on the most intimate area of individual self-determination, is not limited in particular to states of serious or incurable illness or to certain phases of life and illness. To restrict the scope of protection to certain causes and motives would amount to an assessment of the motives of the person determined to commit suicide and to a predetermination in terms of content which is alien to the idea of freedom in the Basic Law. According to the Court, the right to commit suicide, which is protected by Article 2(1) in conjunction with Article 1(1) of the Basic Law, also includes the freedom to seek help from others for this purpose and to receive it if offered.

A German daily newspaper, the FAZ, described the ruling with the slogan: 'Sterbehilfe künftig auch bei Liebeskummer', i.e., '*Assisted suicide in the future also for love disease*' and criticized it strongly[8]. This decision is so important that it should have been taken by the legislator. It is questionable whether the principle of separation of powers is still respected here. Moreover, the decision creates insoluble conflicts of interest. On the one hand, doctors are still subject to the ethical obligation to protect life, on the other hand they must respect the patient's will, even if this will is to die. This implies a contradiction that is difficult to resolve and an unclear legislative situation that needs to be clarified in order to find a fair but difficult balance between the physician's obligations and respect for the patient's wishes.

The judgement is unlikely to end the discussion on the regulation of assisted suicide, as the Court allows the legislator to develop a concept of protection. However, the Court requires 'a strict limitation of state intervention for the protection of self-determination, which may be supplemented by elements of medical and pharmacological quality assurance and protection against abuse'.

But this decision contains a hint that the conflict of interest between the protection of life and the right of every individual to self-determination will be decided in favour of self-determination by the German courts.

III. What has COVID-19 changed in the application of end-of-life rules?

A. Situation in France, Germany and England: Protection of life as an absolute and constitutional guaranteed right?

The right to the absolute protection of life derives from the constitutional principle of the absolute protection of human dignity and the general right of personality[9]. The guarantee of freedom also includes the human right to make free and self-determined decisions in all areas. This principle of respect for the autonomy and will of the individual has constitutional value. It is enshrined in numerous texts at national, European and international level. The European Convention on Human Rights (ECHR) and the Charter of Fundamental Rights of the European

---

[8] Frankfurter Allgemeine Zeitung, Sterbehilfe künftig auch bei Liebeskummer, 26.02.2020.
[9] Lindner, Die "Triage" im Lichte der Drittwirkung der Grundrechte, MedR 2020, 723.

Union enshrine in their Article 1 the principle of human dignity and self-determination of the human being. However, it comes up against the fundamental principle of the absolute protection of life which is at the heart of our constitutions (e.g., Art. 2 § 2 of the German Basic Law – GG) and also in the ECHR (Art. 2 § 1 ECHR). The state has an obligation to protect life as the most precious possession of the constitution. At the same time, Human Rights developed to a protection of the right to die with dignity[10].

1. Situation in France and Germany

One of the ethical foundations and fundamental motivations for the creation of the Claeys-Leonetti Act in France was, that all patients should receive the best care possible, and get the best conditions for the respect of their dignity at the end of their life in accordance with the principles of equity and distributive justice. In France, like in the England/Wales and Germany, health care is accessible and cost-free for every citizen.

The respect of this fundamental right is very difficult, if not impossible, in a situation of a health crisis where sufficient care and treatment are not available and health resource allocation has to be selective[11]. During the COVID-19 sanitary crisis all countries had to make difficult choices for the management of this severe crisis[12].

There has been very little coordination of sanitary measures between France and Germany, and almost none in Europe with Eastern European countries.

In Germany, the management of Covid has been rather uniform compared to other federal countries, such as India or Brazil. However, the federalist structure has allowed more flexibility, especially for the coordination of the healthcare delivery. But some problems have been observed everywhere, such as the high risk of death in nursing homes. In Germany, as in most Western countries, the management of the Covid was more

---

[10] Volker Lipp, « Euthanasia » – a comparative legal perspective, in Rohlfing-Dijoux/Hellmann, Law and culture: Multidisciplinary cross-fertilisation of views on the end of life, p. 114.

[11] *Jochen Taupitz, Verteilung medizinischer Ressourcen in der Corona-Krise: Wer darf überleben?, MedR 2020, 440.*

[12] Ehlers/Bartholomä/Menghin, Rechtliche Regelung der "Triage" – Gesundheitssysteme an ihren Grenzen, MedR 2021, 416.

oriented towards the management of health problems than economic problems. Germany has used curfews only exceptionally, unlike France where curfews have been widely used over long periods of several months. Efforts to temporarily close the German French border were refused on both sides. But other measures in Germany were often judged too restrictive. And other borders, for example to the Czech Republic were temporarily closed and the Schengen space out of order.

However, the problem of limited health care resources was much more pronounced in France than in Germany in the beginning of the pandemic. In France, there were initially (in 2019) 5,433 reanimation beds, 5,954 intensive care beds and 8,217 continuous monitoring beds[13], (total of 19,604 critical care beds). The reanimation beds were later during the pandemic increased to 6,000 beds, while in Germany there were about 8,854 high care beds with invasive ventilation and organ substitution therapy and 13,379 low care beds with non-invasive ventilation (total of 22,233 critical care with ventilation beds)[14]. For this reason, the severely limited hospital capacity was the main reason for the measures restricting freedom in France. And some French patients were brought to German hospitals when hospital capacities in some French regions were exhausted.

But since the fourth wave of COVID-19 the situation in Germany has come to a head, so that in autumn 2021 patients will also have to be moved to other federal states for treatment there.

2. Situation in England

In England the situation in hospitals was quite the same. Big hospital trusts across England had not enough spare adult intensive care beds. 140 acute trusts had 5,500 adult critical care beds, that all were in use. Even before the COVID-19 pandemic in 2019/20, the acute bed occupancy averaged 90.2 %, and regularly exceeded 95 % in winter[15].

---

[13] Figures of 2019 https://drees.solidarites-sante.gouv.fr/article/nombre-de-lits-de-reanimation-de-soins-intensifs-et-de-soins-continus-en-france-fin-2013-et accessed 28 November 2021.

[14] https://de.statista.com/statistik/daten/studie/1109137/umfrage/verfuegbare-und-belegte-intensivmedizinische-betten-in-deutschland/ accessed on 24 November 2021.

[15] https://www.kingsfund.org.uk/publications/nhs-hospital-bed-numbers, accessed on 28 November 29021.

Hospitals hit the limit of their capacity in January 2021. For the raising number of Covid patients, they had to create extra bed and set up beds in overspill areas usually reserved for 'normal' patients. The critical care beds were 3,766 in March 2019 and it was raised to 5,814 in April 2021 and to 5,840 in February 2021[16]. But extra stuff was missing. Intensive care nurses had to look after more patients than reasonable. This was on cost of non-Covid patients and had side effects on the general health care in England.

B. The prohibition of unreasonable obstinacy versus triage issues

Most countries were in the same situation, i.e., a shortage of beds and medical facilities that did not allow for the treatment of all patients in need. If there are not enough resources available to help all citizens in need, how can there be a fair selection of people to whom the available help should be given?[17] The principle of redistributive justice means that the state has to guarantee the same treatment to all citizens in the same situation. Hence, this is not possible if medical resources are restricted. A selection of patients for care has to be operated. This selection procedure called 'triage' can be defined as a procedure that can be used in conflict situations to decide how scarce life-sustaining resources can be distributed as fairly as possible[18].

Even before the lasted aggravations of the COVID-19 pandemic, a latent triage was already operated with patients, who were suffering of other diseases than COVID-19. All non-urgent surgeries of these patients were postponed during the peak of the pandemic with the side effect that the chances for recovery of these patients decreased. The competition of patients around limited medical resources needs to be regulated more closely.

Triage is not specifically regulated by law in any of the European countries mentioned. There are only clinical ethical recommendations, which

---

[16] https://www.england.nhs.uk/statistics/statistical-work-areas/uec-sitrep/urgent-and-emergency-care-daily-situation-reports-2020-21/, accessed on 28 November 29021.

[17] C. Mannelli, "Whose life to save? Scarce resources allocation in the COVID-19 outbreak" Journal of Medical Ethics 46 (2020), pp. 364–366.

[18] https://www.ethikrat.org/fileadmin/PDF-Dateien/Pressemitteilungen/pressemitteilung-03-2021_01.pdf, accessed on 28 November 2021.

are not legally binding. For example, in Germany the Arbeitsgemeinschaft der Wissenschaftlichen Medizinischen Fachgesellschaften (AWMF) has published such non-binding guidelines[19].

Should the selection be based on the criterion of the best chance of recovery, the age of the patient and the estimated time left to live? Many criteria are possible based on health situation, social situation, personal situation and much more.

According to the latest statement by the German Council of Ethics[20], the state should be prohibited from prescribing selection criteria, as in principle all human life is equally protected. To weigh life against life is constitutionally inadmissible. This statement gives physicians considerable leeway, but also imposes considerable responsibility. For physicians, selection is associated with a conflict of duties, a possible violation of professional ethics, and the risk of criminal liability[21].

The oath of physician oblige them to save life in all cases. The duty of selection is against this oath[22].

The selection is also against the principles of absolute guarantee of life and the respect of the will of the patient. So, should we instead of selection criteria apply the principle first come, first served.

The principle of best use of available resources should be the guiding principle. With the imperative that medical resources ought to be best utilized with maximal benefit, priority is often afforded to patients who are judged to benefit the most and quickly from resource-intense forms of care[23]. If a ventilator can save several lives in a row, instead of leaving the ventilator on one patient for a long period of time, should it not be used for several patients over shorter periods? The chances of survival and healing success play a core role. In cases where the maintenance of

---

[19] https://www.awmf.org/leitlinien/detail/ll/040-013.html, accessed on 27 November 2021.

[20] https://www.ethikrat.org/forum-bioethik/triage-priorisierung-intensivmedizinischer-ressourcen-unter-pandemiebedingungen/, accessed on 27 November 2021.

[21] Detlev Sternberg-Lieben, *Corona-Pandemie, Triage und Grenzen rechtfertigender Pflichtenkollision*, MedR 2020, 627; Christoph Sowada, *Strafrechtliche Probleme der Triage in der Corona-Krise*, NStZ 2020, 452.

[22] Sternberg-Lieben, Corona-Pandemie, Triage und Grenzen rechtfertigender Pflichtenkollision, MedR 2020, 627.

[23] Richard Law, *End-of-Life Care in the UK from a Resource Allocation Perspective*, in Rohlfing-Dijoux/Hellmann, p. 150.

The right to life and care in a crisis situation

life sustaining measures should be considered as a medical futility, the priorisation of the resources goes straight to patients with hope for care.

Hence the age of the patient, the social position and profession (if he is a factory worker or scientist with important research work for our societies?) and their family situation should not be taken into account. Life is life and one life can't have more value than another one. But the legislator should procure the medical team with guidelines outlined in accordance with the ethical fundamental principles[24].

The guidelines of the Association of the Scientific Medical Societies (AWMF) recommend taking in account criteria linked to the medical situation of the patient such as severity of the disease, life-threatening pre-existing or concomitant diseases, general state of health and the patient will.

However, the respect of the will of the patient in an exceptional situation such as the COVID-19 pandemic, with overflowing hospitals, insufficient means of care in many countries and emergency decisions, is made very difficult if not impossible[25]. In an emergency situation, there is no time to search for the will of the patient, to follow imposed procedures of collective decision making, to hear relatives etc.[26]. The first aim is to save lives as much as possible.

The recommended procedure is the 'multi-eye principle' where several physicians and care givers take together a common decision. Such a difficult moral decision can not be bearded par one person alone.

On the other hand, the medical decision can be facilitated by the creation of a decision-making algorithm that takes into account the different parameters helping physicians to make decisions under time pressure. Nevertheless, it seems dangerous to automate the decision and neglect the human relationship between the physician and patient as well as the individualisation of this important and irreversible decision.

What about the will of the patient? If the will is expressed the advances directives has always to be taken in account. But in the emergency

---

[24] Brade/Müller, Corona-Triage: Untätigkeit des Gesetzgebers als Schutzpflichtverletzung?, NVwZ 2020, 1792.
[25] Ehlers/Bartholomä/Menghin, Rechtliche Regelung der "Triage" – Gesundheitssysteme an ihren Grenzen, MedR 2021, 416.
[26] *Herbert Grziwotz/ Marc Grziwot, Corona, Patientenverfügung und Triage, NZFam 2021, 189.*

situation the medical team has not always have the time to search for the real or presumed will of the patient. If a person has specified in his advanced directives that he does not want resuscitation measures, one must also ask what consequences this could have in a Covid situation. If only limited medical resources such as ventilation machines are available, artificial ventilation could be dispensed with for such patients, even though they would have a chance of survival, and this pandemic situation was not foreseeable at the time when they made the patient's advance directive. However, all possible illness situations cannot be included in the living will, as it can only be kept general.

The described selection of patients called 'ex-ante triage' may be distinguished from the 'ex-post triage', where one ventilator is already being used by a patient with a poor chance of survival or a very elderly patient, and another is admitted or younger or with a better chance of survival. In this case, is it justified to stop the treatment to benefit the younger patient? Against the wishes of the patient and his family? This will not be possible except the case where the maintenance of medical treatment is considered as a medical futility.

A new aspect for the triage question arises from the possibility of vaccination against COVID-19. Non-vaccinated patients have a higher risk of developing severe forms of COVID-19 requiring artificial ventilation in intensive care beds. Is it therefore justified to consider the fact of non-vaccination in the triage question? What role does vaccination play in the selection of patients for medical care? The German Ethics Council is speaking out against a triage for non-vaccinated patients[27].

The medical treatment outlook should be the guiding factor, i.e., periodisation should take place according to life prospects.

Other criteria such as age, social situation, personal situation should not be taken into account. Nevertheless, two controversial criteria can be used for triage: on the one hand, the relevance of the expected life span and, on the other hand, the criterion of the probability of successful treatment. The second criterion may prove to be a hidden discrimination against people with chronic diseases or disabilities.

This criterion led a group of severely disabled people to file a constitutional appeal for discrimination, which was decided positively by the

---

[27] *Christoph Sowada, Strafrechtliche Probleme der Triage in der Corona-Krise, NStZ 2020, 452.*

BVerfG in Germany on 28 December 2021[28]. Indeed, the BVerfG considered that the triage criterion recommended by the German Council of Ethics entails a risk of discrimination against disabled people and violates Art 3 § 3 phrase 3 GG (the Principle of equal treatment). The constitutional court considered that no one should be discriminated against because of his or her disability when allocating vital resources and in order to avoid any risk, it ordered the legislator to legislate on the issue. According to the Court's reasoning, it is up to Parliament to settle all essential questions. The Court inferred a substantive obligation on the part of Parliament to act.

At the beginning of May 2022, the German Minister of Health Lauterbach presented a draft law on triage, which was withdrawn after a short time due to strong criticism from the public and experts. Since then, there have been no further legislative initiatives. The fact that the legislature has not yet taken any steps to effectively protect people with disabilities from discrimination on the basis of insufficient resources constitutes a violation of the principle of equal treatment. The state has a duty to protect people with disabilities from unequal opportunities. Even if there is no direct discrimination of persons with disabilities, the court considers that when examining the chances of survival and recovery, the health situation of persons with disabilities is often misjudged due to unconscious stereotyping. This is the risk that doctors may assess the overall prognosis of a disabled patient worse than it actually is. There is a risk that the disability will be seen as a comorbidity or frailty, thereby diminishing the chances of successful access to intensive medical treatment. The legislature is in the difficult position of having to legislate on this issue. The court gives the legislature broad discretion and does not, however, provide any further guidance on the triage criteria and the content of the required legislation.

Conclusion

According to fundamental constitutional principles, such as protection of all lives, States are not allowed to set binding guidelines for the trial of patients in a sanitary crisis situation. But it is also unbearable for physicians and the medical team to bear the load of the selection without

---

[28] BVerfGE 28/12/2021, 1 BvR 1541/20.

clear directives. Principles that cannot be respected because of a factual situation cannot be binding. For this reason, the legislator should give guideline for the medical treatment in such situations with the help of Ethical committees and experts. Until now the situation is not resolved in the different European countries.

Bibliographie

Brade Alexander/Müller Maxi, *Corona-Triage: Untätigkeit des Gesetzgebers als Schutzpflichtverletzung?*, NVwZ 2020, 1792.

A. Choong Kartina, Re M (Declaration of Death of Child) [2020]: 'No Best Interests to Consider'? In S. Rohlfing-Dijoux/U. Hellmann, eds., *Law and culture: Multidisciplinary cross-fertilisation of views on the end of life*, Nomos, p. 104.

Ehlers Alexander/Bartholomä Julian/Menghin Daniel, *Rechtliche Regelung der 'Triage' – Gesundheitssysteme an ihren Grenzen*, MedR 2021, 416.

Grziwotz Herbert/Grziwot Marc, Corona, *Patientenverfügung und Triage*, NZFam 2021, 189.

Lindner Josef Franz, *Die 'Triage' im Lichte der Drittwirkung der Grundrechte*, MedR 2020, 723.

Lipp Volker, « *Euthanasia* » *– a comparative legal perspective*. In Rohlfing-Dijoux/Hellmann, eds., *Law and culture: Multidisciplinary cross-fertilisation of views on the end of life*, p. 114.

Mannelli Chiara, *Whose life to save? Scarce resources allocation in the COVID-19 outbreak*, Journal of Medical Ethics 46 (2020), pp. 364–366.

Renger Benoît/Rohlfing-Dijoux Stephanie, *The strengthening of the rights of the patient by the reform of the « Claeys-Leonetti Act » in France and the liability of medical doctors*, in « Interactions between culture and law in India and Europe », Aracne Editrice 2019, p. 141.

Richard Law, *End-of-life care in the UK from a resource allocation perspective*, in Rohlfing-Dijoux/Hellmann, p. 150.

Sowada Christoph, *Strafrechtliche Probleme der Triage in der Corona-Krise*, NStZ 2020, 452.

Sternberg-Lieben Detlev, Corona-Pandemie, *Triage und Grenzen rechtfertigender Pflichtenkollision*, MedR 2020, 627.

Taupitz Jochen, *Verteilung medizinischer Ressourcen in der Corona-Krise: Wer darf überleben?*MedR 2020, 440.

The challenge of vulnerability in the health crisis: Comparative study of the French and German health laws on the protection of vulnerable adults

Charles WALLEIT[1]

The current COVID-19 crisis is characterized by the difficulty of reconciling the exercise of individual freedoms with public health imperatives. Indeed, the measures taken by the French and German governments to contain the pandemic have hampered the exercise of individual freedoms by the population of both countries as a whole, and by dependent elderly people in particular. Whether they live in institutions or at home, dependent elderly people suffer a double penalty. Firstly, they are the most likely to develop a serious form of the disease and succumb to it, but they are also hard hit by the confinement and social distancing measures, leading to unprecedented isolation.

The campaign to vaccinate these same elderly people raises a number of ethical issues, particularly as regards informing elderly patients prior to medical treatment and obtaining their consent. Faced with these issues, we may well wonder whether the legal arsenal provides an effective response in such a crisis situation, where decisions must be taken without delay and judicial control seems compromised.

La crise du COVID-19 que nous traversons est caractérisée par une difficulté de conciliation de l'exercice des libertés individuelles avec les impératifs de santé publique. En effet, les mesures prises par les gouvernements français et allemand pour contenir la pandémie ont entravé l'exercice des libertés individuelles de la population des deux pays dans leur ensemble et tout particulièrement des personnes âgées dépendantes. Qu'elles résident en établissement ou à domicile, les personnes âgées dépendantes subissent une double peine. Elles sont d'abord les plus susceptibles de développer une forme grave de la maladie et d'y succomber,

---

[1] Dr. Postdoc Université Paris Nanterre.

mais elles sont aussi frappées de plein fouet par les mesures de confinement et de distanciation sociale, conduisant à un isolement inédit.

La campagne de vaccination des publics prioritaires que constituent ces mêmes personnes âgées soulève un certain de nombre de questions éthiques et notamment en ce qui concerne l'information préalable à un traitement médical des patients âgés et le recueil de leur consentement. Face à ces enjeux, on peut se demander si l'arsenal juridique apporte une réponse efficace dans une telle situation de crise, dans laquelle les décisions doivent être prises sans délai et où un contrôle judiciaire paraît compromis.

Introduction

The COVID-19 crisis emphasizes the difficulty to conciliate the exercise of individual freedoms with the public health's necessities. The measures taken by the French and German governments to counter the pandemic have led to restrictions of exercise of the individual freedoms for the people in both countries, particularly for dependent elderly persons. May they be home-based or live-in nursing homes, dependent elderly persons had to face double trouble. They were the most likely to develop a severe form of the disease and to die from it, but the lockdown and social distancing measures also have hit them exceptionally hard, leading for many of them to an unprecedented social isolation.

The vaccination campaign of priority groups, to which elderly persons belong, raised several ethical issues, notably the information of those people and obtaining their consent.

Facing those issues, it is questionable if the laws are effective in such a crisis, in which decisions have to be taken without delay and judicial supervision is compromised.

We will first analyse how the restrictions implemented in both countries impacted elderly persons residing in nursing homes (I) and then focus on the problematic of vaccination of this particular public (II).

I. The restrictions implemented in France and Germany to tackle the COVID-19 pandemic

The restrictions adopted in both countries are directly influenced by their respective nursing home system.

In both France and Germany, a large proportion of elderly dependent people reside in nursing homes which are either under public or private management. In France, the repartition is about 55 % private and 45 % public when in Germany only 5 % are under public management. However, the majority of private nursing homes are not profit oriented when most are in France.

From the beginning of the first wave in Spring 2020, the pandemic has shown the influence of the centralized system in France and the federal system in Germany on the emergency lawmaking process. When the French government could impose a strict lockdown from day 1, the German federal government had to deal with the one of each Bundesland, who had the possibility to adopt more or less strict measures. The multiplicity of local measures made it difficult to find common rules at the federal level[2].

In Germany, during the first wave from March to June 2020, none of the 16 Länder applied the same restrictions. Many started with mild restrictions such as:

– limitation of the number of visitors allowed per day,
– limitation of the visit's duration,
– imposing accompaniment of the visitors by carers,
– restriction of the visits to particular days, what have mainly been weekends and holidays.

Others like Baden-Württemberg, Bayern, Thüringen or Mecklenburg Vorpommern started with hard restrictions like a strict prohibition of visits, even relatives, or limited to visitors with symptoms or coming from risk areas.

Depending on the different infection rates, many lifted the strict restrictions for milder ones a few weeks after the beginning of the first wave.

All Bundesländer apart of Berlin and Saarland applied strict restrictions for a certain period.

---

[2] Gangnus A., Hering C., Kohl R., Henson C. S., Schwinger A., Steinhagen-Thiessen E., Kuhlmey A., Gellert P., Covid-19-Schutzmaßnahmen und Einschränkungen des sozialen Lebens in Pflegeheimen, Analyse von Verordnungen und Surveydaten, Pflege 2021, p. 5.

The measures taken concerned not only the prohibition or limitation of contacts with visitors but also the social relations within nursing homes. Physical contact between residents as well as between carers and residents have been restricted in a large majority of the country. Most collective activities have been cancelled and sometimes even individual ones such as physiotherapeutic treatments performed by external people.

Residents have basically been locked in their rooms for a more or less long period of time[3].

The different local rules have not been implemented the same way in every nursing home. Furthermore, the succession of different rulings took a long time to be understood and executed by the nursing homes executives and employees[4]. The accumulation of all those differences makes it impossible to make a nationwide analysis of the violations of nursing homes residents' rights without making generalizations.

In France, the first lockdown was characterized by the prohibition of social contacts between people from different households and social distanciation measures. The latter particularly affected elderly persons residing in care homes. Many of them suffering from degenerative diseases, resulting in a loss of cognitive functions. Refusing these people physical contacts amounts to deprive them from humanity. For people at the end of life, the freedom to have contacts with others is more important than life support. The protection of the carers cannot justify such prohibitions either as they are exposed to the same risks in their normal life[5].

As in Germany, the succession of different rules throughout the pandemic diminished their legibility for the people concerned by the restrictions, but also for those in charge of their application[6].

---

[3] Gangnus A., Hering C., Kohl R., Henson C. S., Schwinger A., Steinhagen-Thiessen E., Kuhlmey A., Gellert P., Covid-19-Schutzmaßnahmen und Einschränkungen des sozialen Lebens in Pflegeheimen, Analyse von Verordnungen und Surveydaten, Pflege 2021, pp. 5–6.

[4] *Ibid.*, p. 2.

[5] *Ibid.*, p. 38.

[6] Défenseur des droits, Les droits fondamentaux des personnes âgées accueillies en EHPAD, 2021, p. 40.

It is important to highlight that the difficulties encountered by nursing home residents to maintain a social life is not a new phenomenon and has already been pointed out before the pandemic[7].

In France, the FIAT-IBORRA report of 2018 highlighted a few of the issues of the French nursing home system. The growing number of severely ill residents due to the aging of the population cannot be coped by the system because of the lack of finance and carers[8]. This context leads to what is qualified as 'an institutionalized' abuse of elderly people[9]. This issue recently became a public debate in France with the scandal of private nursing homes, which focused on the increase of their margin instead of investing in the wellbeing of the older generations.

The residents of nursing homes belong to different groups. Dementia patients, 4th age people[10] as well as younger disabled or mentally ill persons, all living under the same roof. The diversity of the residents makes it difficult to adapt the offer to every situation. Most nursing homes have open and closed areas. As their name suggest they are not favouring the freedom of movement of the residents.

In fact, a majority of nursing home residents are suffering Alzheimer or similar troubles which questions the ability of the carers to collect their consent and guaranty their freedom of movement whilst ensuring their safety[11]. The whole package of rights and freedoms reinforced by the French laws of 2002[12] and 2015[13] is confronted to the reality of the nursing homes.

Two of the goals of the 2015 law were to reinforce the freedom of movement, which should not be in opposition with the protection but part of it, and the assistance to the expression of the consent. For the

---

[7] Trybusińska, D. & Saracen, A. (2019). Loneliness in the Context of Quality of Life of Nursing Home Residents. *Open medicine (Warsaw, Poland)*, *14*, 354–361.
[8] M. IBORRA, C. FIAT, Rapport d'information en conclusion des travaux de la mission sur les établissements d'hébergement pour personnes âgées dépendantes, Assemblée Nationale, Rapport d'information n° 769, 2018, p. 104.
[9] *Ibid.*, p. 8.
[10] Lloyd L. (2015). The fourth age. In J. Twigg and W. Martin (Eds.), Routledge handbook of cultural gerontology (pp. 261–268). New York: Routledge.
[11] M. IBORRA, C. FIAT, *op. cit.*, p. 28.
[12] Loi n° 2002-2 du 2 janvier 2002 rénovant l'action sociale et médico-sociale.
[13] Loi n° 2015-1776 du 28 décembre 2015 relative à l'adaptation de la société au vieillissement.

first one, the government's trust in the new technologies capability to conciliate safety with the elderly's right and aspiration to autonomy and improvement of their quality of life.

There has been therefore experimentations with residents of nursing homes who could consent, after medical approval, to carry a geolocation device[14]. This solution would not have been applicable during the strict lockdown though.

To achieve the second goal, the law improves the procedure of acceptance of the residence contract in ensuring the consent of the resident, the knowledge and the comprehension of his rights. The possibility to appoint a person of confidence for that matter shall ensure the respect of the resident's will.

The Fiat-Iborra report predicts the future generation of nursing homes residents and their relatives to be more likely to complain about their quality of life and to assert their rights[15].

Whereas the German federal government failed to get a country wide report on the situation in nursing homes, the Défenseur des droits issued one last year. The fundamental rights violations listed are identical to the ones observed in Germany.

They are mainly the denial of the freedom of movement during lockdowns, the restriction of the right to family life with the prohibition of visit from relatives, and the denial of exercise of the freedom of religion.

Today, German politicians and lawyers agree to the fact that unlimited visit prohibitions were disproportionate and therefor unconstitutional[16].

The gravity of the fundamental rights' violation depends on the degree of the isolation and the restrictions to the social, religious and cultural activities suffered by every person. This implies a case-by-case

---

[14] Annexe, loi n° 2015-1776 du 28 décembre 2015 relative à l'adaptation de la société au vieillissement.

[15] M. IBORRA, C. FIAT, Rapport d'information en conclusion des travaux de la mission sur les établissements d'hébergement pour personnes âgées dépendantes, Assemblée Nationale, Rapport d'information n° 769, 2018, p. 42.

[16] Hufen F., Zur Verfassungsrechtlichen Beurteilung von Besuchs- und Ausgangsbeschränkung in Alten- und Pflegeheimen aus Anlass der COVID-19-Pandemie, Bundesarbeitsgemeinschaft der Seniorenorganisationen e. V., 2020, p. 38.

The challenge of vulnerability in the health crisis 353

appreciation of the violations making difficult to generalize the violations caused by the restrictions[17].

In any case prohibitions leading to a lonely suffering and death cannot be regarded as justified fundamental rights' violations[18].

Not only the prohibition of outings but also the compulsory quarantine for residents who stayed outside can be regarded as a violation of the freedom of movement (liberté d'aller et venir/Freizügigkeit)[19].

Despite a vaccination rate of 73 %, nursing home residents have not been allowed to go out by the government. This restriction has been brought to the French highest administrative court who issued recommendations for the authorization to exit nursing homes. The court stated that it was the nursing homes executive's responsibility to define the conditions to go out, taking into account the size of the facility, the outing contemplated, the vaccination rate and the proportion of new variants in the region[20]. Despite these recommendations, many nursing homes refused to allow outings of residents, which led the Défenseur des droits to consider that the authorization to leave the nursing homes should not be left to the appreciation of their direction alone[21]. The fear of nursing homes to see their responsibility engaged for the consequences of covid infections could explain the overreaction. A cynical justification for profit-oriented nursing homes could be to keep the beds occupied to guarantee their income. It is important to remember the shock provoked by the first wave hitting the Alsace region in France, when overwhelmed hospitals had to sort out patients with the highest healing perspectives. Needless to say, elderly and dependent people with little chances to return to a normal life did not belong to that group, many have been left to their fate without other treatment than pain relief.

The restrictions adopted in both countries are today highly criticized for their effects on the elderly people's life, and the vaccination campaign has not spared their fundamental rights either (II).

---

[17] Hufen F., Zur Verfassungsrechtlichen Beurteilung von Besuchs- und Ausgangsbeschränkung in Alten- und Pfegeheimen aus Anlass der COVID-19-Pandemie, Bundesarbeitsgemeinschaft der Seniorenorganisationen e. V., 2020, p. 39.
[18] *Ibid.*, p. 37.
[19] *Ibid.*, p. 39.
[20] CE, Ord. 3 mars 2021, n°449759, paragraphe n°11.
[21] Défenseur des droits, Les droits fondamentaux des personnes âgées accueillies en EHPAD, 2021, p. 40.

II. The vaccination campaign in nursing homes in France and Germany

The residents of nursing homes have not only been the first to be locked down and the last to be freed from restrictions in France. They have also been the first to be confronted to the problematic of the vaccination, when there was the least knowledge on the effects of the vaccine. How could they form a valid consent without the basic information?

In respect of the campaign of vaccination, a French national ethic comity has been consulted by the government regarding the consent to the vaccination of vulnerable persons. It recommends transparency in the information regarding the vaccination to be delivered in an adapted manner. It shall be given time to the residents to accept or refuse the vaccination despite the context of emergency. The process of obtaining consent shall be traceable[22].

These recommendations are really difficult to implement in the French context of nursing homes, characterized by the lack of careers and their disposal time for each resident. They do not take into account the easiness to obtain consent to an act from elderly dependent people either. In fact, the latter generally answer 'yes' to every of your question. Without taking a lot of time with each resident to ask the same thing in different manners, it is nearly impossible to guarantee the validity of the consent.

Private profit-oriented nursing homes will be likely to force the consent to the vaccination to guarantee bed occupation.

Health laws guarantee in both countries the research of the will of every patient, even those incapable to express it. Physicians are compelled to collect the patient's consent to any medical act to which vaccination belongs. However, the judicial control of the conformity of the contemplated acts with the patient's will is not practicable in case of emergency.

Only the appointment of a person of confidence enabling her to represent the patient in that matter can prevent for a forced vaccination.

The people drafting advance directives should from now express their will regarding life maintaining measures in case of a pandemic and

---

[22] Comité consultatif national d'éthique pour les sciences de la vie et de la santé, Enjeux éthiques d'une politique vaccinale contre le SARS-COV-2, Réponse du CCNE à la saisine du ministre des solidarités et de la santé, 2020, p. 16.

vaccination. But as in France and Germany courts refuse to recognize the value of advance directives written in general terms: how could people predict in precise terms the occurence of a new virus and decide to consent or no to treatments which the science is still developing?

In emergency situations and when the will of the concerned person cannot be determined without delay, the duty of protection of life should prevail over individual freedoms.

Conclusion

This pandemic makes clear that French and German health care laws are not built to cope with country wide emergency situations. Even worse it shows the inability of self-proclaimed developed countries to offer their elderly population infrastructures capable of providing a satisfying level of humanity and medical care. The incapacity of the law to prevent violations of the fundamental rights and freedoms and the absence of sanction or compensation show the limits of procedures developed for a context of normality.

The german federal system's flexibility can only benefit to the least infected areas. However, the inequality of treatment resulting from it is questionable.

Last but not least, we have to bear in mind that the conclusions we can draw from this pandemic might not be suitable for the future ones.

Brand experience in the COVID-19 age-health and safety as the key factors

Adjnu Damar LADKOO[1]

COVID-19 has toppled the way brands work on customers' experiences. Health and safety are the leading distinguishing factors. A qualitative approach- content analysis of both internet articles and in-depth interviews with Mauritian customers- was considered. All data geared towards- the need to care for your customers; though a close-up of today's consumers' expectations revealed that they are even more diverse and complex. In-home shopping like use of e-commerce platforms is more prominent; even digitally resistant customers have new mind-sets on this. Home-delivery, sanitized products, disinfected spaces like retail outlets or hotels, bookable safe shopping times, touch-free shopping and healthy salespeople are among the expectations of this era's customers. It is a must for branding strategies to include health and safety-in the logos, taglines or brand names and in empowering the buyers to traverse the pandemic safely.

L'expérience de la marque à l'ère du COVID-19 – La santé et la sécurité comme facteurs clés

COVID-19 a renversé la façon dont les marques travaillent sur les expériences des clients. La santé et la sécurité sont les principaux facteurs de distinction. Une approche qualitative – l'analyse du contenu des articles sur Internet et des entretiens approfondis avec des clients mauriciens – a été envisagée. Toutes les données ont montré la nécessité de prendre soin de vos clients; mais les attentes des consommateurs de nos jours révèlent qu'elles sont encore plus diverses et complexes. Les achats à domicile, comme l'utilisation des plateformes de commerce électronique, sont plus importants; même les clients résistants à la digitalisation ont un nouvel état d'esprit à ce sujet. La livraison à domicile, les produits aseptisés, les espaces désinfectés comme les points de vente ou les hôtels, les horaires d'achat sécurisés réservables, les achats sans contact et les vendeurs en bonne santé font partie des attentes des clients d'aujourd'hui. Il est indispensable que les stratégies de marque incluent la santé et la sécurité dans les

---

[1] Senior Lecturer, Faculty of Law and Management, University of Mauritius.

logos, les slogans ou les noms de marque et permettent aux acheteurs de traverser la pandémie en toute sécurité.

Introduction

COVID-19 has changed the facet of humanity and has impacted on many lives as well as on businesses. Marketers who are known to be the agents of change have had to deal with COVID-19 that toppled the way marketing or branding strategies have always been formulated. Each and every customer has his or her own way of feeling about a particular brand, but COVID-19 drastically altered it. New techniques for experiencing a brand have always been in the forefront of many proactive marketers who want to set the demarcating point between their brands and that of competing ones. Yet, COVID-19 made it tough because customers had to be kept away from the experience of physical shopping due to lockdowns and strict sanitary measures. Even e-commerce was affected as more than ever, customers were focused on their health and safety rather than meeting the desires emerging from the branding strategies brought up by marketers. Alongside, suddenly customers had new requirements and anticipations from marketers and their branding strategies. COVID-10 was like a gust of wind erasing the regular way of marketing so as to amalgamate the components of health and safety into the marketing and branding strategies.

Further to the above, the objectives of this research were set as follows:

– To understand what a good brand experience means in a COVID-19 era.
– To identify the expectations of customers from organisations in a COVID-19 age.
– To determine how health and safety factors can be incorporated in customers' branding strategies in a COVID-19 period.

Given that the regular customer buying decision process had been altered, it was of utmost necessity to investigate into the above arena so as to come up with fruitful strategies that could help regenerate the marketing field and businesses in general. The originality of the paper revolves around the merging of branding decisions and the health and safety aspects in the context where both customers and marketers are facing the global challenge set by the COVID-19 pandemic.

I. Literature review

Existing literatures surrounding the above topic had to be scrutinized to know the extent to which this new emerging branding experience had been explored. Google scholar articles were the mainstream of literatures that were considered for this exercise.

A. *Brand experience and customer expectation*

Customers always expect something superior from the brands they are involved directly or indirectly with. This expectation is what leads to what is known as the brand experience. Schmitt (2009) states that they want marketers to provide them with an experience and that they are looking for something real and authentic, and not just ad slogans and messages that are supposed to target cognitions in their mind. As per Nysveen and Pedersen (2014) customer experiences have obtained attention in marketing for decades. Yet, the unprecedented COVID-19 pandemic revolutionized the way that this attention is being taken care of. Communication and interactions as part of co-creation activities are considered important brand-related stimuli with the potential to enhance brand experience (Nysveen and Pedersen, 2014). Indeed, it has been evident that the pandemic made communication a more than ever crucial tool for reaching out to customers and rapid, instant and relevant connection with the latter equally made sense. Schmitt (2009) raised an important question on whether brand experiences are just epiphenomena – that is, when they occur, they are just fun for consumers and do they influence consumer behaviour only in the short term? This question stood good for the present research given that in the future there might not be COVID-19 so should all those new branding strategies not leave a forever impact on the consumers so that it creates competitive edges for the businesses. Since the advancement in communication and interaction with customers, marketers have made use of big data, that is, customer information, in a wise manner such that real understanding of expectations, performance and evaluation could be obtained. The real marketing game is all about relevant experience data so as to capture the feelings about the product, branding, packaging, labelling and all other marketing efforts. Brakus et al. (2009) rightly point out that brand experience is conceptualized as sensations, feelings, cognitions, and behavioural responses evoked by brand-related stimuli that are part of a brand's design and identity, packaging, communications, and environments.

Research had been scantily done about the connection between branding and health and safety dimensions. Thus, it made this research relevant and constructive for not only marketers but other stakeholders dealing with customers and the pandemic. Therefore, it is valid to understand customer expectation and match branding effort with the latter for bringing satisfaction and delight. Burgers et al. (2000) state that to serve the customer right and effectively, contact employees need to know what customers desire. Managers must understand their customers' needs-and then set out to meet (or exceed) these needs (Nadiri et al., 2008). Handling anticipations stretches the needed capacity to create and lead the customer experience. The COVID-19 pandemic urged both businesspeople and academicians to learn about such new desires that customers might be having towards the brand of a product or service so that more proactive branding strategies could be brought forward. With this new virus around, the meaning attributed to health and safety has become clearer. Could new health and safety measures applied during the marketing of products and services represent the future of doing businesses? Since the COVID-19 pandemic started, most customers have been trying to navigate the latter safely. When purchasing products, the customers' brand experience starts from the consideration to the trial, purchase and post-purchase phases. More than ever health and safety are what customers look for and they expect organisations to care for this need of theirs.

B. *Research methodology*

This research adopted a qualitative research methodology given that the research design followed that of an exploratory one due to the newness of the topic explored. Such research designs adopt a more unstructured approach such that the topic can be explored for deeper future in-depth studies. The analysis of literatures along with an amalgamation of data emerging from semi-structured interviews with 10 Mauritians adults, permitted to explore this topic. The purposive sampling technique matched the exploratory nature of the study as well as the context whereby people were not keen to be approached with the fear of the pandemic's propagation. The global strategy itself has been to minimize human-to-human contact either via full or partial cut down of social contacts. As per Rai and Thapa (2015) the main goal of purposive sampling is to focus on particular characteristics of a population that are of interest, which will best enable you to answer your research questions and the sample being studied is not representative of the population, but for researchers pursuing qualitative or mixed methods research designs, this is not considered to be a weakness. The research objectives were converted into broad research questions that were addressed to the targeted respondents and given that semi-structured interviews were used, whenever needed, probing questions were incorporated which depended on the prior responses obtained from the respondents. With the data that were acquired, content analysis was applied, and themes could be identified during the above exercise.

II. Findings and discussions

The research focused on three broad aspects: (1) brand experience, (2) expectations of customers and (3) Health and Safety connection with the first two elements. Hence, the findings could be structured in a similar manner. The themes that could be brought up from a combination of the interviews and some existing literatures, were as follows.

A. Good brand experience

It is to be noted that as per Hwang and Hyun (2012) because individual experience is subjective, different consumers perceive different brand experiences from consuming the same product or service; thus, brand experience is a highly subjective concept. Yet, brand experience is a key element on which marketers need to focus when working on their branding strategies. The first theme that could be generated from the captured data was emotional connection. It revealed that branding strategies that focused on the emotional side of the customers could work wonders. This tallied with Morrison and Crane (2007) who found that emotions play a powerful role in the customer's selection, satisfaction and loyalty toward service brands and the latter also emphasized on why marketers of service brands need to understand the emotional dynamics involved when a customer selects and decides to continue to use a service brand. Below is an excerpt of an interview transcript related to emotional connect of brands:

> "I think in this pandemic period the best brand experience is when the brand can connect with my emotions. I then feel that the brand is standing out from the rest and I feel a sense of belonging to that brand too and interested to be loyal to this brand."

The second theme that could be raised was psychological link and knowledge. As consumers gain more experience with a product or service, they correspondingly develop a deeper knowledge, and can thus form a positive attitude that encourages them to purchase the brand's product or service repeatedly in the future (Hwang and Hyun, 2012). More so, for Kim and Song (2019) strong brand experience leads consumers to reduce their psychological distance toward the brand and to lower their construal level. Below is an excerpt of an interview transcript related to knowledge and branding:

> "If I have adequate knowledge or information about a brand and how it is helping me overcome the pandemic, I feel secure in my mind and choice and can connect better with such brands in crisis periods."

The third theme generated was about the association of the branding experience to the senses. As per Hultén (2011) a sensory experience is defined as an individual's perception of goods or services or other elements in a service process as an image that challenges the human mind and senses. Hultén (2011) further added that academic research has shown that different sensory impressions impact consumer behaviour and perceptions of goods and services whereby the experience becomes an image, forming the mental conceptions and perceptions of interactions and inputs in the service process, which constitutes the final outcome of the multi-sensory experience within a brand perspective. Below is an excerpt of an interview transcript related to connection of branding with the senses:

> "When a brand connects well with my senses like taste or sight or even smell, I can memorise the brand better and even talk positively about it to others."

B. Expectations of customers

What are the expectations of customers from organisations in a COVID-19 age? For this research question, interesting themes could also be brought up and they were as follows:

The first one was to anticipate the needs and wants of customers in the COVID-19 age. The pandemic made many realize that marketers need to be more proactive in terms of research for realising what could make customers happy when it comes to marketing a product or service. The virus has been spreading fast and one of the needs was that of safety so that the health of the customer is not affected due to the act of purchasing products or services. For Bhatti et al. (2020) e-commerce is growing rapidly because of the coronavirus. E-commerce has been one immediate solution adopted by marketers to reach their customers in an unconventional manner. As per Sharma (2020) e-commerce business may employ online shopping websites for retail sales direct to consumers, providing or participating in online marketplaces, which process third-party business-to-consumer or consumer-to- business sales, business-to-business buying and selling, gathering and using demographic data through web contacts and social media, business-to-business electronic data interchange, marketing to prospective and established customers by E-mail or fax (for example, with newsletters), engaging in retail (also referred to as pre-retail or pre- commerce) for launching new products and services. Safety protocols were in the forefront when customers thought of buying products and because of COVID-19 people avoided going out, kept social distancing and preferred to purchase from home. They simply expected that marketers understood the above and tallied their marketing efforts.

As mentioned previously, marketers are known to be the agent of change but this time they had to themselves adapt to changes along with the customers. Adapting to changes was thus another theme that emerged from the findings. The pandemic forces many businesses to rush towards the online platform so that they could continue to sell their products. Some have worked overnight on new online platforms without having the time to give adequate training to their staffs for proper usage of the latter. Moreover, customers had to make it a habit of using the internet as part of their daily routine. Everyone had to adapt as there was no other alternative. Media usage also drastically increased during the pandemic period such as social media platforms both for work purposes and personal uses. Another theme that came up was the re-invention of products/services due to the pandemic. Instantaneous upgraded features had to be catered by marketers of those platforms so as to give their targeted users the benefits that they were seeking and expecting. Businesses who had always dedicated time to research about their customers would know about new products and services that should be created in line with the pandemic. The rest of the companies would have to engage in such research activities if they have not done so before. As per Wang et al. (2020) during the COVID-19 crisis, according to the various degrees of impact, firms usually have different motivations for innovation like to survive the crisis, highly affected firms tend to choose problemistic searches and manage to innovate their marketing strategies to keep their existing business and retain their current user groups while other firms that have not suffered sharp shocks tend to prefer slack searches and make full use of any possible new opportunities in the COVID-19 crisis to devote themselves to marketing innovations to expand their business or gaining more consumers.

Real-time engagement with customers was another prominent theme emerging from the content analysis. With the pandemic, customers did all their marketing activities from their home. Being in isolation from physical businesses implied that customers expected that they be listened to, and adequate responses be provided in a timely manner. Hence, connecting with such customers was vital. For this to happen, companies should have the motivation and guts to take a deep dive into their customer database so as to fully understand the needs and wants of their customers and hence, provide the appropriate responses. Jaakkolla and Alexander (2014) demonstrated that through customer engagement behaviour, customers can contribute a range of resources beyond dyadic exchange, contributing to enhanced offerings and value outcomes at a wider service system level. As per Karpen and Conduit (2020) embracing different paradigmatic lenses theoretically enlightens the multitude of engagement facets and collectively substantiates a broader view of engagement. This led to realising that real-time engagement needs to be considered in different ways and not only for example from the economic perspective but from other perspectives such as spiritual and social too. Real-time engagement would be advantageous for all and for Alshaketheep et al. (2020) brands listen more closely and use social and customer data as a method to recognize new demands and personalize their brand. Below is an excerpt of an interview transcript related to real-time engagement with customers:

> *"I feel amazed when I see that a company is acting upon my expected needs and desires. I can pay a higher price for such a company's products just because I feel they are taking time and effort to study about my likes and choices."*

With COVID-19 came a period of new learnings. New for both the marketers and the customers, but especially for customers who might not have had the habit of learning things as rapidly as would have done businesses given that changes were so quick and fast. Hence, another theme that emerged from the data was to educate customers on new technologies. The pandemic had led to an unprecedented push to learn new technologies that would permit customers to do online transactions safely for ensuring that normal routine life can continue despite facing constraints like social distancing or lockdowns. Information Technology (IT) devices at homes are generally perceived to be poorly configured compared to the work environment IT devices hence the IT devices at home are highly prone to cyber-attacks especially in the COVID-19 pandemic era (Abukari and Bankas, 2020). One tends to believe that businesses should not only secure their own online transactions but also that of their customers. Hence, organisations educating for example customers on cybersecurity measures as part of their corporate social responsibility tasks, could be an interesting way of putting the above into practice.

C. Health and safety incorporation in customers' branding experience

How can the health and safety factor be incorporated in customers' branding strategies in a COVID-19 period? For this research question, major themes that came up during the content analysis were as follows: (1) logo, (2) brand name, (3) slogan or tagline, (4) communication mediums, (6) assistance and (7) empower. Be it the logo or name or slogan, respondents unanimously expressed that all three need to have components that visibly expresses that care and concern is given towards the health and safety dimensions while marketing transactions are being done, be it online or in the traditional manner. Brands are framing the current COVID-19 global pandemic as a force that is bringing people together so brands' marketed notions of 'we' which gloss over inequalities and (re)present everyone as being part of a unified mass of people who are equally susceptible to the negative impacts of COVID-19 (Sobande, 2020). Empathy was indeed in the forefront of the interview discussions and respondents expected that brands would be able to reflect this in their branding strategies. As pointed out by Shah and Tomer (2020) the marketers need to understand that even if there may be a decrease in the sales, staying in the minds of consumers is of utmost importance. Below is an excerpt of an interview transcript related to health and safety with branding:

> "What matters today for me is to take care of my health and that of my family so if a company is genuinely investing in equipment to bring such comfort and protection to me as a customer, I am interested to do business with the latter."

Alongside, it was noted that respondents as well as literatures referred to use of the right communication mediums, assistance and empowerment for reinforcing health and safety measures-related communiqués before, during and after marketing-related activities. Commonly noted mediums were advertising used on various media such as on supermarket trolleys, digital billboards in malls, legible notices in common areas and transport systems amongst others. Moreover, customers were assisted and empowered in maintaining good health through temperature checks and sanitiser stations. Interestingly, for example Olivares-Delgado *et al.* (2020) pointed that luxury hotels' celebrity's engagement was not targeting their promotion but supporting people to respect self-isolation and social distancing, and they used different types of media to stay connected with their customers and to build strong brand reputation. This could undoubtedly be a form of empowerment to preserve their customers' health and safety dimensions.

Conclusion and recommendations

The pandemic has undeniably brought up many challenges for both marketers and customers yet, both seemed quick to adapt. No people-to-people contact, social distancing, controlled movements and lockdowns have made all of us seek new means of moulding into the new settings of life. It could be concluded that companies which invest daringly and sensibly in twisting their marketing activities or transactions towards the behavioural changes due to the pandemic, can quickly grasp market shares and come out as front-runners. Architecting the brand experience will always remain tricky given that it is subjective to each and everyone's way of viewing and interpreting value; each customer has his or her own critical points in the consumer buying process. Newaj and Damar-Ladkoo (2016) state that marketing is the art of delivering value whilst ethical marketing is to provide this value through what is morally right. So, getting as much as possible customer data in an ethical manner is the solution as it can give a clear understanding of the customer's needs.

Despite that customer expectations and preferences evolve rapidly, being empathetic marketers will allow better customisation and meaningful customer experiences. Technology can give relief to merge into the new circumstances of life given that many customers who were earlier digitally resistant are now open to using it. Learning, adapting and thriving along with the customers should be today and tomorrow, the motto of businesses.

Bibliography

Abukari, A. M. and Bankas, E. K., 2020. Some cyber security hygienic protocols for teleworkers in COVID-19 pandemic period and beyond. *International Journal of Scientific & Engineering Research*, *11*(4), pp. 1401–1407.

Alshaketheep, K. M. K. I., Salah, A. A., Alomari, K. M., Khaled, A. S. and Jray, A. A. A., 2020. Digital marketing during COVID 19: Consumer's perspective. *WSEAS Transactions on Business and Economics*, *17*(1), pp. 831–841.

Bhatti, A., Akram, H., Basit, H. M., Khan, A. U., Raza, S. M. and Naqvi, M. B., 2020. E-commerce trends during COVID-19 Pandemic. *International Journal of Future Generation Communication and Networking*, *13*(2), pp. 1449–1452.

Brakus, J. J., Schmitt, B. H. and Zarantonello, L., 2009. Brand experience: What is it? How is it measured? Does it affect loyalty?. *Journal of Marketing*, *73*(3), pp. 52–68.

Burgers, A., de Ruyter, K., Keen, C. and Streukens, S. 2000. Customer expectation dimensions of voice-to-voice service encounters: A scale-development study. *International Journal of Service Industry Management*, *11*(2), pp. 142–161.

Hwang, J. and Hyun, S.S. (2012). The antecedents and consequences of brand prestige in luxury restaurants. *Asia Pacific Journal of Tourism Research*, *17*(6), pp. 656–683.

Jaakkola, E. and Alexander, M. (2014). The role of customer engagement behavior in value co-creation. *Journal of Service Research*, *17*(3), pp. 247–261.

Kim, D. H. and Song, D. 2019. Can brand experience shorten consumers' psychological distance toward the brand? The effect of brand experience on consumers' construal level. *Journal of Brand Management*, *26*(3), pp. 255–267.

Morrison, S. and Crane, F. G. 2007. Building the service brand by creating and managing an emotional brand experience. *Journal of Brand Management*, *14*(5), pp. 410–421.

Nadiri, H., Hussain, K., Ekiz, E. H. & Erdoğan, Ş. 2008. An investigation on the factors influencing passengers' loyalty in the North Cyprus national airline. *The TQM Journal*, *20*(3), pp. 265–280.

Newaj, A. and Damar-Ladkoo, A. 2016. Distorted facets of marketing ethics for alcoholic beer marketing. *Studies in Business and Economics*, *11*(2), pp. 79–96.

Nysveen, H. and Pedersen, P. E. 2014. Influences of cocreation on brand experience. *International Journal of Market Research*, *56*(6), pp. 807–832.

Olivares-Delgado, F., Iglesias-Sánchez, P. P., Benlloch-Osuna, M. T., Heras-Pedrosa, C. D. L. and Jambrino-Maldonado, C. 2020. Resilience and anti-stress during COVID-19 isolation in Spain: An analysis through audiovisual spots. *International Journal of Environmental Research and Public Health*, *17*(23), p. 8876.

Rai, N. and Thapa, B. 2015. A study on purposive sampling method in research. Kathmandu: Kathmandu School of Law, 5.

Schmitt, B. 2009. The concept of brand experience. *Journal of Brand Management*, *16*(7), pp. 417–419.

Shah, M. K. and Tomer, S. 2020. How brands in India connected with the audience amid Covid-19. *International Journal of Scientific Research Publications*, *10*(8), pp. 91–95.

Sharma, K. 2020. A surge in e-commerce market in India after COVID-19 pandemic. *Gap Gyan-a Global Journal of Social Sciences*, *3*(4), pp. 54–57.

Sobande, F. 2020. 'We're all in this together': Commodified notions of connection, care and community in brand responses to COVID-19. *European Journal of Cultural Studies*, *23*(6), pp. 1033–1037.

Wang, Y., Hong, A., Li, X. and Gao, J. 2020. Marketing innovations during a global crisis: A study of China firms' response to COVID-19. *Journal of business research*, *116*, pp. 214–220.

Response to domestic violence due to COVID-19 at international and national levels

Dhan Devi SOOKUR and Nishita Devi HORILL[1]

Domestic violence occurring as a result of COVID-19 has been deemed as the 'shadow pandemic' by the United Nations. It is estimated that globally 243 million women and girls aged 15–49 years have been subjected to domestic violence by an intimate partner during the first year of the outbreak of COVID-19. As the COVID-19 pandemic continues, this number is likely to grow with multiple impacts on women's wellbeing, their sexual and reproductive health, their mental health, and their ability to participate and lead in the recovery of our societies and economy. As a result, many international and regional organisations, NGOs, countries and local governments have responded through relevant measures and initiatives to address and prevent domestic violence. There is no doubt that the COVID-19 pandemic has generated the much-needed momentum around this issue at international and national levels. However, there is still a long way to go and longer-term strategic approaches need to be developed so as to tackle domestic violence.

La violence domestique résultant de COVID-19 est considérée comme la « pandémie de l'ombre » par les Nations Unies. On estime qu'à l'échelle mondiale, 243 millions de femmes et de filles âgées de 15 à 49 ans ont été victimes de violence domestique de la part d'un partenaire intime au cours de la première année de la pandémie de COVID-19. Alors que la celle-ci se poursuit, ce nombre est susceptible d'augmenter avec de multiples impacts sur le bien-être des femmes, leur santé sexuelle, reproductive et mentale, ainsi que leur capacité à participer et à diriger la reprise de nos sociétés et de notre économie. En conséquence, de nombreuses organisations internationales et régionales, des ONG, des pays, et des gouvernements locaux ont réagi par des mesures et des initiatives pertinentes pour traiter et prévenir la violence domestique. Il ne fait aucun doute que la pandémie de COVID-19 a généré l'élan tant attendu autour de cette question aux niveaux tant national qu'international. Toutefois, le chemin à parcourir est

---

[1] Senior Law Reform Officers, Law Reform Commission.

encore long et des approches stratégiques à plus long terme doivent être développées afin de lutter contre la violence domestique.

Introduction

Domestic Violence, also known as domestic abuse, is understood as a behaviour focused on the oppression of another individual, causing significant trauma through physical, sexual, and mental harm, and it is prevalent across all ages, and economic classes[2]. Due to the COVID-19 pandemic, domestic violence cases have increased worldwide at an alarming pace[3].

There has been a 30 % increase in cases of domestic violence in France since the start of the pandemic[4]. Emergency calls to helplines in Singapore have reportedly risen by 33 %[5]. In Brazil, which has been hard hit by the pandemic, there has been a 45 % jump in cases of violence against women[6]. In Colombia, domestic violence calls to a national women's hotline increased by nearly 130 % during the first 18 days of the country's quarantine[7].

In the United Kingdom, 14 women and 2 children were murdered in the first 3 weeks of COVID-19 lockdowns, which is the highest figures in 11 years[8]. Furthermore, it is estimated that globally 243 million women

---

[2] United Nations, 'What is domestic violence?' <https://www.un.org/en/coronavirus/what-is-domestic-abuse>
[3] Moreira DN and Pinto da Costa, 'The impact of the Covid-19 pandemic in the precipitation of intimate partner violence' (2020) IJLP 71.
[4] United Nations Department of Global Communications, 'UN supporting 'trapped' domestic violence victims during COVID-19 pandemic' <https://www.un.org/en/coronavirus/un-supporting-%E2%80%98trapped%E2%80%99-domestic-violence-victims-during-covid-19-pandemic>
[5] ibid.
[6] Brazilian Forum on Public Safety, 'Domestic violence during the Covid-19 pandemic' [29 May 2020].
[7] Lucila Sigal, Natalia A. Ramos Miranda, Ana Isabel Martinez and Monica Machicao, ''Another pandemic': In Latin America, domestic abuse rises amid lockdown', (Reuters, 27 April 2020) <https://www.reuters.com/article/us-health-coronavirus-latam-domesticviol-idUSKCN2291JS >
[8] Jamie Grierson, 'Domestic abuse killings 'more than double' amid Covid-19 lockdown', (The Guardian, 15 April 2020) <https://www.theguardian.com/society/2020/apr/15/domestic-abuse-killings-more-than-double-amid-covid-19-lockdown>

and girls aged 15–49 years have been subjected to domestic violence during the first year of the outbreak of COVID-19[9]. While most victims of intimate partner violence are women, the Respect Men's Advice Line of the United Kingdom has seen a 35 % increase in calls regarding intimate partner violence against men. As the COVID-19 pandemic continues, these numbers are likely to grow.

As a result of which, the United Nations has deemed domestic violence due to COVID-19 as the 'shadow pandemic'[10]. And it can be said yes indeed a shadow pandemic for which there is no vaccine.

Several international and regional organisations as well as countries, including Mauritius, have responded to the rise of domestic violence due to COVID-19.

This article analyses the response to domestic violence due to COVID-19 by:

(I) international and regional organisations;
(II) some countries worldwide; and
(III) Mauritius, before concluding.

I. Response to domestic violence due to COVID-19 by international and regional organisations

A. Council of Europe

The Council of Europe, an international organisation, which has 47 members, protects against domestic violence through the Convention on Preventing and Combating Violence Against Women and Domestic Violence 2016[11]. The Convention is also known as the Istanbul Convention and it is a legally binding instrument.

---

[9] United Nations Women, 'The Shadow Pandemic: Violence Against Women and Girls and Covid-19' <https://data.unwomen.org/sites/default/files/documents/COVID19/Infographic-VAW-COVID19-logo.pdf>

[10] María-Noel Vaeza, 'Addressing the Impact of the COVID-19 Pandemic on Violence Against Women and Girls' (United Nations, 27 November 2020) <https://www.un.org/en/addressing-impact-covid-19-pandemic-violence-against-women-and-girls>

[11] Convention on Preventing and Combating Violence Against Women and Domestic Violence 2016

In response to the increase of domestic violence due to COVID-19, the Council of Europe proposed possible actions and measures that its member states can take under selected provisions of the Istanbul Convention[12].

Some examples of the possible actions and measures include: (i) Granting the police the power to remove a perpetrator of domestic violence from his or her home; (ii) Setting up easily accessible shelters in sufficient numbers and in an adequate geographical distribution; (iii) Making available state-wide 24/7 telephone helplines free of charge; and (iv) Setting up easily accessible rape crisis or sexual violence referral centres which can provide immediate medical counselling, trauma care and forensic services[13].

Besides, the Council called on the European Union and its Member States which have not yet ratified the Istanbul Convention or not fully aligned their national laws with its requirements should do so swiftly[14].

B. World Health Organisation ('WHO'), FIFA and the European Commission

In addition, (i) WHO, the United Nations' specialized health agency, (ii) FIFA, football's world governing body, and (iii) the European Commission joined forces, to launch the #SafeHome campaign to support women and children at risk of domestic violence[15]. The campaign is a joint response from the three institutions to the spikes in reports of domestic violence due to the spread of COVID-19[16].

---

[12] Council of Europe, 'Declaration of the Committee of the Parties to the Istanbul Convention' (Strasbourg, 20 April 2020) <https://rm.coe.int/declaration-committee-of-the-parties-to-ic-covid-/16809e33c6>

[13] ibid.

[14] ibid.

[15] World Health Organisation, 'FIFA, European Commission and World Health Organization launch #SafeHome campaign to support those at risk from domestic violence' (26 May 2020) <https://www.who.int/news/item/26-05-2020-fifa-european-commission-and-world-health-organization-launch-safehome-campaign-to-support-those-at-risk-from-domestic-violence>

[16] ibid.

C. African Union

The African Union consists of 55 member states located on the continent of Africa[17].

In order to assist its member states in addressing, managing, responding and recovering from domestic violence caused as a result of COVID-19, the African Union developed the '*African Union Guidelines on Gender Responsive Responses to Covid-19*'[18]. The African Union emphasized that if African governments implement and adhere to the guidelines, and reinforce them with legal instruments, policy-makers will not only be well informed, but also equipped with the right tools in ensuring an equal future for women and girls in a COVID-19 world[19].

Moreover, in addressing a rise of domestic violence due to COVID-19, the African Union recalled the importance of ratifying, domesticating and implementing the African Charter on Human and Peoples' Rights on the Rights of Women in Africa 2003[20] and African Charter on the Rights and Welfare of the Child 1990[21].

D. Organisation of American States

Headquartered in the US capital, Washington, D.C., the Organisation of American States consists of 35 independent states of America. Its legal framework is found under the Charter of the Organization of the American States[22].

On April 7, 2020, the Organisation of American States published the '*Practical Guide to Inclusive Rights-Focused Responses to COVID-19 in the Americas*'[23]. The guide is intended to support its member states

---

[17] African Union, <https://au.int/en/member_states/countryprofiles2>
[18] African Union, 'African Union Guidelines on Gender Responsive Responses to Covid-19'.
[19] African Union, 'Implementing Gender Responsive Strategies Towards Combatting Covid-19 in Africa' (29 May 2021) <https://au.int/en/articles/implementing-gender-responsive-strategies-towards-combatting-covid-19-africa>
[20] African Charter on Human and Peoples' Rights on the Rights of Women in Africa 2003.
[21] African Charter on the Rights and Welfare of the Child 1990.
[22] Charter of the Organization of the American States 1948.
[23] Organisation of American States, 'Practical Guide to Inclusive Rights-Focused Responses to COVID-19 in the Americas' (2020).

in responding to the global COVID-19 pandemic and to offer tools for responding to cases of violence against women and girls, which have been accentuated by the pandemic[24].

In addition, the Organisation of the American States and Inter-American Commission of Women presented some proposed measures that could be implemented in accordance with the Inter-American Convention on the Prevention, Punishment and Eradication of Violence against Women 1994 to immediately prevent and address cases of violence against women and girls[25].

E. League of Arab States

Arab League, also called League of Arab States, is the regional organisation of Arab states in the Middle East and parts of Africa, formed in Cairo in 1945. It has 22 member states.

In response to the shadow pandemic, the League of Arab States is currently working to adopt its first ever regional treaty to tackle domestic violence[26]. Once adopted, that would represent a commitment of up to 22 Arab countries and will protect an estimated 200 million women and girls by enacting measures to prevent violence and prosecute perpetrators[27].

F. The United Nations

The UN System includes a multitude of specialized agencies, funds and programmes which are seeking to prevent domestic violence due to COVID-19.

For instance, the UN Trust Fund to End Violence which has 144 grantees around the world reviewed all its current grants to identify

---

[24] *ibid.*
[25] Inter-American Convention on the Prevention, Punishment and Eradication of Violence against Women 1994.
[26] Foreign, Commonwealth and Development Office, Westminster Foundation for Democracy, 'UK MPs join Arab League in calling for Internationally legally-binding treaty to tackle violence against women' (25 November 2020) <https://www.wfd.org/story/uk-mps-join-arab-league-calling-internationally-legally-binding-treaty-tackle-violence>
[27] *ibid.*

prospective budget lines that could be quickly reallocated to provide immediate assistance to relevant organisations to ensure the safety of survivors of domestic violence during the pandemic[28].

Furthermore, Twitter, in consultation with UN Women, launched the *#ThereIsHelp* campaign, which provides automatic notification of helplines and other services when a user searches for terms associated with domestic violence[29]. This has so far been launched in Thailand, India, Indonesia, Malaysia, Philippines, Singapore, South Korea, and Vietnam[30].

II. Response to domestic violence due to COVID-19 by some countries

The UN Secretary-General, Antonio Guterres, appealed to all governments to address domestic violence as an integral part of their national response plans for COVID-19[31].

In line with the appeal of the UN Secretary General, there were some countries which developed innovative methods to prevent domestic violence.

For instance, in most of the provinces and territories of Canada, domestic violence shelters were deemed as essential services and must remain open during a lockdown[32]. In Italy, instead of the survivor having to leave the house of an abuser, prosecutors ruled that in situations of domestic violence the abuser must leave the house instead[33].

---

[28] United Nations Women, 'Covid-19 and Violence Against Women and Girls: Addressing the Shadow Pandemic', *Policy Brief No. 17*.

[29] United Nations Women, 'Tech giants partner with UN Women to provide life-saving information to survivors of domestic violence during COVID-19' (24 June 2020) <https://www.unwomen.org/en/news/stories/2020/6/news-tech-giants-provide-life-saving-information-during-covid-19>

[30] *ibid*.

[31] UN chief calls for domestic violence 'ceasefire' amid 'horrifying global surge' | | UN News.

[32] United Nations Women, 'COVID-19 and Ending Violence Against Women and Girls'.

[33] Emma Graham-Harrison and Liz Ford, Lockdowns around the world bring rise in domestic violence (The Guardian, 28 March 2020) <https://www.theguardian.com/society/2020/mar/28/lockdowns-world-rise-domestic-violence>

Argentina took steps to address delays in the judicial processes and has extended protection orders for survivors to 60 days[34]. In Colombia the government issued a decree to guarantee continued access to services virtually, including legal advice, psychosocial advice, police and justice services including hearings[35].

Australia urgently amended its Sentencing Act 1995[36], Sentence Administration Act 2003[37], Bail Act 1982[38] and Restraining Orders Act 1997[39] to allow the justice system to better respond to domestic violence cases during quarantine. The amendments led to the following changes: (i) Allowing the court to impose a requirement that an offender be subject to electronic monitoring under Conditional Suspended Imprisonment Orders and Intensive Supervision Orders; (ii) Permitting a judicial officer to include, as a home detention bail condition, a direction that an accused be subject to electronic monitoring; (iii) Improving access to restraining orders, including enabling restraining order applications to be lodged online; (iv) Creating a separate offence for breach of a family violence restraining order, increasing the penalty to $10,000 from $6,000 and extending the limitation period for prosecuting breach of restraining order offences to two years; and (v) Allowing the Family Court and Children's Court to issue interim restraining orders on an ex-parte basis.

In addition, several European countries, such as France, Germany, Italy, Norway, the Netherlands, and Spain, all adopted a coding messaging system, using a code which is, 'Mask 19', for victims to initiate help-seeking activities[40]. The way the system works is that by communicating the code word (either spoken or written) to a staff in a pharmacy, victims can ask for help without attracting attention, even if the abuser is in close proximity. The staff of the participating business can then contact police or social services on the victims' behalf.

---

[34] United Nations General Assembly, 'Intensification of efforts to eliminate all forms of violence against women and girls' A/75/274 (30 July 2020), 9.
[35] *ibid.*
[36] Sentencing Act 1995.
[37] Sentence Administration Act 2003.
[38] Bail Act 1982.
[39] Restraining Orders Act 1997.
[40] United Nations General Assembly, 'Intensification of efforts to eliminate all forms of violence against women and girls' A/75/274 (30 July 2020), 8.

Similarly, the Red Dot Initiative in India, started by an organization called the Women Entrepreneurs for Transformation, created a coded signal that indicates discretely when a victim is at risk of violence in his or her home[41]. A victim experiencing domestic violence can ask for help by placing a red dot on his or her palm as a distress signal to neighbours, shopkeepers, or in an image to the helpline which has been specifically set up[42].

Italian police officers utilized a YouGov app, originally designed to help young people report bullying and drug dealing, to provide domestic violence survivors with a way to message the police without the knowledge of their partner[43].

Furthermore, an Australian program provided mobile phones and $30 credit to victims and giving domestic violence survivors the ability to connect with support services[44].

In France, the Government created a 24-hour platform for confidential reporting of domestic violence. The Government also agreed to pay for up to 20,000 hotel nights for survivors of domestic violence, to open pop-up counselling centres at supermarkets and to promptly issue legal protection orders for victims[45].

III. Response to domestic violence due to COVID-19 in Mauritius

Mauritius was not spared from a pandemic in the year 2020[46]. The United Nations Secretary General, stated, *'the threat to violence looms*

---

[41] Women Entrepreneurs For Transformation, Red Dot Initiative, https://weft-foundation.com/event/red-dot-initiative/
[42] *ibid.*
[43] United Nations General Assembly, 'Intensification of efforts to eliminate all forms of violence against women and girls' A/75/274 (30 July 2020), 9.
[44] The Women's Services Network, Telstra Safe Connections Program, <https://wesnet.org.au/ourwork/telstra/>
[45] <https://www.france24.com/en/20200330-france-to-put-domestic-violence-victims-in-hotels-as-numbers-soar-under-coronavirus-lockdown>
[46] *'Covid-19: Mauritius to go in two-week lockdown as from tomorrow'* (19 March 2020) <http://www.govmu.org/English/News/Pages/Covid-19-Mauritius-to-go-in-two-week-lockdown-as-from-tomorrow.aspx>

largest where one should be the safest, that is, in one's own home.[47] Indeed, the impact of the COVID-19 pandemic coupled with the requirement to isolate has inadvertently increased the risk of incidents of domestic violence.

According to Statistics Mauritius, this has led to a five-fold increase in the number of cases of domestic violence compared to the same period in 2018 and 2019[48]. It has been reported that as many as 111 victims left the conjugal roof and all of them were women[49]. It further highlighted that out of the reported cases of domestic violence in Mauritius in 2020, 87.3 % were women, while 12.7 % were men[50]. In early 2020, three women were killed on three consecutive days by their intimate partners[51]. Furthermore, the Minister of Gender Equality and Family Welfare, Mrs. Kalpana Koonjoo-Shah declared that a total of 3,094 cases had been reported to the Ministry from January 2020 till March 2021[52]. With regards to cases of child abuse, a total of 4,031 cases had been registered at the Ministry out of 7,310 cases reported for the same period[53].

With the lockdown measures, many women in abusive relationships have been confined with their aggressors and were unable to escape violent situations. Domestic Violence Shelter Director, Mrs. A. Jeanne of SOS Femmes, stated that as the premises of SOS Femme Shelter were not logistically engineered to offer quarantine facilities as per the mandatory sanitary norms, to the women in sheer distress, the victims had to be channelled to the police. She further added that even though provisions for counselling by psychologists and access to lawyers, with regards to advice on protection orders had been put at their disposal, the primary problem remained: the victims were stuck at home with the perpetrators

---

[47] *'UN chief calls for domestic violence 'ceasefire' amid 'horrifying global surge'* (6 April 2020) <https://news.un.org/en/story/2020/04/1061052>

[48] *'DOMESTIC VIOLENCE – Cases of domestic violence escalate in May 2020'* <Covid doc_domestic_violence.pdf (govmu.org)>

[49] *Ibid.*

[50] *'Gender Statistics, Year 2020 – Highlights'* <https://statsmauritius.govmu.org/Pages/Statistics/By_Subject/Gender/Gender_Yr20.aspx>

[51] Dr. Anjalee Dabee, Renooka Beejan, *'A Call to Action Against Gender-Based Violence: Putting Women's Rights at the Centre of the COVID-19 Response'* (4 December 2020) <https://www.undp.org/mauritius-seychelles/blog/call-action-against-gender-based-violence-putting-womens-rights-centre-covid-19-response>

[52] Hansard Debate, 6 April 2021, 155.

[53] *Ibid.*

and that they even ran greater risk when they called at the shelter for help[54].

The Government of Mauritius has undertaken certain measures with the aim to respond to the rising cases of domestic violence.

A. *Outreach programme for victims of domestic violence*

On 3 October 2020, the Police Family Protection Unit (PFPU), under the aegis of the Mauritius Police Force in collaboration with UNDP Mauritius, launched the Outreach Programme for Victims of Domestic Violence. The programme's foremost objective is to encourage people to report cases of domestic violence as early as possible and to ensure that victims are provided with quick and adequate support from relevant institutions. The programme has put in place a mobile service to survivors within the community with the aim of rendering the reporting process more accessible. Easily accessible services have even been introduced to enable survivors to file complaints and to receive legal information and psychological support from professionals. Additionally, the outreach programme also comprises a platform to sensitize vulnerable persons at risk and perpetrators of domestic violence[55].

B. *National strategy and action plan to eliminate Gender-Based Violence (GBV)*

A National Strategy and Action Plan to eliminate Gender-Based Violence (GBV), was launched in the year 2020. It focuses on the elimination of Gender-Based Violence rather than domestic violence. Nevertheless, as domestic violence is the most reported type of GBV in Mauritius, with 4,243 reported cases in 2019[56], it is worth mentioning about this Strategy. GBV is an act of violence directed at a person because of their gender or sex and which is considered as a violation of human

---

[54] Newsletter on *'Gendered Voices'* (Consolidated Issue 01 – 04, 2020), 11. <file:///C:/Users/HP/Downloads/undp-consolidated-gendered-voices-newsletter-2020%20(1).pdf>

[55] *'UNDP supports the Outreach Programme for Victims of Domestic Violence'* (6 October 2020) <UNDP supports the Outreach Programme for Victims of Domestic Violence | United Nations Development Programme>

[56] *Ibid.*

rights[57]. Such acts of violence, coercion and manipulation may encompass, inter alia, sexual violence; child marriage; child trafficking; female genital mutilation or honour crimes. Despite the fact that most GBV victims are women and a majority of policymakers focus on women, it is essential to concede that men and gender-non-conforming individuals may also face gender-based violence.

The key elements of the four-year Action Plan depend upon having a shared understanding of the nature and extent of Gender Based Violence in Mauritius, the commitment of multiple stakeholders, strengthening of the existing legislative and policy framework, capacity building of stakeholders, and a strong monitoring and evaluation mechanism. Four substrategies have been developed in order to address the multifaceted aspects of Gender Based Violence and that are aligned to the National Strategy. Firstly, changing societal norms and beliefs that are against principles of gender equality and equity; secondly, putting the needs of survivors first while holding perpetrators accountable; identifying and redressing discriminatory practices that perpetuate gender-based violence; and monitoring and evaluating any progress made[58].

C. LESPWAR App

Furthermore, a GBV Mobile App, known as 'LESPWAR', was launched on 25 November 2020, which allows a victim of GBV to promptly alert the authorities concerned by the press of a 'panic button' in the App. Afterwards, the Main Police Command and Control Centre (MPCCC) and the Ministry of Gender Equality and Family Welfare are informed simultaneously, and the victim's exact location is displayed through a geo-localisation feature. Subsequently, assistance is provided to the victim, in line with a protocol for intervention, signed between the Ministry of Gender Equality and Family Welfare and the Mauritius Police Force.

---

[57] *'Covid-19 response: What is Domestic Abuse?'* <What Is Domestic Abuse? | United Nations>

[58] High Level Committee on the Elimination of Gender Based Violence in the Republic of Mauritius 2020–2024, *'National Strategy and Action Plan'* (Prime Minister's Office, 25 November 2020) <https://pmo.govmu.org/Communique/PMO%20-%20Natio nal%20Strategy%20TP%20FINAL%20WEB.pdf>

This App is free of charges, may be downloaded on any smartphone, and is accessible to any GBV victims/survivors irrespective of age or gender[59].

D. *Observatory on Gender-Based Violence*

The Government of Mauritius has always prioritized the fight against Gender-Based Violence as part of its agenda. Consequently, a Memorandum of Understanding (MoU) was signed between the Mauritius Research and Innovation Council (MRIC) and the Ministry of Gender Equality and Family Welfare on 23 December 2021 for the running and operationalisation of the Observatory for Gender-Based Violence (GBV)[60]. To that end, the MRIC has secured funding during this financial year to the tune of Rs 13.8 million have been earmarked for the setting up and operation of the GBV Observatory[61]. The aim towards setting up such an Observatory is to strengthen the data capture on gender-based violence in Mauritius, which will in turn lead to collect harmonized data for informed policy making and monitoring and evaluation of initiatives on GBV. A holistic and transparent mechanism will be set up through this platform which will reinforce cooperation and understanding of the actions carried out in matters regarding care for victims; how gender-based violence has evolved in Mauritius and subsequently how public policies may be elaborated in the future to eradicate this societal problem[62].

---

[59] *'International Day for the Elimination of Violence against Women: A National Strategy and Mobile App launched'* (9 December 2020) <https://dha.govmu.org/News/SitePages/International-Day-for-the-Elimination-of-Violence-against-Women--A-National-Strategy-and-Mobile-App-launched.aspx>

[60] *'ICT/Gender: MoU signed to operationalise the Observatory for Gender-Based Violence'* (23 December 2021) <https://gis.govmu.org/News/SitePages/ICT-Gender--MoU-signed-to-operationalise-the-Observatory-for-Gender-Based-Violence.aspx>

[61] *Ibid.*

[62] *'Special Rapporteur on violence against women, its causes and consequences'* (Ministry of Foreign Affairs, Regional Integration and International Trade (Human Rights Division)) 1 <https://www.ohchr.org/sites/default/files/2021-12/mauritius.pdf>

Conclusion

The COVID-19 pandemic has generated the much-needed momentum to address domestic violence which was a pandemic long before the outbreak of COVID-19, but more needs to be done.

The appeal from the UN Secretary General, those recommendations and guidance from those international and regional organisations to eliminate domestic violence lack legal weight necessary to get governments to act. If we want to eradicate domestic violence, there is a need to develop longer-term strategic approaches. There is a need to have a legally binding international treaty addressing domestic violence accompanied with a sustained campaign, preferably led by domestic violence survivors and their advocates for its universal ratification by all states in the world.

As far as Mauritius is concerned, not only should there be strict laws and efficient assistance programmes, but also a real change in the culture and mindset of the population is mandated in order to fight against domestic violence.

Moreover, the COVID-19 is already testing us in ways most of us have never previously experienced, providing emotional and economic shocks that we are struggling to rise above. An increase in domestic violence cases that appeared as a dark feature of this pandemic is a mirror and a challenge to our values, our resilience and shared humanity. We must not only survive the coronavirus, but emerge renewed, with victims of domestic violence as a powerful force at the centre of recovery.

Hommage à Pierre Rosario Domingue

Sabir Kadel

Tout d'abord, je remercie les Professeurs Dijoux et Gunputh de me donner l'occasion de cet hommage à Pierre Rosario Domingue. Et je tiens à saluer la présence parmi nous aujourd'hui de Lydie Domingue, celle qui l'a accompagné et soutenu dans les bons comme moins bons moments, ainsi que ses trois fils, qu'il aimait pardessus tout.

Je suis très heureux que la *Law Reform Commission* soit associée à cette conférence sur le Covid qui, pour tragique que la situation sanitaire soit, constitue l'occasion de repenser plusieurs thématiques du droit, et en premier lieu les libertés fondamentales, dont il sera amplement question par la suite.

Pour ma part donc, j'aimerais dire quelques mots sur Pierre Rosario Domingue, l'ancien directeur de la *Law Reform Commission*, que j'ai eu le plaisir et l'honneur de côtoyer durant deux décennies, et auprès duquel j'ai appris non seulement des pans entiers du droit, mais également des valeurs humaines, dont il était porteur. À l'heure où le monde passe par une crise sanitaire sans précédent, et qui voit s'opposer amis, collègues, parents, en clans rivaux, antivax et provax, anti pass sanitaire et pro pass sanitaire.

À l'heure encore où le bruit des bottes se fait entendre aux portes de l'Europe, et tel Caton l'ancien il y a plus de deux millénaires, on pourrait s'écrier : « *Hannibal ad portas* », et qui fait planer sur le vieux continent le spectre des heures les plus sombres de l'histoire, un colloque international qui réunit, entre autres, deux nations qui jadis se sont fait la guerre, n'aurait pu que réjouir Rosario Domingue, lui qui croyait en la fraternité des peuples, qui pensait qu'il existait un fil invisible, et indivisible, qui unit tous les humains, et qui rêvait d'un monde, où, pour emprunter les mots de Schiller, immortalisés par la neuvième symphonie de Beethoven, « *Alle Menschen werden Brüder* », tous les hommes deviennent des frères.

Car Rosario Domingue était d'abord un humaniste. Le terme « humaniste » est rarement employé de nos jours, on lui préfère d'autres qualificatifs, comme « intellectuel », « moral », ou encore « sage » ; ce qui est regrettable. Car, selon Cicéron, l'humanisme représente « la culture qui, parachevant les qualités naturelles de l'homme, le rend digne de ce nom ». En effet, Rosario Domingue a toujours mis l'humain au centre de ses préoccupations, que ce soit tant du point de vue personnel que professionnel.

Ainsi, tous les rapports produits par la Commission sous son mandat sont empreints d'humanisme. Pour lui, le droit n'est pas là pour pérenniser un rapport de puissance, comme le dénonçait Nietzsche, mais bien pour rétablir l'équilibre entre le fort et le faible, le riche et le pauvre, le célèbre et l'anonyme. Samuel Colt, l'inventeur du célèbre révolver, aurait dit : « Dieu a fait des hommes grands et d'autres petits, je les ai rendus égaux. » Rosario Domingue pensait la même chose, mais du droit. Nous ne naissons pas tous sous les mêmes auspices, au sein des mêmes foyers privilégiés, affublés des mêmes patronymes avantageux. Le droit vient y mettre bon ordre, possédant cette faculté égalisatrice.

Et en cela, Rosario Domingue croyait corps et âme, et c'est ce à quoi il a dévolu toute sa vie, d'abord comme enseignant à l'université, ensuite en revêtant la toge d'avocat, enfin comme directeur de la Commission de réforme des lois. Universitaire de grande envergure, il a formé toute une génération de futurs avocats et magistrats. Tous ceux qui ont suivi ses cours, et j'ai l'honneur d'en faire partie, peuvent témoigner de la passion et de la rigueur qui l'animaient. Il commandait le respect de ses collègues qui l'ont côtoyé, et l'admiration des étudiants qui ont eu la chance d'assister à ses envolées lyriques en classe.

Je me souviens encore du cours qu'il donna sur la distinction entre le meurtre et les coups et blessures ayant entraîné la mort sans intention de la donner. Il prit pour exemple la plaidoirie du grand pénaliste qu'était Gaëtan Duval. Ce dernier, pendant mauricien d'un Jacques Vergès, présenta au jury le scénario suivant, dans une affaire où un homme était poursuivi pour meurtre et où la poursuite se reposait sur le fait que l'intention criminelle était prouvée, car plusieurs coups de couteau avaient été assénés :

« Quand un cafard fait intrusion, relata Rosario Domingue, dans votre cuisine et que prit de peur, vous enlevez votre chaussure pour le frapper, vous aurez tendance à répéter votre geste à maintes reprises. Vous taperez, encore. Et encore. Comme un dératé. De manière hystérique. Non pas tant parce que vous nourrissez une telle haine du cafard que vous souhaitez le voir mort, mais que, saisi de panique, vos gestes dépassent votre intention ».

Par une telle illustration, Rosario Domingue avait réussi à expliquer les subtilités de l'infraction praeter-intentionelle, les affres de la qualification juridique, et le rôle de l'élément moral dans la caractérisation du crime, mieux que ne saurait le faire n'importe quel manuel de droit pénal. Les années passent, il exerce ensuite comme avocat, et daignait se saisir d'affaires que ses confrères rechignaient à prendre, du fait de leur manque de glamour ou à cause du peu de bénéfices financiers qu'ils auraient pu en tirer ; ces affaires qu'il défendait étaient souvent traversées par un leitmotiv : les droits de la défense ; et parfois marquées du sceau de l'infamie, que constitue un excès de zèle des forces de l'ordre. C'est sans doute la raison pour laquelle il avait créé par le passé le module d'études policières, lui qui maitrisait si bien la procédure criminelle.

Mais l'idéaliste qu'il était fut sans doute désillusionné par le système judiciaire, et il finit par délaisser la toge ; remontons *ab ovo* pensa-t-il surement, et il se dit : pour changer le système, il faut commencer par changer les lois. Et il prit les rênes de la Law Reform Commission. Rarement peut-on dire d'une personne qu'elle incarne une institution. Mais cela a été le cas pour lui. Dès les débuts de la mise en place de la Commission, il a littéralement porté l'institution à bout de bras. Alors que la Commission était encore à ses prémisses, il a sué sang et eau, passant des nuits blanches à plancher sur les rapports, et ce afin de lui donner sa vitesse de croisière.

Ayant un sens aigu du détail, il prêtait autant attention à la forme qu'au fond des documents qui étaient préparés. Il repérait jusqu'à la virgule qui était en trop dans la phrase, les mots redondants qui alourdissaient le paragraphe, la disposition de loi qui n'était pas à jour, l'obscure jurisprudence qu'il convenait de mentionner.

Et il aurait pu dire, tel Cyrano de Bergerac : « Tout mon sang se coagule en songeant qu'on puisse y changer une virgule ». Car il avait compris le pouvoir des mots, à même de transformer une infraction formelle en une infraction matérielle ; susceptible de modifier un dol général en un dol spécial.

Tous les rapports de la Commission, et pour lui c'était un point d'honneur, sont rédigés à la lumière des meilleures pratiques internationales, car il avait saisi, ayant cette lucidité, cette clairvoyance, qu'ont les grands juristes, que l'on vit dans un monde globalisé, que le droit ne peut plus se permettre d'évoluer en autarcie. À l'époque où nous vivons, Rosario était une anomalie. Pensant d'abord aux autres avant de penser à lui-même. Attachant davantage d'importance à la fonction qu'au statut. Il était véritablement un pèlerin en terre païenne. J'ai peur qu'on n'en fasse plus des comme lui. Le moule est cassé. Et c'est pourquoi sa perte est aussi grande.

Par tous les traits de son caractère et de son parcours professionnel que je viens d'évoquer, Rosario Domingue aurait salué l'initiative d'une telle conférence, par essence interdisciplinaire, qui convoque des spécialistes de plusieurs domaines, lui qui croyait que le savoir devait être un partage et que le droit ne devait pas être nombriliste, mais être appliqué à l'aune des connaissances d'autres disciplines ; lui qui, enfin, pensait, à l'instar de la professeure Mireille Delmas-Marty qui vient de nous quitter, que si les lois devaient s'adapter aux contextes sociétaux, certaines valeurs sont indélogeables, et certains droits inaliénables.

En temps de crise financière, on a coutume de dire que la valeur refuge est l'or. Rosario Domingue pensait lui qu'en temps de crise sociétale, la valeur refuge, c'est la culture. Et ce colloque lui donne raison. Tous les intervenants qui défileront durant ces journées, et tous les débats animés auxquels les présentations donneront lieu, participeront à une meilleure connaissance non seulement du droit en temps de crise, mais du droit tout court, de ce qui l'irrigue, et de sa raison d'être même. Et en cela, il n'y a pas de meilleur hommage qu'on aurait pu rendre à Rosario Domingue.

Cultures juridiques et politiques

Vol. 1 Stephanie Rohlfing-Dijoux (éd)
La Transmission de Terminologie et de Concepts Juridiques dans l'espace Européen. Allemagne / France / Russie
2012, ISBN 978-3-0343-1094-9

Vol. 2 Otmar Seul & Tomas Davulis (éds./Hrsg.)
La Solidarité dans l'union Européenne / Solidarität in der Europäischen Union. Actes de la 5ème Université d'été francogermano-lituanienne et européenne en sciences juridiques Vilnius, 3-10 juillet 2008 / Tagungsband der 5. DeutschFranzösisch-Litauischen und Europäischen Sommeruniversität in den Rechtswissenschaften, Vilnius 3.-10. Juli 2008
2012, ISBN 978-3-0343-1122-9

Vol. 3 Ralf Alleweldt, Raphaël Callsen, Jeanne Dupendant (eds.)
Human rights abuses in the contemporary world.
Tri-National Workshop, Tbilisi, September 2011
2012, ISBN 978-3-0343-1147-2

Vol. 4 Stefanie Bouquet
La réglementation européenne relative à la discrimination fondée sur l'âge: conséquences sur le droit du travail français. Préface du Professeur Joachim Gruber, Université Paris Ouest - Nanterre La Défense
2012, ISBN 978-3-0343-1174-8

Vol. 5 Izabela Krasnicka & Magdalena Perkowska (éds.) How to Become a Lawyer?
2013, ISBN 978-3-0343-1290-5

Vol. 6 Kerstin Peglow et Géraldine Demme (dir.)
La protection des intérêts privés sur le marché intérieur. La situation des consommateurs et entrepreneurs.
2015, ISBN 978-3-0343-1615-6

Vol. 7   Sam Lyes
Crimes internationaux et immunité de l'acte de fonction des anciens dirigeants étatiques.
2015, ISBN 978-3-0343-1690-3

Vol. 8   Fabien Bottini, Harold Gaba et Pierre Chabal (dir.)
Le régionalisme et ses limites. Regards croisés franco-kazakhs.
2016, ISBN 978-2-87574-335-0

Vol. 9   Otmar Seul, Kaïs Slama, Kerstin Peglow (Hrsg.)
Kulturvermittlung und Interkulturalität, ein deutschfranzösisch-tunesischer Dialog. Politische, rechtliche und sozio-linguistische Aspekte
2017, ISBN 978-2-8076-0133-8

Vol. 10   Stephanie Rohlfing-Dijoux (ed./dir.)
Developing Intraregional Exchanges through the Abolition of Commercial and Tariff Barriers. Myth or Reality? L'abolition des barrières commerciales et tarifaires dans la région de l'océan Indien. Mythe ou réalité?
2017, ISBN 978-2-8076-0126-0

Vol. 11   Sagyngaliy Aidarbayev, Pierre Chabal, Zhuldyz Sairambaeva (dir.) Mutations de société et réponses du droit.
Perspectives franco-asiatiques comparées.
2017, ISBN 978-2-8076-0187-1

Vol. 12   Tomas Davulis (ed.)
Labour Law Reforms in Eastern and Western Europe.
2017, ISBN 978-2-8076-0416-2

Vol. 13   Tai-Uk Chung, Zhuldyz Sairambaeva, Pierre Chabal (eds.)
On the Asian and European Origins of Legal and Political Systems. Views from Korea, Kazakhstan and France
2018, ISBN 978-2-8076-0732-3

Vol. 14   Manuel Goehrs
Coopération transfrontalière et intégration européenne.
Contribution à l'étude du principe fédéraliste
2018, ISBN 978-2-8076-0409-4

Vol. 15 Amandine Cayol, Zhuldyz Sairambaeva, Pierre Chabal (eds.)
The challenge of change for the legal and political systems of Eurasia. The impact of the New Silk Road
2020, ISBN 978-2-8076-1382-9

Vol. 16 Christine Canazza, Stéphanie Rohlfing-Dijoux, Otmar Seul (eds.)
L'Union européenne face au vieillissement de la population active. Analyse et perspectives autour de la discrimination sur la base de l'âge et des conditions de travail.
2020, ISBN 978-2-8076-1454-3

Vol. 17 Patric Kra
Ehe und Familienschutz in Zeiten des demografischen Wandels. Ein Rechtsvergleich zwischen dem deutschen und ivorischen Einkommensteuerrecht.
2021, ISBN 978-2-8076-1469-7

Vol. 18 A mandine Cayol, Hye-Hwal Seong, Remus Titiriga, Pierre Chabal (Eds.)
Eurasian challenges to international economic law. New developments after Brexit and in the context of the COVID-19.
2022, ISBN 978-2-87574-467-8

Vol. 19 Stéphanie Rohlfing-Dijoux & Rajendra Parsad Gunputh (Eds.)
The Intercultural Approach to Covid 19 Management. In Germany, France and the Indian Ocean countries.
2023, ISBN 978-2-87574-790-7

www.ingramcontent.com/pod-product-compliance
Ingram Content Group UK Ltd.
Pitfield, Milton Keynes, MK11 3LW, UK
UKHW021828140426
5217IPUK00017B/1254